"Bishop Carlos Ximenes Belo is a light for the people in their pilgrimage through East Timor's long, dark night. He is a living example to us all that we cannot love God without loving our neighbor. . . . One cannot read Arnold Kohen's book and not be moved. This book gives us all hope."

—Mairead Maguire, recipient of the 1976 Nobel Prize for Peace

"In writing about the experience of a truly extraordinary man, Arnold Kohen presents a fascinating account of one of the most compelling human rights issues of our time. . . . I applaud Kohen for helping to raise public awareness about the plight of this community."

—Senator Russell Feingold

"I shared a jail cell with the Rev. Dr. Martin Luther King, Jr., and saw his leadership qualities, humanity, and sense of humor up close. I have visited Bishop Belo, and believe that he shares those qualities. Arnold Kohen's fascinating book, written in a crisp and engaging literary style based on long knowledge of his subject, is must reading for anyone concerned about justice and human rights. Bishop Belo's struggle for his people, against monumental odds, is an inspration!"

—United Methodist Bishop Melvin G. Talbert, former president of
the National Council of Churches of Christ in the USA

"Interwoven into Kohen's account of more than two decades of the Indonesian army's crushing occupation is his sympathetic, yet realistic, depiction of the admirable character and role of East Timor's Bishop Belo. . . . No reader will doubt how richly Belo deserved the Nobel Prize for Peace."

—George McT. Kahin, Aaron L. Binenkorb Professor of International
Studies, Emeritus, Cornell University.

". . . A detailed, comprehensive and highly readable account of the life of Bishop Belo. It is an important contribution to our understanding of the contemporary history of East Timor."

—John G. Taylor, professor of politics, South Bank University, London, and author of *Indonesia's Forgotten War: The Hidden History of East Timor*

"*From the Place of the Dead* is a richly drawn portrait. . . . A friend of Bishop Belo, as well as that of some of his critics, Arnold Kohen is uniquely qualified to tell this story. And he tells it well. . . . Sympathetic to his subject without being sentimental, Kohen show how, by maintaining a sometimes unpopular but principled path of nonviolence, the bishop has managed to win the respect of East Timorese, Indonesians, and those further afield. . . . It is destined to become essential reading for novice and specialist alike."

—Geoffrey Robinson, UCLA historian and author of *The Dark Side of Paradise: Political Violence in Bali*

"Mesmerizing is the story of Bishop Belo and his heroic people. Once virtually abandoned by the world, international public opinion is being alerted. Read this extraordinary work of literature."

—Martin Sheen

FROM THE PLACE OF THE DEAD

※ ※ ※ ※

THE EPIC STRUGGLES OF
BISHOP BELO OF EAST TIMOR

ARNOLD S. KOHEN

INTRODUCTION BY THE DALAI LAMA

ST. MARTIN'S PRESS ✇ NEW YORK

Book design by Ellen R. Sasahara
Map ©1998 by Mark Stein Studios

Library of Congress Cataloging-in-Publication Data

Kohen, Arnold S.
    From the place of the dead : the epic struggles of Bishop Belo of
East Timor / Arnold S. Kohen : introduction by the Dalai Lama.—
1st ed.
        p.   cm.
    Includes bibliographical references and index.
    ISBN 0-312-19885-X
    1. Belo, Carlos Ximenes.   2. Catholic Church—Indonesia—Timor
Timur—Bishops—Biography.   3. Timor Timur (Indonesia)—Politics and
government.   I. Title.
BX4705.B2924K64   1999
282′.092—dc21
    [b]   98-51285
                                                              CIP

First Edition: June 1999

10 9 8 7 6 5 4 3 2 1

For the souls on Mount Matebian, Mount Ramelau
and other places in East Timor, that they will be remembered;
And that their survivors and descendants may find justice.

CONTENTS

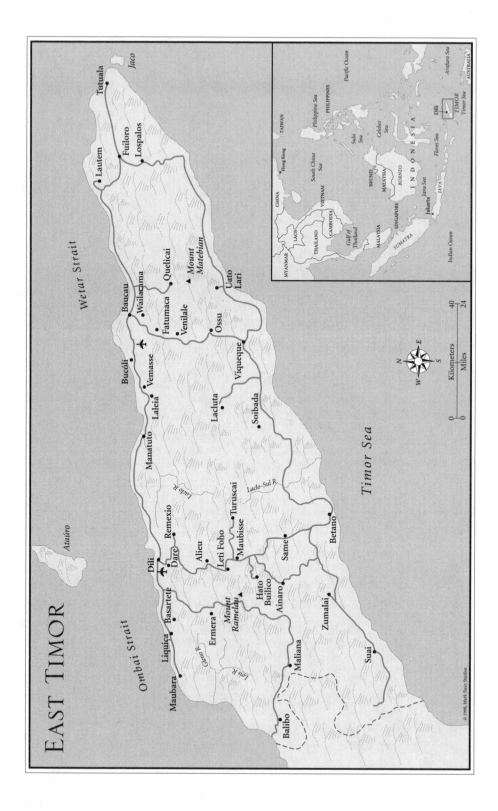

CHRONOLOGY

❖ ❖ ❖ ❖

1948—Carlos Filipe Ximenes Belo is born near Baucau, East Timor, then under Portuguese rule.

1949—The neighboring Dutch East Indies gain their independence as the Republic of Indonesia. East Timor remains a Portuguese colony.

1965—General Suharto seizes power in Indonesia. An estimated 500,000 people are killed in purges that follow.

1968—Carlos Filipe Ximenes Belo goes to Portugal for studies toward the priesthood.

1974—On April 25, the forty-eight-year-old Portuguese dictatorship is overthrown in a bloodless military coup. Political parties are soon formed in East Timor. Carlos Filipe Ximenes Belo returns after a six-year absence.

1975—Civil fighting breaks out in East Timor in August, instigated by Indonesian intelligence operatives. At the instructions of his superiors, Belo leaves to complete his priestly studies. In December, Indonesian forces launch a full-scale invasion of East Timor, accompanied by large-scale atrocities. The United Nations condemns the Indonesian invasion. East Timor is closed to most outside observers. The East Timorese resistance movement takes to the mountains.

1976—In July, President Suharto proclaims that East Timor is part of Indonesia. The United Nations refuses to recognize Indonesian annexation.

Late in the year, Catholic sources assert in a report that as many as 100,000 of a population of less than 700,000 have perished as a result of the Indonesian assault.

1977–78—Large-scale aerial bombardment creates widespread suffering in East Timor's countryside. The head of East Timor's independence movement, Nicolau Lobato, is killed by Indonesian forces.

1979—Massive war-related famine affects at least 300,000 people. Church sources put the death toll from the combined effects of the Indonesian assault at 200,000 or more.

1980—Carlos Filipe Ximenes Belo is ordained a priest in Lisbon, Portugal.

1981—After completing additional studies in Rome, Belo returns to East Timor in late July after an absence of nearly six years.

1983—In May, Carlos Filipe Ximenes Belo is named apostolic administrator, the head of East Timor's Catholic Church, replacing the popular Monsignor Martinho da Costa Lopes, who was asked to resign by the Vatican under Indonesian pressure after condemning atrocities. Soon after, Belo begins to condemn Indonesian military atrocities himself.

1984—Belo sends a letter to Monsignor Lopes, who has gone into exile in Portugal, describing grim results of a new Indonesian military offensive. That July, on receiving the new Indonesian ambassador to the Holy See, Pope John Paul II calls for observance of human rights in East Timor.

1988—Belo is named bishop.

1989—Belo writes to United Nations Secretary General Perez de Cuellar in February, calling for a democratic referendum. "We are dying as a people and a nation," he says; subsequently, his life is threatened. Pope John Paul II visits East Timor in October, and speaks out on human rights. Young people demonstrate for freedom at the end of the papal Mass. Dozens are arrested and tortured; scores take refuge in Bishop Belo's home.

1991—More than 250 East Timorese are killed when troops open fire on thousands of mourners and demonstrators in the Santa Cruz cemetery in Dili, in the presence of foreign journalists. Bishop Belo tries to rescue hundreds who have taken sanctuary in his home.

1992—Amid widespread repression, Belo speaks forcefully against human rights abuses.

1993—Bishop Belo tries to prevent further demonstrations from taking place in East Timor at the same time that he steps up his denunciations of atrocities by the Indonesian military.

1994—When President Clinton visits Indonesia in November, twenty-nine young East Timorese scale the fence of the U.S. embassy, remaining in the parking lot for ten days. Sympathy demonstrations take place in Dili, including confrontations between the military and youngsters outside the cathedral. In the midst of tear gas and high emotions, the bishop defuses the confrontations. At the same time, Belo makes strong statements defending the young people. He is increasingly seen as "the voice of the voiceless."

1995—Religious incidents break out in East Timor with Indonesian settlers, possibly provoked by military units under control of President Suharto's son-in-law, General Prabowo Subianto. Belo negotiates a truce, urging East Timorese youth to avoid confrontations.

1996—In October it is announced that Bishop Carlos Filipe Ximenes Belo has been awarded the Nobel Prize for Peace, together with José Ramos-Horta, chief international spokesman of East Timor's resistance movement. In their citation the Norwegian Nobel Committee calls the bishop "the foremost leader of the people of East Timor." On a visit to East Timor, President Suharto refuses to congratulate Bishop Belo. While visiting Rome, Pope John Paul II tells Belo that he hopes that the Nobel Prize "will be a shield" and enable the bishop "to work more for peace" in East Timor.

1997—Increased military repression occurs in East Timor through much of the year as the Indonesian army clamps down on pro-independence jubilation in the wake of the Nobel Prize. An economic crisis hits Indonesia, leading to devaluation of the currency.

1998—The economic crisis in Indonesia intensifies. Student demonstrations spearhead opposition to the corruption of the Suharto regime. In May, President Suharto resigns under pressure. Bishop Belo works to create a peaceful transition in East Timor, where military rule continues, while stressing that most people in East Timor want a referendum to decide their future.

Belo, who now has the status of a statesman in Indonesia, is increasingly outspoken. In August he condemns military atrocities against "the Muslim brothers and sisters" in the region of Aceh, where mass graves like those in East Timor are unearthed.

September 10–11, 1998—Bishop Belo convenes a meeting of dozens of East Timorese leaders, in an effort to avert clashes and achieve reconciliation among those representing different viewpoints.

October 13–14, 1998—Tens of thousands demonstrate in Dili in favor of a referendum. Bishop Belo appeals for protests to be kept peaceful.

October 30–31, 1998—Despite earlier assertions that many troops were withdrawn in August, Indonesian Army documents cited in the *New York Times* reveal that there really were twice the number of troops the Indonesian government had claimed.

Bishop Belo reports a climate of fear in East Timor's countryside because of Indonesian military movements. The Timorese prelate calls for genuine troop withdrawals.

November 13, 1998—Troops open fire on peaceful Indonesian student demonstrators outside Parliament in Jakarta, killing eight. Bishop Belo condemns the action by the military.

November–December 1998—Massive Indonesian military operations take place in the Alas area of the southern region of East Timor in retaliation for two incidents in late October and early November in which six soldiers and one civilian working with the army were killed. Dozens of houses are burned, thousands are displaced, and at least two are killed and an undetermined number beaten. Bishop Belo states that the military is terrorizing the area, and calls for an end to the operation. Belo adds that massacres will cease in East Timor only after there is a political solution to the conflict.

1999—In a stunning reversal, on January 27, the Indonesian government raises the possibility of independence for East Timor for the first time since the 1975 invasion, and also announces that resistance leader Xanana Gusmao, jailed since 1992, will be released from prison into house arrest. In February, President Habibie states that he would like to see East Timor become independent by January 1, 2000. Bishop Belo appeals for disarmament in East Timor as well as for an international peacekeeping force to help ease the transition to self-rule.

AUTHOR'S NOTE

❖ ❖ ❖ ❖

S INCE LATE 1975, when I produced feature programs for a radio
news service in Ithaca, New York, I have participated in international efforts to draw public attention to Indonesia's invasion of
East Timor. By 1979, involvement in these activities led to a meeting with
Father Reinaldo Cardoso, a Roman Catholic priest from the Azores who
had moved to the United States after twelve years in East Timor, before Indonesia occupied the territory. But in spirit Father Cardoso had never
really left East Timor, and he suffered like no other foreigner over the horrific news he received from former colleagues on the island after Indonesia
closed the territory to the outside world in 1975.

Father Cardoso introduced me to several priests from East Timor. Each
had compelling stories to tell and drew me further into the Timor drama,
none more so than Bishop Belo's predecessor, Monsignor Martinho da
Costa Lopes, whom I met when he went into exile in 1983, and got to know
well before his death in 1991. Dom Martinho, as he was known, was a man
of rare courage and fortitude who nonetheless had the air of someone who
had witnessed more horror than a human being could be expected to bear.

I was quite curious about the nature of the man who had the unenviable task of replacing such an individual. In 1993, I met Bishop Belo, who
had been one of Father Cardoso's students in the seminary in the cool hills
overlooking East Timor's capital city of Dili. Over the next five-and-a-half
years I traveled with the bishop, both in East Timor and abroad, and
worked closely with him on human rights matters as well as efforts to find
a solution to his nation's tragedy.

It was through these various endeavors since 1975 that I came to write
this book. Hundreds of interviews have been carried out with people at
various levels of the Catholic Church, and secular society, both within East

Timor and abroad; with refugees; scholars; journalists; members of Congress and their staffs; and officials of governments, international agencies, and human rights organizations. Although it is based on independent research spanning a wide range of sources, not all of them friendly to the bishop, the book does give prominence to Bishop Belo's memories and viewpoints, which are not widely known and are frequently misunderstood. While it is not an "authorized" biography, neither is it meant to be an exhaustive account of the events under discussion, which would have required a volume twice the size of this one.

Furthermore, though the book obviously concentrates on Bishop Belo, this is in no way intended to undervalue the role of other East Timorese leaders, both secular and members of the clergy, living and dead, known and unknown, who have made important contributions over the past twenty-three years. Although this work deals extensively with the way in which the world has responded to the East Timor tragedy, it has a particular focus, primarily the story of a Catholic bishop who in recent years has become a world figure, and how he has managed to navigate a situation marked by repression and violence, with pressure and fierce demands from competing sides. But this is not only the story of Bishop Belo of East Timor; his experience also may have implications for members of the clergy facing similar circumstances in many other parts of the world.

Finally, although the Suharto regime has fallen, prospects for the future remain uncertain. Therefore, because of considerations of privacy and personal safety, at the request of Bishop Belo the names of several East Timorese who are not public figures have been changed.

Arnold S. Kohen
Washington, D.C.
March 1, 1999

ACKNOWLEDGMENTS

◈ ◈ ◈ ◈

NUMEROUS PEOPLE HAVE MADE important contributions in the course of the researching and writing of this book. Bishop John Cummins, Benedict Anderson, Peter Carey, Geoffrey Hull (for special emphasis on Dr. Hull's work to preserve the languages of East Timor, see note on page 294), Judy Martinez, Thomas Quigley, Martin Rendon, Harris Rich, Geoffrey Robinson, and Dan Southerland and have read all or part of the manuscript at various stages and have offered important editorial advice and comments, as has David Hinkley, whose constant support has been crucial to the outcome of this project.

Over the past two decades, the assistance and friendship of the following, and those mentioned above, have been of great significance: Mia Adjali, Robert Archer, Alan Berger, Michael Chamberlain, the late Edward W. Doherty, Anthony Goldstone, Steve Heder, Herbert Juli, Audrey and George Kahin, Father Edward R. Killackey, M.M., the late Father Bill Lewers, C.S.C., Brenda Hughes Moore, The Right Reverend Paul Moore, Jr., Claretta Nesbitt, Veronica Pritchard Parke, Jefferson Parke, Justin Parke, William Parke, Father Mark Raper S.J., Eileen Sudworth, and John Taylor.

Others have been of help in various ways. In the United States, I am grateful to Arthur Altschul, Michele Bohana, Father Joe Boenzi, S.D.B., John Carr, Father Drew Christiansen S.J., Roger Clark, the late Rev. Gerhard Elston, Carol Bernstein Ferry, the late W. H. Ferry, Chin Fong, Leona Forman, Shepard Forman, Richard Halloran, Robert T. Hennemeyer, Sister Rosemary Huber, M.M., Anne Huiskes, Sidney Jones, Margaret Lang, Robyn Lieberman, Sally Lilienthal, Lance Lindbloom, Vincent McGee, Father Thomas Marti, M.M., Frank Monahan, Aryeh Neier, Tim Rieser, Linda Rotblatt, Ginetta Sagan, John Sharkey, Kirk Talbott, Elizabeth

Traube, the Rev. William Wipfler, Elsie Walker, Cora Weiss, Peter Weiss, Charles White, Nancy Wisdo, and Bob Zachritz.

I would also like to recognize all the members of the East Timor Working Group of the National Council of Churches. Its chairman, the Rev. John Chamberlin (also of East Timor Religious Outreach) has provided many perceptive comments, as have Dennis Frado, Father Peter Ruggere, M.M., the Rev. Max Surjadinata, and Miriam Young, among others.

In Australia, I am indebted to Bishop Hilton Deakin, Archbishop Ian George, Louise Crowe, James Dunn, Jack de Groot, Herbert Feith, Shirley Shackleton, and Pat Walsh.

In Canada, Jess Agustin, Tom Johnston, Jack Panozzo, Sharon Scharfe, and Abé Barreto Soares, a talented Timorese poet in exile.

In Belgium, Isabel Almeida, Bert van Mulders, and Karl Wintgens.

In France, André Aumars, Rene Barreau, Marie-Thérèse Chaffaut, Paulette Geraud, Philippe Guichandut, Catherine Mueniêr, Lidia Miani, Sergio Regazzoni, the late Michel Robert, and Burint Saray.

In Germany, Bishop Franz Kamphaus, Bishop Walter Kasper, Susanne Hitz, Erhard Hitz, Franz Pilz, Margit Schmidt, Andrea Schmidt, Petra Schmidt-Bentum, Ernest Bentum, and Uwe Schmidt.

In Great Britain, I am especially indebted to Max Stahl, as well as Bishop Victor Guazzelli, Steve Alston, Jack Arthey, Claire Bolderson, Kerry Brogan, Carmel Budiardjo, Elaine Capizzi, Cathy Corcoran, Clare Dixon, Tony Dykes, Tricia Feeney, Julian Filochowski, Jonathan Humphreys, Steve King, Liem Soei Liong, Francis McDonagh, Olwen Maynard, Sue Mayne, Stephanie O'Connell, Margaret O'Grady, Catherine Scott, Father Pat Smythe, Paul Valentin, and Lucia Withers.

In Ireland, I am grateful to Tom Hyland, Marian Cadogan, Fionnuala Gilsenan, Donnacadh Hurley, Justin Kilcullen, Maura Leen, Eamon Meehan, Sally O'Neill, and Mary Sutton.

In Italy, I am grateful to Father Egidio Canil, O.P.M. Con., Martin de Sa'Pinto, Father Luc van Looy, S.D.B., and Father Carlos Garulo, S.D.B.

From Japan, the late Kan Akatani, Sister Monica Nakamura, Kiyoko Furusawa, Akihisa Matsuno, Richard Tanter, Sister Jean Fallon, M.M., and Jean Inglis.

In the Netherlands, Bishop Adrian van Luyn, S.D.B., and Victor Scheffers, general secretary of the Justice and Peace Commission and cofounder of the Christian Consultation on East Timor. The steadfast efforts of Scheffers since 1985 have played a crucial role in international interreligious efforts on the question.

In Norway, Bishop Gunnar Staalsett, Bernt Gulbrandsen, Sigrid Lange-brekker, Geir Lundestad, Ernst Basil Rolandsen, Gloria Rosa-Wendelboe, and Francis Sejersted.

In Portugal, Father Mauricio de Bastos e Pinho, S.D.B., Rui Araújo, Father Jose Pachecho da Silva, S.D.B., Fernando Andersen-Guimarães, António Barbedo de Magalhães, Galia Bril, Nuno Brito, Jean-Pierre Catry, Carlos Gaspar, Adelino Gomes, Vicente Guterres Saldanha, Ana Martins Gomes, Francisco Knopfli, Captain (ret.) Rui Leal Marqués, Luisa Teotónio Pereira, Admiral (ret.) António Ramos, João Ramos Pinto, Pedro Ramos, Graça Almeida Rodrigues, Luis de Sousa, Karin de Sousa Fereira, Dona Rui Tereno, and Peter Wise.

In Spain, Father José Luis Rodriguez and Dona Lupe Arano.

My editor at St. Martin's Press, Robert Weil, provided direction and guidance that helped bring this work to fruition, as did associate editor Andrew Miller, who exhibited great sensitivity and skill. Richard Klin provided valuable production editing of the manuscript. Lynn Nesbit was gracious when first approached about this biography. From 1996 through most of the writing of this book, Cynthia Cannell assisted the project with diligence and professionalism. Margaret McMillan proofread the final text with a sharp eye for detail.

This work would not have been possible without the cooperation and patience of Monsignor Carlos Filipe Ximenes Belo, S.D.B., over the past five-and-a-half years. I would like to express my deep appreciation to Bishop Belo and his fellow Nobel laureate, José Ramos-Horta, for their cooperation. Many other East Timorese as well as Indonesians have made crucial contributions, but the dangerous situation that still exists in their homelands makes individual acknowledgment unwise. I would, however, like to mention the late Justino Mota, who died in 1986 from tuberculosis aggravated by his imprisonment after the Indonesian invasion. In his memory, and that of others who have perished, a fund has been established to provide relief and educational assistance through local churches, to families of survivors and others who still suffer inside East Timor. Tax-deductible donations can be made payable to First St. John's United Methodist Church (earmarked for East Timor Religious Outreach), 1600 Clay Street, San Francisco, California 94109.

Above all others, my wife, Korinna, has given me the utmost in encouragement, together with invaluable insights based on her long firsthand knowledge of East Timor. For her part, Maia S.H. has contributed a mixture of support, good sense, and artistic sensibility.

I would also like to thank my mother, Ruth Serotta Kohen, and my father, the late Dr. Philip F. Kohen, for passing on the gumption that helped enable me to take on this endeavor.

Needless to say, whatever assistance I have received, from many different quarters, any errors of judgment or fact in this text are strictly my own.

INTRODUCTION

❖ ❖ ❖ ❖

T HROUGHOUT THE TWENTIETH CENTURY, we have seen far too many brutal attacks on peoples of different ethnic backgrounds and religious faiths throughout the world. I have a great sympathy for the people of East Timor, who, like my own people in Tibet, have been attacked and oppressed for simply trying to keep their own culture and identity alive.

It is heartening to see people who have the courage to resist such oppression, genocide, and merciless attempts to extinguish their culture. Moreover, to my mind, it is especially inspiring when people combine spiritual strength with non-violence in their resistance. Bishop Belo is just such a person. But if men and women like him are to achieve their goals of winning greater rights and freedoms for their people through non-violent means, they need our wholehearted support. I, therefore, welcome very much the story of Bishop Belo and the people of East Timor and urge everyone to read this book.

—the Dalai Lama
May 29, 1998

PREFACE:
DEFENDER OF HIS PEOPLE

❖ ❖ ❖ ❖

B ISHOP CARLOS FILIPE XIMENES BELO began the day as he always did, praying the Psalms and the third part of the rosary at 5:30 A.M. in the little chapel adjoining his modest, Iberian-style shorefront residence in Dili, the capital of the former Portuguese colony of East Timor. On this morning in June of 1997, roosters crowed in the background in the island territory, four hundred miles off the northern coast of Australia, but other than that, Belo was alone, and quiet contemplation had a healing effect. So did the cool morning air: for most anything in East Timor, the early hours were best, before the oppressive tropical heat set in. He had awakened at half past four, his normal time. Already the wiry, diminutive forty-nine-year-old with wavy black hair had jogged inside the tree-lined compound and had done calisthenics. Then he listened to a cassette tape of classical music—today it was Mozart—as he prepared himself for church. Music fortified him: he began and ended the day with it. Whether the Beatles, jazz, or Julio Iglesias, it was a welcome diversion. So were old cowboy movies. Such things lightened the pressure in his life. As always, there was a need to gather strength for the day ahead.

The central event of the morning was the six o'clock Mass. The service was usually full with residents from the surrounding neighborhoods, young people most prominent among them. The assemblage at times numbered in the thousands, with most of them spilling into the courtyard and the street. Mass with the bishop offered the only solace most of those present would receive in a day, and few let themselves miss it. That aside, in the atmosphere of piety in which they lived, most treated their bishop as a symbol of hope who might deliver them from their suffering.

1

Belo scoffed at any suggestions of omnipotence privately with friends, and demonstrated a lack of pretense when he greeted his people. Sometimes Belo would even reject the idea that his words were worthy of the attention of the faithful who came to hear him in his little chapel. For this reason he would often refrain from giving a homily, or would give only a short one. The people would ask for more, but he would refuse, as he did this morning.

There was a special reason why the people wanted to hear him today. Belo had just returned from the United States, where he met President Clinton on June 17, 1997: perhaps there was important news. But the bishop could not be sure of the meaning of his encounter with the American president. He did know that the euphoria that swept East Timor after the announcement on October 11, 1996, that he was awarded a Nobel Peace Prize had been premature at best. The young thought the award might set them free immediately, but thus far little had changed in their daily lives. Therefore, it was best to avoid raising too many hopes about the Clinton meeting.

"Why," Belo would say, "should people want to hear me talk so much? What do I really have to say?" His mischievous sense of humor would take over, as prominent an aspect of his personality as his religious bent. "I have nothing to say," he would tell his parishioners with a little smile, accompanied by a touch of delicious self-mockery. "Enough talk. Enough blah-blah-blah. Better for us to pray silently." And they would do that together, for half an hour or more.

Quiet worship may not have been enough for people anxious for his words, but it satisfied Belo. For him, whatever else he did in life, prayer remained fundamental to his existence, and not only in churchly settings. For a man as tied to his land as he was, prayer took on a special dimension when he was immersed in the natural beauty of his homeland: by the blue sea or looking up into the clear, blue sky or in gardens filled with flowers, he would pray. He especially liked to pray when he heard the birds sing. Without prayer, the bishop felt, it would have been impossible to persist through fourteen long years as head of the Roman Catholic Church of East Timor. He remained, first and foremost, a bishop, a priest, a man of God: he was not a politician in clerical garb.

Even so, Bishop Belo had become known worldwide for his outspokenness in defense of the rights of his beleaguered people. Indeed, the atmosphere just outside his little chapel this day—or, for that matter, any day—made it impossible for Belo to concentrate on purely spiritual matters.

Once again, troops had been breaking down doors throughout the night. They arrived in force, shouting and firing weapons, dragging away suspects. This morning, as was often the case, parents arrived at the bishop's home in search of sons and daughters who had been arrested or "disappeared"; they had nowhere else to turn. Once again, an atmosphere of sheer terror in the community contrasted jarringly with the reflective quiet of Belo's church on the waterfront.

However one chose to phrase it, East Timor was an occupied territory, held against the will of its people by the military might of ABRI, the Armed Forces of the Republic of Indonesia, a nation rich in oil and other resources and the largest country in Southeast Asia. The family of its longtime leader, President Suharto (like many from the island of Java, Indonesia's main power center, he uses only one name), had amassed a fortune—estimated at tens of billions of dollars—largely by trading on their political influence, but Suharto's friends abroad largely dismissed concerns about corruption. Suharto's Indonesia, after all, was a valued trading partner, a "big emerging market," a term coined by an official in the Clinton administration's commerce department. The lucrative opportunities there made Indonesia a highly favored nation in the eyes of the U.S., Japan, Western Europe, and many other countries. Powerful institutions like the World Bank viewed Indonesia as a model developing nation. All of this made the atrocities in East Timor easy for the powerful to ignore.

The fourth most populous nation in the world, with 200 million inhabitants spread over thousands of islands spanning the distance from Maine to California, Indonesia maintains an army of 250,000, many of whom had served in East Timor. The outcome of this unequal struggle, both in terms of soldiers and political influence, was predictable. It is estimated that 200,000 or more, of a population of less than 700,000, died from the combined effects of the Indonesian assault between 1975 and 1979; many others have died since. Bishop Belo has affirmed that the total may amount to 250,000 persons or even more. By way of comparison, about 250,000 people from a population of 4 million perished from the war in Bosnia between 1991 and 1995.

A territory the size of New Jersey—in roughly the land area of the Netherlands—East Timor had become a nation of orphans and widows. Almost everyone had lost a close relative or friend. Whole villages had been wiped out. For the Timorese people, the scale of the tragedy was almost beyond comprehension.

Now, in the vicinity of the 6:00 A.M. Mass at Belo's home, there were plenty of signs of trouble. In normal times, his palm-lined residence on the

Avenida Marginal near the Dili shorefront was surrounded by agents: the headquarters of the local intelligence service was located diagonally across from the bishop's house, apparently in Belo's honor. There was even more activity than usual on this steamy morning in the last days of June 1997.

Today, the Indonesian military, police, and intelligence network all stood on high alert. Truckload after truckload of Mobile Brigade police, their truncheons and dark riot shields at the ready, created the effect of lumbering giants in Dili's narrow streets. Belo and his parishioners tried to ignore the presence of the security forces as best they could. Half an hour before daily Mass began, people began arriving silently. They passed through the iron gate leading to the grounds of the bishop's house and quietly filled every single available seat in the chapel. By six, there was standing room only, and this space was also filled up quickly, mainly with young people. By the time Bishop Belo entered, the little chapel was crammed with close to 150 people. Many more stood outside.

Some were dressed in traditional East Timorese tai, the lovely, intricately designed, multicolored cloth that can take weeks to weave. Others wore simple Western dress. All were East Timorese, bearing the physical traits characteristic of the South Pacific region. A few were nuns with their students, but most were ordinary citizens. One common feature of all the Timorese present was striking: faces marked by deep sorrow. Whatever age or gender, a visible thread of intense suffering seemed to have touched each person's life. In some the suffering had left physical scars. Many appeared to be malnourished.

Their attention to the bishop was rapt, and the devotion throughout the church service complete. In moments of silence, not a single whisper or sound could be heard. The singing during Mass, entirely in Tetum, the lingua franca of East Timor, seemed to be coming out of the depths of people's hearts. When it was time for Holy Communion, each of those present wound his or her way to the altar to share the sacrament.

While the service filled up quickly this morning, as it did every day Bishop Belo was there, people lingered once Mass was over. The service and the moments before they left may have been their only respite from an environment that breathed oppressiveness and the ever-present danger of arbitrary detention, torture, and rape—if not death—for themselves and their loved ones. All the comings and goings through the iron gate were carefully monitored. People did not leave in groups or in conversation with one another. Silently and slowly, they departed by themselves.

The bishop himself left quickly to meet with a group of young men in a plant-lined reception area. On the wall hung a painting of Saint John

Bosco, founder of the Salesian religious order, of which Belo has been a member since 1974. The Salesians, with missions in eighty nations, give special attention to troubled and abandoned youth, and statues at Salesian institutions throughout the world show the Italian-born saint, who lived from 1815 to 1888, extending his protective embrace to the vulnerable young. The painting in Bishop Belo's courtyard depicted Don Bosco trying to navigate his way on a raft in a stormy sea, surrounded by a group of distressed young people. It was a mark of the endless bitter ironies of East Timor that this artwork was a gift from an Indonesian military commander: on all too many mornings, like this one, youngsters pursued by Indonesian security forces would appear beneath this painting, seeking the bishop's help. Some had faces beaten black and blue, at times disfigured so badly they were unrecognizable.

If prayer is one irreplaceable aspect of Belo's life, his identity as a Salesian is another. Surrounded by the persecuted, disconsolate young people at his residence, Belo resembled a modern-day Don Bosco; like Don Bosco, the danger faced by the young people was always uppermost in his mind, the thread that wound itself through all his years as a priest and a bishop.

Even amid such danger, he had a sense of playfulness characteristic of many Salesians: "I am only another sinner!" he would declare again and again. He would list his own failings, sometimes with relish. He knew he had a sharp, mercurial temper. He could be gruff. Still, whatever his faults, Belo was a priest who believed in the Salesian mantra of optimism, hard work, and spirituality. Rarely has this ethos faced such a challenge as it has in East Timor.

The Salesian model of priest as guardian of the young and troubled brings Carlos Filipe Ximenes Belo close to the popular culture of Hollywood, which has captured the imagination of the world. Belo evokes the cinematic Catholic priests in movies of the 1930s and 1940s. Tough but compassionate, played by actors like Pat O'Brien and Spencer Tracy, they rescued slum kids from the clutches of gangsters and the desperate temptations that beset poor youths, unflinching in the face of danger or difficulty. Yet, by comparison, in a nation of orphans afflicted by widespread death and trauma, Bishop Belo's job was at least as complicated as that of any priest, real or fictional, of the modern era.

Thus, seven years earlier, only a short distance from where he was sitting now, Belo had torn off his Roman collar and angrily waved it at East Timorese youth, who demonstrated during the visit of the United States ambassador to Indonesia. The demonstration had brought on retaliation by Indonesian security forces, which badly wounded dozens of youths.

Belo was determined to stop demonstrations that might cause clashes of this kind, and his toughness on that day and many others succeeded in convincing the youths to return to their homes before even greater bloodshed ensued. The bishop had separated young protestors and police in streets filled with tear gas, curtailing the violence before it could spin out of control. He had escorted young people to their homes, sometimes rescuing them from torture or death, although the harshness of the security forces was such that even Belo sometimes failed. He had given sanctuary to numerous youths in his home, although he drew the line at allowing demonstrations or political activity on the grounds of his residence. For all of this, some of the young militants, and their elders in the resistance movement, complained that Belo was weak, that the only way to deal with the Indonesian occupation was to confront it directly. To his ears, these critics talked as if the bishop had superhuman powers. For their part, the Indonesians accused Belo of encouraging the very demonstrations he was trying so hard to prevent.

The difficulty of Belo's position was never more apparent than on this morning in late June 1997, when tension reached a pitch rare even in East Timor. A legendary leader of the guerrilla resistance movement, known by the nom de guerre David Alex, had been captured and killed by Indonesian forces near Baucau, the ancestral home of the family of Bishop Belo's mother. A vast crackdown was under way.

As he finished Mass and walked through the courtyard of his residence, Belo felt sure that there would be new levels of terror. To make matters worse, Indonesian security forces had stepped up recruitment of young East Timorese for militias designed to attack their own brethren. The bishop hoped his presence might help to separate the two sides, and provide protection for others being rounded up by Indonesian forces on suspicion of being associated with the guerrillas. With his driver, António, one of the orphans who lived in quarters to the side of his home, Belo would leave for the area, 70 miles east of Dili, shortly after breakfast.

In addition to his role as driver, António was the one who assisted Belo most closely in the house. Of medium build with quick movements and an easy, pleasant manner, António was perceptive and astute. He was the bishop's eyes and ears, not only on the road, but also in Dili.

As he sat down at the dining room table a few feet from the courtyard, Belo was served a simple breakfast of strong local coffee and fruit by Celestina, the housekeeper. She had come to work for the bishop after her previous employer, a village chief in a mountainous village near where Belo's father was born, was killed by Indonesian forces. Small and thin with short, frizzy black hair in a ponytail, Celestina was diffident, with eyes full of wariness, always testing one's intentions. After what she had seen in the mountains in the worst years of the war, trust was a commodity she would not lightly bestow. From all appearances, Celestina was on the bishop's staff at least as much for her perpetual watchfulness as for her domestic skills.

Overseeing Bishop Belo's household was the sprightly Mother Matilde, a Timorese nun of the Canossian Daughters of Charity, whose headquarters were across the road from the bishop's home. Clad in a light blue habit, at seventy-eight she exuded radiance. Matilde was, like Bishop Belo, from a family of traditional Timorese chiefs known as *liurai*. She grew from strong roots—Matilde's mother had died a few years earlier, at the age of 102—and was fearless: small in stature, under five feet tall, she did not hesitate to look Indonesian military officers in the eye when the occasion arose. This was not the first war she had had to face: the range of Matilde's historical memory was formidable, dating back to her experiences during the years before the Japanese occupation. Meticulous and intolerant of laziness, she ensured that everyone around the bishop fulfilled their role. At the same time, Matilde always had a touch of kindliness, accompanied by a rare understanding and tolerance of human frailty. While she was a source of warmth to those in trouble, all was tempered by toughness and a sharp eye: little escaped her notice.

It was natural that Belo had an affinity for observant people, for he himself could look through people's motives. Even friends had to prove themselves again and again, even if their sincerity was unquestioned. At the same time he was no grand inquisitor: even after he had assessed another's faults, Belo often left room for redemption. Belo's understanding of human foibles was combined with an element that played a big part in enabling him to survive all these years: that of a devilish tease. And in fact, he had nearly been expelled from his seminary studies for mercilessly teasing a colleague.

"Humor is as important as salt in one's food," Belo has often said. "Without salt there is no taste. So humor and enthusiasm are needed, otherwise we spend our lives in grief and sadness and that is not a human life."

He would poke gentle fun at the young men who worked for him. As Belo returned from Mass this morning, he noticed that António and Ignacio, another of the orphans on his staff, had just awakened: "Late again, fellows? And here I have already been up since four-thirty!" The bishop was joking, but the unmistakable message of the disciplinarian was also there.

To some, in a place where a continuing military presence had caused the death of so many people, humor may have seemed somewhat out of place. But the acute sense of irony cultivated by Yiddish-speaking survivors of the Holocaust might help place Bishop Belo's sometimes sardonic wit into perspective. It wasn't gallows humor. It had gone beyond that.

It was part of the riddle of Carlos Filipe Ximenes Belo that despite his traditionalist beliefs, he was no conformist. From his earliest years, he would want to see and think for himself. Even in his boyhood, he would act independently. As much of a believer as he was in Church doctrine, he was no blind follower: he would not run with the crowd.

He was not in the mood for eggs today—the athletic Belo was trying to watch his weight after months of special dinners and desserts to celebrate the Nobel Peace Prize—but had he wanted a hot breakfast, it would have been prepared by his cook, Maria de Fatima, a woman with a hauntingly tragic air of loss. Tall with long black hair, Maria de Fatima had lost her only child because of harsh wartime conditions in the mountains. The father was a leading guerrilla commander. But behind the walls of the bishop's residence, she was safe.

After breakfast, Bishop Belo climbed into his Toyota van. It was best to get an early start: the trip to the east could take four hours, along narrow winding roads. At times like these, many would want to see him, if only for a few moments. António took the wheel, joined by Ignacio in the back. Before leaving the city, the bishop stopped at the headquarters of the Diocese of Dili, about one mile from his house in the center of town near the docks that brought goods—and troops—to East Timor. The news from his clergy in the hinterland was ominous: from all indications Bishop Belo received, military operations, aimed at destroying the armed resistance, were in progress. On the quay in Dili, hundreds of Indonesian soldiers had just disembarked from their ships. They were purposeful and unsmiling, checking their rifles, readying themselves for combat. In addition, thousands of fresh troops had been flown in, and they seemed to be everywhere.

The road climbed the hills along the north coast, filled with army trucks and an assortment of military and police vehicles. Once the bishop gained an international reputation, the treatment he received, at least outwardly, changed greatly from earlier days. Hard-bitten army officers greeted the bishop with apparent respect as he moved through the small towns that hugged the northern coast; they would pay obeisance to Belo, however falsely. There were Indonesian troops of Catholic background who would kiss Bishop Belo's ring, the way the Timorese did, momentarily putting aside their own fierce nationalism; and despite occasional instances of religious tension, it was nationalism, not religion, that lay at the root of the East Timor conflict.

Indonesian troops of different religions recognized Belo's charisma and the power he radiated. The attribute of charisma had a special place in the intricate culture of the island of Java, where more than two-thirds of Indonesia's people live, and from where most of the Indonesian troops in East Timor originate. This charismatic appeal surfaced when he stopped, unannounced, at a small church not far from where he had lived as a boy. Scores of children stopped what they were doing and instantly mobbed him. The scene had a kinetic effect, with the youngsters so energized by his presence that they seemed like a human wave. One was almost entranced by the electricity of the crowd, fighting and pushing to be next to the bishop. Their joyousness greatly pleased Belo. But it was one thing with younger children; as they reached adolescence, as Indonesian domination of their homeland became manifest, sadness set in, coupled with bravery that could prove deadly. The great euphoria of Belo's Nobel Peace Prize had served as only a temporary antidote to the mood of bleak pessimism dominating everyday life.

That dark mood was exemplified by a tune that was popular among the young, including the bishop's drivers, who listened to it on their journeys throughout the island, time and again. The tune was a long instrumental version of the traditional Scottish song "Auld Lang Syne," which means "days of long ago." The rendition of this song in East Timor featured a melancholy violin, set very slowly to local rhythms. "Auld Lang Syne" is a sentimental song in a land at peace, perhaps bittersweet, a staple of parties on New Year's Eve. In East Timor it was transformed into a dirge, expressing the despair over the unchanging nature of the Indonesian occupation. Faced with this, Belo himself would grow somber, and his usually irrepressible humor would temporarily desert him. As they traveled farther to the east, and the military presence became heavier than anything he had ever witnessed, he knew they would face more violence and heartache.

Land Rovers with machine guns, armored vehicles, army trucks, and jeeps dominated the landscape. Like American troops in Vietnam, most of the Indonesian soldiers had little connection with East Timor. As in Vietnam, they were suspicious and hostile toward the local population in areas where guerrillas were active. When an important leader was captured, it was assumed that most of the local population were collaborating with the resistance, and the people would face harsh consequences.

Belo was keenly aware that to the disenchanted youth, the guerrillas served as powerful symbols of resistance against injustice. He also knew that, one way or another, active ties with the guerrillas, or simply suspected admiration for them, could provoke harsh repression, with Indonesian troops always ready to crush signs of nationalist defiance. The resistance movement insisted that attacks on Indonesian troops, and demonstrations in the towns and villages, reminded the world of the feelings of the people. Belo was outspoken in his disagreement: to him, confrontations with the military were dangerously self-destructive. In Belo's eyes, what would become of the people of East Timor if its beloved youth continued to perish? Now that the Nobel Peace Prize had heightened consciousness of East Timor, Belo thought, could it truly be said that one more demonstration, another confrontation, more skirmishes and ambushes were needed to alert the world?

Questions of the past and future were of paramount importance as Belo continued on his journey and moved into the area where the guerrillas had been active over the years. Mount Matebian came into view. It was a majestic sight that filled one with awe. The traditional significance of Matebian, however, gave it spiritual meaning as well as a ghostly aura. Matebian is a fog-shrouded mountain range regarded as a holy site in the age-old religions of East Timor that predated the arrival of Catholic missionaries. Venerated as the place where the soul migrates after death, Matebian had a unique place in the folklore and traditional beliefs of East Timor.

Different strands in the life of Carlos Filipe Ximenes Belo met in the region. As a boy he had lived for two years in Quelicai, a mountainous township at the base of Mount Matebian, the home of his father's side. Nearby there was Fatumaca, the Salesian technical college where Belo taught in 1974 as part of his training to become a Salesian priest, in the days of innocence before the Indonesian invasion. Fatumaca was a refreshing place, where the heat of the lowlands and coastal areas was a distant memory, with a coolness associated with Vermont or an Alpine village. The vistas of Matebian made Fatumaca equal to almost any mountain retreat in the world. Adding to its splendor, Fatumaca was lush with purple and white bougainvillea, shaped and molded into archways and conical designs, giving ordinary corners and crevices the look of a celebration.

A casual observer might have believed that the area, and particularly Fatumaca, was calm on this June afternoon. Inside the chapel, beneath a huge mural of Don Bosco, there were hundreds of students. They studied wood- and metal-working, computers, and automechanics, in addition to agriculture. Fatumaca had its own farm, where an abundance of vegetables and the chewy, nutritious black and red rice grew. There were chickens, little pigs, and buffalo. On the surface, it seemed as if all were harmonious.

But, as Belo soon learned, there had been many arrests of young people in the eastern region. It wasn't clear what had happened to them, but nearly anything was possible: suspected resistance sympathizers had already been beaten, tortured, and worse. As soon as he could, Bishop Belo contacted a friend abroad requesting that he inform staff in the White House about this news and ask the Clinton administration to intercede in Jakarta.

By late afternoon, before dusk, with a brilliant red sun over the horizon of Matebian, the bishop went to chapel to pray. Belo's return to his ancestral region was a reminder of the arbitrary nature of human decision and circumstance. Prayer helped him cope with this uncertainty. Some of his relatives were of a different bent.

There had been warriors in Belo's family tree—fierce ones, especially on his mother's side. In the paternal line, in Quelicai, young Carlos might have become a *liurai*, and had he not rejected the offer, and had his mother not been seized by an unusual piety and desire to support his pursuit of the priesthood, he might have met a very different fate. The range of choices in East Timor was narrow enough so that only a slight alteration in circumstances might have left the bishop in the same position as his boyhood neighbors: Quelicai had become a fearsome place under Indonesian rule, where many people "disappeared." Bishop Belo's main task was to protect the survivors.

The sun was fading. The cool night air would soon follow. From the mountains where he and his forebears were born, from noble Matebian, Bishop Carlos Filipe Ximenes Belo, the man from warrior stock who spurned violence, had become defender of his people.

Chapter 1

What Led to This

▦ ▦ ▦ ▦

To UNDERSTAND THE EAST TIMOR situation, one must look at the complicity or indifference on the part of Indonesia's allies in the United States, Australia, Japan, Europe, and other countries from the time of the Indonesian invasion in 1975—especially in the critical time before the initial assault in 1975, and in the four years that followed. These years were a time of horrific human losses that might have been prevented: the historical record suggests that Indonesia might not have invaded East Timor had its main international allies issued timely warnings.

In a visit they would surely prefer to forget, then President Ford and Secretary of State Kissinger were in the Indonesian capital of Jakarta on the eve of the invasion on December 6, 1975. Kissinger told the press that the United States "understands Indonesia's position" on the question of East Timor. A key CIA official present in Indonesia at the time viewed the Ford-Kissinger visit as an unusually strong American seal of approval. The same official stated that the United States led Indonesia's military resupply effort in a critical period after the invasion, with devastating consequences for East Timor. This was during a time when the United Nations passed ten resolutions, including a Security Council resolution calling for a withdrawal of Indonesian troops "without delay," and negotiations to end the conflict.

Thousands of Indonesian paratroops and marines began pouring into Dili by air, land and sea in the pre-dawn hours of December 7, 1975, after terrifying naval and aerial bombardment of the city. There was valiant resistance by East Timorese military forces, who were vastly outnumbered. They were unprepared for the ferocity of the Indonesian onslaught, which did not spare unarmed civilians.

The human consequences of the Indonesian invasion could be seen right from Bishop Belo's residence: his predecessor, Monsignor Martinho da Costa Lopes, then vicar general of the Diocese of Dili, worked tirelessly to defend the people from assault. One of those Dom Martinho eventually rescued from imprisonment was Maria de Fatima, bringing her to work in his home.

Many who tried to reach the bishop's residence when Indonesian troops attacked Dili were not so fortunate as Maria de Fatima.

"The soldiers who landed started killing everyone they could find. There were dead bodies in the streets—all we could see were the soldiers killing, killing, killing," said Dom Martinho years later, after he had gone into exile. (He was removed from his position as head of the Diocese of Dili in 1983 by the Vatican, after speaking out fearlessly against Indonesian atrocities.) Women who tried to reach the iron gates near the little chapel where Bishop Belo later prayed were attacked with rifle butts. Isabel Lobato, the wife of Nicolau Lobato, the first leader of East Timor's guerrilla army, had her baby ripped from her arms before she was knocked down, stabbed with bayonets, shot, and thrown into the water, a few hundred feet from the entrance to Bishop Belo's residence. To no avail, Isabel Lobato pleaded for her life, begging the soldiers for mercy.

A memorandum on a Washington meeting Kissinger held in late 1975 showed the lack of interest in the human impact of the attack on East Timor, although Indonesian forces waged a merciless campaign comparable to the brutality of the Imperial Japanese Army in World War II. The memorandum, published in *The Nation* magazine fifteen years later, underlined the fact that Kissinger's deputies told him that use of American arms for purposes of aggression was illegal under a treaty between the U.S. and Indonesia. He rebuffed their arguments, stating, "Can't we construe [preventing] a Communist government in the middle of Indonesia as self-defense?" In fact, East Timor was on the remote periphery of Indonesia, and as a CIA official later put it, there was no evidence that it was ever threatened by Communism.

Years later, Bishop Belo, noting that the United States had given its consent for the invasion, observed that "there was no danger whatsoever of a takeover by communists" and that talk of such a takeover "was clearly a pretext." The bishop added that even if this were the case, "Indonesia would still have had no right to invade East Timor."

It was clear that no sizeable invasion by Indonesia could have been accomplished without American weapons: State Department testimony in 1977 established that "roughly 90 percent" of the military equipment available to the Indonesian Army in the 1975 invasion was American-supplied.

These arms were still being used twenty-two years later—a period far longer than the American war in Vietnam, which U.S. troops evacuated the same year Indonesia invaded East Timor.

American military aid was used in the region of Mount Matebian. The OV-10 "Bronco," made by Rockwell International, was a slow-moving counter-guerrilla plane equipped with infrared detectors, rockets, napalm, and machine guns, specially designed for close combat support against an enemy without effective anti-aircraft capability—in short, an enemy precisely like the Timorese resistance. At the height of the war, in the late 1970s, the OV-10 planes would be seen from Fatumaca, flying their bombing raids on Matebian. They would appear as a kind of deadly monster over the mountains and hillsides, creating an inferno unlike anything East Timor had ever seen. Many thousands were trapped and died there.

Before the bombing gathered force, hundreds of thousands of East Timorese were living in areas controlled by the resistance. The destruction of crops generated by the bombing created one of the most devastating famines in contemporary history. Photos of children depicted a situation as horrifying as that in Biafra, Cambodia, the Sahel, or Bangladesh. A Catholic missionary who served in East Timor's countryside for three years after the invasion later said that one third of the people he saw in rural areas during this period died as a result of the effects of the war, especially the raids by the OV-10s. David Alex was one of the guerrilla leaders who survived the battle of Matebian in the late 1970s.

Carlos Filipe Ximenes Belo was spared direct experience of East Timor's trauma during that crucial period: by December 1975, Belo had left the territory and was teaching in the Portuguese colony of Macau, near Hong Kong, when the Indonesians launched their invasion. He completed his studies in Rome only in 1981. Those six years, the worst period in East Timor's history, marked the territory indelibly and left devastating psychological scars on many of his colleagues in the Church, not to mention profound exhaustion. Being away during that fateful period gave Belo a freshness of perspective and spirit that may not have existed had he remained in East Timor without interruption.

Bishop Belo missed a time that marked the lives of even the smallest children. The biography of his driver, António, is typical of that of the youngsters who were held on the island of Ataúro: his father was killed in the war in the late 1970s. Because his mother had died when he was born, António was taken in by family members, who cared for him in areas held by the guerrillas in bush country near the southern coast. From there he was deported to Ataúro, along with many others, in a campaign by the Indonesian military to separate the guerrillas from the local population. The notion that small children posed a security threat embodied the paranoia of the Indonesian occupation. In 1985, Belo went to Ataúro to visit the families there. António appeared behind the church by a prison camp to talk with the bishop, pleading with him for help in leaving the island. The bishop arranged for all the children who were finishing the sixth grade on Ataúro to come to Dili to finish their studies. António left Ataúro, and from then on had lived next door to the bishop's house.

An island visible from Dili, several miles off the coast, Ataúro is the size of New York's Manhattan Island, a geographical comparison East Timor's tiny diplomatic delegation at the United Nations once tried to highlight in a vain attempt to attract press coverage. From the earliest days after the 1975 invasion, there were many prisoners on Ataúro, including Maria de Fatima, with a peak of more than four thousand when António arrived there in 1982.

Despite the tremendous human losses and the cruel injustice, the world protested little over the occupation of East Timor. The international atmosphere began to shift somewhat only after the November 1991 massacre at Santa Cruz cemetery in Dili, in which more than 250 people, mainly youngsters, were gunned down by Indonesian troops. The massacre at Santa Cruz unfolded in full view of foreign reporters, including two British journalists who actually filmed and photographed the bloody scene. With its portrayal of the barbarous cruelties committed by Indonesian troops, and of the Timorese youngsters singing hymns of mercy and taking shelter amid the graves, the film of Santa Cruz brought the horrors of East Timor to an international audience of television viewers for the first time.

But even after this, Indonesia remained a nation of great importance that few were willing to offend. Bishop Belo, whose forceful statements in the aftermath of Santa Cruz nearly led to his removal from office, knew only too well the broad reach of Indonesia's political influence. Still, after Santa Cruz, awareness of the East Timor tragedy had greatly increased, although Belo found it morally reprehensible that some could say that the death of hundreds at Santa Cruz was a necessary sacrifice to draw international notice to a situation that had been ignored.

By the time it was announced on October 11, 1996, that Bishop Belo and Jose Ramos-Horta, the chief spokesman of East Timor's resistance movement, had received the Nobel Peace Prize, the issue of repression in East Timor had come to dominate Indonesia's international image, just as the war in Vietnam had once dogged the United States. A senior German diplomat, for one, complained that his countrymen saw Indonesia as only two things, "Belo and Bali." Bali, a world-famous tourist mecca and cultural cornucopia, was itself the scene of long-overlooked political violence. Unlike Bali, Belo and his country had remained little known until the Nobel Peace Prize. Still, as in Vietnam, a small and supposedly insignificant people had managed to persist against a vastly superior power. In the process, the story of East Timor had become a modern-day version of the epic encounter between David and Goliath. It was not a matter of slaying the giant in the form of a military victory: everyone knew this was impossible. But capturing the world spotlight after many years of seemingly hopeless struggle imbued the story of East Timor with an inspirational quality.

No one was more crucial to this development than Bishop Belo. He emerged as the only one on his native soil with sufficient standing to make himself heard on the international stage. His refusal to bow to demands that he endorse Indonesian rule over East Timor led to a campaign against him, which continued even after he was awarded the Nobel Peace Prize. In 1989 and again in 1991, he had been the object of death threats engineered by the Indonesian military, allegedly by Prabowo Subianto, President Suharto's ruthless and ambitious son-in-law. The bishop took the threats seriously enough, and so did independent observers. During those years, in conversations with visitors, Belo expressed fear that he might share the fate of Oscar Romero, the martyred archbishop of San Salvador, assassinated while saying Mass in 1980.

As if threats of this nature were not enough, from 1992 onward rumors circulated constantly that Belo would be removed from his post by Vatican officials anxious to avoid confrontation with the Indonesian government. Trouble with the Holy See was a central subplot in the East Timor drama. The 1986 Robert De Niro film, *The Mission,* depicting the acquiescence of Vatican diplomats in the destruction of South American Indian missions in the eighteenth century, had become a favorite video of East Timor's native Catholic clergy. Indonesia was using every means of pressure available to assert its control over East Timor, including its contacts in the Vatican, to silence the Catholic Church of East Timor. As late as 1996, Belo was said to be slated for removal. But such rumors were swept into silence when he became the first Roman Catholic bishop ever to be awarded a Nobel Peace Prize since the award's founding in 1901.

These historic facts led to other comparisons that underscore the role Bishop Belo had come to play. The Catholic Church in East Timor under Indonesian rule has been likened to the Catholic Church in nineteenth century Ireland under British rule and Poland under Communism—that is, a Church resisting foreign domination and political repression. As in Ireland and Poland, the Church in East Timor is unified by experiences that have profoundly deepened the faith of its adherents. In a place where simply walking on the street could be deadly, it was the only public arena not controlled by the Indonesian invaders, the only local institution that provided a measure of protection to local people.

The Catholic Church in East Timor quadrupled in size since the Indonesian invasion, and hundreds of thousands of followers of indigenous religions converted en masse. It grew to be the most popular institution in the territory. As its head, Belo became "the foremost leader of the people of East Timor," in the words of the Norwegian Nobel Committee. No less a personage than Pope John Paul II, perhaps paradoxically, given the stance of some in the Holy See, had taken a special interest in the fate of East Timor since his 1989 visit there: John Paul gave his personal support to Bishop Belo long before the Timorese prelate became known to the wider world. The pontiff knew that if he had a choice, Belo would have preferred to stick to religion rather than politics, as various Vatican officials repeatedly admonished him to do. It is not as if Belo has relished or sought trouble with his superiors; in fact, it has pained him deeply, for many years. But the human tragedy in East Timor weighed even more heavily on him, and he, unlike the diplomats or officials at a safe remove in Rome, could not avoid it.

Belo took up his post as local bishop at the age of thirty-five, when he looked as young as one of his seminary students. Later, on his worst days, he would come to have the image of Saint Sebastian, the early Christian martyr: his face would have a look of unbearable anguish at the sight of his people's suffering. Belo once told the archbishop of Dublin, Desmond Connell, that his years as head of East Timor's Catholic Church are "my Calvary," a reference to the place of the crucifixion of Christ. Not every day was bloody, but an air of violence was always present.

Aside from the incalculable human losses East Timor had experienced, the country was slowly being taken over by Indonesian immigrants, in the same way the nation of Tibet was being colonized by China. About half of Dili's population was now Indonesian. The best opportunities—in the civil service, in farming, in street markets, and virtually any kind of business—were going to newcomers. Local culture was slowly being wiped out. The native population, especially the young people, bitterly resented all of this, and confrontations between unarmed protestors and security forces were only one manifestation of their discontent.

The schools introduced by the Indonesians increased literacy to the highest levels ever, and vastly increased educational opportunity. But rather than view this as a benevolent gift, many East Timorese saw Indonesian education as another technique to conquer the territory and subjugate them. The schools were seen as depressing places of inferior quality where the East Timorese were treated as lower beings, forced to relinquish their own culture for that of an alien invader. And as Bishop Belo put it, "We have often asked for local teachers to be appointed, but that never happens."

The Indonesian government never tired of boasting about the many miles of roads they had built in East Timor. Indeed, under the Portuguese, what was now a two-and-a-half-hour drive to Baucau, the first leg of the journey to Fatumaca, had taken twelve hours on an unpaved road that became virtually impassable in the rainy season. Facts like this, trumpeted by the central government in the heavily censored news media at every opportunity, made many Indonésians believe the East Timorese were fairly treated, even pampered. It vexed Bishop Belo to hear this, as though East Timor was merely a construction project.

As is typical in nations with a controlled press, the other side could never make itself heard. The Indonesian media never actually stated that a war was being fought by its troops in East Timor. Nor had it reported on the number of people in East Timor who died as a result. Similarly, the uses to which the new roads were put had not been broached. On this day in June 1997, as on most every day when he was on the road, Bishop Belo's van was one of the few Timorese vehicles in sight. If the roads benefitted anyone, it was the military and other security forces, which needed them to conduct operations. When Indonesian troops first invaded in 1975, there were few good roads, and in part for this reason—staunch resistance was the main one—it took years to subdue the greater part of the territory.

Another crucial fact escaped public notice, namely the deposits of oil and natural gas in the sea between East Timor and Australia, an area called the Timor Gap. A treaty had been signed between Australia and Indonesia in 1989 governing commercial exploitation of this zone. By the mid-1990s billions of dollars in investments were being made there. A group of oil workers told a visiting European near the southern town of Suai that East Timor might be the richest area in Southeast Asia outside the oil-rich Sultanate of Brunei, which itself was one of the richest countries in the world. It is fair to say that East Timor is hardly the miserable, poor, and "unviable" territory that the world had been told from 1974 on, fortunate to be with a nation like Indonesia, which had the capacity to pay for "development." Foreign ministers from Indonesia and Australia were filmed making a champagne toast over the Timor Gap agreement. The world, as then Australian Foreign Minister Gareth Evans had put it when speaking of the legality, or lack of it, of the Indonesian presence in East Timor, was "a pretty unfair place." As Bishop Belo caustically commented, "Maybe the Indonesians want to remain here because of the oil in the Timor Sea. But then, sometimes I think to myself, let them keep the oil but give us our freedom. But they give us neither the oil nor our freedom."

Leaving aside the delicate issue of oil, the words and attitudes of the Indonesians toward East Timor were strikingly similar to those of the colonialists early in this century. Some Indonesians—even the highly educated—referred to the people of East Timor as "monkeys." What the East Timorese thought or felt seemed to matter little. A callous disregard for human life resulted from such attitudes, just as descriptions of Vietnamese as "gooks" had preceded the 1968 massacre at My Lai. Bishop Belo knew this from personal experience. In his first days as head of the Church in 1983, the bishop tried to reason politely with the Indonesian military commander about the atrocities his forces were committing. The commander turned his back and walked away.

Thus, while Portuguese colonialism had had its obvious cruelties, and Portuguese colonists had had their own feelings of supremacy, the Indonesian occupation was regarded as infinitely more repressive and intrusive. Whatever Portugal had neglected to do, and that was a great deal, could not begin to compare with the massive loss of life, dislocation, and destruction of local cultures that had taken place after they left—so much so that more than twenty years after their departure, there was widespread nostalgia for the Portuguese past. It is not too much to say that the Portuguese word *saudades*—an untranslatable word, roughly equivalent to "yearning" or "longing for" someone or something—applied to the feelings of many, if not most, East Timorese for their former overlords.

These thoughts were regarded as heretical by the Indonesian government and its security forces. And there was a price to be paid—by almost anyone—who asked too many questions about Indonesia's stewardship of East Timor: it was not only guerrillas who were seen as the enemy by the military. The father of Ignacio, one of the orphans under the care of Bishop Belo, had worked for the Indonesians. But one night in 1986, after he talked about corruption in the local government, he was taken away, killed, and buried on a beach by Indonesian troops. His remains were found only years later.

History of this kind was invisible to most visitors who came to East Timor. After the international outcry over the Santa Cruz massacre, security forces restricted their roughest activities to places where independent witnesses could not see them. Few Timorese would risk contact with foreigners, much less engage in extended conversations.

In fact, for much of the time since Indonesia launched its invasion, one needed special permission to visit East Timor, and this was impossible for most foreigners (and Indonesians) to obtain from 1976 through early 1989, when the territory was opened to tourists. But even then, tourists were not that many, and visitors were closely watched by a pervasive Indonesian security apparatus. During the years of the greatest bloodshed, from 1975 to 1979, there were almost no independent witnesses present, and it was a simple matter for Indonesian authorities and their foreign supporters to deny reports of atrocities. Nicolau Lobato, the head of the military wing of East Timor's independence movement, which had fielded thousands of troops in a desperate attempt to resist the invasion, was killed on the last day of 1978 with scarcely a word of protest from abroad. At the same time, numerous East Timorese captured by Indonesian forces were brutally executed, many after being promised an amnesty by President Suharto. This, too, elicited no international condemnation.

The Timorese guerrillas managed to regroup in the 1980s under the leadership of Jose Alexandre Gusmão, known as Xanana, who eluded capture until late 1992, when he was taken in Dili. Xanana was given a life sentence in prison (later commuted to twenty years) after a show trial. Nonetheless, there was enough international interest in East Timor by this time to make it impossible for the Indonesian army to execute Xanana, as they had done with Nicolau Lobato and many of his compatriots, and in prison, Xanana attained a stature akin to that of the South African leader Nelson Mandela during his own years of captivity. Indeed, one independent observer confided in 1995 that he himself was told by an Indonesian military commander that without the power of international public opinion, Indonesian forces could simply kill all the young protesters in East Timor. World protest after the events at Santa Cruz cemetery in 1991 made it impossible to take such extreme actions. Still, there were limits on how far Indonesia's international allies were prepared to go in their protests to Jakarta, and killings in East Timor never ceased entirely.

By 1997, the guerrilla movement had been reduced to a fraction of its earlier strength, in spite of its continued significance as a symbol of resistance to Indonesian rule. For years, David Alex, one of the leading commanders after Xanana was imprisoned, had almost dared the Indonesians to capture him, but somehow had remained free against the odds. But the determination of the Indonesian military to seize him reached a crucial juncture after an incident in the latter part of May 1997. The guerrilla army had reportedly taken credit for throwing a grenade into a truck carrying Indonesian Mobile Brigade police, called Brimob. At least eighteen were killed in the fiery explosion in the town of Quelicai, the home of Bishop Belo's paternal ancestors. According to one version of events, it was David Alex who ordered the attack. Within a few weeks, David Alex was captured and killed.

Although the death of David Alex was only one more in a seemingly endless chain that reached back to 1975, there was no denying the momentous nature of the event. He was one of the last major leaders of the original group that had taken to the mountains after the 1975 invasion. He and his men were determined and resilient: sometimes they would lie still for hours to avoid capture, and suffer from easily curable ailments for months or years in the hills due to lack of medicine. They fought on, despite everything, but memories of what had happened in the course of the war had taken an incalculable psychological toll. The year before Alex's death, a British journalist, Dom Rotheroe, spent two weeks with him and guerrillas under his command. He reported that while they were cool and resolute during the day, at night they would moan in their sleep, pouring forth what they and their country had experienced.

The death of David Alex was emblematic of the twenty-three-year history of the East Timor conflict. At the end, Bishop Belo had been told, David Alex was ill, and came down from his forest hideout in search of medical attention. Alex went to the town of Caibada, but sensed trouble. A spy for the Red Berets, elite special forces troops known by the Indonesian name Kopassus—then commanded by President Suharto's son-in-law, Major General Prabowo Subianto—was in the vicinity. A shootout ensued, and Alex was wounded, though not seriously. He should have lived. Instead, the Indonesian military announced that Alex had died of his wounds. There was a quick funeral: his family was not allowed to view the body. Most East Timorese believed David Alex was killed in custody. He joined the many thousands of people who had perished in the region of Mount Matebian in the late 1970s.

The early life of David Alex, like that of many of the guerrillas, could be traced to the Matebian area. David Alex was born in Quelicai, one year apart from Bishop Belo, in the quiet years immediately after World War II. Like Belo, Alex came from a family of *liurais*. Their paths had not crossed in Quelicai—they were from different parts of the township, and Belo lived only two years there as a small child. But their similarities did not end with their origins in Quelicai: Alex also was a teacher at the Fatumaca school, leaving shortly before Belo first arrived there in 1974.

Bishop Belo never supported the guerrilla struggle, and he strongly disapproved of violent attacks no matter what the source. But the bishop also was keenly aware that the Timorese in the hills had few options: either remain hidden and fight on when necessary, or be slaughtered. The bishop knew above all the terrible suffering that had been inflicted by Indonesian forces in the eastern mountain areas where he spent part of his boyhood. It was thus fitting that when the time came for a meeting between a president of the United States and a voice from East Timor, it was a child of the Matebian area who pleaded his people's case.

Bishop Belo visited the first American president to have addressed the issue of East Timor, during the course of his campaign for national office. During the primary election in New York in 1992, Bill Clinton stated that East Timor had been ignored in an "unconscionable" manner. After his election, Clinton sponsored a resolution on East Timor at the United Nations Human Rights Commission, a body that meets in Geneva every year. Clinton went on to discus East Timor with President Suharto in meetings in 1993 and 1994. Then, as trade considerations took on greater importance and American business groups appeared to gain increasing sway over administration policy toward Indonesia, East Timor was downplayed.

Thereafter, allegations of influence-buying accompanied revelations of numerous meetings Clinton held with members of the Riady family, proprietors of the Lippo group, an Indonesian banking conglomerate. Disclosure of these contacts, and campaign contributions made by the Riadys or their surrogates, caused a national stir in the weeks before Clinton's reelection in 1996.

While there is no evidence demonstrating that the relationship with the Riadys had any impact on American policy toward East Timor, reports from those close to the Riadys made it clear that this certainly had been one of their aims. The story became more intriguing on May 27, 1997, less than three weeks before Belo came to 1600 Pennsylvania Avenue for his meeting with Clinton, when the *Washington Post* revealed that Webster Hubbell, a man described as Clinton's best friend and a former partner of Hillary Rodham Clinton at the Rose Law Firm in Little Rock, had visited East Timor in 1994 while working for the Riady group. An Indonesian official was quoted in the *Post* story as saying that Jakarta had been anxious for Hubbell to visit East Timor, and that hopefully this would result in a more favorable U.S. policy from Indonesia's point of view. Hubbell had been paid $100,000 by the Lippo group for undisclosed tasks at a time when he was facing federal investigation for allegedly stealing hundreds of thousands of dollars from his former law firm. Hubbell ultimately pleaded guilty and served more than a year in federal prison.

The credibility of whatever impressions Hubbell had of East Timor was, of course, dubious to say the least. There had been dozens of carefully guided tours under Indonesian government control over the past two decades, few of which were able to stand the slightest scrutiny. Military and police stayed out of sight when dignitaries or foreigners were there, and in the absence of the security forces, one could easily believe (as visitors under the control of the authorities often did) that the territory was at peace. All this could change rapidly, when troops burst into places like the Salesian school at Fatumaca looking for young people they suspected of working with the armed resistance: sometimes accompanied by ferocious dogs, they would terrorize the quiet haven, which received generous funding from the United States and other governments. But it was not clear what, if anything, Webster Hubbell had reported to the White House on his visit.

These various disclosures during the 1996 election campaign and thereafter created an impression of murkiness if nothing else. Coupled with the congressional investigations on campaign influence-buying, it became evident that as much as Bishop Belo wanted to have a meeting with the president, President Clinton also needed to meet with Bishop Belo. It would have been extremely difficult—not to mention unwise—for Clinton to have refused to meet with the bishop. President Clinton had had so many reported contacts with Indonesian businessman, or those with connections to them, that a rebuff to the first Roman Catholic bishop ever to win the Nobel Peace Prize would have seemed unpardonable.

Still, unlike his numerous meetings with the Riadys (which were far lengthier than the fifteen minutes granted the bishop), Clinton did not meet Belo in the Oval Office. The meeting took place in the office of Samuel Berger, assistant to the president for National Security Affairs: President Clinton "dropped by." Similarly, in an earlier meeting with the Dalai Lama, the spiritual leader of Tibet and winner of the 1989 Nobel Peace Prize, Clinton joined a meeting held by Vice President Gore. In each case, the lower status of the "drop-by" meeting seemed intended to pose less of a challenge to the government in question.

For his part, Bishop Belo was delighted that the president of the United States was able to meet with him at all. To the bishop, the very fact that the meeting happened outweighed the rest. Indeed, it was a major milestone.

For his part, President Clinton exhibited all the affability that helped him win two terms in office. After listening with a sympathetic air, Clinton told Bishop Belo that "We will try to be more helpful."

Belo was pleased with the eight color photographs of his meeting with Clinton that the White House gave him the next day. He was soon to return to East Timor, and was happily looking forward to the appearance of the photographs in the local newspaper in Dili, *Suara Timor Timur*. The problem was that this was one of the few places in the world where the photo was likely to be published.

For two days following Clinton's meeting with Belo, wire service reporters tried to get copies of the photos. Though White House spokesman Michael McCurry described the meeting between Belo and Clinton as "very cordial," the White House press office repeatedly refused to release the photographs, a fact not made public at the time. Journalists were stunned by the decision. But it seemed obvious that, like the "drop-by" in the first place, this was another way of downplaying the importance of the meeting. By refusing to release the photos to the press in the first two days after the meeting took place, the White House press office ensured that they would never receive wide circulation; the news value of such material is generally based on its timeliness.

All these details were unknown to Bishop Belo as he rode through the eastern region of his homeland little more than a week after his meeting with President Clinton, when he learned of a wave of detentions in the wake of the capture of David Alex. Belo could not know if the White House would speak to the Suharto regime about this new roundup. In fact, there is no evidence that the Clinton administration took any action. But the bishop was sure that the future was to some indefinable degree in the hands of people of goodwill throughout the world, in seats of power and in other walks of life. Belo would continue to appeal for their help, both in the international arena and in Indonesia itself, even if he often met with frustration. As he had demonstrated time and again during his long years as head of the Church in East Timor, despite all, Bishop Carlos Filipe Ximenes Belo believed in the power of redemption.

CHAPTER 2

FOREBEARS

▨ ▨ ▨ ▨

B ISHOP BELO'S FIERCE determination to protect present and future generations of East Timorese and to alert the world to their situation had its roots in the wounds visited upon his homeland in this century by foreign aggressors, and in the world's historical indifference to its plight. When Indonesia invaded East Timor in 1975, it was the second time since 1942 that a foreign invader brought catastrophe upon the island territory. While little known to most of the world, the people of East Timor played a valiant role in supporting the Allies during the Second World War, sacrificing tens of thousands of lives under Japanese occupation for their efforts. Yet this seemed of little consequence to the outside world.

Indeed, directly or indirectly, East Timor has had a long line of harsh experiences with foreigners, called *malae*, or "stranger," in the Tetum language. (*Malae* originally meant "far," therefore "person from far away.") A pattern of subjugation was established long before the Indonesian invasion, though nothing as shattering as its most recent ordeal. Yet for all the ugliness of the oppression and betrayals that have taken place, East Timor is a land of breathtaking beauty, with incomparable mountain vistas and crystalline springs, some of which spill into Baucau, a coastal town where Bishop Belo's mother had her origins.

His mother's hometown, where the bishop lived for much of his boyhood, is a lush, green hilly town—after Dili, East Timor's second largest town. Baucau is famous within East Timor for its abundance of fresh water coming from the mountains, which forms natural pools and little waterfalls that grace the hills. Bougainvillea and frangipani provide color as well as fragrant air to the front yards along the dirt roads winding through the little town. This verdant region—known as Loro-Sa'e in Tetum, the word for "east" (literally meaning "sunrise")—together with the high elevations inland of his father's home, formed young Carlos's view of the natural world. Those who inhabit this area are mainly people with strong warrior traditions.

The glimmering seaside, as seen from the sometimes twisting road along the seventy miles between Dili and Baucau, is beguilingly pleasant. Mountains rise a short distance from the ocean, some virtually up to the shore. There is little to spoil the view of the beaches, where Carlos played with his three brothers and two sisters as a child. In spite of the brutal tragedy that East Timor has experienced, the people remain deeply tied to their land, perhaps no one more so than Carlos Filipe Ximenes Belo. That rootedness is not a product of fanaticism or fervor, but rather an intimate connection with family, community, the natural environment, and, not least, religious faiths. East Timor is also a place of distinctive and resilient local cultures that have demonstrated a high level of cohesion under conditions that would severely test any of what are commonly regarded as the most "advanced" nations. These factors may help to explain how the people of East Timor have been able to endure untold suffering.

The physical surroundings, to which East Timor's people are deeply attached, vary greatly. There are oppressively hot and humid lowlands, where malaria has been endemic. Mountain locales present a refreshing contrast, not only at Fatumaca, where Belo spent many pleasant days before the war, or at his ancestral town of Quelicai. Mountains, in fact, form a backbone through the center of East Timor, branching out in different directions with varying climates. There are temperate zones where evergreen trees and strawberries grow.

But above all there are the vistas. The view of Matebian from Fatumaca is enchanting; however, although it has great importance in spiritual terms, Matebian may be only the sixth- or seventh-highest elevation in the country, Quelicai the fourth or fifth. The territory's highest peak is known as Tata Mai Lau, part of the Mount Ramelau range, nearly ten thousand feet above sea level. From Tata Mai Lau on a clear day, it is said, one can see all of East Timor. But one does not have to go to as spectacular a vista as Tata Mai Lau or Matebian to find stunning beauty: many places throughout the territory are idyllic, if one can temporarily erase knowledge of what has happened there.

Ramelau is in the western part of East Timor, which is called Loro-Monu, meaning "west," or, literally, "sunset." Far from his boyhood region in Loro S'ae, or "east," it was only a distant dream for young Carlos. But today, Bishop Belo delights in making pastoral visits through the area, and to other mountain zones and rural regions in general. In these areas, at times it is possible for the bishop to find a bit of respite from the unrelenting pressures of his office. Here, too, however, there is no assurance of peace. The situation can be frighteningly deceptive: an apparently blissful setting can turn to horror before one's eyes. Much remains hidden, or seems contradictory, especially to a casual visitor.

In some ways this has always been the case. The diverse geography, with rugged mountain areas interspersed with fertile valleys, forests, and dry coastal plains, can lead to mistaken conclusions about the territory as a whole. What outsiders have perceived in the natural setting of East Timor has depended on their vantage point, and these have varied greatly over the centuries. In his 1915 novel *Victory,* Joseph Conrad called East Timor's capital, Dili, "god-forsaken and pestilential." That may have been true at one time, but the town was largely rebuilt after the Japanese bombings of World War II; the Portuguese made it a pleasant-looking seaside town with a Latin appearance. Approach other parts of the territory from a different angle, and one can see quite the opposite of what Conrad saw: Captain Bligh, villain of the classic *Mutiny on the Bounty,* reached Timor island after forty-one days adrift in the South Seas. Speaking of his first sight of the "remarkable headlands" of the island territory in 1789, he said, "We were greatly delighted with the general look of the country, which exhibited many cultivated spots and beautiful situations." The contrast in views may arise from the calendar. The landscape in many parts of the country can have a charred, gnarled look in the dry season. Like most Timorese, Belo longs for the wet season, when it becomes lush and green with the coming of the monsoon rains, even as Dili turns steamy.

The name Timor is the local word for "east." In the myth of its origin, Timor was said to have been a wandering crocodile from the the north that froze itself into the shape of the present-day island. Located in the eastern end of the Malay archipelago, Timor was first visited by the Portuguese nearly five hundred years ago, when Portugal was the dominant European power in the East Indies. Chronicles of the era show that well before the Portuguese arrived, the territory had been a port of call for Chinese traders for centuries. There were also traders from India, Arabia, and, more than one thousand miles to the west, Java. Bishop Belo's maternal ancestors, who lived near the northern coast, more congenial for navigators than the Timor Sea to the south, may have had contact with some of these early visitors.

The complex geography and climate in the island territory is matched by eighteen distinct language groups in the whole of Timor, fifteen of which occur in East Timor. Local indigenous groups were led by a *liurai,* the traditional chief: in the Tetum language, *liurai* means "village lord." There was tremendous diversity among these groups, and the abundance of languages points to a history of isolation of many tribes. Even in 1997, after the killings and forced resettlement of the Indonesian invasion, which led to the virtual extinction of the speakers of several dialects, Geoffrey Hull, a leading specialist on the territory's languages, still could write that "East Timor is linguistically one of the richest and most interesting regions on earth."

Before the Indonesian assault, the mountains of East Timor were populated by many hundreds of tiny villages that had been largely undisturbed for centuries, with the exception of the Japanese occupation. Bishop Belo's paternal relatives lived here, and here, too, he lived for a time as a child. One of the largest ethnic populations, that of the paternal side of Bishop Belo's family, are the Makassae, a group of about eighty thousand people, mainly located in the eastern mountains. The Makassae are among the oldest settlers on the island, originating in New Guinea. The Makassae are seen within East Timor as a reserved, yet aggressive people: some believe their aggressiveness stems from their belonging to the original group of settlers, who then had a history of fighting off the later arrivals.

The family of the bishop's mother, the much smaller Waima'a, have been traditional next-door neighbors of the Makassae. Numbering only about ten thousand, the image of the Waima'a is that of an intelligent, and industrious people. The Waima'a are centered in the hills above Baucau, where Bishop Belo was born, but their reach extends to the mountains around the Salesian orphanage at Venilale, also near the Matebian region of the Makassae. It is a measure of the distinctiveness of East Timor's ethnic groups that even close neighbors like the Makassae and the Waima'a sometimes have different tongues.

Whatever their differences in language may be, intricate family relations and other forms of kinship have played a crucial role in the lives of all of the people of East Timor, including the family of Bishop Belo, from the earliest times until the present. These relationships remained intact through the colonial period, despite severe disruptions like the slave trade and wars of pacification. While it has had a devastating impact, even the Indonesian invasion has not succeeded in completely disrupting the bonds of clan and ethnic identity that connect the East Timorese to one another.

This strength may stem in part from communities dating back centuries. In religion, there were age-old rituals based on worship of sacred objects, called *luliks*. Luliks are symbols of good or evil, a form of ancestor worship that turns an ancestor into a physical object. A lulik could be in the form of a tree, a body of water, a stick, or even a flag: Portuguese flags from hundreds of years ago that were still held by local tribes in 1975, for example. A lulik could also be a carving, which in Makassae homes often are in the entranceways to protect the families inside, in the manner of the placement of a mezuzza in the Jewish religion.

Forms of worship of this kind, sometimes described as animism, constituted the religions of most East Timorese, including the grandparents of Bishop Belo, who, like the vast majority during their time, were baptized as Catholics only as adults. Regarding these late conversions to Catholicism, it is important to note that in East Timor, unlike other mission lands, one did not see Christianity being fiercely resisted by the native peoples: Timorese pagans gave the Church no martyrs. On the contrary, once the main liurais were baptized, all other Timorese became what one expert called "potential Catholics." The Portuguese did not force them to convert, and the natives were on friendly, social terms with the Church. This helps to explain why, after 1975, they opted en masse to embrace Catholicism: the groundwork had been done, even among people like the Makassae, who had stubbornly maintained their own practices for centuries. In any event, missionaries have usually not had a problem with the mixing of Catholicism with native beliefs as it has occurred in East Timor, especially because local ancestor worship harmonizes with Catholic theology.

The religion of the Makassae, like that of other East Timorese, can also be described as spirit worship. The supreme deity is known as Uru-Watu, a combination of moon and sun. As Bishop Belo has pointed out, the indigenous peoples of East Timor believe in a Supreme Being not dissimilar to that of Christianity.

Traditional beliefs have continued to have a strong influence. Curiously, the origin myth of the Makassae is akin to that of the Old Testament, centered around a flood and a bird who parts the water by kicking it, then nests in a tree that appears. Thereupon, in Makassae myth, a person descended from a hole in the sky, split into two, somewhat like the way Eve was formed from Adam's rib, and became men and women. In Makassae belief there is a pantheon of elders like the prophets of the Old Testament, and their prayers are not unlike those found in the Book of Genesis.

The Makassae have been the subject of more study than the Waima'a, not surprisingly in light of their size and location, centered as they are in such a spiritual setting. The most haunting and most important of the sacred places in East Timor, the mountain range of Matebian, is the spiritual heartland of the Makassae people. Matebian means "souls of the dead." A dark, imposing mountain range, Matebian is where the soul is said to move progressively to the summit, where it unites with the moon and the sun; to the East Timorese, it is similar to heaven. The base of Mount Matebian is east of the town of Quelicai, which climbs ten miles straight up from the coast. Bishop Belo lived near there from the ages of five until seven.

The Makassae, with whom the bishop lived as a small boy, had a simple lifestyle, typical of most indigenous East Timorese. Their principal possessions were a machete, a digging stick or two, a ceramic pot for cooking, a few clothes the women wove themselves, spoons, and rice seeds. Their homes were traditional thatched structures built high off the ground to protect their seeds from rats. Typical food consisted of sweet potatoes, vegetables, rice, and bananas. Life was centered around the family and production of rice in intricately terraced plots in the mountains. Wealthier people owned trade beads of coral and glass, used for dowries.

The Makassae held strong conceptions about relations among families, land, and crops. Like other East Timorese, much of their lives centered around worship of ancestors: the question of whether ancestors were satisfied with their actions on earth was of central importance. People would bring offerings, such as sweet rice, to gravesites, meant to encourage a bountiful harvest. Chickens, goats, water buffalo, and horses played a role in ceremonies for rice planting. Occasionally a buffalo was killed at a feast to appease the spirits of the ancestors.

Relations with other families were built on marriage ties and mutual gift giving. People lived in small clusters of kinsmen and concentrated on planting, harvesting, weaving, and rituals of music and dance. There was a functioning judicial system, led by elders wrapped in traditional cloth.

Historically, the Makassae have been known as a very proud and independent people, and the bishop holds to this tradition. The intensity of Makassae resistance to outside control has been a strong part of their political belief system. But the Waima'a people, ancestors of Bishop Belo's mother, though a far less populous group, have hardly lacked in self-confidence. It is a measure of their sense of strength that Bishop Belo described their relation with the world by the word *nambu,* which in the Waima'a language means "owner of time, earth, and every living thing."

From the earliest times, cultural penetration by the Portuguese was far more important than the actual presence of European settlers. Missionaries were the primary force behind schooling and cultural influence on the indigenous population. From the start, priests played a central political role in coastal settlements of Portuguese soldiers, sailors, and traders, which were created through intermarriage with local women. The mixed-race group was known as the Topasses, from the Dravidian word *tupassi,* which means "interpreter"; in the earliest days the Topasses—Christian Eurasians—were the main vehicle to transmit Portuguese culture. But while they were Portuguese in a cultural sense, the Topasses would not accept domination by Europeans, and resisted outside control. Thus colonists reached the site of Dili, the current capital of East Timor, after being displaced by the Topasses from Lifau, the enclave in the west where Portuguese sailors had first established a presence.

In remote parts of the empire, the Portuguese generally paid little attention to race. What was most important was that natives become Catholic, speak Portuguese, and practice Portuguese culture. Portugal sent few of its women to the colonies, especially not to faraway Timor, and colonists were expected to take local wives (who were first baptized); the children of these marriages were always brought up as Catholics and their education was embedded in Portuguese culture.

Thus, Portugal never needed to subdue Timor directly by force of arms because it used a policy of divide and rule, fighting their wars through local liurai. Given the social structure of the island as a patchwork of small kingdoms, it was not necessary to baptize or make everyone "Portuguese": the fact that their leaders had become vassals of the king of Portugal and subjects of the pope was sufficient to make much of the population potential Catholics.

It was natural that the Waima'a, a small fraction the size of the Makassae or the even larger Mambai in the central mountains, would align themselves with a powerful protector. In this way Bishop Belo's maternal grandfather, Félix da Costa Ximenes, became associated with the Portuguese. Bishop Belo's Makassae ancestors, reputed to be among the fiercest fighters in Timor, were not under direct Portuguese control until early in the twentieth century, even then not completely: an unusually stubborn streak remained. However, Makassae people like Bishop Belo's paternal grandfather began to receive Portuguese education and were incorporated into the colonial system as administrators. This method of rule enabled Portugal to run its colony halfway around the world with a minimum of its own personnel.

From the sixteenth century, Portuguese traders and missionaries had established a scattering of forts and posts throughout the East Indies, leaving a Catholic heritage in the eastern islands of Indonesia that still exists today. But if religious elements lived on, Portuguese military and political supremacy soon faded. By the mid-eighteenth century, the Dutch had largely dislodged the Portuguese from the archipelago. Aside from a few eastern islands that were later sold, the exception was Timor, a continuing object of struggle with the Dutch, who eventually took the western half. A small enclave in the west called Oecussi Ambeno, where the Portuguese had originally landed at Lifau, was retained. Eastern Timor remained a Portuguese possession, together with Ataúro island, visible from Dili, and another islet, Jaco, off the far-eastern tip. Timor was formally divided between Portugal and the Netherlands in a treaty called the Sentença Arbitral, signed in 1913 at The Hague. West Timor remained a Dutch colony until 1949, when, like other parts of the Dutch East Indies, it became part of the Republic of Indonesia.

Far-off observers may wonder about the differences between these two side of Timor island. Since the most recent invasion of East Timor, Indonesia's defenders have tried to emphasize ethnic similarities between East Timorese and Indonesians as a means of justifying the Indonesian claim of sovereignty. In fact, while there was some similarity in languages around the border areas (though the languages of people farther east, such as Bishop Belo's parents, were unrelated to most languages spoken in neighboring Indonesia), the dominant Portuguese cultural influence made East Timor unique, and Portuguese words and concepts heavily permeated the native languages. Bishop Belo himself did not begin to learn the Indonesian language until the age of twenty-seven, which is hardly unusual for people of his generation. Shepard Forman, a leading American authority on the anthropology of the region, has explained that East Timor "did not come under the aegis of the early Javanese/Islamic principalities and, historical conjecture notwithstanding, Indo-Javanese and Islamic influences can barely be noted."

The first contact between the people of East Timor and Portuguese missionaries of the Dominican order is the subject of another traditional legend.

The missionaries, who may have made their first appearance as early as 1514, tried to convince the native peoples to accept them and provide necessities like food and water. The people of East Timor questioned their intentions and were set to drive them away, when the missionaries threatened to have their ship tow the island of Timor back to Portugal. The Timorese still rebuffed the threat: according to some versions of this legend, the native people wanted nothing so much as to cut off the heads of the priests and drink their blood.

"I don't care about your god, and I don't want to know about your religion," the chief of a local tribe is reputed to have told the missionaries. "Sail away before you provoke our wrath."

But before anyone had a chance to make a move, an earthquake jolted the island. While the words of the missionaries had not impressed the people of Timor, the tremors of the earthquake were another matter. Suddenly the natives were petrified of what seemed like supernatural strangers in their midst. The story goes that, convinced that the warnings of the missionaries were real, the Timorese people allowed them onto the island. Thus began a relationship with the Roman Catholic Church, and with Portugal, that has persisted for nearly five hundred years.

This is but one of many legends on the same theme, as Bishop Belo likes to point out. It is a measure of Bishop Belo's wry view of the world that he would laugh at this kind of tale: another example, he would say, of people doing the right thing for the wrong reasons, of acting out of fear, not faith. Belo's practical side takes another view: better to have accepted the missionaries for the wrong reasons than not to have accepted them at all. At the same time, Belo also knows that, despite the fact that some missionaries did praiseworthy work, the people had ample reason to be wary of the newcomers.

The bishop's view of human behavior and, more to the point, human greed is not out of place in assessing the role of the Portuguese priests who first came to Timor with traders, sailors, and soldiers alongside them. But circumstances made it difficult for the clergy to concentrate on spiritual considerations alone. Sometimes the priests functioned as traders themselves, not to mention soldiers. The Portuguese had come to the East Indies primarily in search of trading opportunities in what were then known as the Spice Islands, and from the earliest days, religion helped smooth the way for trade relations. Indeed, when the Portuguese explorer Vasco da Gama made his initial voyage to the Far East at the end of the fifteenth century, his objectives were clear: "spices and Christians," in that order.

On Timor island, it was the precious, aromatic sandalwood tree that was the main attraction. A leading scholar of the Portuguese empire, C. R. Boxer, has cited a Chinese text from the year 1436, commenting that East Timor was "covered with sandal-trees and the country produces nothing else." A world map now in the Vatican Museum drawn in 1529 by the explorer Verrazano recognizes Timor for its aromatic sandalwood resources, whose uses included the making of incense and for medicinal purposes. One of the first Portuguese to visit wrote in 1518 that "There is an abundance of white sandalwood, which the Moors in India and Persia value greatly." The Dominican missionaries were involved with merchants in the sandalwood trade, which was needed to support their missions, which received few if any outside subsidies.

The difficulties between secular authorities and the Church led the Vatican to distance itself from Portuguese goals. By 1622, in the very same year that one of Bishop Belo's heroes, Francis Xavier, achieved sainthood, the Holy See set up a special evangelization unit called De Propaganda Fide, the Congregation for the "Propagation of the Faith." The Vatican also wanted to train indigenous priests in places like Asia. But the Portuguese had little faith in the capabilities of local people; it was only in the late-nineteenth and early-twentieth centuries that the first native priest was ordained in East Timor. Belo himself is the first native of East Timor to be consecrated a bishop.

The establishment of De Propaganda Fide was also a response to the challenge posed by other religions. Early Catholic settlements were built around fortresses to protect converts against attack from Moslem raiders. It was only in the eastern islands near Timor that Catholicism gained significant ground in the early centuries, Islam being well entrenched elsewhere, but there were always hopes that Catholicism would ultimately take root in the more populous areas of the East Indies. Fear of Islam, coupled with age-old hopes of evangelization in the region, continued to shape Vatican attitudes toward the region as a whole, and toward East Timor and Bishop Belo in particular, in the last years of the twentieth century.

For their part, the secular-minded white Portuguese authorities often made things so hard for the missionaries that conversions were limited. A Liberal government in Portugal excluded most clergy from East Timor between 1834 to 1874. In 1875, Father José António Medeiros, who later became bishop of Macau, paid a visit to the territory on what proved to be an historic mission to assess the state of the Church. (He also arranged for the introduction of coffee, cinnamon, and camphor.) After the visit of Father Medeiros, systematic evangelization recommenced, but lack of manpower continued to favor a strategy of baptizing the local liurai and his family, and other leaders of ethnic groups with whom trade relations were needed. This was how Bishop Belo's forebears came to be Catholics. While many liurais had converted to Catholicism by the eighteenth century, even then they would continue to practice their traditional religions, worshipping their lulik.

Being overlooked in this way suited the native population of East Timor: many saw little reason to become Christians. Ironically, Bishop

Belo's father came from such an area, which may have been only 10 percent Catholic by the end of the Portuguese colonial period in 1975. Life in the mountainous interior was far less affected by foreign priests than along the coast. It was not until the early twentieth century that conversions became more widespread, and even that was very little compared with developments since the Indonesian invasion.

Throughout colonial rule, representatives of the Portuguese government were largely based in the capital. Actual settlement by the Portuguese was extremely sparse, even in the twentieth century. To the extent that the Portuguese maintained control of the territory, they did so by playing off one indigenous kingdom against another, making alliances with the liurai where possible.

Although only one was a liurai, both grandfathers of Bishop Belo were closely associated with Portuguese rule. Together the two grandfathers exemplify the colonial policy of divide and rule. Demonstrating the diligence and ambition that has characterized many members of his family, Bishop Belo's paternal grandfather, António Filipe, went to Dili as a young man to study nursing. But during an operation, a Portuguese doctor threw blood in António Filipe's face to see if he had the stomach for his new profession. Proud as he was, António Filipe became so humiliated that he gave up his aspirations to become a nurse. He returned to Quelicai, where he was appointed regional administrator by the Portuguese.

Ill-treatment such as that experienced by António Filipe, and brutal practices such as forced labor, coupled with increasingly harsh taxation, inflamed Timorese resentment, though indigenous life was also harsh, marked by internecine warfare and endemic head-hunting. The native kingdoms long had slave castes. All of these conditions ultimately led to what has become known as the Great Rebellion, led by Dom Boaventura, a liurai from the southern area of Manufahi (now known as Same). Dom Boaventura succeeded for a time in uniting many rival kingdoms. The revolt, which began in 1893, was not completely suppressed for nearly twenty years. After a major uprising took place from 1910 to 1912, the Portuguese Republic was compelled to bring in a cannonship and troops from Mozambique to defeat it. (It mattered little that the Portuguese monarchy had been overthrown in 1908, for as far as the colonies were concerned, there was little change in policy.) Three thousand were killed and twelve thousand wounded on the rebel side; many thousands also died from diseases like cholera. The great-grandson of the Portuguese officer who directed the suppression of the rebellion has spoken privately of family papers documenting the extreme brutality of the operation. As was standard at that time when colonial peoples were suppressed, there were no known protests from abroad.

It was a monumental event in the history of East Timor, and events of the Great Rebellion have been subject to various interpretations. Even today, it is a contentious business, but it is pertinent to the family history of Carlos Filipe Ximenes Belo. While Dom Boaventura has been lionized by some observers, other experts say the uprising began as a squabble between different kingdoms, and that Dom Boaventura rebelled because his enemies supported the colonial regime.

In Bishop Belo's family, the dominant historical memory of this period was not of Dom Boaventura's revolt, but of a towering ancestor who helped Portuguese officers crush it. In fact, there were few Europeans in the army in East Timor. Aside from the troops brought in from Africa because of the crisis, the Portuguese depended on East Timorese soldiers, who had great prowess on the battlefield.

The bishop's maternal grandfather, Félix da Costa Ximenes, generally known as Félix da Costa, was born in 1863. He was a second lieutenant, a position of some prestige. It would have been impossible for Portuguese soldiers to maintain control of the territory without the assistance of native troops, and no one was more reliable than Félix da Costa; he was even entrusted with carrying the Portuguese flag. When he died at the age of ninety-five when Carlos was ten, it was a momentous occasion for his grandson: Félix da Costa was given a funeral with high military honors.

That was fitting, because he was a warrior whose military accomplishments and bravery were legend. Well into the twentieth century, there were two ways in Portugal for the poor to rise in the world: by joining either the army or the clergy. This formula applied to the Portuguese empire as well. But it was nearly impossible for a native of East Timor to become a priest in those days, and Félix da Costa did not have what one would describe as a vocation for the priestly life.

Grandfather Costa was notorious for the collection of heads he amassed during the military campaigns of those years, all the more so for the way he displayed them on a wall near his home in Baucau. As was customary at that time, after he beheaded his victims he licked the blood off his sword, called a *katana* in the Tetum language, and drank the blood from the heads. Bishop Belo makes biting references to his grandfather's savage history.

"There is nothing of them in me," said Bishop Belo, speaking mordantly of his two grandfathers.

Indeed, the paternal side of his family had its own inglorious record during the Great Rebellion: António Filipe was routed by a fierce Makassae army from his perch as administrator in Quelicai and was forced to flee to the coast, where he was evacuated by boat by the Portuguese authorities. This is still a subject of gleeful storytelling by Makassae elders in Quelicai: on a visit by Bishop Belo in the last days of 1997, the subject was discussed, and the bishop joined in uproarious laughter at the expense of his long-departed grandfather, who died in the year the bishop was born.

It may be simplistic, however, to conclude that Bishop Belo's grandfather and those of like mind were simply lackeys of Portuguese colonialism. Their political motivations may have been far more complicated: one school of thought has it that many East Timorese, inward-looking as they are—may simply have wanted to be left alone, and continued Portuguese rule was judged as the easiest way to accomplish that. Area residents say that Dom Boaventura's arch enemy, the liurai Dom Aleixio, whose kingdom was nearer the border area, supported the Portuguese because their weak rule meant his people would be left relatively undisturbed; in contrast, throwing out the Portuguese would lead to a Dutch invasion from West Timor, and the Dutch were seen as interfering with local liberties and more oppressive than the Portuguese.

East Timor's complex relationship with the Portuguese has a strong connection to the situation since Indonesia launched its invasion in 1975, and in Indonesian perceptions of the territory beforehand. First, the absorption of many of the people into the Portuguese world was a voluntary cultural phenomenon, although at the same time there also existed strong resistance to Portuguese rule. If today so many East Timorese refuse to accept an Indonesian identity and are nostalgic for Portuguese days, it is because they have never ceased to think of themselves as Portuguese in a real sense. The Indonesians have been unable to understand this about East Timor: since their own colonial experience was with whites whom they saw mainly as aloof and racist, the Indonesians cannot conceive the extent to which much of East Timor was long ago absorbed into the Portuguese world.

That absorption only increased in the aftermath of the Great Rebellion, and colonization became more direct. The Catholic Church was a status symbol, and it was the children of the liurai and other important officials who were targeted for special attention. Bishop Belo's father was in this category. In contrast, Bishop Belo's mother, Ermelinda, was not allowed to go to school by her father, Félix da Costa Ximenes. But Ermelinda, then around nine, pressed her father with an extraordinarily fierce determination. Félix da Costa Ximenes refused: girls do not need to go to school, he told his little daughter. It was quite a confrontation, between the hulking warrior who had slain many a man, and his small daughter, who even as an adult grew to barely five feet tall. This was in 1924, when even less than five percent of East Timor's native population was in primary school, and only a tiny number of these were female.

Yet, Ermelinda was undeterred: she hungered for the chance to receive an education. So the little girl went back to the schoolhouse and quietly peered inside the classroom, day after day. As the other children received their lessons, Ermelinda looked through the windows and silently watched. Finally, a teacher came outside and asked the child what she wanted. "I want to go to school," said Ermelinda simply. The teacher tried to turn her away, but Ermelinda stubbornly refused. It was at this point that Ermelinda's brother, Lourenço, came to her defense, asking that she be admitted.

The teacher, impressed by the child's tenacity and her brother's support, agreed. Faced with the situation, Félix da Costa Ximenes relented. Stubborn himself, the old warrior recognized genuine persistence when he saw it. Still, a girl going to school was a luxury. He would allow her to enroll, all right, but he made it clear that he would not pay any of the expenses involved: the money for this his daughter would have to find for herself. And find it she did. Having no other way to pay for her school fees, books, papers, and pencils, Ermelinda Baptista Ximenes took fruits and vegetables from the garden of Félix da Costa when her father was not looking, and sold them at the big market in Baucau. It required a good deal of effort, but Ermelinda was set on getting an education, and nothing would stop her.

So it was that Bishop Belo's mother, daughter of the literally blood-thirsty Félix da Costa Ximenes, came to attend school. As one would imagine after all these exertions, the little girl was a serious student and pious as well. Ermelinda showed a particular aptitude for religious studies, ultimately becoming a catechist, one of the few females to do so in those days. Not only did Ermelinda receive an education, she also made acquaintances that altered her life. In her class she met Domingos Vaz Filipe, who, more than a decade after meeting him in class, became her husband and the father of the future bishop.

The bishop's father rejected his birthright as *liurai* in favor of a life as a catechist, which enabled him to move every few years. He was a diligent man who favored going to church over any other community activity. His profession gave him the best of both worlds: religion and travel. Like his son after him, Domingos Vaz Filipe loved to move around in East Timor's picturesque countryside.

As Bishop Belo's parents reached adulthood, the Catholic Church took on an even more exalted role in East Timor. From the late 1920s on, after the rise in Portugal of António de Oliveira Salazar, a former seminarian who ruled as a virtual dictator for four decades as head of the Estado Novo ("the New State"), the Church was a special focus of attention. A major milestone during this era came in 1940, when the Salazar government signed a special treaty, the Concordat and Missionary Agreements, with the Vatican. This agreement regulated missionary activity in the colonies and specified rules governing the appointment of bishops, with a kind of power-sharing relationship between Church and State. It made East Timor a separate diocese from Macáu in 1940, and led to three decades of increased evangelization among the indigenous peoples. After the anti-clerical attitudes and actions of the Portuguese Republic, in power from 1910 to 1926, and the Liberal governments of the nineteenth century, Salazar, a close friend of the cardinal patriarch of Lisbon, was seen by the Portuguese clergy, and the Holy See, as a welcome change.

The Concordat took on a certain notoriety at a time when powerful elements in Portugal flirted with Franco's Spain, Hitler's Germany, and Mussolini's Italy. Although always careful to keep its options open, Lisbon never abandoned its British and American connections. The Concordat provided government financial support for Catholic clergy and institutions, and was seen by some critics as cementing an already unholy alliance between Salazar and the Portuguese Church, which became a promoter of patriotic goals. But for East Timor, the crucial point was that the Concordat placed education largely in Church hands, enabling it to play a central role in what was termed Portugal's "civilizing mission" in the colonies. This helped ensure work for Bishop Belo's parents, and, ultimately, education for their children.

There was little chance to ponder the effects of the Concordat at the time, because the catastrophic events of World War II soon followed—set in motion, in East Timor, ironically enough, by the Allies. There had been little prior contact with Australia, the main exception being a concession granted an Australian company for oil prospecting off the south coast of East Timor. But in the days after the Japanese attack on Pearl Harbor, on December 7, 1941 (the same day that Indonesia would launch its full-scale invasion of East Timor forty-four years later), Australian and Dutch commandos landed on a beach to the west of Dili, over the objections of the

Portuguese, who stayed neutral during the conflict. Although Japan previously had taken no action to occupy Timor, Australia feared that the Japanese could invade its Northern Territory. An article in *Newsweek*—the main mention of East Timor in a major American publication during this period—openly worried about this possibility. The landing of the commandos in Timor, which sits like a tiny umbrella off northern Australia, was supposedly a preemptive strike aimed at heading off a Japanese invasion. In fact, there is doubt that the Japanese had plans of this kind prior to the Australian landing.

Nonetheless, twenty thousand crack Japanese troops ultimately poured into East Timor in response to the Allied move. The Australian forces numbered only four hundred but were provided with indispensable aid by the East Timorese, who responded generously to requests for assistance. Thus the Australians managed to pin down the Japanese for more than a year.

The rugged terrain of East Timor was a major factor in the success of the Australian effort, as it has been for the guerrillas since the 1975 Indonesian invasion and as it was in Vietnam. Finally, however, the rugged terrain was not enough, and as Japanese forces tightened their grip on the area where the Australians were operating, it became too dangerous for the commando force to hold out. The Australians were evacuated, having suffered only forty deaths. In the meantime, the majority of clergy—twenty priests and fifty nuns from eight different orders—left for Australia and Portugal, as instructed by their superiors after diplomatic efforts through the Vatican to ensure their well-being. The acting Portuguese bishop, the highly respected Dom Jaime Goulart, also departed.

Despite their small numbers, and the declared neutrality of Portugal, some Portuguese continued to resist the Japanese after the Australian withdrawal. Among them were opponents of the Portuguese regime, for whom distant East Timor had became a place of enforced exile. About one hundred members of the Portuguese community, one quarter of those resident there, also perished.

East Timorese wartime sacrifices rivaled those of Europeans. Three of the many who risked their lives were Bishop Belo's father, and both his grandfathers. They hid Portuguese officials and supported Australian efforts while serving in a network that provided important information and support. A report from an Australian intelligence agent at the time said that the "penalty for harboring or assisting us or any other whites was death to the chiefs and all members of the villages concerned."

In fact, among the many East Timorese who were badly abused was

Domingos Vaz Filipe, the father of Carlos Filipe Ximenes Belo. Perhaps Bishop Belo inherited some of his heroic behavior from his father: Domingos Vaz Filipe showed unusual bravery in trying to prevent Japanese soldiers from raping East Timorese women, and he suffered the consequences. He received severe beatings and other forms of ill-treatment at the hands of the Japanese that greatly shortened his life. Domingos Vaz Filipe died in 1951 as a result of the long-term effect of the beatings.

This was the legacy with which the future bishop grew up. What happened to the bishop's father came to light only recently through a relative. The bishop himself has never mentioned this important part of his family history, not even when he pointed out to a foreign visitor the caves where the Japanese hid from Allied aerial bombardment during the war. Perhaps he made this omission because so many of his countrymen suffered the same fate: Bishop Belo would say softly, with a touch of sadness, "Nothing special. It was nothing special. It's an old story."

Indeed, the tragedy that befell East Timor during World War II was all too pervasive, even if the heroism of Bishop Belo's father was exemplary: Portuguese census figures indicate that at least 40,000 and perhaps 50,000 or more East Timorese died as a result of the Japanese occupation—more than 15 percent of the population—many from famine that resulted from destruction of crops.

The Makassae ethnic group of Bishop Belo's father and grandfather led the resistance to the Japanese. Makassae leaders were of great help to the Australian commandos in East Timor. Grandfather António Filipe hid Australians and Portuguese in the Matebian area near Quelicai, and gave them food and supplies. António Filipe was fortunate in a way, because unlike others, he did not lose his life as a result of the help he provided, but he was tortured by the Japanese, stretched with a rope between two trees. When the future bishop spent two boyhood years with his grandmother in Quelicai, she would tell young Carlos of his grandfather's ordeal, and it marked his consciousness.

For his part, Félix da Costa Ximenes, the maternal grandfather, ever the survivor and by this time around eighty, escaped the war unscathed. Indeed, those who made the mistake of crossing the old warrior learned the error of their ways, even if they did not live to tell about it. It is a story that Bishop Belo unearthed only since he received the Nobel Peace Prize. The bishop showed an uncharacteristic squeamishness over what he called "that awful story": it literally made him grimace to tell it.

When the Japanese occupied the area around Baucau, old Félix da Costa Ximenes and his brave son-in-law, Bishop Belo's father, did what they could to defend those around them. Portuguese officials in the area were taken to the mountains, where they were hidden. But two of the small group of Timorese informers working for the Japanese learned of this. When Félix da Costa Ximenes hid his family in a cave in the area, the informers were set to betray them.

But Belo's grandfather arranged for the entire family to be moved to another cave where where they would not be discovered. Once they were settled, he went back to the original cave. He brought his *katana,* which Bishop Belo's mother had won as a child in a lottery at school.

The informers arrived and, though younger than he, they knew they were no match for the old warrior. Lacking any alternative, they threw themselves at his mercy and begged for their lives. Félix da Costa Ximenes would have none of their entreaties. With swift motions of the katana, he beheaded each of them. Félix da Costa lived out the rest of the war without incident: no other informers would try to cross him.

Old Félix da Costa was among the lucky ones. As the author and former Australian consul in Dili, James Dunn, has put it, for Australia the Timor campaign was regarded as "one of the epics of the Pacific War. Much less acknowledged are the material and humanitarian consequences for the Timorese people, who were caught up in what was a struggle between two alien cultures . . . few ever fully appreciated the terrible suffering (Australian) intervention inflicted on the people of the territory."

Bishop Belo's father and the rest of the East Timorese were easy prey to the harshest reprisals: the Japanese now considered the East Timorese enemies for the help they gave the Australians and the Portuguese working with them, and set out to exact revenge over the next two years. Villages and crops were destroyed, and executions of local people were commonplace.

Despite their invaluable help, only a relative handful of Timorese were evacuated to Australia. The overwhelming majority of those taken out were Europeans or mestizo. As Japanese retribution continued, the Timorese were desperate for the Australians to reenter the ground war on their side, but this never happened. "They have pleaded with us to arrange an invasion immediately, since the Japanese are very weak, and an invasion would mean an end to their constant suffering," said an Australian intelligence report.

Such Australian participation that did take place was instead carried out at a safe distance: there were large-scale bombing raids by Allied aircraft based in Australia, which left most of Dili and other areas in ruins. The mountain village of Ossu, where Bishop Belo later went to primary school, was also bombed in a Christmas attack, killing hundreds of Timorese.

More than a half century later, little is generally known of East Timorese sacrifices during the Second World War. In at least some instances, well-meaning veterans learned the truth about what the people of East Timor had endured only many years later. "On visiting the island in 1973," one former commando "learned how the friendship so freely given in 1942 had cost the people very dearly in the revenge carried out by the Japanese, after the departure of Australian troops." It defies credulity, however, that the Australian government did not know what had taken place at the time of occupation. While it did almost nothing to compensate the people of East Timor, on other matters the Australian government was diligent. From 1953 on, for instance, Australia has staked claim to what has turned out to be a rich continental shelf in oil and natural gas about sixty miles from the coast of Timor, not far from where the evacuated boats of their World War II commandos had passed.

As for East Timor, the war left the country completely destroyed, the population in a state of near starvation, including the family of the future bishop. By the time the Japanese surrendered, the country's agricultural systems were devastated. Portugal was in little position to help with reconstruction, given the poor economic position of the colonial power itself.

In contrast to the experience of East Timor under Japanese occupation, the Japanese occupation of the Dutch East Indies at once hastened the move toward freedom from colonial rule and developed the military capabilities of the nationalists. Indonesians served in Japanese militia units and were prepared by Japanese officers to resist the return of European colonialism. By the time of the Japanese surrender, Indonesian nationalists were strong enough to declare independence. Indonesia ultimately won the diplomatic backing of the United States for its effort to gain independence from the Dutch, who put up a hard fight that claimed the lives of many tens of thousands of Indonesians. Even earlier, Indonesia's strategic importance had gained the attention of Washington. Secretary of State Cordell Hull had told President Roosevelt in the late 1930s that the crucial resources of the Dutch East Indies, among them oil and rubber, must remain in Allied hands; were Japan to move to occupy this area, it would be reason enough for the United States to wage war against Japan in the Pacific.

In contrast, East Timor was a land without important friends. For the United States, leader of the international Allied effort, the people of East Timor were nearly invisible. Despite their sacrifices and heroism in defense of the Australians, and therefore the Allied cause, Undersecretary of State

Sumner Welles, a close advisor to President Franklin D. Roosevelt, seemed oblivious to their suffering. In a confidential memorandum written in 1943, Welles stated dismissively that "it would certainly take a thousand years" before what was then known as Portuguese Timor would be ready to decide its own future—an omen, perhaps, of later American policy when Indonesia began preparations for the invasion of East Timor.

Why did Portugal keep its far-off colony after World War II? While it may have had little capacity to return to East Timor at that stage, ceding control of East Timor to anyone else would have threatened the basis of Portuguese rule in the rich territories of Angola and Mozambique. Thus Portugal fiercely resisted any suggestion that it leave East Timor: it would be no more prepared to give up East Timor, some in Lisbon said, than the United States would be ready to relinquish Hawaii.

With the beginning of the Cold War in 1945, the Azores air and naval facilities took on increasing military importance for the United States and other Western nations. It had been suggested in some quarters that Australia could take Portugal's place in East Timor as a means of repaying its wartime debt to its East Timorese friends and protectors and gaining a strategic foothold in the area, but Lisbon objected so strenuously that the idea was dropped.

Of course, the relationship between the Portuguese and the East Timorese was varied and complex. On one level, the East Timorese went to their deaths defending some Portuguese officials during the war; on another, there were Timorese rebellions against the Portuguese in some areas. While long and deep ties existed between the colony and colonizer, the onset of more direct rule in the twentieth century was seen as oppressive by many East Timorese. On one side, there was deep Portuguese cultural influence on the territory; on another, many, if not most, East Timorese were impervious to ideas and customs not consonant with their own culture. The Timorese were always among the most difficult people in the empire to govern: it was the only colony of Portugal where a native dialect (Tetum), and not some form of Portuguese, became the lingua franca, used throughout the territory.

In hard times, despite its faults and the lax attitude of some missionaries, the Church was an important source of support. Some priests had defended the people of East Timor against exploitation and physical attack from the earliest days. It would be inaccurate and unfair to see the Church in the colonial period exclusively as an unquestioning arm of the metropolitan power, though some clergy were certainly in this category. There were numerous times throughout colonial history when the Church supported East Timorese groups against Portuguese secular authority. Because of this, over the centuries, Catholic clergy were banned from the colony for decades on end for their trouble.

Starting in the late nineteenth century and early twentieth century, priests tried to ameliorate the effects of forced-labor measures and burdensome taxes. Well before the Indonesian invasion, many individual members of the clergy courageously defended local people, especially in the hinterland, where many missionaries were regarded as community leaders and had higher prestige than the civil authorities. The young Carlos Filipe Ximenes Belo saw the priests who visited his village in this light. Moreover, and quite importantly, friendships between missionaries and native inhabitants have had a fateful impact on the history of the territory until the present.

Reconstruction in East Timor after 1945 was made possible only by the use of forced labor, sometimes under an especially painful whip called the *chicote,* and the dreaded *palmatória* (used to beat the palms of one's hand, sometimes also as a disciplinary measure in Catholic boarding schools where young Belo was subjected to it), remnants of centuries of colonialism. The Portuguese harshly reasserted their authority. Clergy who had been evacuated during the Pacific War returned, including Bishop Goulart, whose integrity won him wide respect from the people of East Timor as he worked to rebuild the Diocese of Dili. For their part, the Catholic population of East Timor showed a staunch devotion to the faith that in many cases was far greater than that of an increasingly secularized Portuguese society. As Bishop Belo stressed in an interview many years later, "During the Second World War when the bishop, priests, and sisters left to seek refuge in Australia for two years, here the people by themselves organized catechism classes, baptisms, and brought [them] to the forests and mountains, and took guard of the objects of the Church . . . it shows the strength of the faith of the people."

And under the guidance of Dom Jaime, as most people called him, the Church was able to provide some degree of comfort to the people. From all accounts, Bishop Goulart, who died in 1997 in his native Azores, was an unusual individual. Like a number of others priests who came to East Timor from the wind-swept volcanic islands midway between New York and Lisbon, Dom Jaime was known for his affection for the indigenous people. When he finally left, he visited numerous towns and villages, greeting many thousands who did not want to let him go. It was a moment of grief. He had been there from the early 1930s as a priest and superior at one of the main schools. Under his leadership, more East Timorese joined the clergy. Unlike most Europeans, who were indifferent to the local culture, Dom Jaime learned to speak Tetum fluently, almost like a scholar. A patient listener loved by many, including non-Catholics and some who otherwise disliked the Church, he was known as a thinker. His portrait, of a tall, bearded figure with warm, penetrating eyes and a kind, reflective smile, still adorns Bishop Belo's study in Dili today. Dom Jaime was in the colony at the time of his future successor's birth.

Although East Timor was underdeveloped and impoverished, the people had the benefit of strong ties to their past and to one another. Local traditions and systems of belief were vibrant, while the Catholic Church provided sustenance to its adherents. With deep roots in family, Church and local culture, Carlos Filipe Ximenes Belo would grow up on a firm foundation.

CHAPTER 3

THE EARLY YEARS

▩ ▩ ▩ ▩

H E WAS BORN while his father was teaching class in the hamlet of Wailakama, near his maternal relatives in the hills around what is now Baucau airport. Domingos Vaz Filipe was known for being highly disciplined and dedicated to duty, and that day, February 3, 1948, was no exception. He left for work from the rice farm where the family was living shortly after sunrise, as usual. Shortly thereafter Ermelinda began to feel pains. It was impossible to take her to a hospital—there was none anywhere near—but several in the family were visiting in anticipation of the birth. So Ermelinda had help with the labor from two of her sisters and also from the venerable Félix da Costa Ximenes, who at eighty-five once again proved his versatility and ability to attend to tasks related to human survival.

The baby, the fifth of six children and the youngest of four boys, was called Carlos Filipe Ximenes. "Belo" was added in honor of his godfather, Abel da Conceiçao Belo, a teacher from the Portuguese mission. But family, friends, and neighbors simply called him Carlos Filipe. His mocking humor would even extend to the name by which the wider world came to know him: "Belo," the bishop later put it, laughingly, was "a fiction."

Ermelinda told Carlos that when he was born, his relatives went to fetch water from a sacred source on a nearby mountain in which to give him his first bath. This traditional ritual was done in the belief that washing a newborn with sacred water makes the child stronger and purer. From his youngest days, then, there was a mixture of the lore of East Timor and strict adherence to the rites of Roman Catholicism. In this case, he was cleansed in the manner of age-old beliefs of the Makassae on his father's side, the group most resistant to foreign encroachment. Whatever their gestures to traditional ritual, few were more devoutly Catholic than his parents. There was never a time when Carlos did not go to church: his father always took him there, and to every religious procession.

Many considered Domingos Vaz Filipe the perfect father, a model of rectitude and stability as well as of unselfishness: the kind of self-sacrifice that he demonstrated in shielding Portuguese officials and local women from harm during the Japanese occupation was something for which he was known in the community.

Despite these auspicious beginnings, tragedy soon struck the family, and some of Carlos's earliest experiences were those of loss and displacement. His father, less than forty years old, succumbed to the cumulative consequences of wartime beatings and died when Carlos was three. The boy was too young to have more than slight memories of him. But there was much more to dwell on than memories. The death of Domingos Vaz Filipe left the family in very difficult circumstances. While he had earned only a small salary as a mission teacher, it was still a regular wage. And it had promised lifetime security: the Catholic Church in East Timor had expanded, and catechists were in demand. All of this security evaporated with his passing: overnight, the income of the family was only one half to one third of what it had been.

Domingos's death put a great deal of pressure on the household. With a small death benefit she received, Ermelinda purchased three vegetable gardens and grew lettuce, tomatoes, beans, and other vegetables. Their life would center around these plots of land, and around the vagaries of the rainfall vital for their crops. All of her children, including Carlos from the age of four, helped their mother tend the gardens, sometimes working from sunrise until evening.

As the Bishop acknowledges, his mother Dona Ermelinda, became the most influential person in his life. The home that Ermelinda provided was grounded in a mixture of warmth, hard discipline, and religion. Her authority was sacred, and was always obeyed by her children. Carlos would follow her through the gardens and the forests, eagerly helping her. He would imitate the purposeful way she moved through the day, performing activities vital to the sustenance of the family. Carlos contributed as much as a small boy could, beginning to wash his own clothes at the age of five. He would do this when he and his friends went to a nearby river to swim and frolic after finishing their chores. If he was lucky, Carlos would bring home fish from the river. This would make dinner into a special feast, adding to their meal of rice, corn, and vegetables, with roasted breadfruit for dessert. "Those were unforgettable days," Bishop Belo recalled with deep nostalgia. "We were never tired."

For young Carlos, they were sparkling times, but they were harsh for his mother, who struggled with the unrelenting demands of caring for such a large family by herself. Dona Ermelinda was perceptive and pious, with a dignified, almost regal bearing. She, like her late husband, was a pillar of the community. Many years later she expressed supreme confidence that she could have remarried. But she had no interest in this, she explained, because "My children were all that I wanted."

Nonetheless, at times there would be a widow's lament. She and other family members would look back on her husband's decision to become a catechist, when he could have been a liurai in Quelicai. The title came with land and other privileges, like the services of loyal workers. Religious as she was, as proud of her husband as she had been, the cruelty of life alone as a mother would weigh on her, and even Dona Ermelinda would sometimes find herself telling the children, "Your father has left us nothing, but your grandfather had everything: water buffalo, rice fields, vegetable gardens."

Ermelinda's in-laws worried over the young widow's burden of raising this large family by herself: six children from the ages of three to fifteen. They wanted to do something to ease her situation, but their wealth, like that of most rural people tied to a subsistence economy, was in their animals, gardens, and fields, not in cash. The only practical way to help was to send for two of the children, one of them Carlos, to live with them. He was then five. It was perplexing for the little boy. Why was he being sent to live so far away? Forty miles may as well have been four hundred in those days. Had he not worked hard, obeyed his mother, and been a good child? Carlos thought to himself. He was sad and upset at leaving.

One of his most vivid recollections as a young boy was being taken by his second-oldest brother, Fernando, then eleven, on horseback on the steep road to Quelicai. Carlos did not attend school in the two years he was there. Neither Fernando nor his eldest brother, José, had been able to get more than a few years' schooling, which was all that their circumstances at the time made possible. Many rural East Timorese, the Makassae people in this case, saw little point in their children attending Portuguese schools, because it took them away from useful work only to learn about Portuguese rivers and kings, which had little meaning for their lives. They would say, "What good did it do to teach the children Portuguese, when the water buffalo only understood Makassae prayers?"

Carlos, in fact, worked full-time taking care of the water buffalo with a cousin. He also tended to dozens of chickens, feeding them and collecting their eggs. He remembers, with a laugh, that the work was very boring. But his mother had given him a tough education, and he did as he was told.

Moreover, he saw that his brother and old grandmother did the same kind of work without protest.

As the bishop now emphasizes, there was nothing unusual about someone having such a hard life at this young age. "At the age of five you are no longer little in the East and in underdeveloped countries, where there is a lack of food and vitamins." Indeed, in East Timor, where there were high rates of infant mortality, malnutrition, tuberculosis, and other diseases, the fact that little Carlos was healthy was a blessing not to be taken for granted.

After two years of using his childhood vigor in attending to the needs of buffalo and chickens, Carlos was desperate to find a way to return to his mother and siblings in Baucau. An opportunity arose, one which illustrates both the observant nature and determined character of the future bishop, as well as the importance of the presence of the Catholic Church in East Timor. The priest who had baptized Carlos, Father Jacinto Campos, a missionary from the region of Trás-Os-Montes, the poor mountain province in northern Portugal, made a pastoral visit to Quelicai.

There were relatively few priests in the countryside; those that existed ministered to a large area and became, in effect, itinerant preachers visiting a congregation perhaps once or twice a month. After giving his sermon in Quelicai, Father Campos started to leave. Before he could do so, Carlos, without telling anything to anyone, walked away from the buffalo he was tending and ran after Father Campos's automobile. Carlos grabbed the steering wheel and refused to let go.

"I want to go home, I want to see my mother," the little boy wailed and cried. His grandmother could not bear to watch the child crying for his mother in this way. Thus, as a result of his eagerness and initiative, Carlos was taken back to Baucau. He remembers receiving a big hug: "I could see the deep regret in her eyes," the bishop recalled.

The incident in Quelicai made a lasting impression on Father Campos. It was the start of a long association between the two: missionary priests like Father Campos helped keep East Timor in contact with the outside world during its darkest years. The encounter with Father Campos in Quelicai had a more immediate effect: shortly thereafter Carlos entered a mission school in Baucau. But joyful as his return to the family may have been, it also involved work in the fields in addition to classwork. Now seven years old, he would labor in his mother's garden every day, returning with dirt all over his body, sweating from carrying firewood from the forest.

In spite of all their efforts, life could be precarious, dependent as they were on the productivity of their gardens and the season of the year. "At home, sometimes we had no food and we had to ask help from others,"

Bishop Belo said. "I remember walking for three hours to visit some families to ask them for a bag of rice so that we had something to eat. . . . I can say we were poor, but this was mainly because my father died when we were little," he continued. "My mother had to deal with many problems, but things could have been worse: there were other Timorese families who were even poorer than we were."

That was undoubtedly true. Despite their daily struggle, his family was relatively stable and successful when compared with the overwhelming majority of the population, which was illiterate and had little access to education: in those days, that meant more than 95 percent, perhaps more than 99 percent, of the native population. Families were also often plagued by inordinately high rates of disease and infant mortality in addition to their economic problems.

The standing of the family of Carlos Filipe Ximenes Belo could not be judged only in economic terms. His grandfathers, one a regional administrator and the other a soldier, had been part of the Portuguese system, and positions like those had long provided the foundation for Portuguese rule. The bishop's parents had gone on to become important in their own right. Although Carlos's father had not earned a large salary, his position as catechist teacher had been a respectable one. According to the system under which East Timorese people were defined by Portuguese colonialism, working as a teacher for the Catholic Church carried a certain status: mission education was central to the "civilizing mission" of the Church. For her part, his mother was well known for her role as a religious coordinator, responsible for arranging ceremonies like confirmations and weddings, and for her charitable work under Church auspices.

As far as the government was concerned, the Church had taken on added status since the signing of the Concordat with the Vatican in 1940. For several reasons, then, the family of Carlos Filipe Ximenes Belo was considered, in Portuguese parlance, "*assimilado.*" In sharp contrast, most indigenous people were classified by the government as unassimilated or "uncivilized": in 1950 these numbered 434,907. Those of the indigenous population considered "civilized" totaled only 1,541, or less than one half of one percent of all the indigenous people in East Timor.

Although the "assimilados" were in a somewhat better position than the "uncivilized" majority, almost all native East Timorese were in an inferior position to Europeans. Statistics of the time show that even assimilados were able to find urban employment that paid, on average, only one thirteenth the wage of the Europeans in East Timor, who then numbered 568. (In addition, there were 2,022 of mixed blood, called mestizos, and

212 people from Portuguese territories in India in East Timor. These three groups generally had the benefits of some education.)

Despite all its problems, Bishop Belo's family was relatively well educated, which at least held out possibilities for a better future. In fact, the Catholic schools at which the bishop's father had taught were much more than a "civilizing" institution in the service of colonialism. Indeed, they offered the best chance for most natives of East Timor to "better" themselves. In order to attend government schools, one needed to be classified as assimilated, but one could not be considered assimilated without a certain command of the Portuguese language. For those who spoke Timorese languages at home, then, one could only get that knowledge in Catholic schools.

But those seeds would not bear fruit until well into the future.

"Every day we worked and our faces were sweaty, but at night, after dinner, we, all the family, gathered in happiness. We prayed the Rosary. Mother often used this chance to speak to and advise her children. After that, we would all sing religious songs," Bishop Belo recalled. "I always enjoyed the nights with my family. It was beautiful, very beautiful."

Carlos remembers being amazed by his mother's faith. With her example, his life was imbued with a strong religious bent. Ermelinda taught him how to make the sign of the cross and to pray the Rosary, and she introduced him to the figure of Christ. During this time, while he was still in primary school, Carlos often accompanied his mother on foot to villages to visit sick people and others, especially those who were members of a Catholic self-help group to which Ermelinda belonged. At every visit she usually made a prayer. Little Carlos often wanted to lead it. His mother recalls that young Carlos would sleep well and happily if he had received a handshake from a priest that day. The family would go to Mass daily, a two-kilometer walk. On the way to primary school, Carlos never missed an opportunity to stop and pray at the chapel nearby.

It was in this setting that young Carlos developed, and it seemed he always knew what he wanted to do, even as he played as a boy. His sister remembers that already as a child, Carlos liked to play at being a priest. He would wrap himself in the traditional Timorese cloth, called a *lipa*, pretend it was a priest's robe, and recite phrases like *Dominus vobiscum* ("The Lord be with you" in Latin). And when he had to watch the family's vegetable garden, where the corn and pumpkins were threatened by attacks from hungry monkeys, young Carlos would peel and slice a sweet potato and make what looked like Communion wafers, which he would then offer to his younger cousins. One day, Carlos and a cousin played "procession," with lit candles. The problem was that they played indoors—and nearly burned down the traditional thatched-roof home of the uncle. When smoke was seen coming out of the house, the uncle and neighbors extinguished the fire, which the playing boys had not even noticed.

The vocation of Carlos Filipe Ximenes Belo was clearly developing rapidly and knew few limits. On another occasion, when he was around ten years old, Carlos took the peel of a grapefruit and fashioned it into a bishop's cap, found himself a stick, which became his crozier, seated himself on a coral, and then asked his young cousins to come kiss the hand of "the bishop."

At times he would stand on a rock by himself and pretend that he was holding a service; many children came to listen to what he was saying. He often held "Mass" in this way. But one day, he heard a noise behind the rock where he was standing. It was Julieta, laughing at him.

All of his playacting was a product of both his spiritual environment and the nature of the life of a child in East Timor in those days. There was no money for anything but the most essential items of clothing, and anything not produced locally required an extra effort to make it affordable. Thus toys were invented by the children themselves. Games and other activities were the product of the imagination or any other form of inspiration that came from the surroundings.

If there was poverty, it existed only in a material sense, because of the great family cohesiveness and togetherness that solidified the community. "In Timorese families, even the poorest," Bishop Belo emphasized, "there are very close relationships between family members and there is much solidarity. Even among cousins of the fourth or fifth degree there is unusual kinship. And there is always help. At the cultural level, my brothers, who were older than me, taught me how to read and write. My older sister taught me how to do homework."

He remembered a courtyard filled with young children including the sylphlike Julieta, who is now a trained nurse. She and others would hang on the arms of their older brothers and sisters. The entire place was filled with the happy noises of children's play.

"Despite the difficulties the family was happy and one rarely complained," Julieta recalled. After sunset, which in both the dry and rainy seasons occurs at 6:00 P.M., there would be dim candlelight or in some homes the luxury of a petromax, a kerosene lamp. There was no television, and radio was a rarity. Storytelling and nurturing of oral traditions provided most of the entertainment.

The walls of Bishop Belo's childhood home were made of dried palm leaves, the roof of straw, the floor of earth. The house, like those of their neighbors, was swept clean of any traces of dust several times a day as people went in and out between the house and the lively courtyard, where chickens, goats, and little pigs would roam around freely. Adjacent to the courtyard was a vegetable garden, with greens, corn, and other crops. There were fruit trees here, mangos, papayas, and bananas. There were coconut palms to quench everybody's thirst with delicious coconut milk.

There was no electricity or running water, so often, at 5:00 A.M., before Mass, Carlos would go with his older brother António to get water from the public tap. Generally the water would be fetched by the older children from communal wells, which were always the site of conversation and play. No one was more playful than António. To hear Bishop Belo tell it, António, two years older, was much stronger and braver than he. António would wrestle with large pigs and other animals. He would take risks others would avoid, like climbing on dangerous slopes. António had an impetuous streak and was more outgoing than the other children. It was the younger Carlos who sometimes had to call António to reason, Julieta remembered.

But Carlos was capable of mischief himself, and this would take various forms. He would sometimes take chicken eggs—rare delicacies that were very expensive—from his mother's kitchen and fry them for his friends. Occasionally he would be spanked. But it was not as if this was because he was stealing. If he was spanked, it was because they were not rich and he could not be allowed to overdo it.

That was because there was a need for special cooperation and discipline if the family was to maintain itself, especially a family with only one parent. It began with basic things, and the children were full participants, even when they were small. The fundamental task was their work in the garden, and they proceeded from there to setting the table and cooking. Each of the six children had his or her assigned day. They used a little outdoor structure as the kitchen, which also served as a storage place for firewood, with a "stove" consisting of a few blackened stones in the middle of which the firewood would be placed. On top an earthen or iron pot could cook nutritious black rice, corn with pumpkin, and other dishes. Carlos liked to cook vegetables, especially a mixture of papaya leaves, squash, and corn stir-fried with sweet-and-sour spices. Even as a bishop, this dish, called *raba raba,* remains his favorite food, which he still cooks when he visits his mother.

As was typical in this subsistence economy, the food they ate was strictly what the family produced itself, with some bartering or sale of surplus on local markets and the occasional sale to the Chinese merchants in Baucau for a little cash income. The Chinese community, which first came to East Timor to engage in the sandalwood trade centuries before, numbered about three thousand when Carlos was a boy, or twice as many as the number of indigenous East Timorese regarded as "civilized" by the authorities. Even the "civilized" did not have their own retail businesses; almost without exception, commerce in East Timor, as in neighboring Indonesia, was conducted by Chinese traders. These merchants purchased produce from the garden of Bishop Belo's mother, which provided income to buy school supplies for her children, just as the garden of Félix da Costa had secretly subsidized her own studies. Many mornings after Mass and before school, young Carlos would go to the market with his sisters to sell vegetables to Chinese shopkeepers so they could buy pencils and pads. These simple school supplies were luxuries not to be taken for granted.

Growing up in East Timor in those days meant a childhood filled with the joys of living in an unspoiled natural environment. Carlos had the liberty of movement that only children in close-knit communities enjoy, where every member helps look after the little ones. Carlos himself would disappear at times to visit relatives in the area, sometimes vanishing for hours or even overnight. He recalls leaving his little sister to visit others by himself. Julieta remembers an instance when he ran away from the beach and they could not find him. But the security of the community was such that there would be no worries about the physical safety of the children.

Interestingly, in light of his future, he was not the favored son. That honor went to his eldest brother, José, ten years older than Carlos. As Bishop Belo recalled, speaking of his mother, "It was always, 'José, José.'" Perhaps because attention was not lavished upon him, he developed an independent streak early on, liking to take initiative and do things by himself. Sometimes it was hard to predict what he might do next. Carlos would switch effortlessly between religious piety and child's play.

"I remember that at night we were usually afraid to go out because of horror stories about the devil, witches, and thieves that would steal children in order to feed them to the great robot, the man of iron at the radio station of Baucau!" He would quietly go outside after dinner, either before or after having prayed the Rosary, and take a long stick to frighten Julieta and his mother. He acted out comical scenes in order to make his mother and siblings laugh. Or he threw stones at the walls, and then would laugh and laugh, making fun of those inside the house. At other times he would simply imitate other people, their way of walking and talking and their gestures.

Carlos was also not immune to the roughhouse scrapping of young boys everywhere. But this was mixed with a more pacific attitude: "I remember fighting with other boys, the usual thing; I used to be in quite a few fights. But then I would regret hitting my colleagues and I promised I did not want to do it and that I wanted to be nonviolent. Then when fighting broke out among my friends, I would try to separate them and stop it."

From his earliest years, Carlos was able to read the moods and feelings of people, of not only close family members, but strangers as well. He could not stand dishonesty, and had an unusual ability to sense when someone was behaving insincerely. Too, he would not tolerate treachery or any form of false dealing. His sister Julieta said that as a boy, if he found his friends cheating, he would grow angry and stop playing with them. He could be very strict and tough. But he also was fair: if he made a mistake or saw he was wrong, he was not slow to apologize.

One other situation in which Carlos would take on a serious demeanor was school. In contrast to his sometimes mischievous ways among siblings, friends, and neighbors, teachers remember a modest, quiet, and studious boy who was always able to talk sense to his colleagues. When told of his early playacting as "bishop" on the coral among his cousins, his spiritual director at the minor seminary, Father José Luis Rodriguez, a Jesuit from Spain, was incredulous.

Whatever the outward appearances, his sights were always set on wider horizons. Various relatives, among them his paternal grandmother, Maria Rosa Filipe, wanted Carlos to take over the position of liurai, the traditional chief of the Quelicai area. After all, lack of money was the family's main problem when Carlos was a boy, and the title of liurai carried with it more than a position as local chieftain: it also meant economic power. A liurai gained followers who would provide labor and render other forms of practical service, and also acted as an intermediary between the Portuguese government and the local people, making the post an added mark of privilege and prestige. For a family that had known hardship since Domingos Vaz Filipe died, all of this would be an important help.

No one seemed more suited to be a liurai than Carlos. To his family and the elders in the region, from the time he was very small Carlos was a clever fellow who always asked many questions of them, questions about the very nature of things. He did not hesitate to debate, even if his opponent was older. Carlos would often have vigorous exchanges with his brother António. They could debate anything, though Carlos put his toughest questions to the village elders. He challenged everyone's treasured assumptions:

"Why does a man have to look for a beautiful woman to be his wife? Why must a married couple donate a deer to the community? And why do people spend so much money on traditional celebrations?" Carlos would ask.

There were so many questions that elders sometimes became angry. But they recognized his intelligence and boldness, sensing that he was a natural leader, and tried without success to make him liurai. Years later, when he and his brother António were at the seminary near Dili, the two boys would return on vacations to Quelicai. Although António was older, much bigger and stronger, the elders would try again and again to convince Carlos, then 13, to become liurai. Carlos would calmly present arguments against it: he needed to study, he said, so that one day he could minister to the faithful.

"*Não vale a pena,*" said the future Dom Carlos to himself, a Portuguese expression that means "it is not worth it," literally, "it is not worth the pain." From his reading and his contacts with missionary priests, Carlos believed he stood a better chance of seeing the world if he joined the Church. Jesuit priests, he knew, were sent to places like Alaska, Denmark, and Macau. Liurais, no matter how many gardens or animals they had, stayed home.

If he had gotten this far in his thinking, it was because Ermelinda had been determined to secure an education for her children. As far back as he could remember she was well informed about the work of the Catholic Church in other places, giving him a sense of the wider world from a very early age. Carlos remembers praying the rosary a great deal for Hungary from the time he was eight, in 1956. His mother had told her children the Russians had invaded Hungary (another place where for many years, like East Timor after the Indonesian invasion, change was said to be impossible) and the pope had asked for prayers.

"Without Mother we might be illiterate now," Bishop Belo recalled. "I know exactly how she fought for her kids. She walked kilometer after kilometer to make sure we were settled in the right place for us to study." As Ermelinda had to struggle to find the money to pay for the church schools that Carlos and his brothers and sisters attended, outside help was always needed. "I remember quite precisely how a missionary priest in Baucau requested that official government assistance be given to my family, to my mother, to sustain us, because my father had been a mission teacher," the bishop recalled many years later. "My mother received nine patacas from the local government administration in Baucau to pay for our studies."

On June 13, 1958, around the time he was playing "bishop," Carlos had his first Communion. After the ceremony, which he attended barefoot—his family had a picnic by a spring in the town of Caibada.

Carlos had begun to think about attending the mission school at Ossu, known to be one of the best. After several years at home in Baucau, at the age of twelve he went to the Salesian school in Ossu for the third and fourth grades. The school was called Collegio de Santa Teresinha do Menino Jesus—the School of Little Saint Theresa of the Child Jesus. Unlike his frolicsome personality at home, in this school, too, Carlos was quiet, and he was known to the faculty and his classmates as very intelligent. In his first year at Ossu, one teacher gave him the Latin nickname "Tacito," because he was so silent.

Later at Ossu, he became more outgoing, and his teacher concluded that Carlos had a flair for languages, geography, history, and literature, but was poor at mathematics and physical science. It was his talent for languages that really stood out and marked him for a career in the Church at a very early age; his teacher thought he should consider going to the seminary. Carlos had already thought of this. His facility at languages made him think of the world at a very early age. And his brother António already had begun seminary studies.

Carlos worried about the cost of the seminary, however. "It was a wonder that we could graduate from elementary school, let alone go to the seminary with its expensive dormitory costs." But the family supported his decision. Ermelinda approached many people for loans until they had covered part of the cost. Carlos's older sister, Aurea Baptista, who had become a teacher at a Catholic school of the Canossian Sisters in Dili, also helped pay his school fees so he could continue his studies.

He arrived at the Seminary of Saint Francis Xavier at Dare, on a magnificent hilltop overlooking Dili and the ocean, at the age of fourteen. All he had in his pocket were two patacas, but a catechist teacher gave him some support. He spent two years at this school, then moved to the upper school in the same place, known as the Seminary of Our Lady of Fatima. Here he received support through Father José Luis Rodriguez, not only because Carlos was poor, but also because he was one of two brothers at the seminary. Father Rodriguez found a benefactor for Carlos in the Orisqueta family of Bilbao, in northern Spain, to pay many of his expenses for five years.

This network of support was sorely needed. Money was so limited that Ermelinda could not come to see the new school with her sons. Three monthly fees were required in advance to cover Carlos's food and other expenses, but they were able to afford only two.

During school vacations, Carlos returned to help his mother tend the vegetable gardens which remained the mainstay of the family income. As Bishop Belo remembers of his summer vacations, "It was a simple life of study and work." His mother would wake him and his siblings early, at 4:00 A.M., often pulling the legs of young Carlos, telling him to get up and get ready to go to Mass. While Belo joked that his mother was as strict as his teachers, in fact, "Life in the seminary was completely different than at home. I faced hundreds of rules that I had to obey," the bishop recalls. "I was lucky that I learned a lot of spirituality at home."

The Dare seminary had much more to offer than discipline. It was in a physical setting of tranquil beauty, with eucalyptus-laced mountain slopes and a view of Dili harbor to rival that of the Portuguese governor's residence. It was surrounded by gardens of flowers of every type native to that region. Dare was the highest institution of learning in East Timor, and the students were mainly Timorese, unlike at the public high school in Dili. Some of the brightest students in the territory, among them many of the future leaders of the country's independence movement, went to Dare, although many did not pursue their studies for the priesthood, leaving to become teachers or civil servants. Carlos became a prominent figure at Dare, through his reputation as a debater and for his thorough and precise discussion of issues. It seemed he never lost the energy to argue. He also loved to read foreign books, whether of history, geography, or German philosophy.

The Jesuits who ran the seminary criticized the colonial system and helped to foster a greater sense of consciousness among the East Timorese students, in contrast to the teachers at the more Portuguese-oriented schools. Still, there were limits to which nationalist expression could go. Symbolic of this was the fact that in class exercises, it was forbidden to speak in Tetum or other native languages. Everything was conducted in Portuguese.

The head student would control the others and make sure they followed the rules. Often this role fell to Belo. As in debating, he was known as very tough and disciplined. Younger students were afraid of him. "We couldn't take it easy if Belo was in control," said one old classmate. "We had to read and memorize all the texts, or else he would punish us." Another remembered that if Carlos heard a student speaking in Tetum, he would crack down right away. The penalty was unusual. Belo would hang a coral stone around the neck of whoever spoke in Tetum. The more a student did this, the more stones were hung.

Despite his toughness, he was a popular student, and was also elected as coordinator of student activities. He was fun-loving and good at uniting the group. He was involved in drama. "He always played a good character," one friend said. "He had too innocent a face to play someone evil." Carlos also played sports; he particularly liked soccer, which he played on the school team. The seminary had musical instruments, and Carlos liked nothing better than to sing songs by the Beatles. He especially liked to listen to romantic songs.

These pleasures notwithstanding, tragedy was never far away. The death of his father was only the beginning of the family's sorrow. His elder brother Fernando, who was supporting the family by working in rice fields and vegetable gardens, died suddenly at the age of twenty-two of an unknown cause after a party at which much palm wine had been consumed. The death of Fernando added to the family's pain and made life still more difficult economically. Carlos and António were at the seminary in Dare when they received the terrible news. Father José Luis Rodriguez, their teacher, remembers the brothers that day, wailing and consoling each other.

They found consolation in the religious life. In December 1962, a few months after he first went to Dare, Belo learned in a lecture at the school of what he called "the apostolic zeal, the audacity, courage, and humility" of Saint Francis Xavier, the apostle to the Orient, who had visited the East Indies. Saint Francis Xavier was one of seven original Jesuits and part of the first missionary expedition sent out by the order's founder, Saint Ignatius Loyola. When he was in India, Francis Xavier had written to Loyola in Rome, from where he headed the Society of Jesus, saying, "Just one letter from you [in the sense of a, b or c], just one single letter and I am ready to obey."

Young Carlos was very impressed by that. He remembers kneeling down at that very moment before his classmates and saying, "I want to be an apostle as you were."

"I prayed to Saint Francis Xavier. Suddenly it came to me that it would be great if I were a person like him. I felt that I was called in my heart," the bishop remembers.

Once the priest had finished his story of Saint Francis Xavier that day in Dare, Carlos ran to the chapel. "I prayed for so long in that chapel," the bishop recalled with great feeling. "I was sure I wanted to be a priest." He declared to himself that he was going to be a religious man inspired by

Saint Francis Xavier. Two months before his fifteenth birthday, he resolved that one day he would join a religious order. It is a measure of his resolve that he held to this idea for years before the opportunity arose to put his aspirations into practice.

As he was to show later in life, Carlos approached his aspirations in a distinctive way, never forgetting his own roots. In light of his admiration for Saint Francis Xavier, it was natural that Carlos first approached the Jesuits. However, he was told that this was impossible. The local bishop, Dom José Joaquim Ribeiro, would not allow any more Jesuits into East Timor, despite the fact that Jesuits ran the seminary in Dare: it was said that Ribeiro felt there was already enough "Jesuit propaganda" there. The Jesuits had a history of conflict with Portuguese authorities going back centuries—dating from the eighteenth-century period depicted in the film *The Mission*. They were expelled from Portugal for long stretches of time, and even when they were allowed in the country, their independence made them an object of suspicion by the Portuguese Catholic hierarchy.

Instead, Carlos was told, it was better to talk to the Salesians, whose missions had begun in East Timor in the 1920s. He did so: Carlos had first heard of Don Bosco when he was twelve, as a pupil in the Salesian school in Ossu. He was the third best student that year, and as a prize he received a book about Dominic Savio, a saintly boy who was a pupil of Don Bosco and died as a teenager.

His decision to join the Salesians caused controversy at the seminary. The rector immediately tried to convince Carlos to change his mind. "I asked for their permission to join the Salesian order," he recalled, "not because I wanted to reject their advice but because I was sure that working for the youth in a religious community was what I wanted to do."

In 1968 he sent a letter to the leader of the Salesian order in East Timor, in Fuiloro, in the extreme eastern part of the territory. Father Alfonso Nacher, a Spaniard, recognized the young man's resolve. He told Carlos to prepare himself to go to Portugal to complete his studies. Carlos became even more confident about the direction in which he was moving. He then went to talk with Bishop Ribeiro. He, too, was not pleased at the news that Belo was planning to join the Salesians.

"Look, Carlos," Bishop Ribeiro said, in the room where Bishop Belo now receives visitors, "you will go to study in the diocesan seminary school in Évora," which is also in Portugal. As Bishop Ribeiro knew, Carlos's brother António would be studying in Évora the following year.

"Excuse me, Bishop, but I want to join a religious order," Carlos replied.

Diocesan priests obey the local bishop and carry out different kinds of work, mainly in the parishes. By contrast, someone who enters a religious order or congregation can be sent anywhere in the world. If Carlos became a Salesian, he might be sent to any of the dozens of countries around the world where they have missions, but he could also come home to East Timor.

That aside, Bishop Ribeiro was known as an ill-tempered man with an authoritarian bent. He originally came to East Timor to serve as an auxiliary bishop to Dom Jaime, who had wanted to stay on with the help of an assistant. Instead, members of the clergy said, Ribeiro made Dom Jaime so miserable that the beloved bishop chose to retire to the Azores instead. But however difficult Ribeiro was, young Belo would not allow himself to be intimidated.

"Why do you want to join a religious order?" Bishop Ribeiro pressed Carlos.

"To achieve perfection," Carlos responded.

The bishop insisted that diocesan priests, too, could attain perfection. Carlos resisted Bishop Ribeiro's entreaty.

"Excuse me again, Bishop, but I already decided this a long time ago and I cannot change," said Carlos, then only seventeen years old.

In 1965, a Portuguese bishop rarely had his authority challenged in East Timor. It took courage and tenacity for Carlos to maintain his position in the face of such opposition. Yet he had no trouble doing so. He was discovering in himself an ability to defy those in authority, even mentors and good friends, if he believed he had to.

There were those who were disappointed. The bishop of Dili later said he was sad to learn that Carlos would become a Salesian. Bishop Ribeiro believed the Diocese of Dili had lost a good candidate for the priesthood. And when Carlos decided he would become a Salesian, he remembers that José Luis Rodriguez, his mentor and spiritual director, was "quite annoyed" because he had known nothing about these plans during the time that he was working to obtain scholarship money for Carlos: Father Rodriguez had believed that Belo would become a Jesuit. But Carlos stuck firmly to his position, and Father Rodriguez remains to this day a good friend, providing considerable help in the hardest of times.

From an early age, just as he had turned aside the entreaties of the elders of Quelicai, he resisted the easy option of bending to the expectations of others. He would not run with the crowd. More than twenty-five years later, facing challenges to his authority as bishop of Dili from all sides, he emphasized, "There must be respect for individuality. That is why I have said, since I was a young man, 'Don't just go with the others.'"

Joining the Salesians, with their emphasis on troubled youth and spirituality, was a logical path from a variety of standpoints. First, there was his own background as a fatherless boy, like Saint John Bosco, who also lost his father as a child. While Bishop Belo would protest his unworthiness of such comparisons with Don Bosco, both were raised by poor but exceptionally pious and disciplined women who made great sacrifices so that their sons might study for the priesthood. Both had to overcome sadness arising from their difficult circumstances. Both emerged with renewed strength and determination to minister to the younger generation, no matter what the obstacles. Hardship would not get the better of them. Indeed, young Carlos learned early on to count his blessings.

Compared with what came later, it was a golden age. Even with the tragedy that Belo's family had endured, this was a time of relative innocence. Poor as they were, there was a kind of sleepy status quo that gave sufficient space for Carlos, his friends, and family to grow. Of course, Carlos was hardly blind to the cruelties of the colonial system. He and his fellow seminarians would go into the community to preach, teach reading and writing, and help fix houses. Everywhere he ministered, he saw backwardness and want: "Whenever I visited villages and saw their poverty, I would tell the children, 'Please study, your life can be better if you are smart.'"

The bishop later recalled how it broke his heart to see how the Portuguese in East Timor treated the indigenous people. He said, "I often saw some of the Portuguese taking palm wine that was for sale by the indigenous people and not give them any money, although the people had walked for a long time to the market in the hope that they would return with some money. They were oppressed and could not defend themselves. Every time I saw these things, my heart ached and I cried inside. But I could not do anything."

His sympathy intensified his desire to see young people improve their lot: it is part of what led him to become a Salesian.

A rich combination of faith and good humor was crucial in Belo's life. For this fatherless boy, life was marked by a certain sadness: And his own personal pain played a role as well.

"I remember clearly as a little boy, sitting on my mother's lap and crying and my mother telling me, 'Be quiet and look at the stars, they were made by our Lord, our Lord loves us and wants us to behave well . . . it is not worthwhile to cry. We must work, pray, and study, and you have to study a lot so that tomorrow you can be a man.'"

Carlos took his mother's advice, and pressed on despite the difficulties. It was hard to imagine anything worse than losing his father, then his brother Fernando. In fact, the family would know still more anguish: Bishop Belo's older brother António died of heart failure when he was still a first-year student at the seminary in Évora in southern Portugal in 1968. Like his brother Fernando before him, he was only twenty-two. António had been playing football when he hit his head against a wall. He vomited blood, and died a few days later, on Wednesday of Holy Week.

Carlos and António had been inseparable from the time they were small boys. Now, buried in Portugal, it was as if António had simply vanished. "It was a great shock for all of us in East Timor as we were commemorating Easter," the bishop said nearly three decades later. "It was the saddest Easter of our lives. We were commemorating the death and resurrection of Christ and at the same time suffering the intense pain of the disappearance of my brother António."

The intensity of the loss is difficult to exaggerate, and its pain still has not receded. Today, it is not photos of her Nobel Prize–winning son that dominate Dona Ermelinda's sitting room in Baucau, although a memento of the award is there. Large photos of her lost sons, two robust young men with radiant smiles and a look of invincibility, occupy the most prominent spot in her home. Even now, she speaks of Fernando and António before all else.

Dona Ermelinda was quite reluctant to allow another son to leave for Portugal, but Carlos showed the firmness that Ermelinda herself demonstrated when she first tried to enter school as a child: "Because António died there, it does not mean that I am going there to die," he told his mother with finality. Carlos showed once again his ability to pursue his mission, despite terrible trauma and the opposition of those close to him.

It was priests such as Father Alfonso Nacher who convinced Dona Ermelinda that she should allow her son to go to Portugal because he had all the qualities to become a good priest. In the end, Carlos pursued his studies in Portugal from 1968 to 1974. On October 6, 1974, he became a Salesian.

Even before his brothers' deaths, Carlos was a cerebral person, with a skeptical streak going back to his sharp questioning of village elders in childhood. The death of his two brothers, both powerfully built and headstrong, had underlined the pitfalls of raw exuberance and overreliance on physical prowess. Carlos himself did not shy from sports, being a soccer fanatic himself. Indeed, he was an excellent defensive player. But he also would become known as a strategist, someone who normally did not allow the emotions of the moment to dominate his thinking.

His brothers' deaths gave Carlos a profound sense of personal loss, well before the cataclysm that struck his country later in 1975, helping prepare him for the role he was to play when he returned from his studies in Europe. There was an unspoken need to fill the shoes of his departed siblings, especially of the indomitable António.

Soon after António's death, in October 1968 Belo became one of a privileged few sent from East Timor to study in Portugal. Carlos saw trains for the first time. Life moved much faster. It was a rude shock in some ways. At home in East Timor friends were very close to one another, while in Portugal things seemed more distant. He was homesick, but he adapted. "We have to adapt in order to survive," he said as he reminisces about those early days, when he received few letters from home because of the slow-moving mail from halfway around the world in Timor.

He encountered racism. One fellow teased young Carlos about the color of his skin, reciting a nonsensical rhyme, *"Um preto da Guiné, lava a cara com cafe"*—"A black from (the Portuguese colony) Guinea, washes his face with coffee." But Carlos was unfazed. He shot back: *"Um sujo Português, branco como porco"*—"A dirty Portuguese, white like a pig."

Belo had always had warm relations with his European teachers such as Father José Luis Rodriguez and Father Armando Monteiro, his main Salesian mentor in Portugal. Racial talk was absurd, but Carlos knew how to make a point. He would not retreat to his ancestral village like his grandfather had done in the face of insults. He would stand his ground.

In the northern town of Mogofores, about two hundred miles north of Lisbon, he completed the last two years of Portugal's rigorous high school curriculum. Thus he qualified to enter the major seminary at Manique do Estoril, a sun-washed coastal area close to Lisbon. "Since then I have been at peace with everything I do."

His self-confidence and inner calm were manifest, and he had plenty of friends. His popularity was based partly on his skill in coordinating soccer games. He ran fairs on the weekends that combined sports, music, and religious pursuits. "We guided the youth at the same time we were having fun," he recalled. He would manage a booth selling drinks and food, with profits financing future events. And he retained his interest in farming: on holidays Carlos would work in rice fields around the ancient city of Évora, where his beloved brother António was buried.

He did not claim to be a saint. One of the reasons he became so fond of the work of Saint Augustine was because of the possibilities of redemption Augustine's life offered. Carlos himself was not above the occasional sleight of hand when it came to survival. As part of a final exam, he was asked whether or not he had read a certain Portuguese poet. He answered yes, although he had not read the particular poet. Somehow the teacher checked no further, and gave Carlos a passing grade. A friend who also had not done the reading told the truth and was given a failing grade. The friend was furious at Carlos, who only laughed, devilishly: he had little interest in unnecessary martyrdom. Indeed, Carlos enjoyed reading poets like Fernando Pessoa and novelists like Eça de Quieroz; *The Sin of Father Amaro,* the epic story of a fallen priest and corruption among the clergy of the nineteenth century, was a favorite, although—or perhaps because—it was considered a scandalous work, banned by the authorities.

Practical matters appeared to interest him more than academic pursuits. The popularity that came with his enthusiasm for sports and his closeness with young people helped him in family visits. Many Portuguese had grown atheistic, Bishop Belo recalls. To some extent this stemmed from the closeness of the Portuguese Church with the Salazar regime. Many who opposed the dictatorship—especially, but not only, the poor—felt alienated and abandoned by the Church. Missionaries had once come to Timor to "civilize" pagan peoples there, but now missionary work was needed in the Portuguese countryside. It wasn't an easy task for Belo.

Although he was often refused, Carlos kept visiting Portuguese families, one by one. They opened the door, but he got a cold response. "So I would approach people through their children. It worked. I became so familiar with them, they even invited me to dinner. They offered me good food and wine. I was happy, though I never expected to succeed. Slowly I got the message across. They started to pray and pray."

Once, the future bishop met with a Communist family. Communists had suffered the most under the Salazar regime. Torture and imprisonment were not uncommon. Most had little use for the Church. "The Communists were the hardest to approach," the bishop remembered. "It took me longer than with the other families. My other friends were not interested in approaching them. I insisted and I visited them very often. We became friends, close friends. It was so touching when they told me they were willing to become Catholic."

For the young seminarian, the years from 1968 to 1974 were quiet. His drawer was full of letters from his family. Julieta became a nurse in Baucau, his older brother and sister married and had children, and his mother missed him and wished she could come to the ceremony marking his entry into the Salesian Order in 1974. He would soon come home.

From the time Carlos Filipe Ximenes Belo went to Lisbon in 1968 until his return, it was the Portuguese-speaking world, not neighboring Indonesia—the Latin world, not Asia—that loomed largest in the young man's mind, and that of his friends. This was natural: East Timor's political status had not changed for centuries, and there was no sign it would do so. In fact, Indian troops took over Goa and two other longtime Portuguese enclaves in 1961, but still, the Indonesian Republic, in the first three decades after it proclaimed its independence in 1945, did not show the slightest interest in seizing East Timor. On the contrary, the legal basis of the Indonesian state was built on the proposition that all of its components had once been Dutch colonies. On several occasions, at the United Nations and elsewhere, Indonesian leaders explicitly denied having any claim, legal or otherwise, to Portuguese Timor. Any move to take East Timor in that period would have been met with condemnation by the United States and other nations then allied with Portugal, who were against the Indian takeover of Goa.

From 1945 until 1965, Indonesia was ruled by the populist President Sukarno, who governed in an uneasy alliance with the army, Muslim groups, and the Communist party (PKI), at the time the largest such party in the non-Communist world. Celebrated as a Third World leader who was a founder of the Non-Aligned Movement in 1955, Sukarno often used strident foreign policy rhetoric as a substitute for action on the domestic front, where he was much more conservative than his fiery image suggested. But as nations throughout the world were gaining independence, the Portuguese colonial regime in East Timor, a relic of long ago in the eyes of many, was spared Sukarno's sharp tongue.

Sukarno's international activities were seen as dangerously "neutralist" in Washington during the feverish Cold War days of the 1950s: the U.S. was increasingly concerned over Sukarno's dealings with the PKI and his opposition to American foreign policies. Moreover, Sukarno maintained good relations with both China and the Soviet Union. There was a failed attempt by dissident army officers with the backing of the CIA to overthrow the Sukarno regime in 1958.

Soon after, in 1959, a rebellion of East Timorese against Portuguese rule around the town of Viqueque followed. The origins of the rebellion were unclear. As was the case in their African colonies in the years that followed, Portuguese authorities moved to crush the Viqueque revolt with great brutality. More than 100 were killed.

For all the later talk about the evils of Portuguese colonialism (which certainly had more than a grain of truth), Indonesia took no action to support the East Timor rebels of that time. The affair was of little interest to Washington, whose main concern during this period, as later, was the direction of the Indonesian government. Thus, the U.S. continued to build close ties with elements of the Indonesian Armed Forces. In 1965, General Suharto, the head of the army's strategic reserve command, took power after a still-unexplained chain of events that began with a coup attempt on October 1, 1965 by members of Sukarno's palace guard. Suharto and others blamed the coup on the PKI, although definitive proof has been lacking. Six army generals were kidnapped and murdered before General Suharto emerged to lead a counter-coup. Some who have studied the 1965 coup have advanced the theory that Suharto may have engineered it himself, because he, alone among the top generals, was at no time threatened.

The Suharto takeover was followed by a bloodbath in which anywhere from 500,000 to one million were massacred, most of them suspected leftists and ethnic Chinese. Despite an official policy of nonalignment that still exists, the orientation of the "New Order" government of Suharto shifted to a heavily pro-American stance.

However significant these changes, there was no difference in policy toward East Timor after the military government of President Suharto ousted President Sukarno. Throughout, the status quo reigned in East Timor until 1975. If anything, cooperation between the Indonesian government and the Portuguese colonial regime improved after Suharto took power. Still, Portuguese officials in East Timor at the time warned that the widespread killing during Suharto's takeover illustrated what would happen if Indonesian forces ever moved into East Timor.

By the 1970s, Portuguese rule in East Timor was relatively mild in relation to the past. For all the squalid and negligent elements of Portuguese colonialism—the high rates of malnutrition, infant mortality, illiteracy, and diseases like tuberculosis and malaria, the lack of good roads and electricity—the cultures of the indigenous peoples of East Timor had been left essentially intact. (The old regime had badly neglected the Portuguese people as well: Portugal was the most backward nation in Western Europe.) Even in the early 1970s, conditions for the 80 percent of the population that lived in small villages and hamlets had changed little since the beginning of the Portuguese presence centuries before. In some mountain hamlets it was not until the early 1970s that the first Europeans set foot there. In those relatively gentle times, outsiders still were seen as strangers and considered intrusive. It was impossible to imagine what would come next.

This was the situation that existed in 1974, when the Portuguese revolution took place, after forty-eight years of authoritarian rule in Portugal and thirteen years of bitter armed conflict in the African colonies of Angola, Mozambique, and Guinea-Bissau (which, like East Timor, had been declared "overseas provinces" in 1951). During those thirteen years it was a blessing for a Portuguese soldier to be posted in East Timor, where there was no danger. Almost the only signs of rebellion appeared in a literary magazine called *Seara* (which means "fields of wheat" in Portuguese), published by the Catholic Church. Before being banned by the Portuguese authorities, *Seara* printed mildly critical essays by some of the future leaders of East Timor's nationalist movements, including the future Nobel laureate Jose Ramos-Horta.

This old world ended abruptly when a movement of captains in the Portuguese Armed Forces launched a military coup on April 25, 1974. From the perspective of East Timor and Carlos Filipe Ximenes Belo, who was listening to the radio that morning and heard the funeral music that was a prelude to the signal for the coup, the proclamations of the Armed Forces Movement in Lisbon turned out to have far more immediate impact than the military putsch in Indonesia nearly nine years before: it set in motion the dramatic events that have altered the history of East Timor from then on.

CHAPTER 4

DISINTEGRATION

❖ ❖ ❖ ❖

T HE STREETS OF PORTUGAL teemed with people celebrating the
collapse of forty-eight years of authoritarian rule. The promise of
an end to the hated colonial wars in Africa was sufficient reason
for rejoicing, but there was also the hope that liberty could take root in
Portugal for the first time since the 1920s. It was a fateful historical moment, a heady atmosphere, with everyone seemingly toasting one another
and talking at once. The twenty-six-year-old Carlos Filipe Ximenes Belo,
who was in Lisbon at the time, was enthusiastic as well. But in a system
where individualism was never a valued trait, he had demonstrated a
strong aversion to following the crowd from his earliest days, and he was
not the kind to become overly engulfed in the wave of emotion that was the
predominant feature of life in the days and months that followed the Portuguese coup. For all of the happiness that he saw in the streets of Portugal,
it was unclear to him what would replace the old system. Belo felt a touch
of wariness almost from the beginning.

While the new freedom held out the promise of a better future for the
long-suffering Portuguese nation and its "overseas territories," within less
than eighteen months the world he and his people had known in East
Timor would be destroyed.

Like young Belo, some of the most powerful officials in the world were
concerned over the outcome in Portugal and its colonies during this fateful period, but not from the perspective that drove the Timorese seminarian. Washington, whose foreign policy was guided by Secretary of State
Henry Kissinger during the Nixon administration, greeted the Lisbon coup
and subsequent developments with alarm, in light of the perceived Soviet
threat that dominated official American thinking in those years.

The great outpouring of feeling after the April Revolution was followed by an even more intense struggle for power by contending forces who had been deprived of public political expression for decades, including the Moscow-oriented Portuguese Communist party. In the eyes of the U.S. government, the old regime might have been a dictatorship, but it was a reliable friend. Now it was gone, and Portugal and its crumbling empire had become prime examples of instability. The future of Southeast Asia was also uncertain, as the war in Indochina was nearing an end. Because of this, Indonesia, the most important nation in Southeast Asia from Washington's perspective, took on even greater significance in the eyes of policy makers like Kissinger. Indonesia and its leader, President Suharto, were seen as bulwarks in the region. In a world governed by power politics, tiny, unknown East Timor could not hope to compete for the support or even the neutrality of the U.S., Western Europe, and other leading players on the international scene.

For a time an atmosphere of optimism prevailed—if not for all, then for many, not only in Portugal but also in East Timor. Public statements that once would have resulted in long jail terms, or worse, became part of the normal discourse. In 1961 the raising of a glass by a student in a Lisbon restaurant with a toast "to liberty" was enough to earn a prison sentence. It was precisely this case that inspired a London lawyer to found the human rights organization Amnesty International. Now, amazingly, almost anything could be said or written.

The passions of the time had captured the imagination of the small student community from East Timor enrolled at universities in Lisbon. Shortly after the April coup, Belo went to a meeting the students had organized at Casa de Timor, their headquarters in the center of Lisbon. A gathering of this kind was a new experience for most of them.

Belo was excited about the prospects for the meeting as he and a Timorese friend at the Salesian seminary set out by train for Lisbon the morning of the gathering. He recalled that he and his friend discussed how they would go back to Timor to found a socialist party that ultimately would spread democracy to Indonesia—after all, hadn't the Socialist Party in Portugal successfully challenged the old regime in Lisbon? Of course, in light of the entrenched military-backed system in Indonesia, of which East Timor was not even a part, it was a fond hope on the part of the two young men—unrealistic, but a measure of the idealism of those days.

Most of the Timorese student community in Lisbon, which numbered about forty, was no less idealistic, but some had far more radical views than that of the moderate sort of socialist party that Belo had in mind.

Among his contemporaries at Casa de Timor, there was Vicente Reis, a

serious student who was the son of a liurai in a small village not far from
Baucau. He had a reputation for quiet courage. There was Rosa Bonaparte,
known as Muki, who was enthusiastic and inquisitive. A visitor from
home, Francisco Borja da Costa, a poet and writer, was a genuine leader.
Soon after, he would write the words to what he hoped would eventually
become East Timor's national anthem, called "Foho Ramelau," populariz-
ing the beautiful peak. Borja, as his friends called him, had a brooding
manner that best expressed itself in verse. Also, there was Belo's former
classmate from the Dare seminary, Abílio de Araújo, who had a reputation
among the missionary priests for his clever ways. He was a musician, later
adapting traditional notes for the song "Foho Ramelau." Araújo had identified himself with a party of the extreme left, the MRPP (Revolutionary
Movement of the Portuguese Proleteriat). He became fond of the political
thought of Mao Tse-Tung, especially that from the ultra-radical period of
the Cultural Revolution of the 1960s, when the Chinese leader attained a
kind of cult status. Araújo possessed a jovial manner that could make him
very convincing to some, at least for a time.

But neither Araújo nor his fellow participants could persuade the future bishop. Belo remembered that he was unimpressed by what he heard
at the meeting, finding much of it "demagogic."

"At Casa de Timor, everybody talked and screamed. It was the talk of
radical students without experience," the bishop recalled more than twenty
years later, insisting that this had been his initial reaction in 1974.

Among other things, Belo felt that denunciations of colonialism that he
heard at the meeting provided few answers. Despite 450 years of historical
ties, East Timor was a distant issue for Portugal, in contrast to Africa,
where more than a million Portuguese citizens had a long-standing stake.
The developments since the military coup made this plain. The talk was
mainly of Angola and Mozambique, of democratization in Portugal, of an
end to feudalism and empire. As the months went on, with far more pressing problems elsewhere, it would grow increasingly difficult even for
well-meaning officials who cared about East Timor to obtain high-level
government attention for this remnant of an Asian empire that had not
been a thriving national enterprise for centuries.

On May 1, 1974, less than a week after the Armed Forces Movement
had toppled the old regime, more than a million people had poured into
the streets of Lisbon to manifest their support for the new freedom, but
there was no mention of East Timor. In response to this lack of attention,
the students at Casa de Timor proposed that a demonstration be held to
bring their concerns about colonialism and the future of East Timor to the

attention of the Portuguese people. For his part, Belo was skeptical that efforts by the students would amount to much. He was suspicious of extravagant language and theories. The future bishop had a disciplined orientation that both his hard upbringing and work in the Church had instilled in him.

In his six years in Portugal, he was involved in the day-to-day struggles of the Salesian religious order. Unlike other orders that place greater emphasis on pastoral or academic pursuits, the Salesians concentrate on highly organized activities that benefit young people around the world. Combined with rigorous spiritual development, they operate an extensive network of job-training programs in agriculture, mechanics, woodworking, carpentry, photography, computers, and many other specific trades. There are recreational programs for youth, including sports and theater: these pursuits function as therapy for those from troubled backgrounds. For example, it would not be unusual to see a Salesian clown travel thousands of miles to entertain children who live in difficult circumstances, from orphanages to refugee camps. Indeed, a special emphasis on friendliness and good cheer has been at the center of the Salesian attitude since the order was founded by Saint John Bosco in 1859. The Salesians run a network of excellent schools, which draw pupils from a wide cross section of society, from the poor to the elite.

Some elements in the Catholic Church may have looked down on the Salesians, seeing their programs as lacking the intellectual weight of the Jesuits', for instance, but they suited young Belo.

The student leaders at Casa de Timor aimed to form a group that would dedicate itself to the independence of their homeland. But as the future bishop saw it, the problem was that the notions expressed that day were fundamentally untested, and most of the students had not yet even obtained their university diplomas. What he had heard at the meeting left him disillusioned.

"I remember leaving there thinking to myself, now everyone is a revolutionary, but that there was little in terms of concrete things," he said. "I felt it was best to maintain a certain reserve." Belo never went back to Casa de Timor.

What seemed like a new era of freedom was, in reality, hardly as open as it appeared. Carlos, like his East Timorese colleagues, had little direct knowledge of Indonesia, but he was keenly aware that its army effectively ran the country. He doubted the Indonesian Armed Forces would tolerate, so close to their borders, the kind of ideas he had heard at Casa de Timor. The people of East Timor had been part of a hermetically sealed Portuguese empire. Few had a clear idea about the nature of the government next door in Indonesia. Belo suspected the students at Casa de Timor did not realize what they were facing. His worst fears would have been confirmed had he known what was to come.

Several members of the student group stopped in London on their journey back to East Timor. There, an academic couple invited the Timorese students to peruse their private library of books on contemporary Indonesia. None of the books had been available in Portugal, so during the week the students from Casa de Timor spent in London, they pursued a crash course of reading. One of their hosts remembers that the students knew little about Indonesia. The group divided up the available books, read what they could, and, after the week was up, undeterred, returned to East Timor, where they plunged into political activities.

At that time, such student groups were common at universities throughout the world, with few serious consequences to anyone, least of all themselves. But unlike most other places, the students from Casa de Timor stepped into an extremely dangerous regional environment, although the atmosphere in East Timor was calm at first.

One of the worse massacres in the contemporary era had been carried out in Indonesia scarcely more than eight years before the coup in Lisbon, without a word of protest from the Western powers or Japan. Indeed, there was clear evidence of substantial foreign approval, including that of the United States, for the actions of the Indonesian military in 1965–66 under its new leader, Major General Suharto.

Removal of the Communist threat in Indonesia was seen as an occasion for rejoicing in influential quarters: The headline *Time* magazine gave the 1965 to 1966 Indonesian massacre was "the West's Best News in Years." Simply scanning books and articles in the library in London the students from Casa de Timor visited would have provided similar examples. By 1974, at least thirty thousand political prisoners remained in Indonesian jails, most held without trial for eight or nine years. International protests over the fate of these detainees had been minimal. None of this was a good omen for the students from Casa de Timor or their countrymen.

While Carlos had been disillusioned by the meeting at Casa de Timor, he had little time to spare for thoughts of it. The year 1974 was not only the time of the military coup in Portugal, it was also the year that he would join the Salesian order, his next step toward becoming a priest. Practical training lay ahead. He was scheduled to return home to East Timor that September to teach at the Salesian training school in Fatumaca for one year. Thoughts of his homecoming and the duties ahead, of seeing his mother,

Julieta, and all the others, not politics, consumed his imagination. Soon he would see his loved ones and become involved in the challenges for which he had been schooled.

So it was that Carlos Filipe Ximenes Belo rose, in early September 1974, at supper in Casa Don Bosco, the Salesian center in Lisbon, to address his colleagues. The building had a magnificent vantage point on the Tagus River, overlooking the newly renamed 25th of April Bridge, which links Lisbon with a region known as Alentejo. Previously called the Salazar Bridge, the letters spelling out the name of the late dictator, who died in 1968, had been torn off the bridge after the coup. It was built by the company that designed the Golden Gate in San Francisco. Like its American counterpart, Lisbon sits on sun-dappled hills, where the Tagus estuary meets the Atlantic Ocean. There is a magnificent quality of light at that point, and Carlos had spent many an evening on the large rooftop patio engaged in quiet thought.

On this very special evening before his departure, he was brimming with optimism. "I am ready to become engaged in the process of building East Timor," Carlos told the Salesians, who were saluting him with a toast of vinho verde, a young wine that is a Portuguese favorite. "I have been preparing for this throughout my years in Portugal. Now the time has come."

The Salesians who heard their young colleague were proud of him. He was mature, level-headed, and sure of his vocation. As they hailed his impending return to his native land, they had no inkling of the trouble ahead. Going to East Timor was not seen as anything unusual, much less as a dangerous assignment. Salesian missionaries had worked in East Timor since well before the Second World War. For them as well as almost everyone else, most notably Belo, the tragedy that awaited the island territory was completely unforeseen.

On September 9, 1974, his plane landed at East Timor's international airport, then located on a plain near Baucau, in the vicinity of where he was born. His first sight of his native land in six years filled him with strong emotion. Unlike some of his fellow East Timorese students in Portugal, Carlos was not one for the life of an expatriate or exile. He might carry a Portuguese passport, but for him Lisbon was not home, though he enjoyed what it had to offer. No matter how much time he spent abroad, he always saw East Timor as his home and the place where he would carry out his mission.

Finally, he was there. His mother and Julieta were older, but almost nothing had changed. Many members of the family and friends awaited him, with a huge feast and garlands of flowers, in a celebration at least as festive as his first communion sixteen years before. It was Ermelinda's nightmare that if he went to Portugal he would never reappear, like her beloved, departed António. But, as he had told her when he left, there was no reason for alarm. Indeed, he came back with a vigor and strength even greater than before. Carlos had only been to Europe, and the ordeals of his life were still ahead, but even then, the family's youngest son had a canny survivor's look about him. He had gone to a place far bigger, more complex and enticing than anything he had previously known, but he had not been diverted from his goals. Already Carlos's quiet confidence had become his trademark: photos of the time show him in a soccer jersey, gazing out with deep-set, intense brown eyes and a look of resolute calm.

Seeing him after all this time was like a dream for his mother and Julieta. After being away for so long, Carlos would be at Fatumaca, together with Father Egidio Locatelli, an Italian priest long known in East Timor for his work in improving access to education for young people. No longer just a student, Carlos was now a Salesian himself. Why, after being halfway around the world in Portugal, he would now be within sight of Mount Matebian, even closer to home than the years when he was at the seminary in Dare! As a small boy Quelicai had seemed so distant from Baucau, but after living twelve thousand miles away, it was next door. He would have occasion to travel through the region, and when he did, he could visit Baucau and spend the night, at his mother's house, as in the old times.

The bishop remembers the eleven months that followed his return in luminous terms, as glorious as the red, white, and purple bougainvillea and foliage lining the pathways of the Fatumaca school. It was a time of optimism unlike any other he had known in East Timor. Something about it filled him with wonder. Perhaps in some way it was the opportunity to render service as a Salesian for the first time, mixed with the spirit of change that dominated East Timor in the period before conflict erupted.

The bishop speaks of this period of his life with a palpable longing. "It was a time that I like very much to remember," the bishop said with deep nostalgia, his eyes brightening many years later. "I taught English, Portuguese, science, and history and organized sporting events. I remember this time with great fondness. I very much liked working with the young students," of whom there were about two hundred at the school. Belo also taught a course about the anti-colonial movements in Africa which had fought the Portuguese army to a standstill.

While he had expressed hopeful sentiments at Casa Don Bosco in Lisbon about engaging himself in the process of building his homeland, the reality was somewhat less elevated. As bright as Belo was, he remained a twenty-six-year-old candidate for the priesthood, someone scarcely in a position to influence the course of events in East Timor. Others ran the Church, and he was obliged to follow orders, not give them. His main advantage was as an observer of a critical time in his nation's history. Here he could apply his keen intelligence without restrictions.

If the future bishop had only a minor position in Church affairs, he had even less of a role in politics, which he had made a conscious decision to avoid, because as a seminarian he was forbidden from participating in such activity.

Three main political parties had formed in the months after the Portuguese coup. The first was the Timorese Democratic Union (UDT), a conservative group made up of landowners, higher civil servants, and others who had prospered under the Portuguese. UDT first called for continuing association with Portugal but later shifted to a pro-independence stance. The second group was the Timorese Social Democratic Association (ASDT), founded in May 1974, favoring social reforms and a gradual movement to independence from Portugal. Just as he returned in September, ASDT changed its name to Fretilin, the Revolutionary Front for an Independent East Timor. The third group, the Timorese Popular Democratic Association, called APODETI, favored the incorporation of East Timor into the Republic of Indonesia; APODETI was by far the smallest of the three groups and could scarcely have functioned without heavy Indonesian backing. Nonetheless, APODETI was against a forcible takeover by Indonesia, and expected Indonesia to maintain the use of the Portuguese language in East Timor: it is in their charter in black and white.

Belo was frequently asked which of the Timorese parties he supported. In fact, he belonged to none of them. But, as with other things, his response was to make fun of the question: depending on what his students wanted to hear, Belo would state the opposite.

"When students who sympathized with Fretilin asked me what my party was, I would respond APODETI," he recalled. "When people from APODETI asked me, I would respond UDT. I liked to provoke them that way so that we could end up having discussions and vivacious conversations."

But he was not indifferent to the political changes taking place around him. The students from Casa de Timor, most of whom had returned home, played a key role in the change from ASDT to Fretilin, and it worried Belo, though he respected Nicolau Lobato, who later headed Fretilin. Lobato had preceded Belo in the seminary at Dare, but he had left to become a civil servant and, lacking the opportunity to go to university in Portugal immediately, took up economics at night in the hope that he might one day study in Lisbon. Nicolau was a sensible figure with a reputation for seriousness and decency. If he had a single fault, it may have been that because he had not been able to attend university himself, he was overly impressed with those who had.

Fretilin was a broad front advocating measures like agricultural cooperatives, health campaigns, and literacy efforts. Carlos knew that changes surely were needed; in the six years he had been away, he recalled, "There had not been the slightest development. The Timorese were poor and thin when I left, and they were the same way when I returned." But the name of Fretilin alone would provide ammunition for the Indonesian regime, which viewed any revolutionary movement with suspicion.

In the early days, Belo was, if anything, more sympathetic towards Fretilin than with the other political groups. Many of the future bishop's cousins were members of Fretilin. He recalled that he liked its nationalist orientation. Only a few days after his return from Portugal—out of curiosity, he said—Belo went with his young niece and nephew, who lived in the Santa Cruz area of Dili, to a demonstration at the governor's palace, where Nicolau Lobato gave a speech.

Nonetheless, after Belo took up his teaching duties at Fatumaca, he was annoyed when some of his students left school to work for Fretilin: East Timor would need educated people, he believed, and in his view, political activity alone was not a sufficient basis for the future. More fundamentally, Belo strongly disagreed with the slogan that "Fretilin is the people and the people are Fretilin." He felt that the wishes of the people of East Timor should be determined by democratic elections, not simply asserted as true by one party or another. But Indonesian maneuvers ensured that no such elections could be held during those years.

Belo did not restrict his skepticism to Fretilin; he had strong reservations about the other two major parties as well.

He saw UDT as the party of the status quo, of the liurais (including his uncle in Quelicai, a UDT member) and senior civil servants who were used to running things. And in light of East Timor's remoteness from Europe, Belo believed that one should not put much weight on the possibility of continued ties with Portugal, the position taken by UDT.

That left the third major party, APODETI, of which his brother, José, was a member. At the outset, Belo was not closed to the idea of joining Indonesia: because of Indonesia's close proximity, it seemed logical. His mind changed in 1975, however, when he heard Indonesian radio broadcasts, beamed into East Timor in local languages by government intelligence agents.

Early Indonesian radio broadcasts attacked Fretilin as "communist," and UDT as "fascist." Some programs began with bursts of machine-gun fire. Later, at times of crisis, the broadcasts condemned specific individuals, which Belo saw as brazenly trying to inflame tensions. "The broadcasts made me sick," he remembered many years later. "The words they used were the language of domination."

At the start, however, soon after his return, life seemed innocent enough. Belo could not have guessed that an elaborate black propaganda campaign, in which the true motives of the actors are disguised and appearances were deceptive, was being played out in East Timor. The territory had been a sleepy backwater for ages, unused to such intrigue. Indonesian intelligence operatives undertook a large-scale operation to incite conflict among the East Timorese political parties. By the time the twenty-six-year-old Belo had returned, his country, and many of the young students with whom he developed a strong bond, were living on borrowed time.

The words on the radio and the tactics behind them came from important factions in the Indonesian military who opposed the idea of independence for East Timor. Jakarta had been willing to tolerate continuing Portuguese colonial rule in East Timor—indeed, it had done so for the thirty years since it declared its own independence from the Netherlands, in 1945—but after first saying it would respect the wishes of the East Timorese people, powerful forces in the military establishment pushed to quash the possibility of an independent state. In part this stemmed from an internal military power struggle and for reasons of the personal prestige of military figures anxious to build their careers. But that was not what the world was told at the time. This was the height of the Cold War: Indonesia skillfully blackened the image of the Fretilin independence movement, a coalition that in reality was more nationalist than radical, to argue that the island territory could become an "Asian Cuba" if left unchecked.

Indonesia had far better access to the world media than anyone else concerned with the problem, and the United States, other Western governments, and Japan were inclined to echo whatever Indonesia said, whether they believed it or not. In short, Jakarta's analyses went largely unchallenged; the fact that no Communist power ever sent a single bullet or military trainer to East Timor never seemed to matter. It was also whispered darkly that an independent East Timor could lead to the breakup of Indonesia, by setting a precedent for others of the hundreds of diverse ethnic groups in Indonesia. But the hard-line Indonesian military had never before lost control of any of those groups in its island empire. Not that it hadn't been tried: as we have seen, in the late 1950s, the CIA moved to overthrow the populist government of President Sukarno by fomenting an Outer Islands rebellion that failed mightily. If it failed then, when the Indonesian Army was far less competent and the Indonesian Republic far more fragile, it wasn't going to succeed now. But knowledge of this sort rarely reached the public. The crux of the matter, however, was that no important nation wanted to antagonize Indonesia—the facts, international law, and the requirements of justice notwithstanding.

First, in September 1974, despite the heavy moral debt Australia owed to East Timor from the Second World War, the prime minister of Australia, Gough Whitlam, said through a spokesman that "an independent East Timor would be an unviable state and a potential threat to the region." This was very important for Indonesia because it showed that the one nation in the region likely to be consulted by the United States and other countries would raise no real objection to Indonesian moves to annex East Timor. In his exchange with Suharto, Whitlam added that whatever happened in East Timor should be in line with the people's wishes, concluding that the Australian public would react negatively against the use of violence. But the Indonesians chose to focus on only the first part of the message. In fact, Suharto felt he had reached such a meeting of the minds with Whitlam that he invited the Australian to a sacred cave of special mystical import near where they were meeting on the island of Java.

Other aspects of what Indonesia and Australia wanted were of a less spiritual nature: Portugal had been driving a hard bargain on the offshore area between Timor and Australia where there was the possibility of significant deposits of oil and natural gas. There was reason to believe that Australia would receive more favorable treatment from the Indonesian government if Indonesia were to take over East Timor.

But Indonesia needed more than simply the backing of Australia. Shortly thereafter, in October 1974, top Indonesian military intelligence figures, led by General Ali Murtopo, a close advisor to President Suharto, traveled to Portugal on a quiet diplomatic mission. Murtopo was a leading figure in Special Operations, called Opsus, Suharto's notorious intelligence network known for political manipulation. At the Sheraton Hotel in Lisbon, the Indonesian delegation met Portuguese officials, including then Foreign Minister Mário Soares and top members of the ruling military council that played a crucial role in policy matters for years after the April 1974 revolution. The Sheraton was located only a few miles down cobblestoned hills from where Belo had recently spent his last night at Casa Don Bosco.

At the Sheraton, Portuguese leaders may have given the impression that they would not oppose an Indonesian takeover of East Timor. Unlike the colonial officials who actually knew something about the nature of the threat posed by the Indonesian military, the Portuguese newcomers had little understanding of the danger that the regime in Jakarta posed to East Timor and, when it came down to it, limited patience. Portugal was in a state of great domestic flux after the April 1974 revolution and its own situation was fragile; it was difficult to know from one month to the next who would be in power in Lisbon. Important voices in the Portuguese leadership had no interest in expending the kind of effort that would have been required to promote a just outcome in East Timor.

In any case, President Costa Gomes later claimed that he had thought East Timor would end up like Goa, the Portuguese colony peacefully absorbed after troops invaded in the early 1960s. But Suharto's military regime was quite different from Nehru's democratic India.

Whatever message the Portuguese group at the Sheraton may have intended to convey, the same day Jakarta launched Operation Komodo, (named after the largest lizard in the world, native to the Indonesian region), bent on the incorporation of East Timor into Indonesia, through military action if necessary. In all the high-level machinations of Indonesia, Portugal, and Australia—let alone other nations like the United States—little thought was given to the wishes of the primary party concerned, the people of East Timor themselves.

The way they actually felt can be gauged by a remarkable event that took place in Quelicai three months after the Portuguese coup. Shepard Forman, an American anthropologist, had spent fifteen months with his family among a kingdom of the Makassae people. Forman mastered the language and culture of the Makassae, and was there with his wife, Leona, a journalist, when the overwhelming majority of villagers petitioned the government for autonomy. As Forman, a New Yorker, put it later, the sentiments of the people of Letemumo "are just as legitimate as the rationale that governs ours." This declaration, and other detailed evidence, left little doubt that this group, one of East Timor's largest, had no interest in joining Indonesia. Indeed, after their experience at the hands of the Japanese, it should have come as little surprise that they did not welcome the idea of being ruled by another Asian military invader.

UDT and Fretilin had entered into a coalition in early 1975, which seemed to offer the best chance for independence: The coalition was pushed by Fretilin moderates like Ramos-Horta. But Jakarta worked over-time to break the coalition, first circulating rumors of an imminent In-donesian invasion in March, interspersed with false stories and a constant pressure campaign on UDT leaders designed to heighten distrust of Fretilin. They finally succeeded in July 1975, when UDT withdrew after re-ceiving an ultimatum from Indonesian military intelligence: either seize power and crush Fretilin, or expect an Indonesian invasion. Jakarta was in-creasingly confident it would meet little international resistance. Certainly it had little to fear from the United States and other powerful nations: it was only after returning from a trip to the United States, Japan, Canada, and other countries in July 1975 that President Suharto for the first time publicly ruled out independence for East Timor.

News such as this never reached Belo, who was still in Fatumaca, which was remote from many of the political developments of the time. On Au-gust 9, 1975, Carlos stayed overnight with his mother and sister. When he left the town of Baucau the next morning, on August 10, none of them had any inkling that he would not return for another six years.

The future bishop left for Dili in the back of a truck, the customary mode of transport, to participate in a teacher training course. Tensions were mounting, and both UDT and Fretilin were mobilizing their sup-porters. Rumors spread that both Fretilin and UDT were ready to use force against their opponents. In one village en route to the capital, Bucoli, there was a large tree trunk placed in the middle of the thoroughfare as a kind of roadblock. The young people of the village, all members of Fretilin, or-dered everyone off the truck for a search.

"I decided that I was going to remain on the truck," the bishop remem-bered. "But then one of the youth yelled, 'You, Father, you have to come down, too.' So I also got off the truck, but they did not search me." The trip continued, in a highly charged atmosphere: "Everywhere there were people waving Fretilin flags."

Belo arrived in Dili on the same afternoon and went to the diocesan compound, called the Câmara Eclesiástica, near the harbor. Ironically, though Australia had taken no diplomatic action to deter Indonesia, there was a lecture that night in the Câmara Eclesiástica by an Australian speaker on anti-Communist policies, hardly what was needed at that moment. Belo spent the night in the Câmara, then was awakened early the next morning, August 11, by a priest who told him not to leave the building be-cause there had been an armed coup d'état organized by UDT. Jakarta's manipulations had finally worked.

UDT seized government installations and means of communications, calling for the arrest of certain Fretilin leaders. For a few days, there was a tense standoff. There were killings and jailings by UDT members in the countryside, and Fretilin retaliated. UDT organized demonstrations in Dili, while Belo remained in the Câmara.

The future bishop once went to UDT headquarters, before full-scale fighting broke out between the two groups. "I was scandalized by what I saw," said the bishop. "UDT commanders were drinking lots of whiskey," but "there was not much thought that would have justified a coup d'état." Their weakness became clear as Fretilin forces advanced rapidly and UDT forces retreated to the border they shared with West Timor.

In fact, Fretilin had the support of most of the Timorese troops attached to the small Portuguese military contingent still present in the territory, and with it, access to the main arsenal of weapons. Thus, when East Timorese troops left their barracks to take the side of Fretilin, they were able to trounce UDT forces, who had their own cache of weapons through friendly Portuguese officers, but lacked popular backing.

With the battle spreading throughout Dili as Fretilin forces were taking over the city on August 20, and grenades and mortars went through the sky, young Belo was near the pier to wait for a boat to take him back to Baucau, which would have put him close to Fatumaca. Traveling by land would have been a problem, the bishop believed, thinking back to his ride to Dili on August 10, because Fretilin controlled the roads and, in light of the fighting, might have stopped vehicles. Road construction vehicles on the Dili-Baucau road had been commandeered to carry troops. A UDT force with the support of friendly Portuguese officers had been advancing on Dili by the Baucau road and passage through that area might have been impossible at that moment.

There were about two thousand people at the harbor waiting to flee to Australia and other places as fighting raged in those days. Many were fearful of what would happen next, including missionaries like Belo's old friend Father Jacinto Campos, who had worked in East Timor for forty years. (Father Campos would settle in a Portuguese-speaking community in the United States.) The last thing young Belo wanted to do was leave his homeland: his main wish was to find a way to return to his students. But when the future Nobel Peace Prize winner tried to get on the boat, "The Portuguese who were in charge of the ship told me that I could not come on board, because the only ones who could leave at that moment were whites and mestizos, not Timorese."

While he waited at the harbor, Belo heard Indonesian radio broadcasts, this time with negative comments about UDT, the very group their intelligence chiefs had urged to launch the civil war in the first place. The Indonesians were trying to denigrate UDT leaders, like Mario Carrascalão, who were as much in favor of independence as their Fretilin opponents. In Belo's eyes, Jakarta's intelligence operatives were trying to do whatever they could to promote chaos. "This was clearly shameless interference by the Indonesians, who wanted to sow bitter fruit in those uncertain times," Belo recalled. "I was so angry."

Carlos, having no choice, quietly took his bag and returned to his room in the diocese. Father Martinho da Costa Lopes, the vicar general, or number-two man in the diocese, was there. "You are young," Dom Martinho told Carlos. "You must go abroad and finish your studies. When things get better here, then you can return."

Father Lopes knew the situation was deteriorating rapidly. However, he was not the man in charge of the Church. That was Dom José Joaquim Ribeiro, the bishop of Dili, and the same man who once tried to talk the seventeen-year-old Belo out of becoming a Salesian. History might have taken a different course had Bishop Ribeiro taken the initiative at that moment: Timorese political leaders were largely Catholic and might have responded favorably had the bishop called for reconciliation and negotiations. In a mark of the deep respect the bishop's office carried, he was able to walk to the harbor to escort nuns for evacuation while the streets were the scene of gunfire between the two sides. During Ribeiro's march to the quay, which some observers saw as fearless, the combatants ceased fire to let him pass, then continued fighting once he had left.

Nonetheless, the bishop's walk to the harbor only addressed one aspect of the problem. The unfolding crisis badly needed his intervention, but Ribeiro deeply disliked Fretilin, which he called "Communistic": Fretilin's program called for an end to the central position the Church enjoyed under Portuguese colonialism, which made the clergy in general highly suspicious of Fretilin. The Portuguese prelate refused to mediate between the contending sides, even as the situation deteriorated. Bishop Ribeiro's attitude left a profound impression on young Carlos, although he himself was highly critical of all parties to the civil conflict then being waged. "How can the Church say in such circumstances that it won't offer to mediate?" Bishop Belo stated with disbelief, more than twenty years after the events in question.

There was ample reason for Belo to feel this way, though he was well aware that the East Timorese groups themselves shared the blame, by resorting to violence against each other. Both sides had committed atrocities, some of which had led to the outbreak of fighting in August, when, for example, UDT units executed a group of students aligned with Fretilin. In the end, at least 1,500 East Timorese were killed in the civil war, according to the International Committee of the Red Cross (ICRC). But it is also true that the conflict could in no way be blamed on the Timorese alone: weeks before, the coalition between UDT and Fretilin had broken down to a large extent because of Indonesian propaganda operations, including circulation of false stories of Chinese and Vietnamese military involvement in East Timor that people like Bishop Ribeiro apparently believed. Meanwhile, Jakarta was working to sabotage any chance of a peaceful solution just before civil war broke out by blocking the entry of a Portuguese mediator. No other nation or international agency was engaged in the problem. The active involvement of the Church in the person of Bishop Ribeiro was the only hope of averting Indonesian invasion: he had, therefore, spurned an opportunity of monumental proportions.

Some longtime members of the clergy were certain that if Bishop Jaime Goulart, Ribeiro's predecessor, had been there, a solution short of bloodshed might have been found. Unlike Dom Jaime, Bishop Ribeiro, who had never learned the Tetum language, was not seen as an effective advocate of the interests of the native peoples of East Timor. Worse, rather than remaining neutral, Ribeiro was perceived to be greatly influenced by a small group of Portuguese officers who had actively supported UDT in the fighting.

If the experience of this time taught Bishop Belo a lesson about the need for mediation by the Church, it also reinforced his natural instinct to avoid compromising the Church's moral authority by taking sides among contending parties. In addition, Belo's skepticism about unsubstantiated rumors became more pronounced.

At the time, because he wanted to complete his work toward the priesthood, Belo felt he had little choice but to heed the advice of Father Lopes and prepare to leave the territory. Together with another priest, Father Victor Vieira, who later went to work in the United States, Belo traveled overland. The twenty-seven-year-old Salesian remembers looking back at the mountains near the town of Maubara that night, thinking he would never again see East Timor. He arrived in the town of Maliana near the Indonesian border at two o'clock the next morning. The future bishop remembers being quite grateful for the lodging he received in a church there: a straw mat with a tablecloth for a blanket on a wooden floor in the sacristy, which became his quarters for ten days. (It was, he said later, a good exercise in humility: when the bishop speaks of that word, he emphasizes that it stems from *humus,* or "earth," in Latin.) Finally, Belo and a group of Dominican nuns and other priests wanted to cross the border, as most everyone else in the area had done to be sure that they would escape the fighting. It was an arduous journey in the heat of the dry season. "We walked all day without a glass of water, no food, not a simple plate of rice, but we were not allowed to cross and had to return to Maliana," the bishop recalled.

About twenty thousand Timorese, some who were with the UDT group and others living in the border area, had crossed the Indonesian side of the border into West Timor. Clergy working on a refugee committee there said the Indonesian government deliberately claimed the figure was forty thousand or more, in an effort to heighten international concern over the scene by the border, the better to justify military intervention and maximize donations of foreign aid.

The Timorese refugees were herded into ten camps in the town of Atambua under Indonesian military guard. Finally Belo and his colleagues were able to go there as well. From what the future bishop could see, the Timorese were regarded as political pawns, and Indonesian soldiers had the attitude of captors. Bishop Belo recalled a visit to Atambua by the Indonesian governor of West Timor, when the refugees were obliged to cheer and shout pro-Indonesian slogans. "It was like a fascist rally," the bishop remembered. "I had just seen democracy in Portugal for the first time, and now I witnessed this." It did not bode well for what awaited East Timor, he felt.

Belo saw the situation moving in an even more negative direction. By night, he said, Indonesian troops entered homes and seized women. The brutality in Atambua would increase months later, when food was cut off after the refugees refused to express support for union with Indonesia. By then, Belo had left.

He stayed in Atambua for a month, enough time, with his quickness in languages, to begin learning Indonesian. By this time it had become impossible to return to Dili or Fatumaca, so his superior in the Salesian order told him to resume his studies abroad. With the assistance of the bishop of Atambua, Belo proceeded to Macau, the Portuguese-administered territory off the southeastern coast of China.

By the end of August 1975, the Portuguese governor, powerless with only a handful of troops, moved with his staff to the offshore island of Ataúro. Fretilin began to run East Timor's administration, while repeatedly asking Portugal to resume control. Lisbon's failure either to take concrete action or to request United Nations intervention opened the door to Indonesian military intervention.

For its part, the United States knew what was happening. William

Colby, then director of the CIA, wrote that Jakarta was sending guerrilla units into East Timor to engage Fretilin forces "and provoke incidents that would provide the Indonesians an excuse to invade should they decide to do so." Washington also retained the capacity to influence events, but made no effort to deter the Suharto regime. Of course, after Henry Kissinger's callous treatment of Cambodia, there was scant reason to expect that East Timor would be any different. In secret documents made public in *The Christian Science Monitor* five years later, the Australian ambassador to Indonesia noted that "The United States might have some influence on Indonesia at present because Indonesia wants and needs American help in its military re-equipment program." (With major problems at its state oil company, Indonesia also needed massive financial assistance from the U.S.)

However, the U.S. Ambassador told his Australian colleague that "He is under orders from Kissinger personally not to involve himself in discussions on Timor with the Indonesians on the grounds that the United States is involved in enough problems of greater importance overseas at present." According to the Australian ambassador's account, the American ambassador added that "the United States would hope that if Indonesia were to intervene [in East Timor] the United States would hope they would do so effectively, quickly and not use our equipment." In fact, congressional testimony by the State Department later showed that "roughly 90 percent" of the equipment available to ABRI was American-supplied. The United States' attitude was shared by the British, whose ambassador in Jakarta said in July 1975, ". . . it is in Britain's interest that Indonesia should absorb the territory as soon and as unobtrusively as possible. If it comes to the crunch and there is a row in the UN, we should keep our heads down and avoid siding against the Indonesians."

The conflict between UDT and Fretilin ended after a short period, and the territory was largely peaceful by early September, though Jakarta falsely claimed that civil war raged for months. Nicolau Lobato exercised discipline on his troops and, by many accounts, took firm action to limit Fretilin reprisals, though he did not always succeed. Still, in contrast to the picture of chaos in East Timor that Indonesia tried to convey to the world, firsthand visits by qualified experts from Australian aid agencies and church organizations produced generally favorable impressions of the Fretilin administration, which sent telegram after telegram to governments throughout the world pleading for diplomatic efforts to restrain Indonesia. After UDT was defeated, Jakarta quietly infiltrated troops in East Timor, advancing the cover story that they were "anti-Fretilin Timorese making a comeback." Anyone directly in the way of Indonesian troops, or, for that matter, the cover story, was dealt with severely. This included five journalists for Australian TV stations who were murdered in mid-October 1975, apparently while filming evidence of Indonesia's secret intervention in the town of Balibó, near where Belo had taken refuge on the floor of a church the month before. But even the killing of the journalists left the Australian government unmoved in its policy of support for Suharto.

Indonesian attacks increased, even as Suharto's government continued to deny any military involvement. Finally, in a desperate attempt to take the issue to the United Nations before Indonesian forces overwhelmed the territory, Fretilin declared East Timor independent from Portugal on November 28, 1975. The Indonesian government, in turn, claimed that a coalition of East Timorese groups had invited Indonesian forces—termed "volunteers"—to intervene.

Meanwhile, Fretilin sent a diplomatic delegation, including José Ramos-Horta, then only twenty-six years old, to New York to appeal to the United Nations.

President Gerald Ford and Secretary of State Henry Kissinger arrived in Jakarta two days before the all-out invasion took place on December 7. An Indonesian attack on Dili was slated for December 5, the day Ford and Kissinger were to arrive. American intelligence operatives learned of this potentially embarrassing timetable, and insisted that the invasion be postponed until the presidential party departed on December 6.

It was on Radio Macau that Belo heard Indonesia had invaded East Timor. Belo was overcome with "an immense sadness: I thought to myself that East Timor had lost its opportunity to become independent forever. First it was a Portuguese colony and now it was going to be an Indonesian colony for the next four hundred years. I thought about the many difficulties that East Timor would have to face." Young Belo walked through the halls of the Don Bosco school, praying intensely hour by hour, thinking of the plight that was descending on his people. But the real test of the faith of Carlos Filipe Ximenes Belo would come later: it would have been hard for the future bishop or anyone else to imagine the extent of the horrors that would follow.

For the second time in thirty-five years, a fierce invader descended on East Timor. Those who witnessed both invasions insisted that the Indonesian assault was far worse than the Japanese occupation. On a somewhat smaller scale, it was like the Japanese rape of Nanking, China, in late 1937 and early 1938, when as many as 260,000 to more than 350,000 of that city's people were slaughtered within months, although for East Timor's population, the next three years were catastrophic, reducing the population by one third or more. Bishop Belo himself has said that more than 250,000 died. By February 1976 alone, it was alleged that sixty thousand people, perhaps 10 percent of the territory's population, had perished.

Indonesian troops arrived in Dili in the predawn hours of December 7, 1975. By the time they landed, a combination of factors had whipped them into a fury. As a disillusioned Indonesian soldier later put it, they had been told they were being sent to East Timor to fight Communist enemies of Indonesia, not people wanting freedom in their own land. Though one of the chief Indonesian planners of the invasion was nominally Catholic, soldiers of Muslim background were told they were sent to fight a jihad, or holy war, against pagan infidels. Then there was the attitude of soldiers from the dominant island of Java. For many of them, the peoples of the Outer Islands of the Indonesian Republic had traditionally been regarded as culturally inferior, all the more so for East Timor, a land that had never been part of the republic, with vastly different languages and customs.

Adding to this volatile mix was the clumsy nature of the Indonesian military operation, marked by poor coordination. Paratroops were dropped by mistake on top of Fretilin units, who put up fierce resistance and inflicted heavy casualties on the Indonesians. Other Indonesian units fired on their own troops. Many of the Indonesian paratroopers rampaged through Dili, enraged by what happened.

The killing was widespread. Even apolitical Chinese businessmen who came into the streets with gifts to mollify the invaders and some members of the tiny pro-Indonesian party were machine-gunned. One priest in Dili at the time said that two thousand people, about seven hundred of them Chinese, were shot in the first few days of the invasion. An Indonesian soldier was killed near what had been the social services building under the Portuguese: two hundred East Timorese were rounded up and executed in retaliation. Two men walking near the bishop's house, close to the waterfront, were executed for the crime of wearing boots of military appearance, their thumbs tied together as they were dragged off. A CIA expert on the area said there was hard evidence of many atrocities. What the CIA knew became public knowledge only more than fifteen years later through the testimony of a conscience-stricken ex-officer.

A crowd of onlookers was forced to count aloud as each of dozens of people, one by one, were shot and thrown into the water by the harbor. The students Belo had met at the Casa de Timor were among the first ones targeted. The poet, Borja da Costa, was shot near the Câmara Eclesiástica, under circumstances that remain unclear. Rosa Bonaparte, who had become the leader of the Popular Organization of Timorese Women, the Fretilin women's organization, was executed on the Dili waterfront; Indonesian soldiers tried to drag her, together with other women, onto a landing barge along with property they had looted. When Rosa Bonaparte refused to go, she was shot. So was the Australian journalist Roger East, the only foreign witness to the invasion, who kicked, cursed, and spat at his antagonists as they made ready to shoot him. Like many others, East's body was dumped in the water. East, who had refused evacuation because he wanted to report on the invasion, became the sixth journalist to be murdered in East Timor in little more than six weeks.

Even the seminary at Dare was not spared. Indonesian planes bombed it again and again. By the time they finished there was little left of the place where Belo and many leaders of East Timor's political parties like Nicolau Lobato had gone to school.

The occupants of what is now Bishop Belo's home had a stark view of the horrors in Dili. Bishop Ribeiro had placed his faith in the Indonesian Army, believing against all reason that their presence would be benign. His mistaken view, that this would be like the bloodless Indian takeover of Goa, influenced authorities in Rome: senior Vatican diplomats now say they were surprised by the violence of the invasion.

Bishop Ribeiro himself was sickened. Grief-stricken, he returned to Portugal little more than a year after the Indonesian assault, leaving the herculean task of caring for the population to his vicar general, Dom Martinho, and the Timorese and foreign clergy who remained. They would see people at all hours, people who came speaking in low voices of terrible things, begging for help. Far from the eyes of the world, it was the Catholic Church in East Timor that shouldered responsibility for tending to the victims.

People in many places were forced to hide in churches night and day for protection. Many young women came to the bishop's house, which was full of those seeking protection from Indonesian soldiers, "who raped at will," two priests wrote. On numerous occasions, Dom Martinho, who became the acting bishop when Ribeiro left, fought to protect the women from harm, constantly lodging complaints with the military. He once told an Indonesian soldier, "If you want to kill, you kill me. These two girls are not going with you."

Unlike years later, when Mother Matilde and her Canossian Sisters were next door comforting the people, there were no women of religious orders in Dili when Indonesia invaded. Fearing what happened in the African territory of the Belgian Congo in the early 1960s, when Catholic nuns were raped by marauding soldiers, the Canossians, Mother Matilde included, were evacuated to Sydney in the months before the Indonesian attack on Dili.

The United Nations passed resolutions, underscoring the principle that the invasion was illegal and that the people of East Timor had the right to determine their own political future. But they had little impact on Indonesia. Speaking of East Timor (and a similar grab by Morocco in the Western Sahara), the then United States representative to the United Nations, Daniel Patrick Moynihan, wrote in 1978 that "the United States wished things to turn out as they did, and worked to bring this about. The Department of State desired that the United Nations prove utterly ineffective in whatever measures it undertook. This task was given to me, and I carried it forward with no inconsiderable success." Moynihan, who soon after became a U.S. senator, subsequently expressed regret for what had happened in East Timor, sponsoring many congressional measures on the question. In the early 1980s, he reportedly told an aide that East Timor was "one of the great horrors of American foreign policy."

The words of a State Department official in early 1976 summarizing the official American position were much more bland: "In terms of bilateral relations, we are more or less condoning the incursion into East Timor." After the invasion, the United States doubled its military assistance to Indonesia. Later in the year, Indonesia received special assistance from Australia, which seized a radio transmitter near Darwin that communicated with Fretilin forces inside East Timor. The Australian action was an important step in tightening the isolation of the territory, most of which was off limits to journalists. For years, most visiting reporters, who almost never spoke local languages and relied on government interpreters, were given carefully guided tours by military authorities, who produced selected "witnesses." Most of the few foreign visitors were easily misled. Thus, within East Timor itself, the press, with few exceptions, had little access to independent information, certainly in the early years and for some time thereafter. The Indonesian public was also kept largely in the dark.

Near the outset, the Indonesian military organized an event aimed at providing an air of legitimacy for its takeover. On May 31, 1976, a "People's Representative Assembly" of hand-picked tribal chiefs asked President Suharto to make East Timor the twenty-seventh province of Indonesia; Bishop Belo later made clear that even those who originally supported Indonesia felt betrayed. Meanwhile, in the months after the invasion, news surfaced of the importance of the Ombai Wetar straits north of Timor island. They were a key route for American nuclear submarines to pass undetected from the Indian Ocean to the Pacific. Military planners wanted to see them in the hands of a proven ally, though it is difficult to see how even a Fretilin government, with no military allies, could have blocked their passageway.

On July 17, 1976, President Suharto announced that East Timor had been integrated into the Republic of Indonesia. In subsequent resolutions, the United Nations rejected the claim, maintaining that the people of East Timor had not had the opportunity to exercise their right to self-determination. But for its part, although most of the territory was still outside Indonesian control, and the takeover of East Timor illegal in the private judgment of some of the State Department's own lawyers, the United States recognized de facto Indonesian control, while admitting that a legitimate act of self-determination had not taken place.

By the end of 1976, little more than a year after Belo left East Timor, a report by Indonesian Catholic priests said that the number of dead may well have been 100,000. The Indonesian Army met determined resistance in East Timor's forbidding interior: a year after the invasion, most of the territory remained in the hands of the nationalist resistance. Gradually a force of thirty thousand Indonesian troops drove into the countryside, bit by bit building the roads that the Indonesian government would boast of years later: the Portuguese failure to pave roads beyond Dili had inadvertently helped buy the Timorese time in their struggle against Indonesian forces.

Thousands in East Timor had served in the Portuguese Army at one time or another and had received some degree of military training. With their centuries-old warrior tradition, exemplified by Bishop Belo's grandfather Félix da Costa Ximenes, the soldiers of East Timor were known for their competence. These men inherited a cache of weapons left behind when Portugal withdrew, mostly automatic rifles. They were fighting a desperate battle for survival. Indonesian forces took heavy casualties, possibly thousands. Information of this nature was kept secret, often even from the soldiers' families themselves. The Indonesian regime was trying to hide the reality of the war from their own people as well as the world at large.

Ironically, the role of conveying such information sometimes fell to Bishop Belo's predecessor, Dom Martinho: "In Dili Hospital, Indonesian soldiers who were wounded asked me to contact their wives. Sometimes I could do this. . . . When I went to Jakarta many wives and children of Indonesian soldiers came to me asking what had happened to their husbands. These women could learn nothing from the military," he said in an interview after his retirement, adding that when he went to Jakarta, he would pay hospital visits to Indonesian soldiers he had known in Timor.

A retired Indonesian officer who refused to do a second tour of duty in East Timor in 1976 sounded remarkably like some disillusioned American veterans of the Vietnam period. "The East Timorese were people just like us. Whether you wanted to or not, you were ordered to go in. Then it was too late; we had to defend ourselves. It was difficult. . . . Once I knew a little about the history, I thought, if I go I'll just be killing ordinary people."

For the first year after the invasion, while the tragedy was unfolding, Carlos Filipe Ximenes Belo continued his education. In January 1976 he received word that his family was unharmed. A few months later Ermelinda and Julieta learned from a relative in Australia that Carlos was well: for six months they had received no news. Beyond the news of his family, however, he knew little. Next to East Timor, he was living in a dream world: Macau was virtually on another planet, a combination of the Orient with a patina of Iberian culture. Belo taught at the Don Bosco school, where the relatively pampered students were a world away from his beloved Fatumaca. He did not realize at the time that in the early days of the invasion, several of the priests at Fatumaca had been stripped naked, forced to sit in the hot sun, and were on the verge of being executed when a Catholic Indonesian Army officer put a stop to it. The students at the school, who at times were arrested and tortured, had far less protection.

In the mountain areas not far from Fatumaca, Bishop Belo's future cook, Maria de Fatima, then eighteen, escaped the war at first. Her home area, in the extreme eastern part of the territory, would take Indonesian forces many months to reach. There was plenty of food in the mountains, the harvests were good, and in some sense life continued as normal. There were sports like volleyball and soccer, as well as a community pharmacy filled with traditional Timorese herbal medicines. Religious services were offered by priests in the area. It almost seemed as if life would go on as before. A Catholic priest who lived in the mountains for three years, Father Leoneto Vieira do Rego, a native of the Azores like Dom Jaime Goulart, the bishop from Belo's boyhood, had lived in East Timor since 1950. He was not a partisan of Fretilin, but found himself in the mountains when the war began. Father do Rego reported later that Fretilin had successfully organized food production and schools, and for some time there was an air of normalcy in areas under the movement's control. This was when Maria de Fatima met Commandante X, a leading member of Fretilin who was a onetime seminarian and also a writer. Life was so normal for Maria de Fatima, in fact, that there was even time to fall in love and have a baby, born in 1977.

Belo was still far from the region where he had spent his boyhood years as a buffalo herder, but he was able to learn more about what was happening at home when he left Macau and continued his studies in Portugal in late 1976. There he met refugees, some of whom he had first known at Atambua in 1975. As a result of an agreement with Jakarta, hundreds had come to Lisbon, led by Father Francisco Fernandes, a highly courageous Timorese priest who had been with them throughout their time in Atambua. From talking with this group, Belo's worst fears about Indonesian military behavior were confirmed.

It was through the accounts of these refugees that the carnage in East Timor drew the attention of the U.S. Congress. Sponsored by church and relief organizations, the former Australian consul in East Timor, James Dunn, conducted interviews with refugees, and gathered numerous accounts of Indonesian atrocities. He was invited to give testimony before a subcommittee in the House of Representatives. The Carter administration, which had recently taken office, brushed aside the allegations. State Department officials downplayed the information Dunn had received, saying it was out of date; the horrors, they seemed to suggest, were all but over.

In fact, with the territory closed to independent visitors, the horrors were well hidden, although they were well known to American intelligence agencies. The atrocities took place in some areas, while they had yet to reach others. On no account could the war be said to have ended.

While it was a fairly simple matter to deny the existence of continuing atrocities from the vantage point of Washington, it was a different question altogether at an open-air Mass conducted in Dili by the Apostolic Nuncio from Jakarta in October 1977. A participant described the event: "A great wave of emotion evolved at the ceremony, made manifest in the tears, the cries, and in the sobbing of the orphans, the widows, and the foresaken, so much so that the Mass was interrupted for a quarter of an hour. . . . It would certainly have been difficult to find someone from amongst all of these people who had not had a relative killed, or unheard of, or a prisoner in one of Indonesia's dungeons. . . . Timor is no longer Timor; it is nothing but an oppressed worm."

It was around this time that Mother Matilde and the Canossian Sisters returned. The people had missed them badly, and were disappointed that they had left. The sisters, at least, could give the people some small measure of solace. There was little comfort in what others were offering: while only scant material aid was being sent, arms exports to Indonesia were being substantially stepped up. On December 5, 1977, at a time when the letter about the open-air Mass was written by a source close to the Catholic Church, the *International Herald Tribune* quoted a Western diplomat as saying that the Indonesians "are running out of military inventory. The operations on Timor have pushed them to the wall." The fight against Fretilin had "virtually exhausted" military supplies, thus "arms salesmen from France, Britain, the Netherlands, Italy, Spain, Switzerland, Belgium, West Germany, and other places discreetly woo the government—their way paved by various embassies." The article could accurately have added the United States to the list: Indonesia received timely help in the form of direct shipments from San Francisco to Dili of a profusion of arms and other crucial munitions, according to a CIA official involved in the process. By contrast, the East Timorese had nothing except what they managed to capture from Indonesian soldiers.

Maria de Fatima witnessed the consequences. Life had been pleasant enough until the bombs began to fall. At this stage most of East Timor's population was still behind Fretilin lines in the mountains. In Indonesia's drive to seize control of the territory, it concentrated much of its firepower on the Matebian area, where more than 100,000 people were living in 1978. It was one of two main areas of resistance, the other being the region around Mount Ramelau. Massive bombing campaigns forced people to move constantly from place to place, making farming impossible. The OV-10 Broncos would take off from the military air base at Baucau, in the very hills where the family of Bishop Belo's mother originated. They turned the majestic mountain range into a zone of misery and death.

Fretilin told civilians that it no longer had the capacity to feed and care for those in the area, which included Maria de Fatima, and urged people to surrender to the Indonesians. Around this time, Indonesian President Suharto announced amnesty for Fretilin guerrillas. But the offer was more for reasons of international public relations than it was real: many of those who took the offer were executed. For her part, Maria de Fatima was captured and sent to Ataúro island.

Belo was in Portugal when these tragedies were taking place. It took more than two years, from 1976 until 1978, before he received another communication from his family, and this was possible only because a relative was able to mail a letter from Java. It was impossible to send or receive mail from East Timor during those years, and largely continues to be so today. In addition, few journalists were allowed to visit the territory. It fell to private groups and individuals to publicize news from East Timor. From a distance, the future bishop learned of the proceedings of the first international conference on East Timor held in Lisbon in May 1979. It featured the renowned linguist Noam Chomsky, the only individual with a significant worldwide reputation to adopt the issue of East Timor in those years. But the Lisbon gathering could do little aside from spreading information from refugees, though this would lead to greater efforts at a later date, especially in generating international pressure to address the famine then gathering force.

No independent witness until then had seen the widespread suffering in East Timor and described it to the world. Then, at last, someone reached the outside world in mid-1979. It was Father Leoneto Vieira do Rego. With the encouragement of Bishop Belo's old mathematics teacher, Father Reinaldo Cardoso, a missionary also from the Azores who had moved to the United States after his service in East Timor, Father do Rego spoke out in New York and Washington in late 1979. The priest had lived for many months under intense Indonesian bombardment of resistance strongholds in East Timor's mountainous interior and had been on the verge of starvation himself. He gave riveting and precise testimony in a two-hour interview at the *New York Times*. While the news article that resulted was sketchy, a hard-hitting editorial followed on December 24, 1979, the first in the *Times* on the subject since the 1975 invasion. It set the tone for sympathetic *Times* editorial comment on East Timor from then on.

Father do Rego, who once edited the Church magazine *Seara* in Dili during Bishop Belo's student days, in peaceful times when the teachings of Pope John XXIII were fresh news, spoke of the devastation of East Timor's countryside by the OV-10 aircraft. As a trained engineer in addition to his priestly vocation, he was able to describe the devastation of the bombing with great precision. Father do Rego's words left a deep impression on *New York Times* editorial writer Karl E. Meyer and others with whom he met. The *Christian Science Monitor* described the white-haired priest as "dignified and mustachioed."

Though Father do Rego was the first eyewitness to come forward, his information was not completely new—it was long known to American intelligence analysts, for example. But the priest's revelations led to further journalistic inquiries. Soon after Father do Rego's testimony, the *New York Times* sent the late James M. Markham, who had reported extensively from Vietnam, to meet Timorese refugees recently arrived in Portugal. In four days of interviews in freezing hotels and a hillside refugee camp at a place outside Lisbon called the Valley of the Jasmine, which Belo regularly visited during those years, Markham, considered to be of the finest foreign corre-

spondents of his generation, slowly elicited accounts of atrocities from ter-
rified refugees of Chinese origin, who feared that their testimony would result in harm to relatives remaining in East Timor. After being assured of
their anonymity, they agreed to speak of their experiences from the Indonesian invasion until their departure in late 1979.

"I felt like I was back in Saigon," said Markham of his encounters with
these refugees, who spoke of "a world of terror" in Dili, which was "full of
informers and spies." "Their accounts were horrifyingly laconic," Markham
added. "Everyone wants to leave," one woman told Markham. "It is the land
of the devil."

As Markham emphasized, it would have been nearly impossible to obtain such accounts within Indonesia and East Timor itself. He stressed that
if he had returned to Indonesia for several weeks, he would not have felt
confident about publishing an accurate story on almost any subject, because of a combination of language and cultural barriers as well as a climate of repression and deception that existed in official circles and other
walks of life. "People would just lie to you," concluded Markham, who had
reported from many different countries under harsh conditions.

In Indonesia, there was always the possibility of corruption. There had
been allegations that the Indonesian regime engaged in vote buying at the
United Nations, and in some instances, there were outright attempts to
bribe expert witnesses and prominent foreign visitors: a leading Western
aid official said that on his first visit to Indonesia in the 1970s, he found an
envelope stuffed with cash on the bureau of his hotel room. The aid official
returned the envelope, with indignation. At the very least, the episode
raised the question of how many others may have been offered an envelope
and not had the integrity to refuse it.

There were more subtle means of pushing the official Indonesian point
of view. All-expense-paid trips to conferences in places like Bali for congressional staff and others close to governments were another way. Former
ambassadors in Jakarta, working on Indonesia-related ventures in retirement, would also act as unofficial but highly influential advocates for the
official point of view. On another level, many foreign journalists dependent on the Indonesian government for residence permits or entry visas
were especially careful about contradicting official points of view.

Still, no matter how great Indonesia's sway among the powerful, the
outside world was occasionally able to get a glimpse of the consequences of
the invasion. For instance, a delegation of Western diplomats, including
the U.S. ambassador to Indonesia, Edward Masters, paid a rare visit to East

Timor in September 1978 and were told of the grim facts: hundreds, possibly thousands, were dying of starvation each month.

Japan came to Indonesia's defense in the United Nations that year echoing Jakarta's line that all was well at a time when a human catastrophe of immense proportions was building. In this political atmosphere, international humanitarian agencies were allowed by Indonesia to begin working in East Timor (having been barred since the December 1975 invasion) only in mid-1979. By then it was too late for many tens of thousands of people, perhaps 200,000 or more. In late 1979 the International Committee of the Red Cross compared conditions in East Timor with those in Biafra and Cambodia, two of the worst humanitarian crises in contemporary history: the head of the East Timor office of the U.S.–based Catholic Relief Services (CRS) said that the problem was "greater than anything I have seen in fourteen years of relief work in Asia."

Before relief agencies gained limited access to East Timor, much of the little food and medical care people received came through the help of the Church. In the years Belo was away, the Catholic Church in East Timor was transformed, spiritually above all, into an institution that shared the people's suffering and provided what assistance it could.

The clergy in Dili, and priests who found themselves in outlying areas controlled by Fretilin, recall having had great moral support from Archbishop Vincenzo Maria Farano, the papal nuncio in Jakarta, who visited them often and traveled as extensively as he could. More than any other Church official from Rome, Farano is remembered with extraordinary fondness, although his courageous stance did not result in any forthright public statements by the Vatican at the time. Farano was tough and humane. On one occasion, he insisted on obtaining the release of a missing priest who was being held in Indonesian military custody after he left Fretilin-controlled mountain areas. Archbishop Farano said he was hoping to say Mass with the priest that day.

The military claimed that they did not know the whereabouts of the priest. Farano stood his ground. "I am here to celebrate Mass with the father," he repeated firmly. Finally, the military released the priest. He and Archbishop Farano said Mass together.

As limited as the actions of the Vatican may have been, they were ahead of those of many governments. Certainly that is the way it seemed to Carlos Filipe Ximenes Belo in his years abroad. Indeed, there is no evidence that the United States or any other major power took any significant action to address the gathering disaster between the time of the Indonesian invasion and the last few months of the 1970s, when grisly photographs of famine victims, mainly children, taken during a rare press visit, brought congressional pressure on the Carter administration to make the crisis in East Timor an issue with Jakarta; public reaction in the U.S., Australia, Britain, and other nations stimulated donations of relief aid. Some Timorese suffered from malnutrition so severe they resembled "survivors from the World War II Belsen or Auschwitz concentration camps," according to the *Far Eastern Economic Review.*

In a sense it came down to Henry Kissinger: few in the foreign policy establishment were anxious to challenge his judgement. A State Department official told the diplomatic correspondent of *The Christian Science Monitor,* Daniel Southerland, that the Carter administration decided when it came to power that it did not want to "get into a contest" with Henry Kissinger over the policy of unquestioning support for Indonesia on East Timor matters.

The consequences of that policy became plain enough. Officials from the United States Agency for International Development visited East Timor and were shocked by what they saw. By late 1979 an estimated 250,000 Timorese had been forced into "resettlement camps," in large part to separate them from the nationalist resistance. One visitor, a refugee-relief expert, called the camps "horrible—as horrible as I've seen anywhere, including the Thai-Cambodian border," then the subject of worldwide outcry.

Speaking of the situation in 1978, Father do Rego said, "I think that more people died in the Indonesian camps than as a result of the war." It was estimated that half a generation of Timorese children may have been rendered mentally retarded by malnutrition. The centrist Washington-based weekly *The New Republic* concluded in late 1979 that "The most intense fighting in Timor has occurred during the Carter Administration's tenure in office—and so have most of the casualties."

Yet some U.S. officials, including U.S. Ambassador to Indonesia Edward Masters, tried to blame the massive starvation in East Timor mainly on lack of infrastructure, the traditional poverty of the region, and drought. In Congressional testimony in December 1979, Masters put the war in fourth place in his list of causes of the humanitarian disaster. The ambassador declined to be interviewed by an experienced journalist who had questions about this and other aspects of his congressional testimony. In fact, Masters was in the same congressional hearing room as Father do Rego, but neither he nor any Carter administration official sought to speak with the priest. The legacy of Portuguese colonial rule was also cited by the American ambassador, although he never explained exactly how this caused the deaths of so many, four years after Portugal had departed. Another State Department official made a blunt comment about the famine to *The Christian Science Monitor* in 1980: "The Indonesians couldn't handle it [Timorese resistance], but they didn't want to let people know how badly they'd botched things. So they just let people starve."

Military action claimed other victims. The dead included Nicolau Lobato, who led the resistance against the Indonesian onslaught: on the last day of 1978, he was surrounded and killed. The future bishop heard the news of Lobato's death on Portuguese television. His immediate feeling, he recalled, was that "It was a great tragedy that they had killed a Timorese hero." Two more of the students that Belo had known from Casa de Timor, Vicente Reis and António Carvarino, were killed by Indonesian forces in the months that followed.

The Quelicai area of Belo's paternal forebears saw some of the heaviest fighting. One measure of his family's present isolation was that Belo had received no news from home, not even a simple letter, since he left in 1975. At congressional hearings in 1977, what had happened near Quelicai was described by Shepard Forman as "the annihilation of simple mountain people." Many of the Makassae people were removed from their land by the Indonesian military so they would be unable to support the independence movement. They were taken from their traditional homelands with their sacred sites to areas along the coast, where malaria was rampant. In these "resettlement areas," they could not practice their livelihoods, and were under constant watch by the Indonesians. It was not the same as "ethnic cleansing" in Bosnia a decade and a half later, though it was something akin to it: it represented what Shepard Forman termed "the obliteration of a cultural system and a way of life that had a lot of value." The inexplicable horror shook the basis of Makassae beliefs.

Simple survival became a frightening daily struggle for the Makassae and other Timorese brethren. An emergency relief operation by the International Committee of the Red Cross and Catholic Relief Services managed to save many lives before it was curtailed in 1981, when Indonesian forces were gearing up for a new military offensive. By then, guerrilla resistance managed to resume, although on a lesser scale than before; still, the Indonesian government was anxious to restrict international access to the territory to limit the chances of further embarrassing disclosures. By 1980 the strategy of Jakarta's policy planners was directed elsewhere, however. They recognized that surviving members of the generation old enough to remember the 1975 invasion and the years that followed might never accept Indonesian rule. But a new generation untainted by such memories would be different, they thought: Indonesian schools and culture, and healthy outlays of government cash, would quell the flames of East Timorese nationalism, given the passage of time. This was the climate in which Father Belo, ordained as a priest on July 26, 1980, returned to East Timor in 1981, after a year in Macau and five more in Portugal and Rome.

CHAPTER 5

RETURN TO THE
FUNERAL PYRE

❖ ❖ ❖ ❖

U PON BELO'S RETURN, only the beauty of East Timor remained.
That much could be said: coastline, mountains, sky, and foliage
on the way to Baucau were mercifully untouched. But many forest areas in places like the road from Dili to the old seminary at Dare, were
cut down to deny cover to the guerrilla resistance. The landscape was not
the same. No one had asked the people, of course; like many other things,
the Indonesian military had simply done as they pleased. It went against
the common law of the East Timorese people to be so flagrantly disre-
garded.

Simply looking at the people was a shock. He was glad to see his country again, but for Carlos Filipe Ximenes Belo it was a sad homecoming in
late July 1981. When he left suddenly nearly six years before, there was deep
anxiety about the future, and most people lived in poverty. It was surely no
paradise then. Now, however, there were all the problems of the old days,
only magnified many times. An atmosphere of mourning, misery, and raw
fright, seemed to hang heavily in the air around them, almost as tangibly as
the soldiers who were strutting through the streets, behaving like conquerors. The society to which he returned was vastly different from anything he had ever known, even at the very worst moments of Portuguese
colonialism.

"The people are now experiencing oppression without end, their rights
are not acknowledged. The people do not have a voice, and live in fear,"
wrote the clergy of the territory in a document of reflection about the time
of Belo's arrival. "Indeed, the people live in a situation of continual war,
and thus must be silent and submissive. But they remain in a very clear po-

sition concerning their ideals. Their faith stands firm and is strengthened, although it is not always able to be expressed in words, but is seen with the eyes of faith by the religious who accompany the people."

Belo's means of arrival tells a small part of the country's story. The former international airport in Baucau, with its long runway in a plain near the hills of his ancestors, was no longer used by civilian planes; it had been taken over for military purposes. So the young priest landed in Dili, spent two days there, and then proceeded to Baucau by road. Father Manuel Magalhães, one of his old Salesian mentors, brought a Land Rover to take him home. Everywhere he looked there were checkpoints, and one needed a special pass to make the journey. Quiet and sleepy when he was growing up, the land of his birth was now like an armed camp.

By July 1981, Belo had been away from East Timor for twelve of the past thirteen years. The most that one might have said of his earlier six-year absence, from 1968 to 1974, was that little changed during that period; East Timor had simply remained poor. The misery from 1975 to 1981, however, was of a profoundly different order. It was like a wrathful punishment imposed by evil forces—no matter which of the island's religious traditions one worshiped. It had an indelible impact on how people lived, died, and on what they believed.

By the time Belo returned, Catholicism for the first time had become the religion of the vast majority of the people of East Timor. Under the doctrine known as *Pancasila,* the five principles of Indonesia's state philosophy, adoption of one of the five approved religions—Islamic, Hindu, Buddhist, Protestant, and Catholic faiths—was expected by the authorities. Only these were legally recognized. In East Timor the pressure to choose one of the five was even greater than elsewhere, since rituals of the native religions of East Timor had become identified in the minds of ABRI with Fretilin guerrillas in the mountains. Moreover, failure to choose could be interpreted as support for atheism, which to the military authorities meant Communism—and from the point of view of the army's ideology, that all but gave them a license to kill.

No practical alternative existed: the people were obliged to make a decision, and in East Timor, Catholicism was familiar. Indeed, in many ways the Church in East Timor was like a tolerant, next-door neighbor of long standing, because whatever its shortcomings, forced conversion had never been its policy. Adding to its mystique was the fact that, well before the Indonesian invasion, white-robed Catholic priests visiting East Timor's countryside were seen by many worshipers of traditional religions as having supernatural powers.

So the overwhelming majority of the people chose Catholicism. They hoped not only for spiritual benefit, but for a degree of protection as well: The clergy tried to defend people from physical attack in the villages and towns, providing refuge in missions and chapels. In a far more concentrated way than in the past, the Church became the guardian of the population, which needed all the moral support and comfort they could get. Taken together, the years from 1975 through 1981 had been, without question, the worst in East Timor's history, even worse than the Japanese occupation, which had ended after less than four years. In the present crisis, though, there was no sign of Indonesian withdrawal.

By the time Belo came home, Indonesia had all but closed the island to the outside world, and it remained that way for more than seven years after his return. Actual events in East Timor were quite different from the reassuring way they were portrayed in Washington, where by now the Reagan administration had come to power. There and in other capitals, government officials spoke of "improvements" in human rights and humanitarian conditions, quibbling endlessly over what had taken place. There was little direct access to the territory by outsiders, most of it in the form of short, infrequent visits by diplomats from countries with close relations with Indonesia, who had little interest in raising uncomfortable questions.

Not only was it difficult for visitors: in many cases people in one part of East Timor itself had little idea of what was happening in other parts of the territory. For nearly two years after his return in 1981, Belo had little information on what was happening outside of his own region. With many people afraid to speak freely with anyone outside their own family, with no newspapers or other means of communication, the situation was doubly dark. Still, governments like the United States and Australia had little problem learning precisely what was going on in East Timor, through their excellent intelligence sources and sophisticated electronic monitoring of the region. But what these nations knew rarely became public.

For the U.S. State Department and Indonesia's other diplomatic allies, it was business as usual. For Belo, what he saw when he returned was the obliteration of the universe he had known. It was, he said many years later, "like a desert."

The future bishop saw a subjugated people. Troops seemed to be traveling in all directions at once, in Dili and elsewhere. As he traveled east on the way to a reunion with his mother, with Julieta and others in Baucau, Belo saw a sad, downcast demeanor on people's faces. It contrasted dramatically with the mood he had witnessed the last time he was down this road, in August 1975, when it was filled with the exuberance of youngsters waving Fretilin flags. Little could they have imagined the harsh fate that awaited them after the Indonesian invasion.

When he was last there, the road between Dili and Baucau had been a scene of glee, of a nervous sort, perhaps. Nonetheless, there had been merriment and great hope. Young Carlos, the Salesian assistant, had sensed misfortune, though how bad a disaster he could not have guessed even in his most pessimistic moments. The youngsters had been naive, in their political enthusiasm of the early days. In some ways, the young people of East Timor of 1975 were little different from the generation that led Indonesia to independence three decades before. The Indonesian armed forces had been founded on October 5, 1945, in part by young people, some known as *pemuda,* who were prepared to throw themselves on bayonets to win Indonesia's independence from the Dutch. One would not have had to travel far in Amsterdam in the late 1940s to hear the opinion that these young, ungrateful Indonesian fanatics deserved whatever punishment they received. Yet many of these people went on to run Indonesia; some, notably Suharto, a young lieutenant-colonel by the end of the war of independence, continued in office many years later.

Thus, however naive they might have been, the youngsters on the road from Baucau to Dili in August 1975, and many like them throughout East Timor, were hardly fiendish criminals deserving terrible retribution. Yet that was to be their fate at the hands of the Indonesian Army. Nearly six years later, the same road Belo had traveled was eerie, with a sepulchral quiet like a funeral pyre. And it was not only that road, it was the whole country.

Father Belo, arriving in Baucau in late July 1981, learned what had taken place from the ones he trusted most. Reaching his mother's house, there was another photo on the wall alongside those of Belo's two departed brothers, and this new photo, like the others, showed a seemingly invincible young man with an infectious smile. It was Carlos's cousin, Aurario Brito, shot dead in 1978 when he tried to surrender to Indonesian forces in Baucau. Aurario, who had worked in the telecommunications department under the Portuguese, was a member of the group around Vicente Reis, one of the students from the Casa de Timor he was a founding member of Fretilin.

Aurario's mother was in Baucau when he arrived, prostrate with grief on seeing Carlos, who was born the year before her son. She fell on her knees and wailed, "Look at what has happened!"

Carlos was grief-stricken himself. The two boys had grown up together, and Aurario's death affected him profoundly, leaving a permanent mark on the future bishop's psyche. Indeed, one could sense a deep wistfulness in the bishop in 1995 when he drove through the region where his cousin met his death. Carlos Filipe Ximenes Belo emphasized the special affection he had for his cousin in a conversation in mid-1998, twenty years after Aurario was killed.

"A number of my cousins were killed in the war," the bishop added quietly, "especially from Quelicai. But Aurario and I went to school together, and his death affected me in a particular way."

The death of Aurario was made even worse by the identity of the person who killed him. The soldier who shot Aurario was a distant relative serving in the Indonesian army. Fear in the area was so intense, and the danger of any kind of identification with Fretilin was so strong, the bishop said, that the family did not feel able to claim Aurario's body until many years after his death. Members of the family took solace within the Church: by 1998, Aurario's daughter, who idolized Carlos from the time he was a young priest, had become a Canossian sister. In addition to tending to the grief within his own extended family, Father Belo was keenly aware from the earliest days of his return to East Timor that there was a pressing need to address the wounds inflicted on society as a whole. There is no doubt that this understanding, and the future bishop's fierce determination to heal the divisions brought about by the conflict in East Timor, had deep emotional roots within his own family.

Belo had heard about the problems. He had read about them. Yet, a man of great religious faith, in worldly matters his skepticism was equally great. Simple assertions meant little to him, ideology even less. But once he had spoken with his family and seen his homeland with his own eyes, he was stunned.

When he went to Baucau, in Vemasse, Laleia, and Manatuto, towns on the road to Baucau, he observed, "There were only women and children; all the men were gone." He was alarmed. What was the meaning of this? No independent outside observers had been allowed to remain, even the International Committee of the Red Cross, which generally works on a confidential basis, avoiding critical public statements except under emergency conditions. In 1981 the ICRC was told to leave: The Indonesian regime wanted no foreign witnesses to what they had planned.

Belo did not have to wait long to see what his mother had told him was true. And if it seemed as if soldiers were moving in all directions at once, it was because they were. A major operation known as the "fence of legs," which would last through September, was in full force as he arrived.

East Timorese males between the ages of fifteen and sixty were forced to march in front of Indonesian troops to flush out Fretilin guerrillas still active in large sections of the countryside. In the "fence of legs" operation, many of Belo's countrymen endured unfathomable conditions for weeks in tropical heat, forced to march up and down the steep mountains for which the territory was known. His own brother, uncles, and cousins were among thousands used as human shields as they were taken by the Indonesian military from village to village. CIA sources told a senior U.S. Senate Intelligence Committee staff member that the Timorese death toll was two thousand, many of the men perishing from exhaustion and disease. Others said it was higher.

Belo did not have to suffer hunger and thirst himself, or undergo a forced march, but great trials lay ahead of him. He could not know it at the time, but his own pain was only beginning. Not only would he feel the trauma of his return, but in the years that followed he would suffer estrangement from many of his fellow priests, conflict with Indonesian military authorities and Vatican officials, and, ultimately, confrontation with the youth of East Timor. His own personal Calvary would involve a particularly harsh form of isolation.

Even so, the young Salesian never regretted his decision to return home. He had not hesitated to come back. An inner voice told him that it was his lot to share the pain of his people. He was young and fresh, and truly happy to be home. Carlos Filipe Ximenes Belo had not gone through years of rigorous training to apply his skills elsewhere. The East Timorese needed him, and he would serve without complaint. Although he had been away for many years, there was never any question of his staying in comfortable exile in Portugal, which, as a nation where the Salesian order is held in especially high regard, would have welcomed this young priest.

Almost half a lifetime ago, when Carlos was seventeen, his bishop had worried that as a Salesian, Carlos would be lost to the Diocese of Dili. In 1979, Bishop Ribeiro, who by then had returned to Portugal, invited Belo to his home in Évora to convince him that he must go back to his people in East Timor. Carlos went out of courtesy, but like his earlier choice to join a religious order, he did not need a lecture or words of wisdom: his decision, as he once told Ribeiro, had been made long ago. He enjoyed Portugal, loved the hospitality and graciousness of the people, and, next to Timor, felt most at home there. He knew the customs and nearly every region of the country. But he could not see himself staying there. He never allowed the pleasures of Lisbon or Rome to sway him. It was not that he was incapable of enjoying himself there, but whatever occurred in these places was quite secondary to his primary purpose in life, which was serving the poor, either in his own country or, failing that, perhaps in Africa or Latin America. Many years later, when there was talk that he might be removed from his post as bishop of Dili, Belo dismissed the idea that he might go to live in Portugal with a wave of the hand, using that old Portuguese expression: "*Amigos, amigos, negocios aparte*"—"Friends are friends, but business is business."

Similarly, he had no desire to conduct campaigns from abroad, and he steered clear of militancy. The priesthood was his vocation, not political activism. In fact, while in Portugal, he avoided activity that might have made it impossible for him to return. His mission was in East Timor, no matter who ruled the territory.

Some disapproved of his decision to return under these circumstances. An old friend in Portugal, whom he knew from the seminary at Dare, berated Belo. Before slamming down the phone on Carlos, he demanded to know how he could return to live under Indonesian rule, a traitorous act in the eyes of some exiled nationalists. To go back to East Timor it was necessary for Belo to obtain an Indonesian passport, and that meant taking Indonesian citizenship. Symbolic issues like this meant little to the practical-minded Belo: "I am working for the people, no one else," he said.

Finally he had his chance. After a week in Baucau with his family, Belo took up the post of master of novices at the training school at Fatumaca, where he had been before he left East Timor in 1975. And as he settled into his new task, he learned more about the horrors that had taken place since he left.

People had a weary look about them, something he was familiar with from the hard times his family had known when he was growing up. With the loss of his father and two brothers, the future bishop's family had known more grief than most. Yet even then, they also knew how to laugh, and were confident that ultimately they could rise above sorrow. The situation he found after returning from his studies in Europe was vastly different: a look of oppression was worn by nearly everyone. Worse, the war was far from over.

The guerrillas of Fretilin always managed to regroup. Belo's Christian philosophy could not countenance the loss of a single life, or justify violence in any form. But he knew that the situation was hardly straightforward: if the guerrillas surrendered, they would in all likelihood meet the fate of many of their compatriots who had done so in the late 1970s, including his cousin Aurario: summary execution.

In any case, as a junior priest newly returned after so many years away, no one was asking him for his opinion. As he settled into Fatumaca, once again Belo was able to play a role as an observer, this time of the changes that had taken place since 1975, especially in the attitude of the youth.

Everyone, it seemed, was in mourning, for many of the students he taught in 1975, which now seemed like a Golden Age, had died in the war. Belo remembered the spirit of the young people then, before the war, and shuddered. In 1981, "the environment had completely changed. It was one of grief, tension, and sadness, where the military dominated and people lived in constant fear," he recalled.

It was bad throughout the territory, but it was particularly grueling in his father's ancestral village in the Matebian region. If his mother's area had become a military base, his father's had become a killing ground. Belo remembered Quelicai well from his childhood of tending buffalo and chickens, later as a place to debate the elders together with his brother António, but in his absence it had become known as a place of execution: "To speak of Quelicai makes our heart thump and our hair stand on end, for Quelicai means certain death for those called there," said a letter written by a priest before Belo returned.

It was little better elsewhere. Almost exactly when Belo returned home in 1981, and the "fence of legs" campaign was proceeding with grim fury, his predecessor had reached his limit. The end of Dom Martinho's tenure as apostolic administrator of East Timor can be traced to his strong reaction to that Indonesian military sweep. Dom Martinho wrote that "the Catholic Church, running all risks, had to denounce to the world the atrocities committed during four days of the siege near the Rock of Saint Anthony in Lacluta, where more than five hundred Timorese were killed" in September 1981. The victims included pregnant women and children, whose heads were smashed against rocks.

Monsignor Martinho da Costa Lopes, one of the first native priests in East Timor, was born in 1918 in a village not far from Bishop Belo's birthplace. He endured prejudice at the hands of the Portuguese, and developed a combative streak. A stout man of medium height, he became known for his stubbornness, one manifestation of his fierce strength of character. But he had a lighter side that alternated with his darker moods. Dom Martinho played the accordion, and well. He was a sports fan, with a particular interest in boxing. He could be kindly, or he could exhibit a volcanic temper. The strain of the war had taken a toll on Dom Martinho's well-being, and his deeply lined face showed it. His voracious appetite for food was legendary, but it had been tempered by the sorrows of the conflict, and he had lost a good deal of weight as a result. By 1983 he exhibited a deep melancholy. The people called Dom Martinho "the bishop," although he did not officially hold that position. Dom Martinho, like East Timor itself, was in a kind of limbo. Then as now, the United Nations considered the Indonesian occupation illegal; the Vatican followed the position of the United Nations, so Rome did not extend official recognition to the Indonesian claim. Therefore, because of East Timor's unsettled status, the Diocese of Dili has continued to be administered directly by the Vatican, rather than through the Catholic Church of Indonesia.

Under these conditions, no permanent bishop can be named. The pope instead has designated an apostolic administrator, or acting bishop, for the post. In 1981 that was Dom Martinho, a man of the system, the one-time vicar general who had told the twenty-seven-year-old Carlos Filipe Ximenes Belo to leave East Timor during the civil war. Far from being a radical, in many ways Dom Martinho was an old-school conservative. Like his former boss, Bishop Ribeiro, he had been prepared to accept the Indonesians had they behaved decently. But after a lifetime of obeying the rules, Dom Martinho saw his people being slaughtered, with barely a word of protest from abroad. Nonetheless, he tried to work quietly with the Indonesian military for more than five years to persuade them to treat the people of East Timor with respect. Finally he concluded that this approach had been all but fruitless. "I decided that because there were no other means, I should speak openly in accordance with the Church's prophetic mission," Dom Martinho said later.

In the park near his church on the Dili shorefront area of Lecidere, the place where Bishop Belo would later preside, Dom Martinho, a masterful orator, condemned the atrocities, cautiously, without naming Indonesia directly. It was before a group of twelve thousand people, on October 13, 1981, the day commemorating Our Lady of Fatima. He received death threats as a result. The situation did not improve, and before long he became more blunt.

Years later, an Indonesian priest spoke in awe about Dom Martinho's raw courage—for instance, the time when the Indonesian Defense Minister of the time, Andi Mohammad Yusuf, came to Dili to review his troops.

"This one, this one, this one, that one!" cried Dom Martinho, pulling out of line the military officers responsible for atrocities and pointing his finger at each of them. No one could silence this venerable priest.

On November 19, 1981, Dom Martinho sent an anguished letter to a friend in nearby Australia that is the best record of what he said during that time:

> The news from Timor is quite bad. However, it is necessary to have the courage to receive it, considering that it is based on the truth.
>
> With the military operation that took place in July, August and September, it seems as if a cyclone had swept Timor from end to end, leaving the island in a true tragedy: the death of innocent children of two to three years of age, pregnant women and defenseless people massacred only because they did not want to lose their identity among the nations of the world. Approximately 500 people were accused and killed without hesitation or pity, exclusively for the crime of not wanting to integrate into the Republic of Indonesia, preferring above all to be slaves in their own independence to being well-off under the paw of others. After all this we come to the conclusion that the military operation undertaken by Indonesia in Timor not only did not produce the desired effect, it was actually counterproductive. The question of Timor cannot be resolved by shooting, only through dialogue.
>
> But let us leave this to the politicians, considering that the policies adopted until now have been an authentic disaster. The Indonesians would like to excuse themselves with material development without the participation of the Timorese people, who are now reeling from hunger, disease and all kinds of physical misery. The greatest wealth of Timor is the Timorese people, without which everything else would have no sense. Let us ask God to enlighten men so that they can understand that above all it is human dignity that should be valued, in accordance with the teachings of the last Papal Encyclicals.

Gradually, Dom Martinho's letter, and others that he had written, found their way to the international press, where they received attention at a time when news reports on East Timor were rare. The letter led to debate in the Australian Parliament, and was published in the official record of the U.S. Congress. Actions like this, and his reputed support for Fretilin, ultimately led Jakarta to put pressure on the Vatican to ask Dom Martinho for his resignation.

As Dom Martinho said later, when he met Cardinal Casaroli, then the Vatican Secretary of State, it was a matter of politics, pure and simple. After all, at almost the same time in Nicaragua, Cardinal Miguel Obando y Bravo—himself a Salesian, like Belo—was seen as giving moral support to contra guerrillas seeking to overthrow the Sandinista government, but Obando remained in office.

Already resigned from office, Dom Martinho told Cardinal Casaroli when they met in Rome, "In matters of theology I believe the Vatican is infallible, and I am obedient. But in matters of politics, you are only human, and you are wrong about East Timor." The Secretary of State of the Vatican—who, Dom Martinho said, bore at least some of the responsibility for preventing him from meeting with the pope until he had already left his post—was hesitant, and did not look at him directly.

As Cardinal Casaroli knew well, East Timor posed an extremely difficult problem for Rome, one with considerations well beyond the issue at hand. Indonesia was an important nation for the Catholic Church, just as it had been when Portuguese and then Dutch sailors made their first trading missions in search of spices in the sixteenth and seventeenth centuries. Now as then, it was at a crossroads of civilizations, with Muslims, Hindus, Buddhists, and Christians converging on the vast archipelago. To some in the Vatican, on a religious level at least, Indonesia was as strategically significant as the military and economic importance of its sea-lanes and oil reserves. Indonesia was the largest Muslim nation in the world, playing a leading role in the interreligious dialogue between Christians and Islam. The strain of Islam practiced in Indonesia was remarkably tolerant, at least in its mainstream tendencies; Catholics were relatively free to evangelize in Indonesia, unlike in many areas of the Muslim world. This alone was a fundamental reason why important voices in Rome wanted to downplay the issue of East Timor. The Indonesian government provided generous assistance to Catholic schools and hospitals.

In a nation of more than 150 million at the time, the 4 to 5 million Catholics of Indonesia were a distinct minority. But some members of the Indonesian Catholic community were extremely powerful, especially in the years 1974 through 1988. There were prominent Catholics in government ministries, in the military and intelligence establishments, and among the wealthy Chinese business elite, members of another vulnerable minority. Catholic leaders in Indonesia would speak darkly of their fear of a Muslim ascendancy, while some in the Vatican hinted at the danger of the Indonesian Catholic Church being destroyed by unnamed enemies. At the same time, the military government of President Suharto had long kept Muslim fundamentalists under control, resorting to repression without hesitation.

There were other reasons for avoiding confrontation with Jakarta. On a humanitarian level, the need to channel aid to East Timor through Catholic agencies, especially between the emergency years of 1975 and 1982 (for most of this time, the Church was the only available route for outside aid), also lent itself to a policy of discreet silence on the part of Rome. Other top Church sources—including leaders of the Church in East Timor, and at times Dom Martinho himself—stressed that it was crucial to address the situation on a practical level. The question of strong public statements by the Vatican under these thorny conditions was problematic at best.

Vatican diplomats would argue that they were only being realistic. According to the conventional foreign policy wisdom of the time, which influenced Rome, East Timor would surely reconcile itself to Indonesian rule sooner or later.

Dom Martinho put it another way. "It was the great dream at the Vatican to expand the Catholic Church in Indonesia," he said later. "The little ones are being sacrificed for big interests."

But as he and a range of Catholic bishops have also emphasized, there was a world of difference between the attitudes of Pope John Paul II and the Vatican bureaucracy. The pope, Dom Martinho said, had been very kind to him when they met privately in Rome, showing "great awareness" of the plight of East Timor. Dom Martinho affirmed that it was "an encouragement to me." It was just as Edward W. Doherty, the late American diplomat turned adviser to the U.S. Catholic bishops, once said: "Vatican diplomats are like any other diplomats, no different than the Americans or the French or the Russians: their main purpose is to improve relations with the government of the country where they are accredited."

The contribution of the Catholic Church could hardly be judged on the basis of the policies in the Vatican bureaucracy alone. Dozens of people like Edward Doherty, often in close cooperation with secular organizations, worked to bring about justice for East Timor through pressure on their governments; In Doherty's case, it was by helping to alert the State Department, Congress, the news media, grassroots Church constituencies and, above all, the American Catholic bishops themselves. Had it not been for the weight of such people working quietly within the Catholic Church in many places around the world, the plight of East Timor would have been far worse.

And some non-Catholic religious organizations, notably the New York-based Women's Division of the United Methodist Office for the United Nations, played a pioneering role in supporting many of the same efforts, using their facilities to inform the public and the diplomatic community from the earliest days of the Indonesian invasion.

Most of this could scarcely be seen by the clergy of East Timor at a time when news of what was happening in their own land was difficult to obtain. As the storm swirled around Dom Martinho and his letters, Carlos Filipe Ximenes Belo was hard at work in Fatumaca, where after a year he had been promoted to the position of superior. Even though Belo had hosted a retreat for the clergy there, he had not been informed of the existence of Dom Martinho's letters.

It was a fateful time. In early 1983, Pope John Paul was with his friend Don Egidio Vigano, the rector major of the Salesians of Don Bosco. The Salesian order was reputedly favored by John Paul for its exemplary work, and its reputation for fealty to Rome. Some said one reason the pope had a special affection for the Salesians was that they were known to him from his parish church as a young man in Poland during the German occupation in World War II: the Nazis had arrested the Salesians from that church, sending them to a concentration camp, where twelve priests and one novice perished. It was significant that the future pope, then twenty-four, maintained his nonviolent stance after this episode: when the Polish armed resistance tried to recruit young men from the parish, Karol Wojtyla managed to convince most of them not to join.

Sitting with Father Egidio Vigano many years later contemplating another violent situation, John Paul had a difficult decision to make: he was given three candidates to replace Dom Martinho, who had been asked to resign, as apostolic administrator. The first two, John Paul told Father Vigano, were highly experienced and competent, having lived through the conflict during the past eight years. The third was one of Don Egidio's own, Carlos Filipe Ximenes Belo.

"I will choose this young priest," Pope John Paul II declared to Egidio Vigano. "And may God hold me accountable for the action I am taking today."

Much later, Belo said, "My responsibility before God comes from having been the last" of the three names submitted to the pope.

When he first heard the news, Belo went into a state of shock. He was at Fatumaca on April 15, 1983, when he received a telegram from the papal nuncio saying he should come to Jakarta as soon as possible. When he arrived, he was informed of the Pope's choice.

"Now go to your room, and after praying, sign this paper saying that you accept," the nuncio told him.

He could not refuse, Belo said, "because for us Salesians a request made by the pope is a command."

His Salesian sense of obedience was undoubtedly a factor in his selection by Rome, especially after Dom Martinho's growing recalcitrance. Belo would not be a problem, some Church authorities felt. For their part, the Indonesian government apparently believed that Belo's youth would make him easily controllable, timid, and meek, in contrast to Dom Martinho.

The Salesian order ran several schools and social programs in East Timor and, because of its desire to stay in the territory, its members refrained from public criticism of the Indonesian occupation. Like many other religious orders around the world and in East Timor itself, the Salesians adopted a position of cooperation with local authorities. The price of remaining where they were was public silence. Some therefore assumed that Belo was a man who would not rock the boat. Belo's independent-mindedness was little known in 1983, and it might not have helped him if it were.

Indeed, Belo was under so much stress at the news that he locked himself in his room for a long time of reflection. When word of Belo's nomination spread through the Diocese of East Timor, the reaction was negative. While it had been difficult to return to Fatumaca two years before, Belo's new role was a challenge of an entirely different order. Even his own mother seemed to believe that Belo was too young for the job. The circumstances were impossible; Dona Ermelinda tried to insist with her son that he refuse the assignment.

"I myself knew that I had no parish experience," Belo remembered of that time. "The two years that I was in Fatumaca, I was helping out in the villages in the area, saying Mass, and administering the sacraments, but I had no experience on how to organize a parish."

His family knew that an added problem was the delicate question of Dom Martinho, who was already a priest when Belo was born. He was the one who had advised young Carlos to leave during the civil war to complete his studies abroad, surely never imagining Belo would one day be his successor.

"I was a kid," he said in 1993. But Belo was not just any kid, his capabilities notwithstanding. It was the local parish priest who had helped the family obtain government assistance after his father died. In fact, Dom Martinho was the priest from the Baucau area who came to Ermelinda's aid so that little Carlos could attend school. Now, after a lifetime of service to the Church, Dom Martinho was being succeeded by this young fellow, who at thirty-five looked even younger.

His mentor from the seminary at Dare, Father José Luis Rodriguez, was likewise incredulous. It was only a short time since he had seen Belo off when his former pupil left Rome for Timor in 1981. Then in 1983 he encountered Archbishop Puente, a fellow Spaniard, and was informed that the papal nuncio was thinking of appointing Belo as the new apostolic administrator.

"But how can that be, he is so young and was only ordained two years ago?" said Father Rodriguez.

"Tell me if you know someone better prepared than he: he is young, yes, but he is prudent, spiritual, well educated and has no political prejudices," the nuncio replied.

But at the moment many observers were inclined to believe the worst about the new apostolic administrator and the motives of those who engineered his appointment. A showdown was coming, the start of an extremely difficult and painful situation for the young priest, whose appointment came amid an atmosphere of intense distrust of Rome's motives. In their 1981 reflection, the clergy stated that they did not understand "why the Indonesian Church and the universal Roman Church have up till now not stated openly and officially their solidarity with the Church, people and religious of East Timor. Perhaps this has been the heaviest blow for us . . . we felt stunned by this silence which seemed to allow us to die deserted." From the perspective of the Timorese clergy, the Holy See somehow could have mobilized international public opinion on East Timor's behalf, but had failed to do so.

Belo was slated to be installed as apostolic administrator at the pro-cathedral in Dili, the Church of Saint Anthony of Motael, on May 12, 1983. The evening before at 6:00 P.M. the clergy came to address the nuncio inside the bishop's residence. There a spokesman read a list of facts to be considered, describing to the nuncio the situation in East Timor.

"The new apostolic administrator is young, has no experience, we do not accept him, and refuse to be present at the ceremony tomorrow," the spokesman concluded. In fact, most Timorese priests thought Belo was a stooge.

Then came Dom Martinho. Conserving his dignity, he stated that he was obeying his superiors, who had asked him to hand in his resignation. "I do the will of God and accept it in a spirit of faith and humility," he said.

The group of clergymen present then asked Belo for his response.

"I am also obeying," Carlos Filipe Ximenes Belo said simply. "The Holy See asked me to take the position. I am doing what was requested of me."

It was a time that inflicted lasting wounds on both sides. Prior to becoming apostolic administrator of Dili, Belo's life was one of simple service to the Church and youth of East Timor. He was deeply hurt by the hostile reception.

The Vatican may have inadvertently invited a rebellion among the East Timorese clergy. When Bishop Ribeiro retired in 1977, the papal nuncio at the time, Archbishop Farano, encouraged the priests of East Timor to vote on a replacement. This time, no election was suggested. Instead, according to local clergy, Archbishop Puente said it was "the Holy Spirit" who had ordained that Belo would become apostolic administrator—a proposition that, in the heated atmosphere of the time, became the object of ridicule.

Shortly after going into exile, Dom Martinho characterized the views of the Timorese clergy, as well as his own:

". . . There were many native Timorese priests with ability and a good intellectual and apostolic preparation. They were not very pleased because they were not consulted about this replacement, and since they had not been consulted they felt left out of the process. They said, 'Here's a young lad just out of the seminary coming to run the diocese over our heads.' It's human nature . . . Mgr. Ximenes [Belo] was not very well received."

This disagreement played right into Indonesian hands, as had happened during the Indonesian drive to create discord in 1975 among the Timorese political parties. In 1983, the Catholic Church was the target. Indonesian military authorities were anxious to divide the native clergy, to weaken the one institution in the territory of international consequence. Belo and the priests, placed at odds with one another, were targets of a campaign of rumor-mongering and deceit that continued for many years.

The priests, many of whom were seen by independent observers as authentic heroes of the war, found it easy to believe the worst of Dom Martinho's replacement. On one level, they saw him as an outsider installed at the behest of the occupying power—although there was no evidence that Belo was at all friendly toward Indonesia's military occupation. In addition, the fact that he had been abroad during the traumatic years of 1975 through 1981 was interpreted as a sign that the Vatican wanted someone unmarked by that period. In fact, Belo had a very clear idea of the human consequences of that time, which could be seen every day since his return and which he knew from the experiences of his extended family.

Until now, from his post in remote Fatumaca, Belo had been far removed from this kind of intense internal conflict. The distrust he encountered left Belo wounded.

It is, however, hard to see how things could have been otherwise. Nearly ten years later, rumors surfaced that Carlos Filipe Ximenes Belo would be removed from his post, just as Dom Martinho had been. One can only imagine the reaction among the clergy in 1992 if Belo had been replaced, let alone by a much younger man recently returned from many years abroad. Whatever the obligations of clergy toward obedience and faith, their loyalty surely would have been to Belo at that stage. Any successor would have encountered a nearly hopeless task in attempting to win the trust of his colleagues, no matter what his goodwill or talent.

So it was in 1983, even if the circumstances surrounding the resignation of Martinho da Costa Lopes were far more complex than most observers have been willing to acknowledge. At least some of Dom Martinho's friends knew that his nerves were nearing the breaking point. How could they not have been? With perhaps a third of the population dead as a result of the war, Dom Martinho had led the mourning for countless victims. He found out late in life, in the cruelest possible manner, that power and brute force often were more potent than principle or religious piety. This awareness grievously injured his spirit. At nearly sixty-five years of age, it was far from clear that Dom Martinho would have lived long had he stayed in his job as apostolic administrator.

Not everyone in East Timor regarded Belo's ascendancy with suspicion. Mother Matilde had long known of Carlos Filipe, as they still called him. From the time he was a boy he was known as studious, smart, and capable—one of the bright young men of the Diocese of Dili. Mother Matilde and other religious sisters thought he should be given a chance. He had the makings of a leader, and he was known as a disciplinarian. Perhaps the young people needed that. As a Salesian, Belo knew how to reach the youth; Dom Martinho was a more distant figure. Of course, there were other priests who had more experience than Belo, but whether they had his physical endurance was questionable. Their nerves, and their health, like that of Dom Martinho, had weakened after eight years of war and pestilence. Perhaps the diocese needed someone who could stand up to the punishment: Belo, a football player, was like a young bull.

It was true that Carlos Filipe had a temper that could sting like a *chicote*, the Portuguese whip of old. Dom Martinho, too, had a penchant for anger. Both had fierce pride and, when pushed too far, fury. The old Portuguese bishop had picked Dom Martinho to be his vicar general, while the papal nuncio had promoted Carlos Filipe many years later. Both choices may have been based to some extent on the toughness the two men had in common, thought Mother Matilde later.

Belo needed all his toughness for what followed. Dom Martinho's departure inflamed bad feelings that already were rife. He had wanted to remain in his homeland, but was told by the nuncio it was advisable to leave. It was impractical for Dom Martinho to take all his belongings into exile in Portugal. Even his prized accordion, used for the entertainment of friends, was left behind in a corner of an office at the partially rebuilt seminary at Dare. However, he did take documents and photographs with him that illustrated the horrors in East Timor. The general assumption was that Belo would say little about these matters, in keeping with the wishes of the Vatican.

His boyish appearance and shy demeanor conveyed an image of fragility to some observers. An international aid worker remembered arriving at his residence and asking a youthful-looking priest, who looked like a student, if it was possible to meet with the bishop.

"I am the bishop," answered Carlos Filipe Ximenes Belo, who seemed to be taken aback. The visitor thought that such impressions must have made it even more difficult for Belo to be taken seriously, not least of all by the senior priests.

The mood Belo faced from his first day in his new position was illustrated by the fact that all of the Timorese priests boycotted the ceremony that marked the transfer of authority the day before.

Belo retreated to his residence, taking solace from the coconut pastries, roast pigeon, and other dishes prepared by Maria de Fatima. For a time the young priest gobbled cakes, putting on weight. It was a very disagreeable period, but he fought off depression, remembering the lesson of the master of novices of the Salesians in Portugal, Father Armando Monteiro, who quoted a saying by Saint Francis de Sales, for whom the Salesians were named: "A saint who is sad is a sad saint."

Belo repeated this saying like an incantation: he did not want to be downcast. But even this offended some people. "Why are you smiling so much?" asked an older priest. "A bishop must be a serious person!"

Belo knew, however, the difference between being serious and gloomy. Dwelling on his rejection by the priests served little purpose, and there was so much he had to learn in his new position. The Waima'a self-image ("owner of time, earth, and every living thing") Dona Ermelinda imparted to him had produced a steely self-confidence. So he reached out to the people, visiting parishes, hamlet after hamlet, traversing the territory with his youthful energy. Dom Martinho, for all his devotion to his parishioners, no longer made frequent forays into the rugged countryside, a difficult proposition for anyone because of the condition of the roads. At first, in the interest of doing his pastoral work, Belo accepted the Indonesian offer of a helicopter so he could reach remote villages. But during these visits he was accompanied by someone who was obviously a spy, posing as a pious assistant. So Belo took to going by road, despite the difficulties. Bit by bit, Belo developed a popular following.

Mainly, however, he calmed himself by walking alone and praying hour after hour, reading the Gospels again and again. Slowly, meditative prayer helped him through the adversity that he faced.

One of his early acts in the religious sphere involved the implementation of an earlier decision by the Diocese of Dili that was of great importance to his prayerful people. The diocese had asked the Vatican to allow Mass to be said in the Tetum language, rather than in Indonesian. Rome agreed. This had the effect of promoting a uniformity of expression in Church settings that provided a degree of autonomy for the people. Fittingly, the first prayer books printed were named for Monsignor Martinho da Costa Lopes.

The religious aspects of his job were straightforward in comparison with the rest, and Belo soon faced the harshness of the Indonesian military leadership. Risking reprisals, a mother came to Belo with a heart-rending account of how her son had been shot by Indonesian troops while tending his crops. Comforting the woman, he said he would seek justice for her. But when he approached the army commander at an event the next day, the military man quickly turned his back on Belo. When the young prelate later returned to the commander and other military officials with complaints of atrocities, Belo received the same treatment time and again. Years of this had driven Dom Martinho to speak out.

In a separate interview a few months after he left Dili, Dom Martinho stated that Belo "took up his new position with no experience of how the Indonesians have treated our people . . . But I strongly believe that he will, little by little, realize what is going on, and begin to do what he can."

Belo took office at a fateful moment. After denying since 1975 that there was any armed resistance to Indonesian rule, the military concluded a cease-fire with the Fretilin guerrillas; an extraordinary set of photographs appeared showing the smiling Fretilin commander, José Alexandre Gusmão, known as Xanana, with his Indonesian counterpart, Colonel Purwanto, the military commander of East Timor. Mohammad Yusuf, simultaneously defense minister and armed forces commander in chief, a veteran of the war of independence from the Dutch and a native of the island of Sulawesi, saw the conflict in East Timor as a dead end for the Indonesian army. General Yusuf reputedly advocated a degree of autonomy for East Timor, and opted for a "hearts and minds campaign," as it was known locally: the cease-fire was its centerpiece. After a semblance of peace for a few months (which showed, if nothing else, that the conflict could be ended quickly with some rather simple moves), in August 1983 the cease-fire broke down. The end of the cease-fire was linked to the ascension in 1983 of a hard-line armed forces commander in chief, General Leonardus "Benny" Murdani, who reversed the softer policies of General Yusuf and Colonel Purwanto.

An immediate explanation of the resumption of fighting was that Indonesian soldiers attending a local celebration had raped Timorese women, provoking retaliation, with sixteen Indonesians reportedly killed. In the Indonesian version of events, the killing of the sixteen was an unprovoked attack on unarmed engineers. What is beyond dispute is that the incident set off a ferocious Indonesian response, with at least several dozen and probably hundreds of Timorese massacred. Belo traveled to the area, near Viqueque on the southern coast, to investigate. "I saw the graves," he later told an interviewer, marking the first time that he made a public statement on Indonesian atrocities.

A full-scale offensive came quickly. "This time, no more fooling around," said Armed Forces Commander Murdani, who added that there would be "no mercy" for the guerrillas.

On October 13, 1983, Belo raised his voice in the church of Lecidere against "arrests and violence" following the procession of Our Lady of Fatima. Indonesia was powerful, Belo said, but "They could win without convincing." Rather than bringing guns, they should give "flowers and books, and meals for the people." It was a moderate statement, but General Murdani, a Catholic himself who reputedly had some influence in Rome, was not pleased.

Four months later, the situation worsened. In a February 16, 1984, letter to Dom Martinho, now exiled in Portugal, Belo wrote of how the Indonesian military was gathering villagers, as in the 1981 "fence of legs" operations, to hunt the guerrillas, detailing grim atrocities:

> People have been imprisoned (in Dili alone, 600 people) and now they are going to be tried in military courts. Other people have disappeared. . . . In the areas of Lospalos, Viqueque, Baucau and Ainaro the war exists and the population is encircled. They suffer from sickness, hunger, lack of liberty and persecution. [The In-

donesians] already started again to mobilize the civilian populations. . . . We are surprised how in this country with so many battalions, helicopters, tanks and bombers they still need the support
of the local population . . . leaving their ricefields and gardens. It is
misery, Monsignor! The Red Cross cannot enter the prisons, nor
can I celebrate Eucharist for the political prisoners. . . . [In some
areas] there were "public judgments," meaning people implicated
for having contacts with the mountain areas were killed in front of
other inhabitants by knife, cutlass and by beating with sticks and by
their own family members . . . and [the Indonesian military] laugh
with contentment, rubbing their hands together and saying that it is
not their fault. . . . It is a macabre situation that we are living. This
is more or less a pale image of what we are going through. I ask you,
Monsignor, to continue to pray for us and to launch an appeal to
the free world to open its eyes to the barbarities of which the Indonesians are capable.

The Church itself, wrote Belo to his predecessor, was being "persecuted
and accused, schools are being searched and the students are being interrogated." Perhaps in retaliation for Belo's statements, the residence of the
Salesian priests in Baucau was savagely searched by the Red Berets, the elite
unit of ABRI.

Belo's letter to Dom Martinho came to the attention of the *New York
Times* and the *Washington Post* and was a central element in a letter by 123
members of the U.S. House of Representatives to Secretary of State George
Shultz when he visited Jakarta in July 1984. Shultz raised the issue of East
Timor publicly with his Indonesian counterpart. The Indonesians blamed
Belo.

A few days before Shultz went to Jakarta, Pope John Paul II brought up
East Timor on receiving the new Indonesian ambassador. The pope noted
that Rome had "earnestly recommended respect for human rights," and
said, "It is the ardent wish of the Holy See that all the rights of individuals
be respected," adding, "The Holy See continues to follow the situation with
preoccupation and with the hope that particular consideration will be
given in every circumstance to the ethnic, religious and cultural identity of
the people."

In his meeting with the Indonesians, Shultz was told by Indonesian
Foreign Minister Mochtar that Belo's letter had influenced both the
congressional group and the pope. This was "unfortunate," the foreign
minister said. But in an interview with Michael Richardson of *The Age*,

(Melbourne, Australia) published on July 16, 1984, Belo concluded, boldly, "I am ready to be removed if that is the price of defending human rights and the rights of the Timorese. The truth should be published." In this interview and a subsequent report in the *Washington Post*, the Timorese prelate said the situation in East Timor had become "very critical," with a new Indonesian military operation "terrorizing" the population in their drive "against Fretilin and anyone suspected of being a Fretilin sympathizer." Belo said that Indonesian Red Beret troops had executed ten Timorese the month before at Baucau airport because they were suspected of having links with Fretilin. But he spared no one: Belo noted that "It is the East Timorese people who suffer from the Indonesian side, and from the Fretilin side." He said Fretilin guerrillas "also terrorize people, burn houses, steal and take food." The bishop added, "But I don't think those in Fretilin are communists. Their real aspiration is for self-determination. But everyone who wants self-determination in East Timor is called communist by the Indonesian authorities."

Belo stressed that the Indonesian government was "colonizing the territory with its own population, with the result that the Timorese had become second-class citizens in their own country." He emphasized that "If Indonesia is determined to colonize East Timor by force . . . there will be more resistance from the Timorese." Belo called for a new cease-fire and greater autonomy for East Timor as "a first step," and said that he wanted to explain his proposals to President Suharto and General Murdani, but had not had the opportunity to do so.

For his part, after Belo gave these interviews, the papal nuncio advised him to stick to his pastoral work.

Whatever the requirements of diplomacy in its relations with Indonesia, the Vatican could have had no doubt of the actual situation in East Timor: as in most places in the world, the quality of information available to the Holy See was first-rate. A confidential document of July 1984, the year after Bishop Belo's appointment, stressed that "Military operations on a large scale are a characteristic of life in East Timor," resulting in "difficulties in cultivating the land, with consequent food shortages and sickness." There was "displacement of civil population for military and security reasons," accompanied by "disappearance of persons, arbitrary detention and torture." The Vatican document noted as well that Belo had "made various attempts to mediate in the dispute," without positive result, but that he had succeeded in gaining permission for priests to visit prisons. And as Bishop Belo knew only too well from his early days in office, when even international relief officials were not permitted to own a radio, there was "isolation of the territory from the outside world." And, there was "imposition of an alien language and culture in all sectors of the administration, including the schools."

After he began to voice his concerns, Dom Martinho's young successor, supposedly a weak figure amenable to Indonesian wishes, was placed under constant surveillance, virtually unable to leave his residence without being closely followed. A European visitor, one of the very few during this time, recalls walking with him on the shoreline across the street from his residence. Belo complained, "I am like a prisoner here."

Indonesian authorities were, of course, doing their own complaining to the Holy See. When a critical document with Belo's name attached to it was highlighted in April 1985 in the *Washington Post*, on the eve of a visit by President Reagan to Portugal, there was a quick response from Vatican officials. The papal nuncio issued a denial of the authenticity of the document—in Bishop Belo's name. The document, was, in fact, genuine, but the denial diplomatic in nature. Belo had not actually written it: it came from the Council of Priests. Nor had he authorized its release. But the whole chain of events in connection with this document reinforced the earlier impression that Belo was timid and easily controlled.

Soon after, in June 1985, Belo visited Rome for his first audience with the pope. John Paul II told him to "fight the suffering of the people and seek a right solution for Timor." But it was evident that the situation was complicated, and the Vatican was under heavy Indonesian pressure. In a 1994 interview, the bishop recalled the 1985 meeting: "His Holiness said to me: 'I understand your position. I pray for Timor. I suffer for Timor. But, on the other hand, the Church in Indonesia also needs our attention.'"

For whatever reason, over the next three and a half years, Belo's words received little international notice. In fact, the bishop seemed to make few public statements during this period. Timorese resistance leaders contended that he had bowed to pressure from Indonesia and the Vatican to remain silent. But he displayed a common touch that endeared him to his parishioners. When he heard that Indonesians were complaining about the attitude of the East Timorese population, he stated pointedly in church one day, "Whoever does not feel well here should go back to their own country." When he began another sermon, he referred to the omnipresent surveillance, dryly displaying his mordant wit: "Whoever has the tape recorder, don't forget to put it on."

By now the Indonesian government regretted that they had ever let Dom Martinho leave. In his letter of February 1984, Belo had asked his predecessor "to launch an appeal to the free world" on East Timor's behalf, and Dom Martinho did so, never giving up, even when he became discouraged at the lack of immediate response. He went to the United States, Japan, and Germany, but everywhere the problem was similar: it was not morality that mattered, but rather "commercial interests," as Dom Martinho put it.

Sometimes at night on his travels to foreign cities, Dom Martinho would grow despondent. He would say that Western nations speak of spiritual and ethical values, but only material values count. "Do these people we're meeting with really hear us?" Once he added, "Does God really hear us?"

In Washington just before President Reagan traveled to Indonesia in 1986, Dom Martinho met with staff of the Committee on Foreign Affairs of the U.S. House of Representatives. He raised what he saw as the central issue, the need for the people of East Timor to be free of Indonesian overlordship, so that they might determine their own future. Since 1976, every United States administration has recognized Indonesian rule in East Timor, while withholding full legal recognition of Indonesian sovereignty because of the manner of Indonesia's acquisition of the territory. In practice, no American government challenged the Indonesian stance, and that is the way Dom Martinho saw Washington's position, legal distinctions aside.

The senior committee aide asked blandly about the position of the State Department on this question. Dom Martinho answered that they recognized Indonesian control of East Timor. The aide replied, "Then you're out of luck."

It was the kind of bureaucratic answer one might expect from any government agency, perhaps from a motor vehicles bureau. But Dom Martinho had not missed a deadline, or committed any other breach of regulations. And although his hosts at the Committee on Foreign Affairs may have momentarily forgotten, Dom Martinho had not come from the kind of place where he could possibly accept what they were saying. The words "out of luck" especially grated on him.

Wearing black slippers and a black clerical suit, at the age of sixty-eight he seemed to jump across the room, almost as if he were fighting a duel with an enemy.

"*Out of luck?*" he cried out with real rage. "You send the arms that kill my people, and then you tell me I'm *out of luck?*"

The man who had said Dom Martinho had been "out of luck" looked for a moment as if he had been struck dumb. Like many of those who work in the deferential atmosphere of Capitol Hill, he was not accustomed to being addressed in that manner. Dom Martinho made his point, however. His message to Congress would not be forgotten.

Belo knew how to speak strongly, too, but it was more complex where he was, and he had to keep his feelings in check. Although he had made forthright statements on the suffering of his people, critics spoke as if he lived in a free country and were able to speak his mind on all occasions. Actually, it had been little different from Dom Martinho. In a TV interview in early 1983 in his study—now Belo's study—Dom Martinho, a few months from resignation, was reticent, noticeably frightened. Visibly perspiring, his eyes blinking nervously, Dom Martinho spoke only in the most oblique terms of the horrors that were commonplace in East Timor. Thus, two years after he resigned, when Belo was the center of controversy over the Council of Priests document, Dom Martinho was understanding when discussing Belo's predicament over lunch in Lisbon.

"We cannot know," Dom Martinho said softly, "the kind of pressure the Indonesians are putting on him. They did the same thing to me, and often I had no alternative but to do what they wanted." As much as his removal hurt him, Dom Martinho was gracious when he spoke of Belo, during his visits to Washington, enunciating the words "my successor" with respect and dignity.

The international environment with respect to East Timor was hardly hospitable in those days. The Reagan visit to Asia in 1986, including a stop in Indonesia, for instance, was dubbed "The Winds of Freedom," although there was no evidence to justify the name, even in words. In a sign of things to come, articles appeared in the *Sydney Morning Herald* before the Reagan visit to Indonesia trumpeting "the Suharto billions," fortunes made for family and friends through business favoritism. It was an incredible financial feat—Suharto had begun life poor, was a house servant in one of the foster homes where he lived, assisting the woman of the house in sewing garments. Except for a brief period as a young man, when he worked as a bank clerk, Suharto never left the public payroll.

In retaliation for the stories, Australian journalists were barred from Indonesia for the Reagan visit. So was *New York Times* reporter Barbara Crossette, in her case because of a *New York Times Magazine* article by the paper's editor, A.M. Rosenthal, who made tough criticisms of Suharto's anti-democratic practices.

The White House announced it was aware of Suharto's sensitivity on the question of his family finances and considered his business practices "an internal matter." The White House said Reagan also would not raise what the *Washington Post* called "the even more sensitive question of East

Timor," which more than one hundred members of Congress, led by Representative Tony Hall (Democrat of Ohio), were pressing Reagan to give "serious attention" to in his meetings with Suharto.

East Timor's resistance, still aggrieved over the departure of Dom Martinho, remained displeased with his successor, who had no interest in collaboration with them. But from Belo's point of view, if he had been critical of Bishop Ribeiro for taking sides against Fretilin in the civil war of 1975, he also could not support Dom Martinho's later support for Fretilin. Both, in Belo's judgement, had crossed the line into dangerous, unacceptable ground for a Church leader in East Timor.

Xanana, the resistance's leader and a skilled writer and poet, argued that a Polish priest assassinated by the Communist regime for working with the Solidarity trade union is rightly considered a martyr, and others who helped Solidarity did so without reprimand from Church authorities, whereas priests in East Timor who speak out on behalf of their people's human rights are criticized for engaging in politics. Xanana went further, stating that if Belo would appear to be supporting integration with Indonesia, this would not be considered "political" in the eyes of Rome.

Belo would have agreed for the most part with the comparison between Poland and East Timor, though he emphatically avoided political partisanship. At times when he advocated autonomy for East Timor (rather than independence), the bishop saw himself as taking steps that might address the grave consequences of the conflict, which had the potential to continue for many years with no solution. When he met Xanana in 1986, Belo saw no immediate possibilities for self-determination.

The real problem, as Belo saw it, was that in comparison with the Church in Poland, the Church in East Timor had little backing from Rome and, during most of the 1980s, little international support of any kind, as Dom Martinho had known only too well.

In fact, by the late 1980s, there was a growing unarmed urban resistance movement that was similar to Solidarity in some ways, as East Timorese fled rural areas for the relative safety of the towns, which were growing rapidly in size. But again, this was not Poland: until the late 1980s, East Timor was all but cut off from the outside world, and the military could behave as it chose. The bishop believed that if he actively encouraged the non-violent resistance movement, it could provoke a harsh reaction by the Indonesian military, and he then would bear responsibility for the consequences.

Of course, there was still the issue of the armed resistance, which had not existed in Poland, though the Nicaraguan situation showed that, so far as the attitudes of Church authorities toward violent insurrection were concerned, it was not a black-and-white matter. But Bishop Belo abhorred violence from any quarter, and he could not support any guerrilla group, whatever its aims. At bottom, he did not want to see more people die like his beloved cousin Aurario.

And whether or not others agreed, he saw his fundamental obligations as those of a churchman with religious and humanitarian objectives, not the aims of a political leader: in the end, many who tried to convince Belo to support their political goals, no matter which side of the spectrum they were on, would find themselves frustrated.

According to Belo, he had his own priorities at the time. In a secret meeting in 1986, Belo recalled telling Xanana that the guerrillas should stop attacking civilian targets—that no matter what the justification, this was no strategy to pursue. Xanana later contended—wrongly, according to Belo—that the papal nuncio had pressed Belo to convince Fretilin to surrender.

Belo countered that he told Xanana that the resistance leader should embark on a political struggle rather than rely on armed struggle. "Please change your strategy," the bishop recalled pleading more than a decade later, "You'll never win this way."

From Belo's point of view, it was clear by 1983 that the Timorese guerrillas could not succeed militarily, and that further armed conflict would only bring needless suffering to the people who, he emphasized, were his primary concern. Xanana, on the other hand, had lived through many years of privation, in a desperate fight to survive and, as he saw it, defend the people from Indonesia's occupation and ultimately bring peace through continued resistance. During Belo's first six years in office, according to the guerrilla leader's 1994 autobiography, Xanana viewed the Timorese prelate as someone under "great political and psychological pressure" to accommodate the aims of the Indonesian regime, and, from Xanana's standpoint, Belo had done so. The divergent perspectives did not leave much space for common ground at that stage.

In their meeting late one night in April 1986 at the Fatumaca school near Mount Matebian, Belo perceived Xanana as guarded and distant. To Xanana, who had been fighting for more than a decade at that point, the new Timorese prelate was apparently a total stranger, their disagreements aside; the bishop himself has said that he believes Xanana had not even heard of him before his 1983 appointment. And Xanana was nearly as unknown to Belo, who only had seen the future resistance leader from afar in Baucau in the 1960s when the two were seminarians (Xanana is two years older). Belo would not see his face again until photos of the 1983 meeting with Colonel Purwanto surfaced.

In spite of disagreements with the resistance, as time went on the opposition that Belo initially faced softened considerably, although hard feelings on both sides never completely vanished.

But as far as his churchly work was concerned, Belo visited every town and hamlet he could. Within two years, he had been to all the parishes in East Timor, had spoken to groups of people from all walks of life, and was able slowly to establish a climate of cooperation with the priests.

His old mentor Father José Luis Rodriguez, who had lived in East Timor for many years, returned for three months in 1987, and saw Belo's acceptance by the people firsthand: "During one of these visits when I accompanied him, he confirmed three hundred Christians, married fifty couples, and spent hours in the confessional as any priest. He met with the housewives, the young people, all during the two days that particular visit lasted."

Belo's residence in Dili bustled with visits of people in need who besieged him, some for food, others for clothes for their children so they could go to school, still others so that he would intervene on behalf of a family member who was a political prisoner. Drawing on his great stamina, he did for each whatever was possible.

In March 1988, Belo went to Italy to mark the one hundredth anniversary of the death of Don Bosco, held in the saint's birthplace in Turin. Then, at the Vatican he met again with Pope John Paul II. In the months ahead, it was announced that Carlos Filipe Ximenes Belo would receive a promotion.

CHAPTER 6

BISHOP

❖ ❖ ❖ ❖

ONA ERMELINDA HAD difficulty believing it. Here was her son, the same naughty one she would pull by the legs at four o'clock in the morning to awaken for Mass, the boy who had worked from the ages of five to seven and was fortunate to have gone to school at all, becoming the first native-born bishop of the Diocese of Dili. It was truly like an apparition, received in a dreamlike state, as the Vatican ambassador, Archbishop Francesco Canalini, performed the ceremony on June 19, 1988. Reminiscing how she raised six children by herself, struggling for every single pencil and pad of paper, the event seemed like a gift from God. Dona Ermelinda had deeply regretted that she was unable to attend Carlos's ordination ceremony in 1980. Now, not even eight years later, there was this! Visitors came from Europe, people she had only heard of but hadn't met, like Dona Lupe and Don Emilio Arano, who had paid for the last seven years of her son's priestly studies and acted as his surrogate family during his years abroad. The couple traveled from Spain for the occasion.

Unlike his installation as replacement of Dom Martinho, there was no controversy this time. Whatever their initial misgivings, the priests had grown to accept the young man, who, they now realized, had a good deal of backbone, even if they did not always agree. Now, the East Timorese clergy who surrounded Belo were smiling. All told, Dona Ermelinda was content, because before anything else she was a woman of the Church, and the dissension that marked his appointment in 1983 had hurt her. Thus after five years as apostolic administrator, Dom Carlos Filipe Ximenes Belo was ordained titular bishop of Lorium, an ancient diocese in Italy no longer functioning, while still holding the position of apostolic administrator of the Dili diocese. Although the political status of East Timor remained unchanged, and therefore Belo could not be named ordinary of the diocese, naming him as bishop of a titular see was nonetheless a sure sign of the Vatican's confidence in the young prelate. He had turned forty only a few months before.

It seemed wonderful to Ermelinda, Julieta, and other family members who attended this historic occasion. But the scene, like almost all large public events in East Timor, had a deceptive quality. The festive ambience was real enough, but behind the big smiles and inflated language, almost everyone knew that this was only a momentary pause in the normal course of their life of fear and intimidation. Even the bishop's own family had to think twice before paying what would in any other setting be a normal visit. They were reluctant to visit him, for fear of being subjected to questioning by the police, who would ask what kind of information they had provided. "What," the secret service would demand to know, "did you tell the bishop?"

Of course, much of the family lived in Baucau, and it wasn't easy to travel to Dili, though Carlos was able to stop at the family home on his trips. But his other sister, Aurea, lived nearby, in the vicinity of the Santa Cruz cemetery, about a mile from the bishop's residence. She rarely came to visit her brother, essentially for the same reason as most of the others, to avoid being made an object of interest by the Indonesian secret service. Although this day was a bright spot in their lives, tomorrow would be as harsh as before.

These concerns, normal as they were in East Timor, were well hidden amid the pomp of the bishop's installation ceremony. Almost everyone, it seemed, was pleased with the promotion of the Timorese prelate. Artists from the island of Java were flown in for the occasion. In the weeks beforehand, Archbishop Canalini had raised high hopes: "By being elevated to a bishop," the nuncio said, "Father Belo can exercise his duties more officially and take fuller care of people in Dili." Indonesian state television made much of the event, which lasted four hours and was attended by thirty thousand people, including ten Indonesian bishops.

Shortly after Belo was initially appointed in 1983, the Indonesian Catholic bishops sent him a letter of solidarity. But they quickly came under tough military pressure, and thereafter remained close to the government line. Now a spokesman for the Indonesian Conference of Catholic Bishops stated forthrightly the top priority of the Indonesian government and those within his church who were influenced by it: "It is only a matter of time" before the Diocese of East Timor became an official part of the Indonesian Church, he said. With the blessing of the popular young bishop, the rest of the people of East Timor—or, at least, most of them—would adopt the same attitude, so the Indonesian regime hoped.

Despite the fanfare and praise, the newly appointed bishop was hardly complacent. Quite the opposite: never someone overly impressed by the praise of others, Belo was preoccupied with the pain of his people, which was unmistakable beneath the appearance of good cheer. Despite the majesty of his installation and the joy of his family and friends, it was evident to the new bishop that the situation for the East Timorese was not improving. The youth, the center of his ministry, were seething with resentment. The Indonesians may have built roads and schools in East Timor, but this had no importance alongside the anguish of recent history.

One of the darker parts of that history took place across the water from where they were now standing. As children scampered in the background after the ceremony—frolicking the same way he had as a boy—and the crowd took light refreshments, Ataúro island could be seen from the garden of Bishop Belo's residence. Not long before, Ataúro, called the "isle of goats," had been home to thousands of Timorese prisoners. It was something no one who had been there could ever forget; Maria de Fatima, the cook, and António, the bishop's assistant, were always reminded of their captivity on Ataúro whenever they walked through the bishop's garden and gazed northward.

There was an irony in the talk of peace and human development that pervaded the bishop's installation ceremony, with Ataúro literally on the horizon. Indonesia's public relations agencies in the West spoke of the age-old poverty now being alleviated in East Timor. But Maria de Fatima knew there was plenty to eat in East Timor's countryside until the bombing began. It was only on Ataúro that she and her fellow prisoners were given putrid food that made them sick.

That wrenching memory was a small thing in comparison with the larger tragedy. Most of the women her age were widows, living with heartrending visions of husbands or fiancés dead in the prime of life. Some couples were separated by the war and were unlikely to be reunited, even if the men remained alive in the mountains. Mother Matilde had an enormous task in trying to provide some comfort to these women. The preponderance of single women and near absence of men of a certain age were noticeable on this day, as during all public events. By itself, this meant a severely reduced generation to come, but there was even more.

In 1985 Bishop Belo had strongly denounced a forced birth control program introduced by Indonesia that limited families to two children. This was enforced most rigorously in the countryside, where the power of the military was supreme. It proved more difficult to impose in Dili. Objections to the program went far beyond religious belief. In East Timor, underpopulated to begin with, such a program took on an air of genocide. "With so many dead," Bishop Belo said, "we have no population problem here." But the birth control effort, too, was presented by Indonesian authorities as evidence of "development."

António, among others, was startled at the glowing words about Indonesia's stewardship. Friends his age—he was then about seventeen—were milling about, sullen and bitter, in large part at the smug attitude of the Indonesians. They were small children when the Indonesians invaded, four years old in António's case. By 1988 they had received Indonesian education throughout their school years, giving them a familiarity with their occupiers that earlier, Portuguese-speaking generations did not possess. But the notion that education would somehow create affection in a place where a third or more of the population had perished from war-related causes always seemed a strange illusion. Like António, many had spent their early years first under siege in the mountains, then on Ataúro.

Over time, Ataúro, became notorious. The *New York Times* published an item on Ataúro when Suharto came to Washington in 1982 for a state visit, and the prison island was featured in letters circulated by members of Congress. This probably helped free Maria de Fatima—the Indonesians had learned from experience with long-term political prisoners that it was not a good idea to hold too many for too long in any set place. Far better to keep them in anonymous locations for relatively brief periods, then release them to where they could be easily controlled. This way, they could head off international pressure of the kind that in the case of Indonesia itself ultimately led to the release in the late 1970s of tens of thousands taken political prisoner during the events when Suharto took power. But some of the Timorese "released" from Ataúro in the early 1980s, especially men identified as Fretilin members, were taken into the countryside and quietly left in camps, where they died of starvation or disease, at a time when the Reagan administration insisted conditions were getting better.

Ataúro did not disappear overnight as a penal colony. It was still there in 1985 when a delegation of West German members of parliament visited. Joint pressure with their American colleagues finally convinced Indonesia to close Ataúro prison. By that time António and Maria de Fatima were living within the walls of Bishop Belo's residential compound.

Even as visible places of repression like Ataúro were shut down, Belo's anger was rising over Indonesia's dominance. By the time Belo was made bishop, much of Dili was Indonesian. Whatever the surface appearance, it was an atmosphere in which nobody lived in safety. A simple knock on the door triggered fear. From time to time even priests were beaten, and there were other actions directed against the Church, such as the destruction of religious statues, for which, it was believed, the military paid Timorese agents. Groups of young people wandered about in Immaculate Conception Park, where the ceremony had just ended, clearly directed by Indonesian military intelligence, which occupied the building opposite the residence of the Canossian Sisters, next door from Belo himself. As in all situations where people become desperate—whether in France under the Nazis, Sarajevo at war, or Kuwait under Saddam Hussein—some people had their price. For Belo, this kind of corruption of their society bothered him almost as much as the sacrilegious acts themselves.

If anyone was self-satisfied when Belo took his new office, it was not he, but the Indonesian government. Because the situation appeared calm, top officials in Jakarta had come to believe their own rhetoric, and were set to allow tourists to visit East Timor at the beginning of 1989 for the first time since the December 1975 invasion. Not since Indonesian troops arrived had any foreigner been allowed to visit East Timor without special permission.

A gesture like this was needed, because East Timor had remained a difficult issue for Indonesia. For instance, East Timor "dominated" congressional and press commentary when President Suharto came to Washington for a state visit with President Reagan in 1982, according to the *Far Eastern Economic Review*. Before and since, Indonesia faced criticism not only in the U.S. but also in parliaments throughout Europe, Japan, Australia, and Canada, among other places. Shutting Ataúro was one response, another was a trumpeted release of East Timorese political prisoners in 1987. Nonetheless, in the months after Bishop Belo took office, nearly half of Congress signed letters calling on the victor of the 1988 U.S. presidential election to make East Timor a priority issue. Although President George Bush was unlikely to do so, the very mention of East Timor in this manner stung the Indonesian military. By opening the territory, the Indonesian regime thought it finally resolved its international public relations problem.

But publicity was one thing, reality quite another. That became manifest in the period when President Suharto visited East Timor in November 1988, his first trip there in ten years. Security forces struck hard before anyone could launch open protests. It was also the biggest show of force by the Mobile Brigade riot police, the Brimob, in many years. Hundreds, most of them young, were arrested in the period prior to Suharto's visit.

The military crackdown was bad enough. But there were no foreign journalists present, and from the perspective of the outside world, all that existed was the government's soothing statements. Bishop Belo heard them on Indonesian radio and television, and they infuriated him. He had tried to be reasonable, working to inform the authorities, and the Vatican, through proper channels. Invariably, he was told to be patient. Always, there were promises of a better day, somewhere in a future that never seemed to arrive. Now there was this.

Belo walked around his compound, remembering the words of peace and reconciliation of the ceremony months before. It had been said that his new position would enable him to take better care of the people, but thus far his elevation had done nothing to bring changes. Worse, things now seemed to be moving backward, with arrests on a scale that had not been seen in years. And these were not simply detentions: almost everyone who fell into the hands of the security forces received brutal treatment.

In the midst of this, Jakarta tried to make it appear as if Belo were a government ally. It seemed the authorities expected him to bear what they were doing in silence. Carlos Filipe Ximenes Belo was amiable and diplomatic when necessary, but he had not become bishop to be used by anyone. If anyone thought otherwise, they would be disabused of their error. Belo thought hard, then drafted a statement on the recent developments, to be read in churches throughout East Timor on December 5, 1988.

He minced no words. "We disagree with this barbaric system and condemn the lying propaganda according to which human rights abuses do not exist in East Timor," said Bishop Belo. Interrogations of those detained, he emphasized, were "accompanied by blows, kickings, and beatings." This, Belo insisted, was "the norm in East Timor."

His statement reached foreign publications, including the Sunday *New York Times* of January 22, 1989, which produced the headline, "Bishop Says Indonesia Tortures in East Timor." His words on December 5, 1988, were his most forceful denunciation of Indonesian atrocities since he became apostolic administrator in 1983.

A new phase of Belo's life as bishop had begun.

He had been in his post for nearly six years now. Almost eight had passed since he had returned from his studies abroad. But whatever he had said was only a small reflection of the smoldering rage and spiritual suffering of East Timor's young people. It was not merely a matter of being poor or disadvantaged. Don Bosco had tended to the needs of children victimized by the social upheavals of the industrial revolution in nineteenth-century Italy. In East Timor, it was different: on top of the material want, the very cultural and national identity of the young was threatened with extinction by an aggressive conqueror.

Now, the unarmed youth were prepared to defy the invaders. And if hundreds had been arrested when Suharto visited because of their suspected opposition to Indonesian occupation, Belo knew that this sentiment was close to universal among the East Timorese, especially the young people.

Nearly ten years before, when Belo was still studying abroad, it was argued that the young would grow to accept Indonesian rule. But now, in early 1989, a key advisor to the government was saying the same thing, while writing off the current group: "Forget about this generation," said Jusuf Wanandi, one of the planners of the campaign to seize East Timor in 1975 and director of the Institute for Strategic and International Studies in Jakarta. "They will never love us. We need to wait until the next generation comes of age, and that will take a decade."

The situation came to a head at the end of the school day on February 6, 1989, when a Timorese youngster came to the door of Bishop Belo's residence in tears. He had been humiliated at school, he told the bishop. The Indonesian teachers did not respect him or his classmates; they looked down on them, insulted them. What they were taught had nothing to do with being Timorese. The new settlers who were streaming into East Timor were also treating them badly; the young boy and his friends felt they had nowhere to turn. They were not at home in their own country.

Bishop Belo knew his people, and especially the youth who are his special calling, were being marginalized. Something about the story of the little boy that day touched Belo and moved him to act.

It was a pivotal moment for the bishop. He knew that he could do his absolute best to emulate the life of Don Bosco. He could play with the children as the saint had done, he could teach them sports and theater and take them on walks that were integral elements of Don Bosco's educational system. Still, in the end, the youngsters would be rudely pushed aside if things were allowed to stay on the course imposed by the Indonesian regime.

And so it happened late on the afternoon of February 6, 1989. His action was not a dramatic gesture in the style of Dom Martinho: Belo did not jab his finger in the direction of military officers responsible for atrocities, or engage in direct confrontation; in all but the most unusual of circumstances, that wasn't his way. Yet what Carlos Filipe Ximenes Belo said that February 6 was something even the revered Dom Martinho never stated directly while he was in office, even when he had the chance to do so, in the presence of Indonesia's highest authority, President Suharto himself: that the people of East Timor should be able to vote on whether or not they wanted to be part of Indonesia.

Belo, a man of deep feeling and emotion, nevertheless focused on practical results. He felt that if he didn't say something, if something was not done, before long the distinctive culture of East Timor would be eradicated, the place overrun with settlers. It would be too late. People were suffering "physical, moral, and psychological abuses," as he later described it. So Belo, who can write well in several languages, went to his study just before dusk and wrote a short, graceful letter to the secretary general of the United Nations at the time, Javier Perez de Cuellar:

> . . . I am writing to your Excellency to bring to your attention that the process of decolonization in Portuguese Timor has not been resolved by the United Nations and should not be allowed to be forgotten. We, the people of Timor, believe we should be consulted about the future of our land.
>
> As the person responsible for the Catholic Church and as a citizen of Timor I hereby request your Excellency to initiate a genuine and democratic process of decolonization in East Timor to be realized through a referendum. The People of Timor ought to be heard through a plebiscite on their future. Until now they have not been consulted. Others have spoken in their name. It is Indonesia which says that the People of East Timor have chosen integration but the people themselves have never said this. Portugal hopes that time will resolve the problem. But in the meantime we are dying as a people and a nation.
>
> Your Excellency, you are a democrat and a friend of human rights. I ask you to demonstrate by deeds respect for both the spirit and the letter of the UN Charter which gives to all peoples the right to decide their own destiny, freely, consciously and responsibly. Excellency, there is no better democratic way of knowing the supreme wishes of the Timorese people than by the conduct of a REFERENDUM promoted by the UN for the People of Timor.
>
> Thank you for all your sympathy for the People of Timor.

Sending a letter may have seemed like a simple matter, but not in East Timor, where all mail was censored. The letter, which was posted from outside East Timor, was written at a time when East Timor was largely cut off from the outside world, with visiting foreign journalists a rarity and the people subject to widespread repression. In confronting this conspiracy of silence, Belo risked his life. It became a decisive document in recasting the terms of debate on the East Timor issue. Years later it remained a benchmark of an acceptable solution. Bishop Belo viewed the situation in simple terms. The fate of future generations was at stake. He was only making a simple request, basic to democratic life, in asking for a free and fair election supervised by the United Nations to allow the people to choose.

The bishop's act was motivated in the most profound sense by his religious calling, by something basic to his identity as a Salesian priest: responsibility to troubled youth. Yet his fateful decision brought on an unrelenting campaign of intimidation and death threats.

It had long been known that the bishop was under surveillance, his mail intercepted, his phone tapped. But now it became clear that even within his own residence, Belo was closely watched. The day after the letter was sent to the United Nations, the general public in East Timor already knew about it. "Very strange," Bishop Belo observed. "They are right inside my circle. A carbon copy of the letter had been taken from a place which only people close to me know anything about."

He could not have hoped to keep the letter secret indefinitely, but the fact that it leaked out like this so soon after he wrote it illustrated what life had really become, and why the need to be free was so urgent. Indeed if he was monitored in the manner of the Soviet KGB, Bishop Belo also was vilified in a manner reminiscent of victims of the dictator Joseph Stalin. Indonesian authorities tried to slander and discredit him, while speaking respectfully to his face. They questioned his competence. The same kind of pressure the Indonesian regime had applied on the Vatican to remove Dom Martinho was now directed at Belo, and it was of a particularly venomous type, even extending to efforts in some quarters to cast doubts on his mental stability.

Indeed, the whispered Indonesian propaganda about Dom Martinho's faculties and those of his young successor became strangely similar: both, it seems, had become unbalanced, taking almost identical lengths of time to become this way. As Dom Martinho told an interviewer after he went into exile, "After six years I decided I should speak out because there were no other means." With Belo, six years in office elapsed before he sent his letter asking for a referendum.

If there was to be any lasting change in East Timor, the United Nations would have to be a crucial player. Under the terms of the last relevant resolution passed in 1982 by the General Assembly, the UN secretary general was to carry out "consultations with all parties directly concerned, with a view toward exploring avenues for achieving a comprehensive settlement of the problem." But for years there was scant progress.

Before his letter was made public, the Timor problem was gradually fading as an international issue. The letter received no reply for years, but still, Belo had challenged Jakarta in its most vulnerable spot.

Indonesia's rulers could have had few illusions about the outcome of any fair election. The late General Ali Murtopo, then one of the country's foremost intelligence chieftains, had tried to assess the possibilities should Indonesia decide to hold a referendum in East Timor. In the late 1960s Murtopo had arranged a heavily manipulated "Act of Free Choice" in West Papua, the former Dutch half of the island of New Guinea, later named Irian Jaya by the Indonesian government. In this way, the United Nations recognized Indonesian rule there, even as indigenous lands and natural resources were seized, with human rights abuses rampant.

Drawing on his Irian Jaya experience, Ali Murtopo sent a group of operatives to East Timor in 1983, disguised as house painters, to gauge local feeling. Away from the staged receptions and ceremonies normally presented to the world, Ali Murtopo's men found unmistakable hostility; it was clear that Indonesia would lose badly in any genuine election. As far as Ali Murtopo was concerned, the idea of a referendum was dropped. With a few hundred strokes of his old mechanical typewriter, Belo revived it, completely undermining the claim, which Jakarta was tirelessly promoting, that the East Timorese, and their new bishop, had come to accept Indonesian rule.

Belo had not written the letter at the instigation of anyone; by doing so, he established his own independence. Bishop Belo made it clear that it was the duty of the United Nations to discern what the people wanted. It was not for their bishop or the clergy in East Timor, which warmly endorsed Bishop Belo's letter, to say for them. As for the Portuguese government, Bishop Belo was telling them that the future of East Timor had to be decided by the people there, not by the old colonial power; negotiations between Portugal and Indonesia alone, as conducted by the United Nations until then, excluded the East Timorese. Finally, Bishop Belo was signaling to the Holy See, at very grave risk to his own standing and his very job, that the problem must be handled in a free and democratic manner, despite the objections of some Vatican policy makers who gave overriding priority to relations with Indonesia.

It was Bishop Belo's conscience, free of anyone's manipulation or control, that became a thorn in Indonesia's side. The problem of Belo was far more difficult for Jakarta than that of Dom Martinho, who was nearly sixty-five when the Vatican asked him to step down. In contrast, it was hard to see how Rome could find an acceptable rationale for replacing Belo. He had only turned forty-one in February 1989—a rather young age to be a bishop, let alone a former bishop. Since his days as a seminarian, Belo had a reputation for sensible behavior. After all, at the time of his installation six months before, Belo was the object of much praise from the Holy See.

Once he had sent that letter to the United Nations, the favored, moderate, realistic young bishop almost immediately became depicted as a kind of devil. But Vatican diplomats soon learned, to their discomfort, that this modest young prelate, who appeared to be so gentle, could not be bullied. The papal nuncio was livid over the letter to the United Nations. Archbishop Canalini publicly stated that the letter was a "personal initiative" of Belo's that did not represent Church policy. Canalini sent a letter to the bishop demanding that he retract what he had told the UN secretary general if he still wanted the pope to make a long-awaited visit to East Timor later that year. A document was prepared for Belo to sign, which stated that he regretted everything and that, with this admission, he would once again enter "the ranks of the true Catholic bishops." With the attitude Belo had displayed in writing to the secretary general, he was, said Canalini, "the only Catholic bishop in the world who had overstepped the line."

From the time he was a boy, Carlos Filipe Ximenes Belo reacted against pressure, especially of the variety dressed in emotional and exaggerated language. The greater the sound and fury, the more he would stand firm. He was the kind who would think quietly, fold his arms, and react with cool simplicity, like a judge on a Makassae tribunal. That is what he did with Archbishop Canalini. "Your Excellency," Bishop Belo simply asked the papal nuncio, "which sin have I committed against Catholic morals and doctrine?"

Despite the fact that what he had done was hardly a sin—if it was, then many cardinals and bishops in Eastern Europe who had crossed swords with Communist regimes over the future of their nations were sinners, too—the conflict with Rome pained Belo deeply. He was a man of the mainstream Catholic Church and, despite his strong sense of conscience, was scarcely a rebel. If there had never been a conflict in East Timor, Belo might have been content teaching school and organizing youth activities. But his people were threatened and the bishop could not be indifferent.

Although Archbishop Canalini had threatened that the pope would not travel to East Timor if Belo did not retract his letter to the United Nations, the visit of John Paul II beckoned. The Indonesian government, hoping to show a peaceful East Timor and pave the way for international recognition of its claim to sovereignty, wanted the trip to proceed as planned. The Catholic Church in East Timor was seen as the main obstacle to Indonesia's designs. Gain the support of the pope, the Indonesian reasoning went, and this would force Belo and the local Church into line.

There were those who believed that a visit by the pope could imply full-fledged Vatican recognition of Indonesian rule; some in the clergy of East Timor felt, therefore, that the pope should not come. Moreover, there were objections to the location of the papal mass at Taci-Tolu—"the three lakes," in Tetum—the site of a notorious killing field on the seacoast outside Dili. A group of clergy wrote to the pope, protesting the papal visit. They thought Bishop Belo should join them.

Belo strongly disagreed. This would be the only opportunity to have the pope visit East Timor, one that should not be missed. If he came to East Timor, at least the pope could see the Church, and the situation of the people for himself.

Bishop Belo's view was strongly supported by the Indonesian-appointed governor, Mário Carrascalão, the onetime UDT leader during the 1975 civil war. Circumstances had led him to work for Jakarta, but of all the four governors installed by the invaders, Mário Carrascalão was the most independent-minded. Dom Martinho had had a good opinion of him, and he also enjoyed close relations with Belo, who from his earliest days as head of the diocese said that Carrascalão was "working very hard . . . for the people." Though Carrascalão had little real authority—power was chiefly in the hands of the military—he and Belo shared practical problems and difficulties: their relationship made life less lonely for both of them. In a pastoral letter in April 1989, Belo addressed the objections that were being voiced in the Diocese of Dili:

> The Pope knows that in Timor there is suffering, there is death, there are abuses of human rights. . . . He does not want to return from his visit [to Asia] without giving his Timorese children a word of comfort, of hope and of moral and spiritual support . . . he knows that his gesture [of visiting East Timor] is susceptible to political interpretations, but he is willing to run the risk of bad interpretations so that he may come visit the people of East Timor. The

Pope does not come here to defend integration, nor does he come to defend independence, nor to indicate political solutions to the problem of East Timor.

His outspokenness put him under siege. In July 1989 there was a threat on Belo's life while he was on the way to preach in Baucau. On the winding roads on that seventy mile journey, one could be killed with ease, and simply making such a threat created a climate of severe tension. The same thing happened later that year. According to Timorese soldiers who passed the news onto the Church sources, the threats were set in motion by Lieutenant-Colonel Prabowo Subianto, President Suharto's son-in-law. The commander of the soldiers, Gilberto Freitas, "disappeared," in what was billed as a helicopter accident in January 1990, "because he knew too much," Church sources said.

As the pope's visit approached there were increasing threats against Belo, other priests, and the Church in general. Finally, the bishop made his own threat: he sent a letter to the Indonesian military commander, the governor, Archbishop Canalini, and the Indonesian Bishops Conference, warning that unless the "dirty campaign" ceased, the Church in East Timor would ask the pope to cancel his visit.

Once it was established that the pope would visit, there was disagreement over what language would be used for the Mass—Indonesian, Tetum, or Latin—and over what the pope would do and say on his visit. An emissary from Rome told one of Belo's deputies in the months before the visit of John Paul II that the East Timorese clergy should be moderate in their demands: "We are not going to sacrifice all of Christendom on account of 400,000 Catholics" in East Timor, the emissary said. While no one was asking for such a sacrifice, it was a revealing expression of the nervousness of Vatican policy makers, who were under excruciating pressure from Indonesia.

The stakes were high, as a well-placed observer at the United States Catholic Conference, the public policy arm of the U.S. Catholic Bishops, stressed the week before the pope's visit to East Timor. Already, some analysts had perceived a softening in the stand John Paul II had taken in 1984. If the pope downplayed the problems in East Timor during his visit, this would send a certain signal to the American bishops and other Catholic bishops around the world. While many Church organizations are free to craft their own positions, the appearance of a lack of interest in Rome would be universally damaging to East Timor. The U.S. bishops had made a statement in 1987 that carried influence in Congress. In turn, international relief experts credited congressional expressions of interest with affecting the behavior of the Indonesian military in East Timor. A weakening of political will could have frightening consequences.

The Indonesian government's decision to invite the pope to East Timor carried other risks. Dozens of Western journalists would accompany the pontiff on his travels. A papal visit marked the first time the media would shine a worldwide spotlight on the area since Indonesia launched its invasion in 1975. Unlike the small groups of journalists on carefully controlled tours from early 1976 through mid-1989, the Rome-based Vatican press corps was neither beholden to Jakarta nor subject to its control. Unlike Jakarta-based foreign journalists, who worried about renewal of residence permits, or foreign correspondents, who needed to obtain special permission to report from Indonesia, the large numbers of journalists with the pope could report without fear of retribution from the Indonesian regime—an unprecedented opportunity in East Timor's recent history.

But at the same time, however, Indonesian authorities had ample reason to feel in control of the situation. At no time in the previous fourteen years had any group of East Timorese carried out a public demonstration during a visit by foreign journalists. To have done so would have risked torture or death. In a move aimed at silencing the opposition in the weeks leading up to the papal visit, thousands of fresh troops were brought in to beef up the contingent of thirty thousand already estimated to be in East Timor.

Bishop Belo told a reporter some weeks before the papal visit that he was speaking out because he had seen people suffering "without a voice to speak openly, frankly, and freely. Priests and bishops can speak but the ordinary people cannot speak. If they do, they face interrogation or torture." Soon after he said this, some in the military suggested that Bishop Belo and his vicar general, Father Alberto Ricardo, should be imprisoned, and foreign priests expelled.

The pressure continued to build. Shortly before the pope arrived, Belo told a reporter that, because of his letter to the United Nations, and the regime's apparent fear of what the bishop might say next, the military "are threatening me psychologically. They send me anonymous letters. They say they want to kill me." And still pressure mounted. As the pope was set to arrive in Indonesia, where he would spend three days before his visit to East Timor, threats against the Indonesian Church surfaced, warning that Catholic schools and hospitals might suffer if things went badly. Under tense circumstances, John Paul II nonetheless began, on his arrival, with what could be seen as a subtle reference to East Timor: "At times, nations are tempted to disregard fundamental human rights in a misguided search for political unity based on military and economic power alone. But such unity can easily be dissolved."

Finally, on October 12, 1989, Pope John Paul II arrived in Dili. It was the first (and only) visit to East Timor by a world leader. In a memorable tableau, John Paul was photographed by the Vatican newspaper, *L'Osservatore Romano,* embracing a joyous young Belo when the pope arrived at Comoro airport. It almost seemed as if the pope was protecting Belo from a throng of Indonesian security agents hovering about them.

The pope asked Belo to join him in the limousine ride from the airport. Aside from the driver only the two were present. The bishop was pleased to be alone with John Paul. The bishop himself was in need of priestly comfort. Tens of thousands of parishioners, many dressed in bright colors, were waving alongside the road. In this atmosphere suffused with tension, the opportunity to point out the parish churches on the road to Dili provided a refreshing break for Belo.

Feeling that the pope was there on a pastoral visit, Belo restricted his conversation in the limousine to ecclesiastical matters. There was plenty for the bishop to relate, much more than they had time to cover. He told the pope of the hundreds of thousands of conversions to Catholicism in East Timor. It was Belo who was head of the diocese when Tetum became the language for Mass, and it helped draw people closer to the Church. John Paul seemed pleased with what he was hearing, and expressed satisfaction that he had been able to come.

Belo explained to the pope the strong devotion of the East Timorese people to the Church. As the bishop later emphasized, "Our people have a simple faith, but are very, very profound in this faith. It is not intellectual, not theoretical, but a kind of emotional faith, a living faith."

On their first stop John Paul II was to bless the newly built cathedral in Dili. Some observers focused their attention on whether the pope would kiss the ground upon landing in East Timor, a sign that he had set foot on the soil of a sovereign nation. John Paul did not. But at Bishop Belo's request, when the pope arrived at the cathedral he knelt down, kissed the ground, and prayed for a long time. The impression it created was that he had, indeed, made the desired gesture recognizing East Timor as distinct from Indonesia. While there, the pope met with East Timorese priests and received firsthand accounts of conditions in the territory. John Paul II wept, and told the native priests that he wished that more could be done for them. What the pope said in public in East Timor during his visit was significant; what he said privately to the clergy convinced them of his strong commitment to the people of that beleaguered land.

Having received encouragement from the pope, Bishop Belo managed to steer his way through a diplomatic minefield. Originally the pope's Indonesian schedulers did not want him to stop in Dili at all; Belo insisted that an hour be spent there and that the cathedral be blessed by John Paul. The next issue was what language to use while meeting with the clergy at the cathedral, something of enormous symbolic importance. The government preferred Indonesian. The local clergy wanted Portuguese or Tetum. It fell to Belo to reconcile these contending perspectives.

He solved the problem by stating, "Holy Father, here in the Diocese of Dili all the clergy speak Italian." The pope smiled and responded that "One notices immediately that the Diocese of Dili is a diocese directly connected to the Holy See, so that is why all the clergy here speak Italian." The pope's open acknowledgment of East Timor's disputed diplomatic status further convinced the native clergy that he was sensitive to their problems.

Finally, it was on to the most difficult destination of all, Taci-Tolu. There the pope placed a crucifix in a cushion on the ground, again creating the impression that he was blessing a distinct nation. At the cathedral the pope was able to learn about the history of the site chosen by the Indonesian government for the papal Mass, a place where people had been thrown from helicopters, buried, or "disappeared."

In his homily at Taci-Tolu, John Paul II was blunt:

> What does it mean to be the salt of the earth and the light of the world in East Timor today? For many years now, you have experienced destruction and death as a result of conflict; you have known what it means to be the victims of hatred and struggle. Many innocent people have died, while others have been prey to retaliation and revenge. . . . Respect for the rights which render life more human must be firmly ensured; the rights of individuals and the rights of families. I pray that those who have responsibility for life in East Timor will act with wisdom and goodwill toward all, as they search for a just and peaceful resolution of present difficulties. . . . Your land is much in need of Christian healing and reconciliation.

While derided by some critics as too mild, the papal statement was all the signal that many Catholic organizations around the world needed.

Dona Ermelinda and Julieta had come from Baucau to join the 100,000 people at Taci-Tolu for the event. Mother Matilde, Maria de Fatima, Celestina, and the orphans from the bishop's compound were there. From their standpoint, after so many years of suffering in near oblivion, they were pleased at not having been forgotten by the pope. Nevertheless, attendance at the Mass was only a fraction of what had been expected.

"There are checkpoints everywhere," a priest told journalists. "Soldiers ask for documents many people do not have. Other villagers have not come fearing they'll have problems when they return home." Many thousands more might have been there if not for the obstacles put in their way.

For his part, John Paul II did not forget what he saw at Taci-Tolu. An instant after the pope pronounced the final words, *"Ite, missa est"* ("Go, the Mass is over" in Latin) a group of about thirty young demonstrators raised large banners with slogans praising the pope and calling for independence and human rights for East Timor. They rushed to the altar. It was the first incident of its kind since the Indonesian invasion, and several European newspapers and agencies (among them Italy's *La Stampa*, Spain's *El País*, and Reuters) were there to record what happened.

"Long live the pope!" they shouted. "Long live independence!"

"Holy Father, they are saying that they are happy you have come here. They are expressing their aspirations for freedom," Bishop Belo told the pope, who nodded in understanding.

Indonesian police attacked the unarmed demonstrators with large wooden truncheons, sticks, and batons. Authorities in plain clothes were seen throwing metal chairs at the demonstrators. A Reuters wire photo circulated throughout the world, dramatically illustrating that the East Timorese were not reconciled to Indonesian rule. The demonstration spoke eloquently about the level of discontent in the territory, with youngsters willing to risk their lives to make their feelings known to the world.

This incident was said to have had a lasting impact on the pope: an Italian journalist observed the pontiff staring attentively at the mêlée before walking to the sacristy with a bitter smile. From that point on, it was said, John Paul II no longer relied solely on the diplomats in the Vatican's Secretariat of State for his information on the situation in East Timor.

The pope, with his personal experience of German and Soviet occupations of his native Poland, was not indifferent to the dilemma of a young prelate attempting to cope with volcanic social forces bred by an unwanted foreign occupation. For whatever sort of briefing John Paul may have received in advance about Bishop Belo and East Timor, the situation on the ground had its own resonance.

Indeed, the visit of John Paul II did more to place East Timor on the world map than did any single action from Indonesia's invasion in December 1975, until 1989. In the end, few observers were really satisfied with the visit, but then again, it was difficult to see how everyone could have been pleased in light of the contrasting expectations that had been created. From the perspective of the East Timorese resistance, anything less than an outright denunciation of Indonesian rule and recognition of East Timor's right to self-determination would have fallen short of what was right and proper. But from the perspective of the Indonesian government, the goal was full-fledged recognition of Indonesian sovereignty over East Timor, with incorporation of the Diocese of Dili into the Indonesian Catholic Bishops Conference. The visit provided nothing of either sort. At the pope's next general audience after returning to Rome, he said that "it was necessary and fitting to stop to visit with the Catholic community of this island, whose members have suffered so much in recent years," adding that he was impressed with the "living church" there.

The demonstration at Taci-Tolu resulted in the beating and torture of those brave enough to attempt it. The pope's visit wasn't the end of it. Indonesian troops raided the school at Fatumaca: even that provided no refuge. Military intelligence attempted to blame the demonstration on Father Locatelli, an apolitical Salesian missionary at Fatumaca who had then been in East Timor for twenty-five years. This charge was put out by the Indonesian Ministry of Information and ABRI's information department, and was aired on Radio Australia; according to Timorese soldiers working with Intel, this propaganda was organized by Suharto's son-in-law, Prabowo Subianto. Indonesian authorities even made an effort during the demonstration itself to frame Fatumaca students who were present at the Mass, an evident act of retaliation against the Salesians for Bishop Belo's independence.

In the weeks after the papal visit, Bishop Belo's home became a place of sanctuary for dozens of youngsters fleeing the military. Members of Congress and human rights organizations were voicing concern over numerous reports of abuses in the wake of the pope's visit. One of the groups concerned was the New York–based Human Rights Watch. At the request of the Asia committee of that group, of which he was a member, Paul Moore Jr., then just retired as Episcopal (Anglican) bishop of New York, made his first visit to East Timor.

Bishop Moore had been badly wounded as a young lieutenant at Guadalcanal, a watershed battle of the Pacific War in 1942, and had gone on to build a distinguished life as a promoter of civil and human rights and as an anti-war spokesman and advocate. He developed ties throughout the American media and political circles and worked with world figures like the Reverend Martin Luther King Jr. and Archbishop Desmond Tutu. From his wartime experience, Paul Moore knew terror better than most. But he maintained that in all of his experience, which also included fact-finding missions to South Africa, Central America, Vietnam, and the former Soviet Union, he had never before seen fear of the kind that he saw in East Timor.

It was a mark of life in East Timor in those days that at first Bishop Belo was too frightened to talk with Bishop Moore, who was dressed in his clerical garb, when the latter came with a letter of introduction from a priest who knew the bishop. It was a bad time and Belo's phone had been cut off the day of the pope's visit so that journalists could not reach him. For some minutes the two churchmen and Brenda Moore sat in uncomfortable silence. Only after patient urging by Mrs. Moore did Belo begin to open up: he told the Moores about his preoccupation in those days, that he feared he would meet the same fate as Archbishop Oscar Romero, who was assassinated while saying Mass in San Salvador in 1980.

The Moores were impressed by the determination and hardy spirit of the youthful demonstrators taking refuge in Belo's compound. But the youngsters were facing an uphill battle. Once the press departed with the pope, it remained difficult for East Timor to hold the attention of the world. Governments were now no more anxious to raise the issue than they had been before: Australia, to cite a striking example, signed the Timor Gap agreement on Dec. 19, 1989 with Indonesia only weeks after the pope returned to Rome. Carving up the potentially rich offshore area south of Timor island in a profit-sharing deal, the agreement was celebrated in an exuberant champagne toast in a jet overflying the zone by the Australian and Indonesian foreign ministers.

Despite the shift in international interest, in January 1990, another group of youths had the courage to air their grievances, this time to the United States ambassador. The young East Timorese felt they had a special reason to address their complaints to Washington—the U.S., after all, had been Indonesia's leading backer from the very beginning.

The American ambassador, John Monjo, and his staff were staying where most visitors stayed. On the surface it seemed harmless enough, but the Hotel Turismo, across from the beach, less than a quarter mile from the bishop's house and a few hundred yards from the military commander's villa in the other direction, was filled with spies. Most of the waiters and other hotel employees may have had little choice if they wanted to feed their families. Jobs were extremely difficult to find, and employment at the Turismo put one in contact with foreigners, whose hard currency made them rich, if only for the time they were in East Timor. The Turismo was a great market for handwoven traditional cloth and silver coins from Mexico that had surfaced in East Timor decades before, and this could mean a good deal of money in local terms. As for the spying, it wasn't done in a malicious way, but with a smile and an air of gracious hospitality. Still, everything you did, and everyone who came to meet you, would be closely observed. Sometimes rooms were thoroughly searched'when one was away, and listening devices were said to be planted throughout the premises.

The hotel was much the same way as when the Portuguese left in 1975, although it had seen numerous guests since. It was apparently owned by one of the military companies that controlled East Timor's commerce, but management was indifferent. The place needed a new coat of paint, and there were cobwebs amidst the potted plants. In reality, the Hotel Turismo was like a haunted house. The journalist Roger East was a guest during the days before the Indonesian invasion in December 1975.

Roger East apparently had felt ill and wanted to stay in the hotel, where he was comfortable. But Indonesian troops came, dragged East out of his hotel room, and took him to the wharf, where they killed him.

Shirley Shackleton, the wife of Australian TV journalist Greg Shackelton, one of the five reporters killed by Indonesian troops in October 1975, came to the Turismo in late 1989, a few months before the people from the American embassy. She came to East Timor in search of answers about what had happened to her husband, who also had stayed at the Turismo shortly before he was killed. At the Turismo's restaurant one night, in the courtyard, she confronted one of the masterminds behind the 1975 invasion, General Murdani. Not surprisingly, he claimed he knew nothing of the case.

The Turismo was where the youths came to meet with the ambassador, John Monjo. At his confirmation hearing before the U.S. Senate in 1989, Monjo was questioned extensively on East Timor. A letter signed by more than a hundred members of Congress had raised concerns about the fate of those detained and tortured after the pope's visit. This seemed to explain Monjo's trip there, though one could not expect any grand changes in policy as a result. But for the Timorese students who came to call on him at the Turismo, Monjo was America's representative. That meant something to them, and they, like most of the young, were growing increasingly anxious to make their feelings known.

The ambassador's visit was another warning sign of trouble to come. Monjo and his staff were met by perhaps one hundred young people who wanted to discuss their grievances with him. They did so for one hour in the Turismo's courtyard. No sooner did Monjo leave, however, than security forces roared in, bloodying dozens, some seriously. To the young people wanting to express their frustration over the Indonesian occupation and their desire for independence, the encounter with the U.S. ambassador had been worth the sacrifice: it was the first time they had reached a top American official, and they were prepared to take their punishment. But to Bishop Carlos Filipe Ximenes Belo, it was only more bloodshed, with no concrete result other than misery, and the potential for more of the same.

Belo was enraged—and not only at the security forces. His fatherly instincts boiled over as he surveyed the scene at the Immaculate Conception Park, a short distance from the Turismo.

There were some muttered complaints from the youth about Belo. The bishop was too weak. The bishop was old and soft. The bishop had sold himself to Indonesia. Perhaps someone else could do a better job.

Belo, then only a few days short of his forty-second birthday, had had enough of such talk. "All right, you run the diocese, I'll go to the mountains!" he thundered at the young people, then tore his Roman collar off his neck, furious over what he saw as their reckless behavior. He was using his special brand of biting sarcasm to make some points: that he was a churchman—not a guerrilla in the mountains, nor a militant, nor an agitator—and he was not going to support their confrontational ways.

For their part, the young people had been complaining—and would go on complaining—that the bishop was *katuas,* a word in Tetum with multiple meanings. In this case it meant "feeble" or "lacking in youthful vigor." *Katuas* can also be defined as "wise" or "venerable," but that is hardly what was intended here. Belo, still in football player's shape, made it clear to the young people that while he could equal them in physical courage, they were lacking when it came to wisdom. They disagreed, loudly.

The bishop was unimpressed with such bravado.

"You monkeys!" he chided them, addressing them in a sharp yet affectionate way. "You have no guns, you have no way to defend yourselves, you will only get yourselves killed! Go home, I tell you, go home!"

After some more protests, they did. Bishop Belo had succeeded in protecting them for a time at least. He appealed to their parents, insisting that they needed to use all their authority, in this family-oriented society, to restrain the youngsters while they still could. But there was to be little respite.

Within weeks of the incident at the Hotel Turismo, General Murdani issued fierce warnings. Speaking to a private meeting of local officials, Murdani railed, "Don't even dream of an independent state . . . we will crush them all! I repeat, we will crush them all!" speaking of opponents of the regime, and in particular of Fretilin. He was especially indignant that the East Timorese youngsters had dared to confront the American ambassador. Some in the Indonesian military had said at the time of the invasion that it would all be over within days or weeks. More than fifteen years later, East Timor remained a big problem for Indonesia. But by 1990, for all their symbolic importance, Fretilin guerrilla forces had greatly diminished in size and effectiveness. The real problem for Indonesia, as became increasingly clear after the pope's visit, was the youth, many of whom were small children or had scarcely been born when the invasion first took place. The Indonesian Army could contain the relatively small number of guerrillas left in remote areas, but the young people were something else entirely. Unarmed, with little more than their ideals to sustain them, the youth of East Timor would not back down, no matter how badly they were beaten or tortured. That kind of fortitude in itself was unnerving. And no matter how the bishop tried to restrain them, to protect their lives, they were prepared to continue their struggle for independence.

Despite the pope's expressed sympathy for Belo during his 1989 visit, in 1990 there were rumors that Belo would be replaced. As with the ouster of Don Martinho in 1983, it wasn't a matter of what was right or wrong. At bottom, that was the maddening part for Belo. Had he been a heretic or had he committed a grievous sin, he could have accepted his punishment with grace. Belo had been raised on traditional theology and simple ideals of goodness and mercy; in the most basic terms, he was straightforward and expected the same of others.

Why was the young bishop, who had been embraced so warmly by papal nuncios in 1983 and 1988 and by the pope the previous year, being treated in this manner? Belo was the embodiment of the Church, its symbol and its leader, just as the authorities in Rome wanted him to be when he was first appointed. Only Rome's perceptions of Belo had changed. It was not Carlos Filipe Ximenes Belo who had gone through any transformation. It was instead a question of how a small group of diplomats and policy makers in Rome viewed the importance of East Timor alongside what they saw as the long-term interests of the Roman Catholic Church, in which Indonesia counted for more.

This treatment did not surprise Belo's predecessor. Martinho da Costa Lopes and his successor had at least one thing in common, whatever their differences: both spent their lives obeying the rules, only to find themselves charged with excessive zeal in defense of their people against physical attack. Dom Martinho always knew that it was difficult for East Timor to attract the sympathy of the world because of its smallness, compared with mighty Indonesia. He knew that East Timor had only moral appeal. To him, therefore, moral gestures were important.

To make one such gesture, East Timor had aromatic sandalwood, the main attraction for early traders. Indonesian invaders had stripped much of the little sandalwood left in the territory but some remained, and a crucifix made of the precious wood was delivered to the U.S. Catholic Conference in Washington, on the instructions of Dom Martinho da Costa Lopes, in December 1990. (Monsignor Lopes had grown increasingly despondent. He answered a birthday greeting he received that November with gratitude, but added, "I have lived long enough." A few months later he died in Lisbon at the age of seventy-two.)

Dom Martinho's gift was meant to thank the American Catholic hierarchy, notably John Cardinal O'Connor of New York. As chairman of the then committee on Social Development and World Peace, O'Connor had quietly helped Monsignor Lopes contact the Reagan administration and the news media during his visits to the United States, and had sent a letter of support to Bishop Belo shortly after the cardinal assumed his post in New York in 1984. The gift from Dom Martinho was meant also to thank the American Church for its diplomatic support of the East Timorese Church and people, dating back to the late 1970s, including numerous behind-the-scenes intercessions in addition to its 1987 statement. The sandalwood crucifix was a quiet plea to the American Catholic hierarchy that East Timor not be abandoned in the rush of contemporary affairs and, more to the point, that Church politics not be allowed to dominate the moral dimension of the East Timor tragedy.

That danger was growing. By late 1990, a neutral observer may have been forgiven for believing that the question of East Timor was slowly being pushed aside in vital parts of the Catholic world. While it was not true of John Paul II—his 1989 visit had convinced him that grave human rights problems continued—much of the Vatican bureaucracy had little patience for this vexing issue, and for the increasingly independent-minded bishop of Dili.

A year after the pope's visit, only a few months before the sandalwood crucifix from East Timor was taken to the U.S. Catholic bishops, Carlos Filipe Ximenes Belo was waiting, day after day, at the headquarters of the Salesians of Don Bosco outside Rome. He had been summoned for a meeting at the Secretariat of State on his *Ad Limina*, a visit to the Vatican which all bishops make every five years. Day after day, no one was available to see him. He spent time walking through the lush gardens, planted with fruit trees and vineyards, praying the rosary, but his frustration grew. Finally, after fifteen days of no response, Belo telephoned the Secretariat of State and exclaimed in exasperation, "I have traveled more than ten thousand miles to be here, yet you keep me waiting as if I were a catechist!"

The bishop was subsequently called in for a meeting, and then made to wait for nearly two hours. Finally he was told that the official with whom he had an appointment was busy, and to come back the next day. Angry at this treatment, the bishop left and did not return.

Through well-placed friends in Rome linked to his Salesian religious order, Belo found a way to see Pope John Paul II at his summer residence, Castel Gandolfo, where he told John Paul of the physical torture being inflicted on the young people and abuse of the population in general. Vatican bureaucrats were known to filter the information that actually reached the top, and Belo had no option but to speak directly to John Paul, who now had his own experience of East Timor from the 1989 visit.

Meanwhile, word went out from unfriendly sources in Rome that Belo was another Oscar Romero, the martyred archbishop of San Salvador, who had also run afoul of the Vatican. When both Romero and Belo were first appointed to their posts, it was believed that they would have cozy relations with their respective governments. Both, however, had turned out differently than expected. For those in Rome, Romero had been too critical of the Salvadoran regime, and was seen as too sympathetic to the cause of change—despite the fact that he privately expressed his unhappiness at occupations of churches aimed at publicizing protest demands. In Vatican eyes, according to a leading Catholic expert, "Romero was not playing the game the way a bishop should." It did not help Romero that the Salvadoran military had important friends in Church circles.

This was 1990, the war in Central America had not yet ended, and feelings remained raw. The sensitive position of Catholics in Indonesia, combined with the fact that General Murdani, then Indonesian defense minister, was able to mobilize his own Catholic network against the outspoken bishop, further contributed to making Belo the object of the Vatican's wrath. It was ironic, for even as Carlos Filipe Ximenes Belo was being shunned by at least some high authorities in Rome over his outspokenness (his 1989 letter to the United Nations calling for a referendum, and his continuing refusal to endorse Indonesian rule were at the heart of the matter), he was also heavily criticized by those who saw the bishop as too obliging to Indonesian authority.

After weeks of quiet prayer in the gardens of Salesian headquarters in Rome, Bishop Belo made a pilgrimage to his early Jesuit roots. He visited the Sanctuary of Saint Ignatius of Loyola in northern Spain, where he also reflected on the arduous life of his hero, Saint Francis Xavier. He visited the city of Avila to say Mass in the Convent of Saint Teresa of Jesus and to request that a monastery of the Carmelites be founded in Dili, a wish that was granted. Bishop Belo also paid a visit to Father José Luis Rodriguez, his old friend and Jesuit mentor from the Dare seminary, who was now in Santander. There Belo expressed thanks for the help the Church in East Timor was receiving from different towns in the area at a time when few others were showing any interest. This quiet network of international help, centered around the Salesians and old friends like Father Rodriguez and the Aranos, offered a crucial source of spiritual as well as material support. It provided an uplifting contrast to the political struggle that was increasingly surrounding Bishop Belo and the East Timorese Church.

It was around this time that the bishop told the chief delegate of the International Committee of the Red Cross stationed in Indonesia, Pierre Pont, that "my position is very difficult, but I have to see that the people of East Timor will not be hurt." Pont, stationed there from 1989 to 1993, a defining time for the bishop, recalled a balanced individual who always tried to find reasonable solutions with the Indonesians, at the same time that he maintained the respect of the Timorese, which was a combination rarely easy to achieve.

For its part, the armed resistance often saw Belo as an obstacle, because of his ornery independence. This quality had kept him apart from the internecine conflict of 1975, and on a different level, from the battle between the Indonesian army and Timorese guerrillas: he could visit one side, then move on to another side, always maintaining his distance, keeping a critical perspective.

It wasn't long after his return from Rome that Belo once again was asked to take sides. The chance many had been waiting for since 1975 was approaching. It was announced that a Portuguese parliamentary mission was to visit East Timor in November 1991 under the United Nations' auspices. East Timorese resistance leaders saw this as a prime opportunity, perhaps their only chance, to alert the world to the horrors of life for the East Timorese and to their aspirations for the future. The United Nations had never recognized Indonesian sovereignty over East Timor, not only because the Indonesian presence resulted from an illegal invasion, but also because there had been no valid process of self-determination to which all former colonial peoples are entitled: the decolonization process carried out by Portugal in 1975 had been interrupted by the Indonesian invasion. Because of these related factors, the UN continued to regard Portugal, in legal terms, as the "administering power" of the territory, giving the old colonial ruler a crucial role in any political outcome for East Timor. But even this central position understates the importance of the Portuguese role in the eyes of the East Timorese: after a relationship stretching back more than four hundred years, and after the almost unimaginable suffering of the past two decades, Portuguese deputies visiting East Timor were seen, however unrealistically, as saviors coming to the rescue.

Belo was skeptical and worried. He had lived in Portugal during a decade of study and subsequently made a number of return visits. It was like a second home, but he knew that nothing happened quickly there: no single trip by parliamentarians would liberate East Timor, no matter what anyone believed. On the Indonesian side, they were determined to keep up appearances, no matter how grotesque the pretense: as part of a multimillion-dollar tourism promotion campaign, "Visit Indonesia 1991," there was a poster issued of the "Taci-Tolu area," the onetime killing fields, alongside a traditional Timorese thatched house of the kind the bishop lived in as a boy. Under these circumstances, there would only be trouble, Bishop Belo thought.

In July 1991 Bishop Belo had his second secret meeting with Xanana Gusmão, five years after the first one. At this juncture it was more than two years after Belo sent his letter to the United Nations calling for a referendum, and the bishop's credentials as defender of the people of East Timor could hardly be doubted; in his writings, Xanana had expressed appreciation for Belo's letter and acknowledged its importance.

This time, the bishop said, the meeting was held in Ossu, where Belo had studied as a child. Xanana asked him to hold a special Mass for the Portuguese parliamentary visitors in the cathedral in Dili. Belo believed that a big demonstration by the resistance would follow.

"We can't use the Church, the liturgy, the Mass, for this purpose," Bishop Belo recalled telling Xanana. Moreover, the bishop said he thought that such an event could lead to a confrontation that might result in bloodshed. Belo was mortified at the notion. Doing such a thing would have been "very dangerous," he said many years later.

As the Portuguese visit neared, tensions mounted. Much of this was far from the world view, but in a letter to the *New York Times* on January 22, 1991, Bishop Moore had warned that the growing confrontation between the military and the youth movement might lead to a Tiananmen Square–style massacre. Bishop Moore presciently called for international pressure on Indonesia to avert further violence in East Timor before it was too late.

From their perspective, far removed from the double standards of world politics, the youth of East Timor saw no cause for pessimism in recent events. In the aftermath of the Iraqi invasion of Kuwait, East Timor became, for the first time, a small part of the biggest news story of the day. On the fifteenth anniversary of the Indonesian invasion of East Timor in December 1990, a *New York Times* editorial, noting a letter signed by a majority of members of the U.S. House of Representatives, spoke of the need to take a diplomatic stand on East Timor, especially in light of recent developments in Kuwait, where a small nation was also overrun by a brutal neighbor. Months later, television reports of the liberation of Kuwait by a coalition of nations led by the United States and Britain received close attention from East Timorese young people—the powerful communications satellites purchased by Indonesia from American companies had the effect of linking East Timor with the outside world as never before. And the youth of East Timor, like youth everywhere, were too idealistic to accept the "realism" of many of their elders, even their bishop.

Indeed, Bishop Belo himself later told Indonesian military leaders not to blame him for the actions of the young people, that Indonesia had brought television to East Timor and must accept the consequences. Indeed, television, which seemed like a bad joke when news of its coming first appeared in the late 1970s, turned out to have a revolutionary impact. The young put on the television in Dili and watched the collapse of the Berlin Wall and the massive Western response against Iraqi aggression on CNN. They saw the end of the Soviet Union and independence for the Soviet-occupied Baltic States. This new wave of historical change on the one hand and the Indonesian occupation of their homeland on the other struck a chord in East Timor that could not be silenced. After the momentous changes in the world unfolding before their eyes, why should they accept their fate under Indonesian rule as "irreversible," as the politicians described it?

The Indonesian regime was determined to stop the youth from being heard. In a letter to Bishop Manuel Martins of Setúbal, in Portugal, Bishop Belo issued a plea for help. There was, Belo said, "a campaign of terror. . . . Anyone who approaches the Portuguese will be killed. There is no climate of freedom. The Portuguese will not be able to have contact with the Timorese because they have been threatened and indoctrinated." The people had been told that "nobody should say anything or take part in demonstrations because, if they were to do so, they will all be killed after the deputies leave."

Still, the youth were set on making themselves heard. It came as a great shock, then, after a year of anticipation, and so many feverish expectations, when Portugal canceled the parliamentary visit scheduled for early November 1991, at the last minute. The reason, ostensibly, was Indonesia's objection to one of the journalists slated to accompany the Portuguese; the Indonesian authorities were always anxious to control the news coverage East Timor would receive.

Whatever the reason for the cancellation, there was deep disappointment at the news on October 26 that the visit was off. Many in the East Timorese resistance had prepared for months for this occasion, working to make signs and banners. They had exposed themselves to danger: the omnipresent "Intel," the Indonesian spy network, knew who had planned to do what. Now there would be retribution, but no rewards, for their sacrifice.

Sitting on the porch of his residence, in early November 1991, obviously being watched by a man outside the gate, Bishop Belo told Clare Dixon of the London-based Catholic Fund for Overseas Development, (CAFOD), "Half the population of East Timor is paid to spy on the other half." Intel was now even insulting him and other members of the clergy with its spying. Dili swarmed with troops and informers, even at the Areia Branca beach a couple of miles out of town, where soldiers jumped from a truck and clicked their rifles: it seemed like Nazi-occupied France or Holland, Dixon recalled.

Provocateurs were known by a special name: *bufos*, Portuguese for "clowns." In some instances it was impossible to know who was actually working for whom. Someone known as a key leader of the clandestine front of the East Timor resistance, for instance, was observed during that period openly riding a motorcycle through Dili, seemingly without fear. Senior clergy, having lived through the Indonesian occupation from the beginning, had developed keen instincts on what was possible in that setting: they firmly believed that this particular leader must have been working for Intel. Of course, there was always the possibility that this leader was a double agent, someone pretending to cooperate to get inside the Indonesian intelligence system.

As Bishop Belo noted, the battles between Intel and the pro-independence Timorese they were watching grew especially intense during those months. Before the cancellation of the visit of Portuguese parliamentarians to East Timor, many young people sought refuge at the Church of Saint Anthony of Motael on the waterfront of Dili, about a mile from Bishop Belo's home down the Avenida Marginal. The military tried to make them leave, since they would have been the first to demonstrate upon the arrival of the Portuguese parliamentarians. But after the visit was canceled, the young people stayed on. Late on the night of October 28, 1991, military vehicles circled the Motael church.

Fighting broke out between pro-Indonesian Timorese and the young people in the church, one of whom, eighteen-year-old Sebastião Gomes, was killed, as was a Timorese man working with the Indonesians.

Bishop Belo was awakened. He arrived at the Motael church at 3:00 A.M. and saw Sebastião's body on the street. The Indonesians turned the body around and tried to claim he had been killed with a knife. But the bishop—and the Indonesian-appointed governor, Mario Carrascalão—saw the bullet holes in his body. The bishop had known Sebastião Gomes, who only two weeks before went with him to inaugurate a church in the town of Lolotoi.

Making a gesture to victims on both sides, Bishop Belo held a funeral Mass for Sebastião Gomes and the other Timorese who had been stabbed during the same incident. In his early morning sermon, the bishop minced no words: "You young people need to reflect! The bishop and the priests will give you protection! But you need to think with your heads on your shoulders. Breaking the windows of the church, taking the lives of others, slandering the bishop, breaking holy objects, this is all that happens these days. They broke the statue of Our Lady in Comoro. In Lahane, in Bobonaro, they speak ill of the bishop, the priests, and the nuns."

The bishop added, bitingly, "This has only happened after Integration, the time of Merdeka ["freedom" in Indonesian]. It never happened in the colonial time under the Portuguese government."

Then Belo directly pointed his finger at those who held ultimate authority in East Timor: "I was there at three in the morning. The news put out by TVRI [Indonesian TV] was false! False! The truth turned upside down! [The report had blamed the Church for the two deaths.] We live in a country where bad is good, light is dark, and there is no justice! The death of these two people is their responsibility!" the bishop concluded, accusing the Indonesians.

Claire Bolderson of the BBC interviewed Bishop Belo at length in Dili during this time. He was "deeply, deeply troubled, downcast, almost distracted," she later recalled. "Frustrated and angry. He told me, 'Something bad is going to happen. The situation is very, very tense. It is the worst I have ever seen it.'"

The sense of dread was almost overwhelming. But Belo had so little power to affect the course of events. Everything seemed to be spinning out of control. East Timor was being pushed relentlessly toward another conflagration. It seemed as if the people were powerless to stop it. Belo felt fury rising within himself. The governments of the world had taken no action. From the United Nations came a deafening silence.

He prayed and prayed for deliverance, but it seemed as if he and his people were engulfed by evil. It grew harder and harder to get any rest at all. Bishop Belo begged the young people to calm themselves. If only they would take heed, he felt.

But many of the youth, marked by heroism and a feeling of invincibility in the face of overwhelming force, were determined to make themselves heard. In 1989, Bishop Belo had told the United Nations of the agony of his nation, but East Timor had received little response. Now, in late 1991, this new generation, unwilling to be cowed by fear, would take further steps to determine its own destiny.

CHAPTER 7

SANTA CRUZ AND BEYOND

◈ ◈ ◈ ◈

. . . Please pray for me, because now I have to confront two sides: Indonesia and
the [East Timorese] youth. . . . The [Indonesian] soldiers continue to accuse me
of promoting demonstrations and the young people accuse me of having
sold out to Indonesia, because I do not allow them to have
demonstrations at my residence. . . .

—CARLOS FILIPE XIMENES BELO,
letter to the author, September 5, 1993

I DID NOT KNOW about the demonstration. I only heard the shots,"
he recalled much later. The sounds of machine-gun fire reached the
home of Bishop Belo as he walked through his courtyard on the
morning of November 12, 1991 at ten past eight. He feared the worst. Then
the rector of the seminary arrived and told the bishop that there had been
indiscriminate shooting at the Santa Cruz cemetery: many people, most of
them youngsters, were dead. The bullets came from U.S.-made M-16 rifles,
the kind used by American forces in Vietnam. The Indonesian Army had
made them a staple of its military gear.

Bishop Belo was at once enraged and heartbroken when he realized
what had happened. "Why was I not told?" the bishop asked again and
again. For months, Belo worried that something like this might take place,
and now it had. Why had no one told him what they planned to do? Perhaps he might have been able to stop them, the way he had ended the
standoff near the Hotel Turismo during the visit of the U.S. ambassador
the year before. If only he had known. Years later, after he received the
Nobel Peace Prize, the bishop said balefully that he must have been the
only one in East Timor who had not known what was planned for Novem-

160

ber 12, 1991. It was, of course, logical that he wasn't informed, because he would have tried to stop it.

Santa Cruz was the biggest challenge to Bishop Belo's faith and philosophy of nonviolence in his tenure as head of the Diocese of Dili, an event that recalled the massacre at the Rock of Saint Anthony in the town of Lacluta in 1981. For Belo, Santa Cruz was one of the greatest horrors imaginable: hundreds of his beloved young people killed and wounded, while he, a Salesian priest charged with protecting them, had been powerless to prevent it. Despite his best efforts, there were those among the young people whom he could not convince: some were determined to capture the attention of the world, no matter what the bishop might say or the consequences for themselves. But that was not all: Belo believed there were those working for Intel who may have provoked the confrontation, just as they had done at the Hotel Turismo.

What there was to know about events on the morning of November 12, 1991, was confusing. There was an early morning procession to the Santa Cruz cemetery, led by the family of eighteen-year-old Sebastião Gomes, who had been killed two weeks before. It was a commemoration march of a religious nature that began with Mass at the Church of Saint Anthony of Motael, right where the young man was murdered on October 28. Marchers were to place flowers on Sebastião's grave in the Santa Cruz cemetery. Church officials announced that the Gomes family did not want the procession to be used as a vehicle for a political demonstration. The commemoration was to be a solemn occasion of mourning.

However, some came to the Mass with a different mission: senior Catholic Church officials said that the procession was joined by young activists carrying banners reading, "*Viva* Independence!" "*Viva* Timor Leste!" and "*Viva* Xanana Gusmão!" Xanana was still holding out in East Timor's mountainous interior, despite numerous Indonesian attempts to capture him over the previous decade. He had called for a demonstration to take place during the Portuguese parliamentary visit, but exactly what Xanana had in mind for November 12, 1991, was unclear. Who, if anyone, actually ordered the use of banners and slogans remains a mystery. Some contend that events were manipulated by General Murdani, representative of a hard-line faction opposed to the more conciliatory General Warouw, then East Timor's military commander.

Throughout the war, demonstrated by General Jusuf's 1983 cease-fire and the testimony of disillusioned veterans who took part in the invasion, there were individual officers and units who were more humane and more willing to compromise than others, although few, if any, were willing to grant independence for East Timor. Still, in the atmosphere that existed in 1991, General Warouw was considered a liberal, and this may have made the November 12, 1991 procession possible.

Perhaps three thousand persons marched to the Santa Cruz cemetery, a walk of a mile and a half. The mourners were led by women holding flowers, with many little children in attendance. Some marchers had lost their entire families over the previous sixteen years, yet, surmounting all apprehension, they were taking the chance to express their feelings. It was a special day for another reason: officials from the United Nations were visiting; General Warouw was meeting with the UN Special Rapporteur on Torture, Pieter Kooïjmans of the Netherlands, and that was the immediate reason for the demonstration.

Moving out of Saint Anthony's Church by the old Portuguese lighthouse, the marchers walked along the seaside near the harbor. Indonesian troops and police looked on with hatred and disgust, yet there was no interference by the authorities. Army troops and police stood on the side of the road holding long polished wooden sticks. As the procession passed the Governor's Palace, the Indonesian array of force was evident. They could have stopped the march at any moment.

Flags of the nationalist resistance movement were unfurled. The procession continued on to the Santa Cruz cemetery at a brisk pace. Suddenly there was a brief scuffle as an Indonesian major waded into the crowd with a group of soldiers bearing fixed bayonets. The major threw a young woman to the ground as he tried to grab a nationalist flag she was carrying. Some accounts say the major was then stabbed by the boyfriend of the young woman. The stabbing, later cited by Indonesian authorities as the reason for the tragedy that day, was hardly noticed at the time, and to this day it is not clear what happened. Despite that burst of action, no one made any move to stop the procession or the demonstrators alongside them. They were still half a mile or more from the cemetery. As they proceeded, their high spirits mingled with anxiety, and for good reason: the assembled East Timorese were walking into an ambush which some Church leaders are convinced had been set for them well in advance of November 12.

As the marchers mingled, some inside the cemetery, some outside, Indonesian troops arrived and opened fire on the crowd at point-blank range, without warning or provocation. It had all the appearance of a planned, disciplined operation. The fusillade lasted several minutes—no one could be sure how long. When the shooting started, prayers for Sebastião Gomes had only just begun. The soldiers jumped out of their trucks, and fired directly into the crowd. There was no call to disperse, no opportunity to avert tragedy.

While the origins of the massacre at Santa Cruz remain obscure, the consequences are no mystery. Mayhem followed, as hundreds of people fled for their lives. Boys and girls were chased down by Indonesian soldiers and shot in the back. Some comforted themselves by praying. When at last the shooting stopped, dozens lay dead or wounded amid the gravestones. It was a scene of martyrdom, as scores of young people dove behind graves while the few that could scrambled into the small cemetery chapel. Like the young in Soweto, South Africa, fifteen years before, the young in Dili, East Timor, were defenseless before heavily armed troops.

Hundreds of young people fled to Bishop Belo's house for help, some running, some in taxis. The bishop, angry that he had been informed neither of the memorial Mass nor the march, nor the demonstration, at first would not let them in. But he quickly yielded. The area was filling up with military and police, concentrated on the beach across the street. The bishop's residence was encircled; there were troops all over the place. This was no time for lectures.

"Hide us, or they will kill us!" called a teenage girl in a blood-drenched dress.

"Come inside, all of you!" the bishop responded. They poured into the garden behind the house. More kept arriving until there were 315 of them. The bishop arranged medical care for the wounded at Church clinics, and then sent for bread. He also called Governor Carrascalão and asked him to come see them. Above all, the bishop recalled, he tried to remain calm, as more and more mothers arrived, crying that their children had been killed. Belo's ability to maintain his composure under strain was severely tested.

One of the mothers was his elder sister, Aurea. Three of her children were present at Santa Cruz, right by their home. She wept and pleaded for help. But he could give his own sister no special assistance. "I don't like nepotism!" was the bishop's vehement answer. His pain was still evident when asked about this seven years later. "Nephews?" he said emphatically. "How could I favor my nephews? What about everybody else?" He made wide gestures describing the wrenching scene outside his residence, where dozens of desperate mothers were voicing their own grief and supplication.

Indeed, there was no time to lament his personal anguish, for nearly every Timorese family in Dili had someone who was either killed, wounded, or missing, and as bishop he had equal responsibility for them all. Belo hurried to Santa Cruz with his vicar general, Father José António da Costa, and Dona Helena Carrascalão, the wife of the Indonesian-appointed governor. Mário Carrascalão, known as sympathetic to the youth movement although there was little he could do to help them, had been there earlier.

At the cemetery, the bishop reacted with disbelief. Dozens of people were ripped apart by bullets, lying in the dust amid the pastel-colored graves and crypts in the fierce midday heat. The bishop struggled not to lose his balance at the sight of such brutality and the crying of the mothers. Soldiers were at the cemetery when he arrived. Obviously shamed by the bishop's presence, they moved away and hid when they saw him.

The bishop noticed a trail of blood leading to the chapel. Belo went inside and saw that there were six seriously injured young people, some beaten, others with gaping bullet wounds. They were feverishly praying and singing hymns of mercy. The bishop knew one of them, Tomás Ximenes, a mission teacher from the coffee-growing town of Ermera.

"Oh, Bishop, I am hungry and thirsty," Tomás Ximenes screamed in agony.

"There was nothing I could do but give him my blessing," because the military would permit no more, Belo remembered later, his face lined with regret. Even the International Committee of the Red Cross (ICRC) was not allowed to enter the Santa Cruz cemetery that day.

Belo saw a line of sixty young people, all of them students, whose shirts had been stripped to tie their hands behind their back. "Why did you do this without letting me know?" the bishop exclaimed, still livid that he hadn't the chance to prevent the bloodletting.

Belo left the cemetery feeling sick. He knew he had to move quickly. The 315 people on the grounds of his residence could not stay there for long: after the pope's visit in 1989, and at other times, troops had threatened to invade the bishop's compound to arrest those taking refuge. The situation was far more explosive now. If they could be taken home, perhaps they could escape harm. The bishop phoned the police at about eleven that morning, and received their agreement not to interfere.

Then Bishop Belo asked for the help of an Indonesian priest known for his ties to the military; perhaps this connection would help those in danger. Belo and the priest, together with Mother Matilde, began to transport young people in groups of nine and ten in a trooper car and other vehicles. There were more than twenty secret service men in front of the bishop's house taking note of who was leaving and how many people were in each car.

Between the hours of 1:00 and 6:00 P.M., the bishop personally escorted the young people back to their homes. But at about 5:30 P.M., the bishop noticed that they were being shadowed by a motorcycle and a car. As he returned to his house, many of those he had taken home had returned to his residence in taxis, fleeing troops in hot pursuit. Mother Matilde's car was almost hit by a military vehicle tailing her. Belo stopped the operation for the night.

The extent of the double-cross by the police was unclear. The next morning Bishop Belo went to the military commander, insisting he be allowed to see the dead and wounded. Finally he was permitted to visit the military hospital: there were more than one hundred there. The bishop was unable to speak with most of the wounded: he was only able to go around to the wards. But he did talk with some of the youngsters who had come to his home for protection: to the bishop's horror, many in the hospital were the same young people he had taken home the day before. He thought they had escaped to safety. But there they were, "many of them severely beaten and some of them injured so severely that they were beyond recognition."

Bishop Belo prayed to himself, silently vowing, "I must tell the world about these horrors no matter what they do to me."

Belo learned that the group of sixty young people he had seen at the cemetery had been taken away in police cars to Comoro military headquarters. There they were beaten and tortured. When he visited the hospital, he saw that their faces were smashed.

Of his three nephews who were at Santa Cruz, only one made it safely back home. Another went into hiding for many weeks and then was able to escape to Australia. The third, António, namesake of their lost uncle, was shot in the head and shoulder. He was taken to the military hospital and was among the people the bishop was able to see there in the days that followed.

António suffered extensively and was beaten in the chest while the military told him, "It was your uncle who made you do this." It was, as Bishop Belo had said earlier, the truth turned upside down. In fact, António was beaten when the military learned he was Belo's nephew. But at least the bishop had seen him alive; they now could not simply dispose of him. António survived and escaped to Macau.

Although Bishop Belo gave his family no special help, they were luckier than many others. The wounded that the bishop had seen in the hospital on November 13 were only the beginning. There were more than one hundred the first morning he went there, but on the following day, only eighty-nine remained.

"Many of them I never saw again, because they were killed by the military," the bishop later affirmed.

Belo learned from a guilt-stricken soldier that many of those who survived the massacre at the Santa Cruz cemetery were taken away and executed by Indonesian security forces. People were brought to a government building in Dili, the bishop learned later. There prisoners were killed "with big stones, and with iron bars and with injections of a special substance that killed them." As for the six people Bishop Belo encountered in the cemetery chapel, including the mission teacher Tomás Ximenes, they simply "disappeared."

"I never saw any of them again," Bishop Belo told Philip Shenon of the *New York Times*. "Since I knew the teacher, I went to look for him. I went to the hospital. I went to the mortuary. I could not find him. His family says he is still missing." So were hundreds of others. Bodies were taken away and buried secretly. Some were reportedly placed in a container dumped at sea. Others, because they were too frightened to seek medical assistance, died of untreated wounds.

It was more than a week before the ICRC was allowed to enter the hospital where the victims of Santa Cruz had been taken. The authorities clearly wanted to delay ICRC visits as long as possible, perhaps because the ICRC surgeons would be able to recognize bayonet and stab wounds on people who had already been shot.

ICRC delegates met Bishop Belo, who was extremely worried about the wounded. Despite the hard exterior he sometimes exhibited, the bishop showed enormous empathy for his people, an attribute especially noticeable in crisis situations, said Pierre Pont. Pont, then ICRC's chief delegate in the Indonesian area, saw the bishop on numerous occasions over a five-year period from the time of the papal visit in 1989.

While he was depressed about what had happened at Santa Cruz, Belo also had to endure threats against him from Intel and the army. The atmosphere of terror was so intense even the bishop seemed frightened. Meanwhile, in the outside world, the Indonesian government was trying to advance the idea that what had happened at Santa Cruz was only an "incident," an emotional outburst by a handful of irresponsible elements totally out of character with Indonesian rule in East Timor.

But the bishop and his people soon had help of a kind that had never existed in the past. For sixteen long years, from the time Indonesian forces had begun their attacks across the border in 1975, the East Timor tragedy had remained largely hidden from outside view. There were no foreign witnesses to the 1981 massacre at Lacluta, which may as well have been at the end of the earth. Nations providing military aid and diplomatic support for Indonesia's East Timor campaign benefited from this obscurity: if the events themselves were to a great extent invisible, all the more so the specifics of how they were carried out. Thus the United States and other countries providing help for Indonesia were able to avoid the kind of scrutiny that would have revealed their indefensible actions to the public.

All of this took a dramatic turn on November 12, 1991. What was different about Santa Cruz was that it was filmed by a British filmmaker, Max Stahl, who was making a documentary, subsequently entitled *Cold Blood: The Massacre of East Timor* for Yorkshire Television. No foreigners, let alone journalists, had ever witnessed such things and lived to tell about them. As the Indonesian military closed in on him, Stahl buried two videotapes in the cemetery and, miraculously, managed to retrieve them later. The footage would eventually come to haunt Indonesia.

Other foreigners, too, were present in the cemetery. Among them, twenty-year-old Kamal Bamadhaj, a student and a New Zealand citizen, was shot at Santa Cruz and bled to death while a Red Cross truck carrying him was stopped by the military: His mother, journalist Helen Todd, wrote a gripping article on Kamal's death for the *Wall Street Journal.* And three journalists, two of them American, were badly beaten. Amy Goodman of Pacifica Radio, and Allan Nairn, a freelance reporter then on assignment for *The New Yorker,* were at the front of the demonstration: Nairn's skull was fractured by Indonesian soldiers wielding rifle butts. British photographer Steve Cox took photos of the badly wounded inside the cemetery chapel and elsewhere. The soldiers threatened Cox by putting a gun to his head and a bayonet to his throat, which gave him nightmares even years later, and his cheeks were pummelled until they were raw.

Witnesses said the cemetery was cleaned the following night. Blood-spattered chapel walls were whitewashed. But despite the desire of Indonesia and many other governments to relegate the Timor issue to its previous obscurity, Stahl's videotape and the testimony of the other journalists created a dynamic of its own. In 1983 Senator Gordon McIntosh, an Australian parliamentarian, told Representative Tony Hall, the longtime leader of East Timor efforts in Congress, that the defenders of Indonesia's military regime had imposed such stringent standards of proof that "one almost has to bring them dead bodies before they will accept your information." On November 12, 1991, they got more than a few. The atrocities in East Timor became undeniable.

Foreign journalists were soon expelled from East Timor after what came to be known as the Santa Cruz massacre. The day after the carnage in the cemetery in Dili, Saskia Kouwenberg, a Dutch freelance reporter, managed to smuggle Stahl's tapes out of East Timor, then out of Jakarta, and to

Amsterdam. By Saturday night—the massacre had taken place on Tuesday—the horrors of Santa Cruz were witnessed anew on television throughout the Netherlands. In front of a huge screen in the freezing cold of Maastricht, protestors wept. They had come from all over the continent to call for action by the European community. The video was aired in Britain by the beginning of the following week. In the United States, officials had begun to try casting doubt on the accounts of the two American journalists at Santa Cruz; Stahl's videotape, presented in part on the *CBS Evening News* on November 21, not only demolished such efforts, it enraged members of the United States Congress across the political spectrum. Gradually, news of the Santa Cruz massacre would reach many more around the globe, shocking millions of viewers.

Max Stahl wrote that the morning after the massacre, "there were smiles on the faces of many Timorese." The reason, he wrote that week, ". . . was because the foreigners had been there and filmed the event, and the foreigners, for once, were also beaten up and this they believe will be noticed. This, they believe, may lift a little the curse which is worse than oppression and death for Timorese, the curse of their total and relentless isolation in their struggle."

But for all the wonders of the media age, Bishop Belo's international phone line had been severed. He was desperate to make contact with the outside world, but could not. "My telephone has not been functioning since October 28. It is not a coincidence. Every time there is a special event here, my phone doesn't work," Belo told one of the remaining journalists in East Timor shortly after November 12. He could still receive local calls, however, and he added mordantly, "I have received anonymous letters and phone calls, certain of them calling me pig."

In fact, almost all phone service between East Timor and the outside world was suspended. Worse, in the aftermath of Santa Cruz, there was a concerted effort on the part of the regime to implicate the Catholic Church. Priests suspected of opposing the Indonesian occupation and assisting foreign journalists were subjected to long interrogation sessions by the military—lasting five, six, and seven hours without interruption each day, with few breaks, for a number of weeks, marked by "psychological assaults like in a Soviet prison." It was "as if the shooting on November 12 had been done by the priests and not by the Indonesian military. They are trying to act as if it is the Church that is culpable, rather than their own acts," members of the clergy said. Bishop Belo was not interrogated, perhaps, one priest suggested, out of fear of the Vatican.

Still, quiet threats were issued against the Catholic Church in all of Indonesia. Worries about retaliation, Timorese Church leaders said, explained the silence of the pope, who only a few months earlier had declared, "I hope this problem of East Timor will be solved in a way that respects the principles of justice, human rights, and international law."

To the clergy who had been there throughout, an atmosphere descended of all-pervasive fear worse than any since Indonesia's 1975 invasion, with terrible tension and death threats hanging in the air, the streets empty of civilians and filled with soldiers. "If anyone speaks even one word in Portuguese [rather than Indonesian]," recounted a priest, "it is treated as a crime against the state, with big trouble for the 'offender.'" People were afraid to talk with one another, even when eating at the same table, let alone to write letters or try to place phone calls. It was dangerous even for priests to get together to console one another.

The peril for ordinary people was starkly illustrated by the case of Fernando de Araújo, a twenty-six-year-old leader studying in Indonesia. In the days immediately following Santa Cruz, he told friends to contact the human rights organization Amnesty International in London. He also organized a demonstration in front of foreign embassies in Jakarta. This protest led to an indictment of Araújo, for which he received nine years in prison; Araújo, who received a Reebok Human Rights Award in 1992, won release only in 1998. Combining draconian punishment like this, mass roundups of suspected opponents of Indonesian rule, who were shipped out of Dili, and threats to decimate the youth, the Indonesian military hoped to prevent information from reaching the international community.

The military also tried to force Bishop Belo to make statements favorable to their cause. But despite their strongest efforts to coerce the bishop, they were unable to silence him. Questioned by one reporter on his intentions in the near future, Belo said that his duty was to remain among his people and "suffer in joy" while waiting for better times and a peaceful solution to the problems of East Timor. But more than anyone, he worked to inform the world of his people's distress.

"The majority of Timorese, whether in urban or rural areas, want the right of self-determination and independence. But they are afraid to express themselves," he told journalist Adam Schwarz of the *Far Eastern Economic Review*, going even further than in his 1989 letter to the United Nations.

To little avail, Belo offered an olive branch to the Indonesians. Asked about tensions between the government and the Church, the bishop responded, "We must avoid this; we must try to live side by side." Asked to comment on what happened on November 12, he simply stated that it "reflects the pain being felt by the people here."

In his Christmas Day homily, the bishop offered a double-edged message. On the one hand, he urged, "Let us look ahead in the spirit of Christ, to where there is no more enemy, no conflict, and no ethnic problems." But he stressed that for many this was a "gray Christmas," because the November 12 tragedy had left their loved ones dead, wounded, or imprisoned: "We are all outraged. We are living in fear, not in peace. We suffer, hate, cry, and lose hope."

Even on Christmas, Indonesia's public relations drive continued, brazenly stating that Bishop Belo and his clergy "threw an open house yesterday morning which lasted until noon. Among the guests were leaders of the provincial government and the military."

"I invited no one," Bishop Belo told a journalist from the Portuguese press agency, but at that point his telephone (which had been restored) was again cut. They called again, but when the same subject was discussed, the call was again interrupted, a familiar pattern for the bishop.

It was the day after Christmas when the Indonesian government chose to release its official investigation of the Santa Cruz massacre. The choice of date was strategic. Public relations agencies working for the Indonesian government knew that many journalists and political figures in Europe and North America were on Christmas break, so it was an excellent day to avoid scrutiny of the report, which vastly understated the severity of the killing. The government's official investigation had ignored Bishop Belo's testimony, and much more. But two generals were soon removed, including General Warouw, the military commander in East Timor (however, few believed he was the one who ordered the troops at Santa Cruz to open fire). One prominent expert on the Indonesian military, who said that Suharto saw the Santa Cruz events as a major blunder, noted that it was the first time that any Indonesian army officer of that rank "had ever been so publicly humiliated" during the Suharto era. In addition, a high-ranking general, Feisal Tanjung, and Army chief of staff Edy Sudradjat, headed a military "Honor Council" that conducted its own investigation of Santa Cruz. Although the extent of its actual impact was unclear, experts believe that there was a shake-up of most of the command structure in Dili. And for the first time, there was a great deal of critical reporting on East Timor in the Indonesian news media, provoking unprecedented domestic debate on the issue, and encouraging the Timorese resistance movement.

Still, for all of these developments, Bishop Belo felt that many ABRI leaders remained unrepentant, judging from the day-to-day behavior that he could see. Shortly after Santa Cruz, Indonesian Armed Forces Commander, General Try Sutrisno (later to be vice-president), had exploded over questions from the media: the protesters, he said, were delinquents who deserved to be shot and "we will shoot them." Others continued to express similar sentiments.

Public reaction forced the European community and the United States to condemn the violence, and by the end of 1991, the prime minister of Japan, Indonesia's largest aid donor and trading partner, proclaimed that the issue of East Timor was "important." Amid the international outcry, ten members of the Indonesian security forces were tried for disciplinary offenses in connection with the Santa Cruz massacre. All received sentences of between eight and eighteen months, mainly served under house arrest, and were reportedly released well before serving their full sentences. In stark contrast, East Timorese accused of organizing the demonstration at Santa Cruz on November 12, 1991, and a subsequent demonstration in the Indonesian capital of Jakarta received sentences ranging from five years to life: Several of these prisoners were still being held in late 1998. As Bishop Belo knew well, foreign protests had not prevented such injustices from taking place. Well-placed sources in the clergy stressed that, far from showing contrition toward the families of the victims of Santa Cruz, the Indonesian military persecuted them as if they were the criminals.

In response to international criticism, Suharto created the National Human Rights Commission. Despite early concerns that it might simply do the government's bidding, in its first year of operations it was surprisingly independent and critical, and conducted public investigations of some of the worst abuses in Indonesia itself. This may have pressured the military to court martial some lower ranking soldiers. But in East Timor, the Commission did not begin operations until years later, and when it did, the Commission's office was located next to the military command. This, combined with a general mistrust of Indonesian institutions and the fact that the person who ran the office was seen as incompetent and indifferent, severely undermined local confidence in the Commission's effectiveness, whatever its intentions and performance elsewhere. This was a pattern in East Timor. The discrepancy between words and deeds was described by Mário Carrascalão after he left office in 1993 after ten years in his position:

"The main conclusion that I draw from my tenure as governor in East Timor is that there is a large gap between what Jakarta says it wants to do in East Timor and what actually happens in East Timor."

Some observers believed that the removal of the two generals and court martials of lower ranking officers had little concrete impact but were the very least the Suharto regime could do to appease an outpouring of international protest, and public disquiet in some quarters of Indonesia itself.

Just after the Santa Cruz massacre, U.S. Representative Tony P. Hall of Ohio, the most vocally concerned and active member of Congress since his election in 1979, was angry and distressed at what he had seen and heard, both on television and in personal accounts. Confronting the late Dante Fascell, then the longtime House Foreign Affairs Committee chairman, Hall asked bluntly, "Why haven't we done anything to call Indonesia to account? Why have we always allowed Indonesia to get away with murder?"

As Hall remembered it at the time, Fascell's reply was equally direct: "Because George Bush's friends and Henry Kissinger's friends won't let us do anything." Fascell spoke of corporate giants—like AT&T—with huge interests in Indonesia that had the lobbying power to prevent congressional sanctions on favored governments. Indeed, several months before, Bishop Paul Moore Jr. had met a senior State Department official, in the presence of two Republican U.S. senators. The official did not contest the gruesome history of East Timor since the Indonesian invasion, and acknowledged that 200,000 people may have perished since the Indonesian assault. But, he countered, America's commercial interests in Indonesia must be cultivated and protected; AT&T had just signed a contract to provide 300,000 phone lines to Indonesia.

Influence of this kind, coupled with the complete absence of television coverage of the horrors in East Timor until Santa Cruz, gave Congress little reason to pass or even consider legislation. No sanctions against Jakarta had ever been voted, although shortly after the 1975 invasion, Representative Tom Harkin (Democrat of Iowa) proposed that U.S. military aid to Indonesia be cut off; the measure lost by a three-to-one margin. Even after Santa Cruz, the New Orleans–based mining concern Freeport McMoran, a company with a long history in Indonesia, on whose board Henry Kissinger served, lobbied Congress to refrain from taking strong action; it was joined by others.

But even as Hall and Fascell were speaking, and despite the efforts of corporate giants to stop significant congressional action, things had begun to change. Many members of Congress were approaching Hall, telling him that after Santa Cruz, they now fully understood why he had been concerned about East Timor for so long. And Bishop Paul Moore's cousin, then Republican Senator Malcolm Wallop of Wyoming, led a group of fifty-two U.S. senators, including then Senator Al Gore, in writing a strong

Bishop Belo in 1968, standing in the center, behind his
mother, Dona Ermelinda. His sister Julieta is at right.
(Courtesy of Bishop Carlos Ximenes Belo)

Belo circa 1972 as a student in Portugal.
(Courtesy of Bishop Carlos Ximenes Belo)

Bishop Belo with Father Alfonso Nacher, a Salesian teacher from Spain, circa 1982. *(Courtesy of Bishop Carlos Ximenes Belo)*

Dom Martinho da Costa Lopes, Belo's predecessor as head of the Catholic Church of East Timor, at a Timorese refugee camp outside of Lisbon, Portugal, in 1985. *(Courtesy of Korinna Horta)*

The Pope's visit to East Timor in 1989, when Bishop Belo served as his host. *(Courtesy of Bishop Carlos Ximenes Belo)*

Bishop Belo with children near Baucau, 1995. *(Courtesy of Korinna Horta)*

Bishop Belo in Dili, 1995. *(Courtesy of Korinna Horta)*

This young man is wearing a Bishop Belo T-shirt,
which is very popular in East Timor, 1997.
(Courtesy of Korinna Horta)

Bishop Belo standing in St. Peter's Square, Rome, 1996.
(Courtesy of Salesians of St. John Bosco, Rome)

President Clinton greeting Bishop Belo in the White House in 1997, with the
author at far right. *(Courtesy of the White House Press Office)*

Left, East Timorese traditional leader near East Timor's sacred mountain, Ramelau, 1997.
Right, A woman from a mountain region waiting to see Bishop Belo, 1997.
(Courtesy of Korinna Horta)

East Timorese traditional leaders gathering to meet Bishop Belo at
pilgrimage to Mount Ramelau, 1997. *(Courtesy of Korinna Horta)*

Bishop Belo addressing traditional
leaders and local villagers near
Mount Ramelau, 1997.
(Courtesy of Korinna Horta)

Ceremonial horn
blowers at Ramelau, 1997
(Courtesy of Korinna Horta)

Bishop Belo at the tomb of St. Anthony in Padua, Italy, 1997.
(Courtesy of the Messenger of St. Anthony, Padua)

letter to President Bush on the issue. Wallop noted that many of his fellow conservatives were especially disturbed by the *CBS News* segment that appeared on November 21; indeed, until then, the Bush administration had taken an equivocal position. After seeing the grim footage of Santa Cruz, Secretary of State James Baker told a Republican congressman that he was deeply disturbed by what had happened, though this did not prevent the Bush administration from continuing military aid to Indonesia. Bishop Belo transmitted a private appeal stating that if action was not taken by the United States, he feared that the people of East Timor "would disappear." This led to strong bipartisan congressional pressure on the Bush administration, led by Hall, Wallop, and Republican Representative Frank Wolf of Virginia, to make diplomatic overtures to Indonesia to stop the killing that continued after the Santa Cruz massacre. According to Church sources within East Timor, these actions ultimately had some impact, though they were too late for many. Priests said there was a direct connection between occasions when the Indonesians relented in their repression and actions by the American Congress, editorials in the mass media, and statements by the American government. (Bush himself openly expressed sympathy for the plight of the East Timorese on two occasions, including once after he left office.)

American public reaction grew. Within months of Representative Hall's conversation with Fascell, whose staff remembered well their exchange with Dom Martinho years before, the House of Representatives voted to cut off funds for United States military training to the Indonesian Armed Forces. The Senate followed suit, though the Clinton administration later circumvented the intent of Congress by allowing Jakarta to purchase the training with its own funds. Other nations took action as well. The Netherlands cut aid to Indonesia, as did Canada and Denmark. The terms of debate had shifted, though the response was mixed. Shortly after Santa Cruz, despite protests, American, Australian, British, and Japanese oil companies signed new deals in the Timor Gap area, even as the Indonesian government seemed to do everything it could to downplay what had happened, both at Santa Cruz and beyond. And while the Netherlands had cut assistance to Indonesia, Suharto reacted by rejecting Dutch aid. The Intergovernmental Group on Indonesia (IGGI), an international donor coordination group headquartered in the Netherlands, Indonesia's former colonial ruler, then disbanded. The IGGI had provided tens of billions of dollars in loans and other credits to Jakarta during the Suharto regime; another aid group with the same purpose was convened under the auspices of the World Bank, not missing a beat, let alone an aid payment. Washington's diplomatic backing continued, with substantial aid programs, including arms sales, left untouched. Norway, Sweden, and Finland in November 1991 issued a joint statement condemning the massacre. But within the year all three had signed a new economic cooperation agreement with Indonesia.

Nonetheless, the film from Santa Cruz awakened Portugal's sense of historical obligation. No country in the world had a stronger human connection with East Timor than Portugal, but for the Portuguese government, there had always existed a fear of isolation that comes with diplomatic disapproval by the United States and the big European powers like France, Germany, and Britain, all close friends of Indonesia. For Lisbon, Timor was a very difficult issue. But the sight of East Timorese praying in Portuguese and cowering in terror in a cemetery built in the Portuguese style had a huge impact on the Portuguese people. Public sentiment forced the government's hand. As one Portuguese diplomat confided, before Santa Cruz it would have been possible for the Portuguese government to conclude a deal with Indonesia over the heads of the people of East Timor, but after Santa Cruz, any such deal became untenable.

While the climate of opinion had shifted in Portugal, rumors surfaced in 1992 that the Vatican was thinking of removing Belo from his post. A special envoy from Rome had visited East Timor just before Christmas 1991 on behalf of Pope John Paul II, telling the bishop and the clergy, "Be strong, don't be discouraged, the Holy See is with you." In fact, no less a personage than General Murdani expressed annoyance with the Vatican emissary (who, the general said, "confused human rights with the right to secede"). But the views of the pope's special representative did not mesh with the stance of the Vatican policy-making machine. A new, hard-line Indonesian military commander, Brigadier General Theo Syafei, launched harsh verbal attacks on Belo, warning the bishop to stay out of politics, as if a measured defense of his people's well-being amounted to that. As part of a wider move to besmirch Belo, one military commander had gone so far as to invite the bishop to a nightclub on Bali, in the hope of engineering compromising photographs. Naturally, Belo refused the invitation. But it was a small sign of what the military was prepared to do, and by this time, a strong campaign had been mounted to discredit Belo in Catholic Church circles.

The Holy See was not immune to such pressures, and appeared to be brushing aside moral considerations. Diplomatic sources directly in contact with the Vatican embassy in Jakarta said that a high-ranking official there was consistently trying to cast doubt on the severity of the situation in East Timor, and was "ready to believe anything of the government."

Belo could not accept this: had he been faced with the Machiavellian designs of secular political or military leaders, that would have been understandable, albeit distasteful. But he was totally unprepared for such behavior within the Catholic Church: it affected him profoundly, especially after what had happened at Santa Cruz and beyond.

A little more than two months after Santa Cruz, Bishop Belo returned to the cemetery with Hilton Deakin, the auxiliary bishop of Melbourne, Australia, who was making his first visit to the island. By then the death toll from Santa Cruz, in the initial shooting and in subsequent weeks, had been estimated to be at least 271; when all subsequent "disappearances" are taken into account, the number may be considerably more. No independent survey of the dead and wounded was ever allowed. Because of this, a precise figure on casualties has been elusive. (The official death toll was much lower: First, Jakarta said it was 19, then raised it to 50.)

Despite numerous international protests and the pleas of the families, Indonesian authorities produced the bodies of few of the victims. It was a severe blow to their relatives. In both the traditional religions of East Timor as well as the Catholic faith, proper burial of the dead is a crucial matter. Children were disoriented because one or both parents or brothers or sisters were taken to jail. All of this had a terrible emotional impact on Belo and his parishioners. As Bishop Deakin remembers it, Bishop Belo, after all the statements and toughness and weeks of enforced calmness, after all the anguish and suffering of that time, allowed himself the indulgence of weeping at dusk over the graves.

Three months after Santa Cruz, and a few weeks after Bishop Belo shed tears in the cemetery, a priest commented that "the Indonesians are saying one thing internationally and doing the opposite in East Timor. People are still being arrested and maltreated. Prisoners are being held in hamlets throughout the territory. Things are getting darker and darker. But the more the Indonesians persecute people, the more people of all ages resist. The persecution makes people stronger than before."

Several months later, the priest said that "the net is tight and spreading all over the island. Prisoners are in isolation. The torture and sophisticated interrogation of prisoners are having results and bring more people to secret prisons. Under terrible torture, some of the young people give up and reveal what they know."

Even the elusive Xanana Gusmão was not immune. He was arrested in

Dili on November 20, 1992, a few days after the first anniversary of the Santa Cruz massacre. He had been sleeping in a house where he was hiding, barely a mile from the cemetery.

After two weeks, during which he was held incommunicado, Xanana went on Indonesian television. Appearing dazed, he asked the Timorese guerrillas to lay down their arms. At the same time, the military said the Catholic Church would issue a Christmas pastoral letter calling on them to surrender to certain churches. Once again, even the Christmas season was subject to official manipulation.

"It's just a fabrication," the bishop retorted to a Portuguese interviewer for the newspaper *Público*. "This was cooked up by the military so that people would believe it. There is nothing whatever about any church being designated for this."

His fear, of course, was that the guerrillas would give themselves up, only to be tortured or killed. What the bishop wanted was a genuine peacemaking role for the Church, as he told an Indonesian paper: "Let's all lay down our arms and have dialogue with bare hands, using our brains and our hearts. Treating each other as equals. Not with the attitude, 'You're wrong and I'm right' or vice versa."

Told that this was not possible "if one of the sides is still in the bush," Belo responded, "In this world, everything is possible. If we want something to happen, it will be possible."

As for Xanana's TV appearance, Bishop Belo was the only one in East Timor in a position to make a frank comment: "I don't know what happened to make Xanana change so fast," Bishop Belo said archly. "I don't know for certain what happened, but for the past seventeen years if any prisoner has spoken in the way Xanana has spoken, it has happened as a result of torture."

Others drew the same conclusion. Mário Soares, then president of Portugal, said so, and his well-known democratic credentials helped stimulate an editorial in the *Washington Post* on Dec. 6, 1992, the fourth in that newspaper since Santa Cruz. Speaking of the "arrogant and clumsy show of power" with regard to the latest incident, the *Post* concluded that "A wise Indonesian government would deal with Mr. Gusmão in a political process. . . . How can it be in Indonesia's interest to remain a colonial power?"

Belo confirmed that the situation had worsened since Xanana's arrest. While Xanana's life was spared, there was a massive roundup of his suspected supporters.

"When these people are taken to prison, the first thing they do is beat them up," the bishop told Portuguese Catholic radio in February 1993. "I have received letters from prisoners and former prisoners telling me about all kinds of torture, electric shocks, burning of genitals with cigarettes, placing people in barrels of cold water, and whipping, until they say they are Fretilin collaborators."

Belo added that those arrested were "forced to confess that the bishop and the priests organized demonstrations." The bishop stressed that the Indonesian military "look for ways . . . of persecuting the Church in a veiled way: arresting catechists, brothers, the priests' close helpers in the parishes, stopping the young people from attending liturgical meetings."

Asked if he was ever physically afraid, the bishop said, ". . . I know that this is a place where any day I could be found with a bullet in me. To die and stop speaking, and stop walking, of this I am not afraid."

After all the suffering and terror Bishop Belo and his people had known, the election of Bill Clinton held out the promise of a new American policy. Soon after President Clinton took office, the United States in March 1993 supported for the first time a resolution on East Timor at the United Nations Human Rights Commission in Geneva. This move put America on the side of the victims in East Timor, and influenced European nations as well as Australia to support the resolution.

A few weeks after the Geneva resolution, *New York Times* reporter Philip Shenon was able to visit East Timor, the first occasion the *Times* was allowed to do so since Santa Cruz. Political detainees are tortured "just like two plus two is four," Bishop Belo told Shenon. "We lack the freedom to speak, to walk where we want, to have different opinions." The bishop cited an Indonesian intelligence officer who told a prisoner, "We only need your land, we don't need people like you Timorese."

"The people of East Timor need the help of President Clinton and the United States," Belo concluded.

Reporters, including Shenon, were allowed to visit for the trial of Xanana Gusmão. What happened there was typical. When the resistance leader tried to read a defense statement (making it clear that his earlier statements on TV were the result of coercion), he was silenced by the court. "In a mockery of justice, Indonesia has only tarnished itself, not its prisoner," *The New York Times* editorialized on May 29, 1993.

Just after Xanana was sentenced to life in prison, Bishop Belo made his first visit to the United States and Canada. He was invited to attend a gathering of the American Catholic Bishops in June 1993 in New Orleans, where he was met by his old teacher from East Timor, Father Reinaldo Cardoso, for many years a resident of Rhode Island. Since the 1970s, Father

Cardoso had played an indispensable behind-the-scenes role in establishing fruitful international links for the Diocese of Dili.

The visit gave Belo the opportunity to convey his views to a group in a real position to help him. Walking with three hundred fellow bishops to a special Mass at Saint Charles Cathedral in the city's French Quarter was a welcome break from the grinding pressures of life in East Timor. There was time for a bit of his favorite music at Preservation Hall, home of the famed Jazz Band, and for the purchase of some tapes to take home with him. All in all, it was an invigorating interlude for the bishop.

In private discussions in New Orleans, Belo was quite direct about the predicament he felt East Timor was facing. The social situation in East Timor was deteriorating so badly, the bishop said, that it was vital to find some way to improve the situation. Some form of autonomy, he stressed, was vital in the near future, though this did not imply any backtracking on his part regarding a referendum on self-determination. To illustrate the depth of sentiment in the territory, Belo described a group of youngsters, perhaps seven or eight years old, who always were at demonstrations; one boy had survived Santa Cruz.

During one demonstration, a large number of young people were sitting in front of the doorway leading to the bishop's residence. He asked the younger children, those who were about seven to nine years old, what they wanted.

They responded brightly: "We want independence."

Belo asked them: "What is independence?" and they responded, "Independence is to govern ourselves!"

"You little monkeys, you don't even know yet how to wipe your noses, but you want to be independent," the bishop teased.

But he himself walked away, shaking his head, incredulous that children so young were thinking in such terms. This, Bishop Belo stressed, almost more in wonderment than anything else, is what he—and the world—must deal with in East Timor.

Bishop Belo also emphasized that he was under excruciating pressure on several fronts. Many abroad took for granted his outspokenness, failing to grasp the harsh reality of East Timor, where every word had to be carefully weighed. Months before, he had cautioned an interviewer, "You are speaking in Portugal, where you are living in a democratic climate. We are living in a different world." But difficult as Belo's circumstances were at home, while away his situation became more complex still. Under Indonesian law, he could always be banned from returning home. Thus, it was impossible for the bishop to make many strong public statements while outside East Timor: paradoxically, he was the one East Timorese freer to speak inside East Timor than anywhere else.

The bishop, a churchman first and foremost, was keenly interested in the development of a new seminary in East Timor to replace the one that had been destroyed by Indonesian bombardment at Dare. There, candidates for the priesthood would be free of the endless political pressure to support the government that they faced in Indonesian seminaries. The construction of a new seminary was his dream, a place where the students could be themselves, and he would tell this to anyone who would listen. While this was of little interest to those who viewed East Timor only in terms of politics or human rights, it won him points among his American colleagues, including John Cardinal O'Connor of New York, who hosted the bishop for breakfast at his residence. O'Connor was amazed at the number of new vocations in East Timor: "That's more than the whole Archdiocese of New York!" the cardinal exclaimed.

During these discussions it also became evident that Belo was a sensible, conscientious cleric, not the firebrand Church diplomats had led them to believe. As for relations with Rome, when asked by the American bishops about Vatican policy on East Timor, Bishop Belo simply replied with a discreet smile, "I don't understand Vatican diplomacy."

The bishop also went to Canada, where the Canadian Catholic Organization for Development and Peace continued a tradition of solidarity with the East Timor Church established when Dom Martinho visited that country in 1983. Canada had been one of the few nations to immediately cut aid to Indonesia in response to Santa Cruz. In comparison with the inaction of other nations, it was a courageous move, reflecting public opinion aroused by a movement of church organizations and secular groups that had been active on East Timor for many years. Many were looking forward to Belo's visit. But after the Canadian government let it be known that the Indonesian government was tracking the bishop's movements, he responded by keeping a low profile, restricting his schedule in Canada to a few private meetings. Belo was soon to return home and was anxious to avoid confrontation with the powers who controlled Indonesian borders.

On his way back to East Timor through the West Coast, Belo stopped in Oakland, California, to see Bishop John Cummins, who had been to East Timor in 1990. Belo was accompanied in the San Francisco area by David Hinkley, an official of Catholic Charities and a former chairman of Amnesty International, USA. Asked to describe his main task in life, Bishop Belo responded without hesitation, "Saving the young people of East Timor from throwing themselves on the funeral pyre of their own history and their parents' history." He made it plain that he could never comprehend how anyone could frown upon his insistence on the physical protection of his people.

Despite such sentiments—or perhaps because of them—Indonesian pressure on Rome intensified. Just after he left America, rumors again surfaced that the Vatican embassy in Jakarta was saying that "Belo has to go."

The bishop's growing international contacts and credibility may have had something to do with this. He had quietly seen senior government officials in Canada, and while in Washington, he went to the White House to see Anthony Lake, President Clinton's National Security Advisor, stressing that the most important thing was for Indonesia to withdraw its troops from East Timor. He made similar arguments at the State Department. Perhaps more worrisome from the point of view of the Indonesian government, Belo also had quiet meetings with key members of Congress, including Representative Tony Hall.

"People could see he was the real thing, a man of God and a man of peace," recalled Martin Rendon, a senior advisor to Hall who had followed the East Timor issue for much of the two decades he worked in Congress. After meeting the bishop, Hall—as a national legislator, he was eligible to do so—"felt able to nominate Belo for the Nobel Peace Prize with conviction," Rendon said. It was not a matter of religion, however: Hall was not a Catholic, but an evangelical Christian, and had taken up the plight of various oppressed groups, including the Ahmadi Muslims, a minority in Pakistan.

Reinforced by the bishop's visit, a broad bipartisan group of forty-three U.S. senators asked President Clinton to raise the issue of East Timor with President Suharto when the two leaders met in Tokyo in July 1993, at the summit meeting of the Group of Seven industrialized nations. Clinton reportedly gave him a gentle lecture; an account that followed said that President Suharto was offended by the young American president. At that time, the talk was of "Asian values." Countries like Indonesia were making so much economic progress with such high growth rates, based on discipline and order, that they challenged the right of outsiders to bring up unpleasant subjects like East Timor, the rights of Indonesian workers, and similar issues.

The situation to which Bishop Belo returned in July 1993 was as difficult as ever. The difference was that he felt far less isolated: the bishop had seen for himself that senior Church officials, members of Congress and Parliament, and others in North America were behind him. He was soon visited by three members of the Swedish parliament, who left shocked by the atmosphere of terror, calling for an arms embargo on Indonesia until a free election under United Nations control was held. Unbeknownst to the bishop, he received additional support from the Swedish delegation: soon they too nominated him for the Nobel Peace Prize, as did Japanese and Portuguese members of parliament.

In early September 1993, Bishop Belo wrote: "On Sundays, the churches of Dili are guarded by well-armed Indonesian troops because they fear possible demonstrations. . . . So much fear has been created . . . that Catholics are now afraid to approach the Bishop and the priests. . . . The youth are constantly under surveillance, they are tense and I believe that one day the whole thing might explode."

Sure enough, on September 5, 1993, a group of U.S. congressional staff members came to Dili. The military staged a show of force to discourage demonstrations, patrolling all of the city of Dili and its surroundings. Violence was in the air, as the power of armed force made itself felt. Many hundreds of unsmiling troops moved through the area, sending the message that they were ready to crush any disturbance.

Several dozen young people, however, refused to be intimidated. They were, in fact, exuberant over the possibility of bringing their plight to the attention of the American Congress. But the bloodshed at the Santa Cruz cemetery had already sent a terrible message to the world, one that did not need to be repeated. In the view of the bishop, fresh from his visit to Washington, the young people did not realize how little could be achieved by still another sacrifice.

The youngsters came to Bishop Belo's house for the 6:00 A.M. Mass, but there were too many to fit into the small chapel, so they went outside on the patio. Afterward some of the young people hid in bedrooms, bathrooms, and the kitchen of the bishop's house to wait for the right time to demonstrate in front of the congressional staff. There were about one hundred in all, and during the day more arrived. Belo wanted to do everything possible to avoid a confrontation with the military, who were only too anxious to have a bloody showdown with the youngsters.

The bishop had earned a reputation as a tough disciplinarian, but he was no martinet: he knew how to be fair and he knew when and how to relent. So it was with young Profirio, a close friend of one of the orphans who lived in his house. Profirio confronted Indonesian security forces to the point of recklessness. Bishop Belo gave Profirio sanctuary, but let it be known he would tolerate no political activity in his residence. Belo's word stood. Now he was faced with dozens of Profirios, but the principle remained the same: because the Church played a vital role as a go-between,

Belo would not allow his home to be used as a base for political demonstrations.

In fact, most of the youngsters left when the bishop asked them to do so. But one group managed to remain hidden in the bathrooms. "When I found out about this just before the arrival of the congressional staff delegation, I picked up a broom and personally went from room to room and around the house to find them, and told them that they were ill-behaved, because they had entered my house without asking permission and said that they should leave and I even hit a few of them on their bottoms," the bishop recalled.

The bishop escorted them to the entrance. But the house was surrounded by military, police, informers: altogether about two hundred people. Staying was no option—that was what the security forces were there to prevent. "After a lot of discussion with the young people, I decided to drive them myself in a truck and drop them off near their homes," he said. "That way, there was no demonstration."

The congressional staff arrived. Intel men were waiting for them, and maintained a heavy presence right outside the bishop's window. They were obviously trying to eavesdrop. Before they left, the fifty young people he took home had been filmed by Indonesian intelligence outside the residence. As for the Americans, the Indonesians may have scattered the demonstrators, but it was all too apparent to the visitors that they were in a police state. By now Belo was furious with the military's heavy-handed presence.

"Bishop Belo went to the window, looked at the eavesdroppers, and slammed the window shut," one of the congressional staff remembered. "It was incredible."

Belo may have had a premonition of what would follow: once again, as after Santa Cruz, there had been a double-cross. The following day, Indonesian troops captured the youngsters the bishop had escorted home. "They took them to headquarters, and these young people who had not even demonstrated before the congressional staff were barbarously beaten and tortured," the bishop wrote indignantly in a letter to me at the time.

Belo was extremely depressed over what had happened; it was another diabolical ruse by Indonesian intelligence, with terrible consequences, both for the victims and, in another way, the bishop himself. He had tried to make peace, and now, a measure of responsibility for the outcome was laid at his doorstep.

He, as much as anyone, understood the frustrations of the young. Belo may have been poor as a boy, and he may have been fatherless, but he had never been plagued by the despair that had come to pervade the lives of young people in East Timor now. And as tragic as the death of Belo's own father had been for Dona Ermelinda and her children, the event that had caused it, the Pacific War, was long over, enabling the family to rebuild their lives in relative calm. The present generation of East Timorese youth had no such luxury: many had not only lost parents, but also grandparents, uncles and aunts, other family members, as well as friends and neighbors. Life in East Timor during the youth of Carlos Filipe Ximenes Belo was carefree in contrast with theirs.

In the aftermath of the congressional visit, Belo was pressed between two sides. While the youth were upset with the bishop over his refusal to allow the demonstration to take place at his residence, the Indonesians were fomenting a campaign against him. Throughout East Timor the military were spreading the story that the bishop had organized a demonstration on September 5 (though none had taken place) and had hid the participants. In Belo's eyes, it was a campaign to discredit him. Far worse, there was the torture of the young people.

A few days after the youngsters were tortured, Belo told a Swedish journalist, "In many villages, people cannot even go out to their rice or coffee fields. This military organization has to be got rid of. People have to be allowed to speak out freely, to go around freely, and to create a clearly peaceful, free, and democratic civilization. Here, there is a dictatorship."

Fittingly, the same month the congressional staff visit took place, legislation proposed by U.S. Senator Russell Feingold passed the Senate Foreign Relations Committee.

The Feingold amendment stipulated that before arms sales are made to Indonesia, the Clinton Administration should consider several criteria, including whether the Indonesian government had accounted for those missing in connection with the Santa Cruz events and punished those responsible for the massacre, taken steps to address the cases of political prisoners held in connection with Santa Cruz, restrained its forces in East Timor and "implemented stated plans to decrease the military presence . . ." Although the Clinton administration opposed this broad-ranging measure, Indonesia's friends were worried by Washington's renewed focus on East Timor. Australia's prime minister at the time, Paul Keating, went so far as to criticize Clinton and Congress for putting too much pressure on Indonesia. For Keating, who was quoted as saying that the "stability" of the Suharto regime was "the single most beneficial strategic development to have affected Australia and its region in the past thirty years," silence on human rights was best. But Clinton hardly needed advice from Keating: he already was beset on a number of fronts to back off from his administration's early stance on East Timor.

As it happened, the next foreign trip Bishop Belo made was to Australia, mainly to minister to the community of Timorese refugees there. On the second anniversary of the Santa Cruz massacre, Bishop Belo presided over a special Mass at Melbourne's Saint Patrick's Cathedral. "Think of the future and how to build a new generation—a future based on peace and justice and reconciliation," he told the mainly Timorese audience.

"The Timorese, they tell me, 'Bishop, it is very difficult to forgive those who killed my father, my son, my husband,' but above all we are Christians," the bishop told a journalist after the service. "I respect the dead and I pray for them and we pray this event will not happen again. But for me it is more important to put in the hearts of the young people that we must live in hope to become a new society."

In a sensitive article for *The Age,* a leading Australian paper, columnist Mark Baker noted that "It is clear that on this, one of his few visits abroad, Bishop Belo does not feel free to speak his mind. The Timorese-born bishop travels on an Indonesian passport and he is believed to have been threatened with expulsion. . . . But while choosing his words with great care, he speaks none the less. And what he says leaves no doubt that the situation in East Timor remains grim and volatile."

Belo spoke of his frustration in trying to promote negotiations. "I told the governor, I told the commander, please give the opportunity to have a dialogue. But . . . it is not a dialogue but only a monologue: they invite the young generation to accept the status quo."

Unlike on his visits to the U.S. and Canada, Belo did not meet with government officials in Australia ("It's a pity—they might learn a lot," Mark Baker wrote). It was said that the Australian Catholic Church, which sponsored the Belo visit, wanted to avoid an embarrassing situation for all concerned. But Cardinal Edward Clancy of Sydney called for a stronger stand on human rights by the Australian government. "It is time the Australian Church does something, because during the Second World War many Timorese died for the Australian people," Belo told a radio interviewer after he returned to Dili. "So now it is time to pay, to show the solidarity."

Meanwhile, most East Timorese could not find decent employment. At this very time four hundred young people were brought to Java by interests controlled by President Suharto's eldest daughter, Siti Hardiyanti Rukmana, known as Mbak (the Indonesian term for "elder sister") Tutut. The four hundred were promised training and good jobs, but when they arrived, they were given low-wage work in terrible conditions. "Many of the young East Timorese in Jakarta suffered like slaves," Bishop Belo wrote. "Two of them have died already. Others are being persecuted and beaten. It is great injustice and suffering."

In May 1994 the bishop gave a sharply worded press interview to the French Catholic newspaper, *La Croix*. "Integration with Indonesia is still a dead letter in the hearts of the people as long as the Government treats us as a conquered province," he stated forthrightly. There would be no solution so long as the East Timorese could not "express themselves freely about their own future."

When questioned on whether "it is realistic" to expect a referendum, Belo responded, "We are different from the Indonesians. Our history and our culture are not the same. Realism demands that the people of this island are given a voice. . . . To denounce injustice is also part of my duty as Bishop."

Bishop Belo said he sometimes felt "cheated, even furious, to see that the drama" of East Timor was forgotten. "High-ranking Church authorities" gave the "impression that they are more concerned about caring for the Indonesian Catholics" than supporting the Timorese. "I am not speaking about moral, spiritual, pastoral support, which is real. I am talking about active support, I mean political support." East Timor, the bishop said, remained "a taboo subject" for the Church.

Although Belo would not take sides among the parties in East Timor, he believed that making a general appeal for his people's basic rights was an entirely different matter. He felt it was the responsibility of the Church in Rome to defend the people, as well as his own.

Soon after, there were new insults to the Catholic Church in East Timor by the Indonesian military, which took the form of outright desecration when soldiers trampled on Communion wafers in a church in the town of Remexio, south of Dili, in late June 1994. The military commander apologized, but men identified as army intelligence agents made obscene comments to Timorese nuns at the local university the following month. Some saw these incidents as deliberate provocations designed to create unrest and therefore justify the military's presence to maintain order. The bishop himself believed that the religious incidents had been concocted by the military to misrepresent the nature of the conflict, which was mainly political, not religious, in nature. But whatever their source, such assaults on the religious feelings of most East Timorese made it seem as if their last redoubt of dignity was under attack. Enraged, Bishop Belo told the press that "East Timor is like hell. Christians are constantly being arrested, beaten, and intimidated by police."

He later described a typical incident, in which jailed youth were forced to swallow rosary beads: "They say to young people 'Go on, eat your God, so He can come and help you to escape from this prison and this torture. . . .' They come to me and say, 'Bishop, physical suffering does not matter. What is most painful is the enjoyment they get out of mocking our faith and our religious sentiment. . . .'"

Important voices in Congress were appalled by the religious incidents. Even senators who only a few weeks before had led an effort against a ban on arms to Indonesia did not contest action to send Jakarta a message. Around the same time the U.S. Catholic bishops issued a statement noting that the invasion of East Timor and subsequent policies had "been described by serious observers as nearly genocidal." The U.S. bishops called for "new initiatives" by the United States "to encourage both the resolution of the political crisis and full compliance on issues of human rights." (There were also statements by Jewish and Protestant groups and leaders such as Bishop Melvin Talbert of the United Methodist Church, who later became president of the National Council of Churches.) Bishop Belo distributed the U.S. Catholic bishops' statement throughout East Timor. Fearful of a stronger measure like the one organized by Senator Feingold the year before and prodded by Senator Patrick Leahy (Democrat of Vermont), chairman of an important foreign aid committee, the Clinton administration finally agreed in July 1994 to a ban on the sale to Indonesia of light arms and crowd control equipment that could be used for lethal purposes in places like East Timor.

Earlier in 1994, Belo pointed out that "the City of Dili is gradually becoming a Javanese City . . . waves of immigrants continue to occupy the southern coast's fertile lands." But there was fierce resistance to these encroachments, and the bishop knew that it was the young people who first and foremost were addressing the problem of self-determination, that it was they who were the most nonconformist. During civics class for lessons on the *Pancasila*—the five principles of Indonesia's state philosophy—they would defiantly raise questions such as this one: If the preamble of the Indonesian constitution says we must eradicate colonialism and neo-colonialism from the face of the earth, why does Indonesia not give freedom to East Timor? "Shut up and stay out of politics," their Indonesian teachers replied. This kind of effrontery was an unsettling challenge to their authority. But the students only became more determined to confront their Indonesian overlords.

"The young people involved in the events of the 12th of November at Santa Cruz are still being hunted down," Bishop Belo said. "It is unacceptable that the Timorese, the first owners of this land, are being progressively relegated to being second-class citizens. It is unacceptable that the Indonesian army and police continue to carry out raids and arbitrary arrests."

In early November 1994, Carlos Filipe Ximenes Belo called for the removal of Indonesian troops guarding the Santa Cruz cemetery. Their presence at the site, he stressed, "only creates anger and hatred among the people."

Far from being intimidated by the events of Santa Cruz and harsh repression in the wake of the capture of Xanana Gusmão, the youth movement in East Timor only became bolder. Soon there would be the first visit to Indonesia by a president of the United States since Ronald Reagan visited there in 1986. For the youth, it was an ideal opportunity to bring East Timor's story to the attention of the world. For Carlos Filipe Ximenes Belo, it would pose another difficult test of his ability to manage a highly volatile situation.

CHAPTER 8

"IF I HAVE TO GO TO HELL, I'LL GO TO HELL"

▨ ▨ ▨ ▨

L IKE THAT FATEFUL DAY of the bloodletting at the cemetery, Bishop Belo did not know that any action had been planned. But there was no reason why he should have been forewarned of what took place on November 12, 1994, because events had shifted from Dili to the American embassy in the Indonesian capital of Jakarta, 1,250 miles to the west. There, twenty-nine young East Timorese, many of them students, jumped out of taxis carrying banners and scampered over a seven-foot iron fence with sharp metal spikes on top. It was early morning, and they managed to carry this off while security was light. Chanting "Free East Timor!" the group occupied the parking lot of the embassy compound, where they set up a display of posters calling for an end to genocide in East Timor. One simply said, "We need freedom."

Some of the twenty-nine survived the carnage at Santa Cruz and had been in hiding since. Now they were staging a protest not only to mark the third anniversary of the massacre, but also to demand a full international investigation of the Santa Cruz affair. The East Timorese presented a well-worded, respectful letter addressed to President Clinton, and vowed to stay where they were until their demands were met. As if to signal their peaceful intentions, the twenty-nine gathered to say Catholic prayers as night fell on November 12.

The same day, demonstrations also broke out in Dili, sparked by the murder of an East Timorese, Mário Vicente, in the Becora marketplace. The Indonesian said to have committed the deed, from the island of Sulawesi, was one of many small traders who had come to make a living but ended up dominating Dili's markets. (At the top, Suharto and his associates developed a monopoly on East Timor's trade in timber, coffee, marble and other products.) Thousands took to the streets in a protest far more widespread than anything the town had seen since the Indonesians invaded. It was something that would have been unimaginable before the 1990s. Youngsters marched, and their elders, even old women and men banging pots and pans, joined in. Over the following days, Bishop Belo's struggle to deter violence would be tested on all sides.

"It was the first time that this happened—an uprising throughout the city, with everyone in the streets shouting that the Timorese are also a people, with their dignity," the bishop said at the time. "It means that the patience of the Timorese is running out. . . . People have to live, and their sense of survival outweighs the risks," Belo added. "The Timorese have no opportunity whatsoever in their own country because the structure is set up in such a way that they are becoming increasingly relegated to an inferior level."

The urgent need to win the world's attention was what drove the Timorese students to enter the United States embassy. They were a group of bright, active young men mainly in their twenties, with tastes in music and dress that were little different from those of their contemporaries in Western countries. Led by a polite, well-spoken student of English literature with a ready smile, thirty-year-old Domingos Sarmento Alves, they had planned carefully, even reading books on the cultural attitudes of American diplomats.

Most important, the action was timed to coincide with President Bill Clinton's visit to Indonesia for the Asia Pacific Economic Cooperation (APEC) summit meeting in Bogor, forty miles from Jakarta. APEC, dedicated to promoting trade, had grown to be a pet project of the Clinton administration and other regional powers; the location of the 1994 summit in Bogor was intended as a plum for the Suharto government, designed to showcase Indonesia's economic accomplishments and investment opportunities. Instead, the bold action by the East Timorese at the American embassy signified the return of the unwelcome ghosts of East Timor at the worst possible moment, from Jakarta's standpoint, when the largest group of foreign leaders and media representatives in history was visiting Indonesia.

The Timorese in the embassy called for the release of Xanana Gusmão and other political detainees, and requested that the United States act as a mediator between Indonesia and the Timorese resistance. They also asked for a meeting with President Clinton or Secretary of State Warren Christopher. Although neither set of demands was granted, their plea—that the world pay attention to the East Timor tragedy—was treated with respect by the vast majority of international news media. Television beamed horrific images of the Santa Cruz massacre throughout the globe as background to the current crisis. The embassy protest highlighted the continuing effects of Santa Cruz, including the plight of the families of prisoners as well as the families of those who had "disappeared."

For several days, the East Timorese at the U.S. embassy received more international media attention than Santa Cruz had received when it first happened: the presence of President Clinton and other leaders put East Timor at center stage. There were reports on television on numerous occasions—CNN ran updates almost every half hour for the four days Clinton was in Indonesia. As the London *Economist* put it, "The demonstrations, both in Dili and Jakarta, served their purpose. International television coverage of the summit was juxtaposed with pictures from East Timor and the American embassy compound."

Editorials in the *New York Times,* the *Washington Post,* the *Boston Globe, USA Today,* the *Times* of London, and the *Globe and Mail* (Canada) gave serious attention to the East Timor problems during the embassy crisis. The *Wall Street Journal* questioned whether continuing Indonesian rule in East Timor was worth Jakarta's while. Many called on governments to protect the embassy protesters and their compatriots in Dili. Judging from the tone of the editorial coverage, the fence-jumping initiative of the young people had struck a chord in the American psyche, and their point had been made forcefully, well beyond the United States.

The scenes of the young people in the embassy had overtones of the Chinese democracy movement in Tiananmen Square before the bloody crackdown five years before. But with the world's major news organizations so heavily focused on Jakarta during the APEC meeting, it would have been a public relations nightmare for the Suharto regime had the embassy standoff ended violently, and the United States certainly was conveying that message. Nonetheless, the situation unfolding within East Timor itself was far more dangerous.

Bishop Belo had been apprehensive all along. In some places in Dili, it seemed as if pandemonium had broken loose, but much of this atmosphere had been created by agents provocateurs working for Indonesian military authorities. A feeling of menace was unmistakable. Clinton and other foreign leaders had left Indonesia once the APEC meeting ended on November 16, and with them, CNN and most others moved elsewhere. Journalists were in Dili, too, but they were far less numerous, and were there on only a short-term basis. Soon the press would leave, and with them whatever protection they provided. Demonstrations within East Timor were easy prey. With few foreign witnesses on hand, the potential for bloodshed in East Timor at that juncture was apparent.

To the bishop, conditions seemed ripe for a violent confrontation. The whole chain of events in connection with the U.S. embassy and the demonstrations in Dili had greatly embarrassed President Suharto and his regime. Right before the eyes of the world, twenty-nine young men had made the Indonesian Armed Forces look impotent or incompetent. Before it was over, another general, the commander of the Jakarta Metropolitan Region, would be fired. A desire for retribution was in the air. Now, on November 18, in Dili itself, another group of demonstrators was planning another action in solidarity with their compatriots who remained in the American embassy.

Bishop Belo was in the middle of teaching a five-day training course for priests; that day there was a discussion on "models of the Church." A memorial Mass was to be held at Dili Cathedral in the late afternoon to honor the foreign missionaries who had served in East Timor. But at 10:00 A.M., a local official came to see Bishop Belo at the request of the military commander to tell him a demonstration was planned at the cathedral to coincide with the Mass.

The bishop was worried and more than a little suspicious upon hearing this. He interrupted the course he was giving to the priests and asked them if they would agree to have the Mass changed to another day: Belo's idea of "models of the Church" did not include allowing demonstrators to utilize Mass for their own purposes. That aside, it was clear that Dili was in an explosive mood. A United Nations specialist, Bacre Waly Ndiaye of Senegal, had recently concluded that the conditions that produced the bloodshed at Santa Cruz were still present. Belo, of course, did not need a voluminous report to know that another massacre could happen at any time.

The bishop knew that people had legitimate grievances, but in his eyes another confrontation would do little to improve their lot. Although some of the priests objected, the bishop shifted the date for the Mass to December 7.

Although the Mass for that afternoon had been canceled, many came to the cathedral anyway, young people chief among them. Some left when they saw what was going on, with the area encircled by police, military vehicles, and Intel people. Soon tear gas began wafting through the air. A demonstration by several hundred young East Timorese began as they pulled out banners at a prearranged signal, calling for independence and the release of Xanana Gusmão. It was just the kind of action Belo had hoped to avoid.

Still, the demonstration at the cathedral was peaceful until government agents threw a volley of large rocks. "This," the BBC's Philip Short reported, "was the provocation which turned the whole thing violent." The Indonesian military seemed to be trying to start a mêlée that would give security forces and troops a pretext to attack. Riot police hovered nearby. More tear gas was being fired at the demonstrators every moment. Reporters on the scene called it the worst trouble in the streets of Dili since Santa Cruz: in some ways the scene at the cathedral was a carbon copy of what had preceded the carnage at the cemetery.

"The potential for violence was shown graphically," the BBC continued, "by what happened to a Timorese bystander," a young man who helped a German TV crew back to their hotel as they were caught in the midst of the stone throwing at the cathedral. Philip Short provided an eyewitness description of what happened next: "Fearing that the police might have seen him with them and that he'd later be accused of having been a demonstrator himself, he asked the Germans to go with him to a police post so he could explain what had happened. When they arrived, special unit officers set on him and beat him so severely that half his face became an unrecognizable mass of bruises. . . . For some hours afterward, no local doctor would come to treat him because they were too frightened of being involved.

"They thrashed the living daylights out of him—he owes his life to the German crew, who seized him and dragged him away from the police as they were beating him. . . . Now, if the Indonesians mete out that kind of violence to people who were not involved in the demonstration, one can only too readily imagine what they do to people who were."

The young man's battered face was later shown by the BBC to a worldwide audience. Further bloodshed seemed certain, as the standoff at Dili Cathedral continued for two hours. It showed every sign of spinning out of control, as more and more rocks were hurled by the Indonesians in plainclothes and the Timorese demonstrators scattered. The protesters were trapped. Some hurried inside the cathedral to escape the rocks, where they sang and prayed.

The military commander, Colonel Kiki Syanakri and Father José António da Costa, the parish priest for the cathedral and vicar general of the diocese, were trying to break the deadlock, without success.

The scene illustrated the paradoxes of East Timor in the mid-1990s. While there were still grim brutalities, and some experts did not believe that the reprimands and investigations had a major effect on ABRI's behavior, some Indonesian military commanders seemed to be more careful than before Santa Cruz, at least where outside observers might be present. In some instances, though by no means all, there was a greater degree of fear among military commanders of damaging their careers by being connected with human rights violations, though various experts on international human rights questioned the extent to which lower-ranking officers and troops shared these concerns. Nonetheless, as illustrated at the cathedral in Dili on November 18, 1994, there was also some worry about arousing international interest, already at a high level because of the Clinton visit and the action at the U.S. embassy.

At 5:00 P.M. aF priest came to Bishop Belo's residence to ask him to talk to the young people. In fact, the two opposing sides had asked for the bishop to mediate between them. While some of the military people saw Bishop Belo as an adversary, others genuinely respected him. Regardless, when things threatened to get out of hand, they would call the bishop. Whether he liked it or not, he was compelled to respond, because the lives of others were in his hands. Belo interrupted his work and hurried to the cathedral.

Belo would deal with the Indonesian military and the Timorese youth in his own way. The Santa Cruz events had had a profound effect on his own psyche; he remained haunted by the thought that he might have been able to stop the confrontation had he known about it in time. Now, three years later, he was determined to avoid a repetition.

In the blazing heat, made even more wilting by the tear gas that filled the square by the cathedral, Bishop Belo walked to the center of a group of furious military and police commanders.

The majority of young people did not want to surrender. As a foreign eyewitness observed, Belo kept a certain distance from the Timorese youth, who had the kind of respect for the bishop that did not permit any kind of familiarity. In fact, in this setting, he did not appear to be particularly sympathetic to the young. The bishop would protect them without giving vent to his emotions. Belo might have wanted to chastise them, but that was for another time.

Large numbers of riot police seemed to be everywhere, with batons, shields, and heavy helmets, backed up by army troops. The bishop was accustomed to these displays of overwhelming force.

"These security disturbers have to come with us," a military commander told the bishop. He demanded that the young people be taken for interrogation. Belo would not allow this.

"You called me here," Belo said firmly to the military and police commanders, "and I say that nothing should happen to these young people. Take your troops and police from the area, and I'll find a solution."

"These hooligans are stupid and shameless and can only live by hiding behind the skirts of the bishop and the priests," a commander screamed.

"Everyone must leave the area," the bishop replied quietly to the Indonesian commanders. "Then there can be peace."

Then the bishop spoke to the young people. "I ask you to go back home. In the end you will only be the victims. You are ignorant and stupid! You only cause trouble, using the cathedral for your political purposes!" Belo told them forcefully.

They sat down and hung their heads. Still, the standoff continued. The military would not compromise.

"I grew tired of arguing back and forth with the military at the cathedral," the bishop recalled, "so I sat myself down in a bus between the two sides, folded the arms of my black suit, and just stayed there and refused to budge until the demonstrators were allowed to go home without threat of police reprisals."

Belo's demands were simple: to the military and police, no retribution against the demonstrators. To the demonstrators, go home, call off the protest, and stop using the Church for political purposes. He knew that if the protesters left with the security forces, torture was a near certainty. What had happened the year before during the visit of the American congressional staff? And it could easily be death for at least some of them, like after Santa Cruz. Back then, the International Committee of the Red Cross representatives in Dili had not been allowed to help, but now the bishop insisted that they be permitted to escort the young people home. He could accept nothing less than an absolute guarantee of their safety.

Neither side was satisfied with what Belo was asking of them, but in the end they granted the bishop's wishes: at his request, the military called for two buses. The bishop sent a priest in each of them. He used his own minivan as well, with António as driver. Together, they took the four hundred young protestors back to their homes. At Bishop Belo's behest, they put their banners away. Back in their neighborhoods, they rejoiced over their narrow escape. It would not be the last brush with disaster. But for now, the confrontation at the cathedral in Dili on November 18, 1994, was over.

Bishop Belo then went home himself. The German TV journalists were waiting to ask him to visit the young man whose face had been battered. He had been brought to the Hotel Turismo nearby. Lying on a bed, his head was completely swollen. When he saw the bishop, he made the salute of the

Catholic Boy Scouts, of which he was a member. The bishop returned the salute. These are the brutalities the Indonesian military are capable of, Belo thought. This is just what might have happened to the others.

Despite his ability to pacify the situation, complaints about the bishop surfaced that very day. Some believed the Mass should have been allowed to go forward. Belo would have none of it. "The Church is not here to be a political instrument or to be politicized," he declared. "The Church is here to carry out its mission as intermediary. It is here with everyone, and for everyone." He was always prepared to assist those in trouble, Belo stressed, but he would not allow the Church to be used for propaganda purposes.

As he returned to his residence that day, he reflected on the near disaster at the cathedral. Who could say what would happen next? He would do his best to restore calm, but would the Indonesian security forces attack the young people once the journalists were gone? In a place like East Timor, one could never know. His appeals for restraint were not enough. He had done what he could to calm his parishioners, issuing pastoral letters, giving sermons, and still the young people would be beaten. Authoritative diplomatic sources said that, in the absence of growing international pressure, Indonesian forces would have simply killed all of the young protesters of East Timor, as they had killed so many of their elders. But as vital as this international restraint was, it could not resolve the underlying crisis.

The world needed to hear what the real problem was, even if Belo had to walk a tightrope to do it: powerful people in Jakarta would be upset, they would put pressure on the papal nuncio there to discipline him, but he could not be silent. In an interview published on November 22, 1994, in the *New York Times,* he spoke of arrests and beatings of protesters and said, "It was an act of courage for East Timorese people to speak up." He emphasized that the solution would be a vote on independence. President Clinton, who had told President Suharto in a meeting the previous week that the people of East Timor should have more control over their own affairs, did not go far enough, Belo said. "He should be more direct," the bishop told the *Times.* "He should say they should withdraw from East Timor."

One problem was that Clinton's visit had sent a variety of signals. He reportedly expressed concern about East Timor in his meeting with Suharto, after being besieged with questions by reporters. But Clinton left public statements to his secretary of state, who said that the American relationship with Indonesia could never reach "its highest level if the people of the United States don't have confidence that there is an effort here to respect the human rights of all the citizens." It was hard to know what that statement really meant: Clinton refused to meet with human rights groups in Indonesia, while stressing the importance of commercial ties; tens of billions of dollars in contracts were signed with American businesses during the visit. Another element, less visible at the time, was that a group of old friends from Arkansas had been brought to Jakarta for the occasion by an Indonesian businessman named James Riady, who had gotten to know the Clintons while living for a number of years in Little Rock.

The same day the interview with the bishop was published in the *New York Times,* an agreement was reached for a peaceful conclusion to the action at the American embassy. The Indonesian regime allowed the twenty-nine Timorese safe conduct out of the country on November 24, 1994, when they flew to Portugal. Emotional photos of the arrival of the young people in Lisbon captured their deliverance from a difficult ordeal.

As for the young people at the cathedral, they may have been rescued on November 18, 1994—unlike previous occasions, there were no obvious reprisals this time—but it did not end there. On a pastoral visit to the countryside that Christmas Eve, the bishop went to inaugurate a new chapel in the town of Atsabe: even in this tiny place the young used the occasion to express their feelings, crying, "*Viva* Timor Leste! *Viva* Xanana Gusmão!"

"It shows how profoundly they live the political problems of East Timor," said the bishop. "These young people lost their parents, so many of whom died in places like Matebian. Today they live in a difficult situation and I understand very well why sometimes they carry out demonstrations against Indonesia, because they lost their parents and families."

"There is a lot of suffering, a lot of pain," lamented the bishop in 1994. "I am deeply distressed when young people are taken away, interrogated, tortured. Their courage and strength to resist impresses me. They tell me, 'It matters not that we suffer and die. This is our country.'"

The bishop understood the problem in a direct way. For more than ten years, he had opened his residence to a group of orphans, ensuring that they received proper care and education. Though they were sprightly fellows who showed all the resilience of youth, they also represented a tragic cross section of East Timor since 1975. Belo regarded them as part of his family.

"I try to be their older brother and help compensate for the loss of their parents," he told a visitor in 1995. Indeed, it would be little exaggeration to say that Bishop Carlos Filipe Ximenes Belo had been trying to compensate for the loss of thousands of parents since he returned to East Timor in 1981.

Of the orphans living in his home, António was special. In fact, António was like a younger brother, but of an unusual sort. He had learned to use his wits from the time he was very small, well before Bishop Belo first met him on Ataúro island, and he had developed sharper instincts than people twice or three times his age. So he became a mixture of sibling and lieutenant. And like many junior officers of the best sort, while António was obedient to the chain of command, he was not uncritical of his superiors—if not openly, at least in his own mind.

António and his cohorts were certainly capable of an occasional snicker when the bishop was in one of his bad moods, and like other assistants to important people, they knew when to approach their boss and when to wait until later. António and the other young men in the bishop's compound were helpers with keen intelligence, and carried their own weight.

The young men did so in ways that were crucial for their community. António and the others had seen their fathers disappear. The danger of confrontation with the Indonesian military was something they did not need to be taught. Thus, when things got rough Belo was not alone. If the young people in Dili or elsewhere were engaged in a standoff with the authorities, which was happening more and more, the orphans around the bishop could serve as informal intermediaries and, at times, sources of information and wisdom.

But no matter how much Belo did, the future looked more and more bleak to many of the youth of East Timor. It was inevitable that there would be persistent grumbling, before and after the confrontation at the cathedral. Why had the bishop acted as he did? Why was he not at one with their aims? Indeed, why did he even seem to oppose them?

"Sometimes as bishop I have to use ugly words because it is much more important to me that they will not suffer, will not be beaten, not be tortured, and not be killed, because my conviction is that if the youth of East Timor disappears then tomorrow we have no people to build East Timor" was Belo's answer. He was aware of an implacable reality: much of his own generation, people who would now be in their forties, had perished over the previous two decades.

The reality few recognized was that Belo was on the horns of a dilemma more complicated than most anyone could imagine. He was beset by all sides, forced to maintain a balance between irreconcilable interests. Belo had few allies—almost no one, in fact—who accepted his independence, or were even willing to understand its necessity. Almost everyone wanted to enlist him for their cause, and were deeply offended when he rejected their overtures. It was a measure of the respect he commanded that a wide spectrum of people—the military, politicians of many stripes, businessmen, foreign embassies—used his name, almost always without his consent, to endorse their own positions. No matter what he did, someone blamed him. No matter how he tried to accommodate them, they wanted more.

His unwillingness to follow anyone's line made for a kind of prickliness that grated on some people's nerves: most would prefer to do without complications, and Belo was anything but simple. People would complain about this, and, irritated, he would answer, "Why must I be predictable?"

The bishop had to deal with myriad forces that would have long before exhausted a lesser individual. He had to contend with the Indonesian military and a welter of government factions and agents, sometimes working at cross purposes: all of them wanted Belo to facilitate acceptance of Indonesian rule, something that he could not and would not do. There were the papal diplomats and foreign policy makers in the Vatican, who wanted an absence of conflict with Indonesia on matters relating to East Timor, refusing to accept that this was impossible for the bishop to provide. Then there were his own Timorese clergy, who often expected far more than any bishop could do under the circumstances. There were the young people, who also exaggerated the bishop's influence and power. Finally, there was the armed resistance, which more than once was furious at him.

Though Belo made no secret of his independence, the organized resistance to Indonesian rule in East Timor complained that they could not rely on him: "The only consistent thing about Bishop Belo," a leading guerrilla commander once griped, "is his inconsistency." Some accused him of being "soft" on the Indonesians.

"I accept their criticism," he said with a laugh in an interview with the Portuguese newspaper *Público*, in the period when he rescued the situation at Dili Cathedral. "Let them come and take my place. Let another, harder bishop come and take my place."

For years the threat of removal from his post as bishop of the Diocese of Dili by the Vatican had been a sword of Damocles looming over the head of Carlos Filipe Ximenes Belo. There was persistent talk that a new diocese would be created in Belo's hometown of Baucau, to which he would be shifted—that is, demoted. Although they had already seen Dom Martinho removed, many in East Timor and elsewhere judged Belo's behavior, inexplicably, as if the precariousness of his position were not a factor. Many of his own clergy in East Timor second-guessed him, from both radical and conservative points of view.

On top of this, he was deprived of normal family contact, and all of this made for a lonely life. But if that is what it was, he could stand it. Belo's task was to resist the blandishments of the opposing sides, to rise above his personal pain. In his own nonviolent way, he was like a warrior. But his task was far more difficult than simply leading the troops into battle with traditional swords: armed combat was straightforward by comparison. In many ways, he was quite alone, and he knew it.

Belo's troubles were made even more difficult by some basic facts and figures. Of more than 900 million Catholics worldwide, only about 100 million lived in Asia—all told, only three percent of Asia's population; half of those were in the Philippines. Christianity in general was seen as a Western implant in Asia, making matters all the more delicate. Indonesia was one of the leading countries in the region and evangelization in Asia was seen as "the principal object for the mission of the new millennium," in the words of a leading Vatican official. By comparison, tiny East Timor had little to offer.

Around the time of the standoff at the cathedral, Bishop Belo's frustration was evident on this point: "The human person is more important than numbers," he offered, when pressed on his relations with the Vatican. But, Belo added, with a touch of deep sadness, "Even though we are few, over the years we have all contributed towards a Church which is on the side of the poor and the oppressed, which the Indonesian Catholic Church has not done because, just like the times of Fascism in Portugal, it is a Church that collaborates with the authorities. Only a democratic revolution will change things."

Still, the more the world learned, the more international scrutiny East Timor attracted. "The dead are beginning to be noticed," he said hopefully.

"They [the Indonesian military] see me as an enemy. They say that it is I who am holding back the integration process, and there are rumors and even governmental meetings about sending me away from here," Belo stressed.

"They could replace the bishop, as they did Monsignor Lopes. Anything is possible. Unfortunately, politics and diplomacy enter into religious affairs, and sometimes carry more weight, and bishops are changed according to the wishes of the powers that be, he said with a hint of bitterness."

Carlos Filipe Ximenes Belo concluded, with irony: ". . . I am waiting. If they send me to Africa, I shall go to Africa. If I have to go to hell, then I'll go to hell. My duty is obedience."

A name grew up around this stubborn bishop who refused to be pressured by any side: cabeça dura, local argot for "hard head." In Indonesian they say "keras-kepala," which means "obstinate" or "mulish," that Belo's head is like a stone, that he will not allow himself to be used.

"*Keras-Kepala* is what the Indonesians say because they say I don't speak with them, they say I don't have dialogue with the authorities. When they have celebrations, for Christmas, for instance, I do not participate, or when they invite me to ceremonies marking the seventeenth of July, the Day of Integration, or the seventeenth of August, Independence Day, or the fifth of October, Armed Forces Day, I am never there, I do not attend. So they say I'm not collaborationist . . . they say that I talk a lot of politics, I am *cabeça dura,* but not only that, sometimes they say I'm a Communist, I'm Red; others call me up on the telephone and call me pig, traitor. I get everything, I must have patience!"

Belo, of course, was all too anxious to have dialogue: his complaint was that the military authorities only wanted a monologue. "The government understood the message, but it will not sit down at the table to talk to the people because it is an arrogant, dictatorial government, and only they can be right. As long as there is no democratic spirit in the military ranks, nothing will ever be achieved," he stated boldly in his interview with *Público.*

Bishop Belo had reached such a point of exasperation after more than ten years of informing the government of his views. The military would let him speak, but most often, they would turn a deaf ear. And for all the talk of wanting Belo at celebrations, he even had to watch the food that was delivered to his house, like the cake a jittery woman brought to his residence some years before, which killed the dog that ate it.

If Belo could be described as *keras-kepala,* it was partly because he persisted in pressing his case. Two weeks after the cathedral standoff, evidently as a result of international pressure, the bishop was invited for the first time to address hundreds of newly commissioned Indonesian police in Dili. Like other Third World police forces, they had become good customers for the latest riot equipment. "East Timor does not need modern technology, but humanitarianism," Belo told them.

Within days of his appearance at the police meeting, the BBC reported severe ill-treatment of people taken into custody during the unrest in November. Soon, Bishop Belo was mediating in the streets once more, this time in his childhood city of Baucau, where the marketplace was burned by local youths on New Year's Day 1995 after an Indonesian immigrant killed an East Timorese man. The bishop would cool the situation temporarily, but the marketplace, the same place where he had sold fruits and vegetables as a boy, would remain a hot spot.

A small, symbolic fact helped explain why the marketplace was a target of frustration. Timorese officials prominent in the local administration in the region had tried for years to convince the Indonesian government to build a few short miles of road so that the excellent local rice and produce from particularly fertile areas could be brought to the Baucau town market. But despite their repeated efforts to achieve this modest goal, the requested roads had never been built, and the Baucau market instead sold vegetables and rice imported from the western part of the island—that is, the Indonesian side—hundreds of miles away.

Several months later, back in Dili, a new challenge emerged for the bishop. Roaming gangs of masked thugs terrorized neighborhoods in Dili and other towns at night, beating suspected opponents of the government, who in turn organized themselves in vigilante groups to fight back. The gangs were called "ninjas," and Belo believed the military was behind this new phenomenon. President Suharto's son-in-law, Prabowo Subianto, by now a Major General, was said to be a key actor in the creation of the "ninjas," whose activities were aimed at the main threat to Indonesian control of East Timor by that time, the young demonstrators in the urban centers. That threat was made only too clear after the near-uprising in Dili at the time of the Clinton visit to Indonesia.

The bishop held a meeting of the military and police at his home to craft an agreement to end this new round of violence. Meanwhile, the Church called on the population "to create a climate of peace." At a Sunday Mass, Belo appealed for calm and asked the Timorese not to take justice into their own hands.

Despite criticism of the bishop on various fronts, it was clear that he had the support of the East Timorese people. They saw Belo as their defender—as he put it, "the voice of the voiceless," a phrase first used to describe Archbishop Romero. It was his combination of moral and spiritual authority, toughness and humor, that enabled Carlos Filipe Ximenes Belo to help bring representatives of all East Timorese groups together in 1995 for the first time since the Indonesian invasion. Paradoxically, the meeting stemmed from an Indonesian effort to undermine United Nations diplomacy, which, although it had shown limited effect, had at least kept East Timor alive as an international issue. With the back-room sponsorship of President Suharto's eldest daughter, a small group of Timorese politicians convened meetings in London and elsewhere, dubbed "reconciliation talks." But Bishop Belo refused to recognize the legitimacy of these gatherings unless the United Nations had a role and the meetings were made broadly representative: why, Belo asked one of the organizers, are you going to luxurious hotels in London to seek reconciliation, while excluding major East Timorese groups? The result was that, finally, a compromise was reached, in which a series of meetings called the All-Inclusive East Timorese Dialogue was held in Austria beginning in June 1995.

Before that, Bishop Belo paid his first visit to Portugal in five years, to attend ceremonies marking the one hundredth anniversary of the Salesian order there. It was an emotional return. On a pilgrimage to Fatima in May, where tens of thousands participated in a procession, he was treated like a hero, amid news reports raising the possibility of a Nobel Peace Prize. Surrounded by friends in the Salesian community, he clearly felt at home, with hundreds of priests, nuns and laypeople there to wish him well. There was a gathering sense of excitement. Timorese refugees greeted the bishop with thunderous chants: *"Belo, amigo, o povo está contigo!"* ("Belo, friend, the people are with you!")

The bishop's increasing popularity and ability to unify widely disparate groups was in evidence at the Austrian meeting in early June. Representatives of the resistance were there, as were Timorese allies of the Indonesian government—or, at least, some who had been well paid by Jakarta—as well as independent participants. There were also people with ties to both sides, one of whom commented: "The room suddenly fell silent as soon as Bishop Belo spoke. . . . People were so strongly attentive that one of the participants remarked to me, 'Man, every time the bishop speaks, everybody sits with their mouths open, taking in every bit of what he is talking about.' Sometimes people disagreed with what he said but they would say so respectfully. I think our interaction with the Bishop was very healing.

"The role of Bishop Belo was the most determining one. After UN officials opened the meeting, participants did not know where to begin because it was the first time the main protagonists had met after a fierce battle. They looked at each other nervously and suspiciously."

But the bishop asked the group to pray together and rise above their past differences. He stood above politics. They knew it, and responded to his entreaties. No matter what divided them, they remained Timorese first and foremost: even those with high positions in the Indonesian government could never be secure, with their family members always facing an inescapable atmosphere of violence. So the group, including one current and one past governor, unanimously adopted a declaration on human rights, culture, and other matters affecting life in East Timor. More than that, there was a real sense of enthusiasm over the meeting.

"Belo managed to win the respect of all sides," said one independent expert. "He had the effect of creating a positive and constructive atmosphere. He had a moderating influence both during the meeting and in the months before."

It became more evident than ever that Carlos Filipe Ximenes Belo, though not a political leader, was East Timor's most broadly acceptable public figure in the global arena. The Suharto regime was thoroughly alarmed at the bishop's unifying role, both at home and abroad. It was perhaps for this reason that the authorities would not allow him to visit Xanana Gusmão in prison; he had asked that the bishop hear his confession. The bishop's message, that Xanana should renounce armed struggle in favor of dialogue with the occupiers, was deeply threatening to Jakarta: Indonesia could cope with military challenges, but its moral arguments were flimsy, and Belo's growing prestige only underscored this vulnerability. It would be far easier to diminish the East Timor issue if Belo were out of the way. There were signs that the regime was redoubling its efforts to discredit him and have him removed. It became urgent that Bishop Belo gain increased international support.

As the talks in Austria ended, Bishop Belo flew to Washington to address the international policy committee of the U.S. Catholic Bishops, reminding them of the harsh conditions East Timor faced. "To cope with this tragedy, a sense of history is vital. We draw inspiration from the perseverance of our predecessors who defended the faith under harsh circumstances of foreign occupation in places such as Ireland and Poland"— nations, of course, where many of Belo's American colleagues had roots. After meeting the bishops at their headquarters near Catholic University, he spent time in prayer at the National Shrine of the Immaculate Conception. Belo was also able to renew contacts made in Washington on his first visit.

The bishop went to New York, where, very briefly at least, anonymity coupled with the vibrance of Manhattan provided a tonic for him. Belo's main business was at the United Nations, to which he had written six years before asking for help that remained elusive, despite the best efforts of certain officials there. Only in 1994 did he receive a reply: "The United Nations is committed," wrote UN Secretary General Boutros Boutros Ghali, "to make every effort for a final, just, comprehensive and internationally acceptable solution." The bishop was not impressed. "At least," he said dryly, "after five years I got a reply."

Belo was not any more impressed once he finally had the chance to meet the secretary general, who seemed keen to distance himself from the East Timor question. He said that the United Nations was counting on Belo; "You are the man on the ground," Boutros Ghali told him, as if that gave the bishop the power to negotiate a solution to the conflict.

Belo was skeptical of the secretary general's grand talk. "Why are they giving me all the responsibility?" the bishop said later. The answer may have been that Boutros Ghali was then running for reelection to his post and needed Indonesia's goodwill: the East Timor issue would not advance his ambitions. In fact, Boutros Ghali's own staff privately spoke of his lack of interest in the question.

Certainly the security of the UN secretary general's office left something to be desired: though the meeting with Belo was private and unannounced, somehow word had spread. Two Indonesian officials were waiting for the bishop when he left the meeting, anxious to know what had been discussed. It was almost like home.

Between his visits to Washington and New York, the bishop traveled to Rhode Island for a reunion with his old teachers. Not only did he see Father Cardoso, his mathematics instructor at Dare, but the bishop also paid a visit to Father Jacinto Campos, whose car Belo had chased in Quelicai as a boy of seven in his desperate plea to return to his mother in Baucau. Forty years had elapsed since that fateful encounter, which resulted in the future bishop's attending school, and may well have altered the history of East Timor beyond recognition. Father Campos beamed as he looked at his former charge in a sitting room at the Church of the Holy Rosary in the city of Providence. The visit was well timed, for Father Campos died only a few months later.

During those weeks Bishop Belo reflected on his life after twelve years as apostolic administrator of the Diocese of Dili. Throughout that time he had taken no vacation. From nearly the break of dawn, announced by East Timor's omnipresent roosters, the bishop would plunge into one activity after another, beginning with 6:00 A.M. Mass and only ending at nine o'clock, even later if there was trouble; often, there would be little respite from sunrise until past midnight. Belo took this in stride. It was, he noted, as Don Bosco once said: "This lifetime is for work, we will rest in the hereafter."

But the pressure had taken its toll. Despite the success of the meeting in Austria and the talk of the possibility of a Nobel Peace Prize, as Belo traveled from Rhode Island through Connecticut on a Saturday in June 1995, he was considering resigning his post.

A few weeks earlier in Lisbon, the bishop told journalist Max Stahl, who had captured the Santa Cruz massacre on film and now was interviewing Belo for a documentary on his life, that "I am ready to be removed. . . ." After Lisbon, Belo traveled to Rome, only to be disheartened by his meetings with the Vatican bureaucracy. It was his first *Ad limina,* or five-yearly visit, since 1990. Once again, the pope was kind to him: John Paul II apparently made a point of stressing that he had "retained active interest" in the fate of East Timor to papal biographer Tad Szulc and others. But Belo's contacts with the Secretariat of State were still difficult: however much he was applauded elsewhere, such was not the case in certain quarters in Vatican City.

As someone who had followed the rules of his faith since his mother awakened him as a little boy at 4:00 A.M. for Mass, the bishop was dumbfounded by suggestions that he had somehow deviated from the proper religious path. To Belo, his situation was unique: as he had told the American Catholic Bishops, "There is probably no diocese on earth that has seen a third or more of its people perish." It came down to what Dom Martinho had said in frustration many years before: it was politics, pure and simple.

One week after traveling through the Connecticut countryside with thoughts of resignation, he crossed the Atlantic. Bishop Belo arrived in Brussels on a brilliant Saturday afternoon. It was the bishop's first trip to Belgium, and he was having lunch in a restaurant corridor behind the Grand Place, the ornate, gilt-covered medieval town hall in the center of the city. The restaurant was packed with diners amid a stunning array of fish and seafood, as were all the other establishments nearby. It seemed difficult to find an empty space anywhere. The people were not only in the restaurants. The meal finished, Bishop Belo walked through various parts of the city center. He moved quickly from place to place, shaking his head in disbelief at the crowds.

That night, the bishop proceeded to the Church of Saint Joseph for Mass. On a Saturday evening, there were scarcely twenty-five people in the large, elegant neighborhood church: all but two were elderly women. One was a crippled youth, the other a young man from Africa. Afterward, Belo shook hands with the priest and the congregants. He stepped into the street. Even in the rain, hundreds of people milled about a flea market of no special charm. The bishop simply could not comprehend why there were so many people in restaurants, shops, and street markets, and yet, amid all that prosperity, there were so few in church. It was not only Belgium: one could see the same in all too many places in Europe, the United States, and Australia. The following Sunday, in France, he found the main church in one town was shuttered at an hour when thousands would have been present at his church and dozens of others in East Timor.

To be sure, the bishop was grateful for the hospitality he was receiving from the Belgian Catholic aid agencies who invited him, Broederlijk Delen from the Flemish-speaking community and Entraide et Fraternité from the French-speaking segment of the nation. The next day there was a pleasant visit to the cardinal of Belgium, Godfried Daneels, a well-respected moderate. In France the following week, his hosts were the Catholic Justice and Peace Commission and the French Catholic Committee against Hunger and for Development. These agencies and others like them were the most reliable international supporters of East Timor over the past two decades. The bishop knew that solidarity from groups like these helped lighten the immense burden of poverty in nations throughout the world.

In some ways, Belo's lack of comprehension was mutual. Some in the richer nations saw only the suffering, poverty, and injustice in East Timor, never stopping to wonder—and it was a matter of wonder—how Bishop Belo and his parishioners had managed to sustain their spirits through more than two decades of horror.

Traveling in East Timor, with or without the bishop, one saw this great spirituality immediately, as Pope John Paul II made clear after his visit. Churches are filled to capacity, with people of all ages, especially the young, overflowing into the street.

The pride and self-confidence of Carlos Filipe Ximenes Belo would show after seeing churches in the wealthier countries with few worshipers. "Our churches are full," he said with the triumphal air of a rich man. "There are many thousands of children and young people at services. There are more vocations for the priesthood than we can manage."

Bishop Belo's focus on the spiritual development of East Timor's people, especially the youth, and his disdain for the excesses of consumerism matched the emphasis of Pope John Paul II on these matters. His ministry was doing precisely what the pope recommended for the rich countries, which nonetheless went their own way. Was it that people now worshiped at the altar of material objects? In East Timor, people had almost nothing in terms of worldly goods, but spiritually they were at one with their Church. Still, bureaucrats in the Vatican, some from the very nations where churches were increasingly empty, would say that the bishop should stick to his pastoral work. It rankled.

To be sure, it was not the same everywhere he went: some church services in the countries he visited were well attended. There was the splendor of the world-renowned Cathedral of Notre Dame in Paris, where Cardinal Jean-Marie Lustiger invited Bishop Belo not only to concelebrate Mass on a Sunday evening, but also translated Belo's words from English into French before thousands of people in that ancient cathedral, a magnet for pilgrims from around the world. Belo was impressed by the service and touched by the warmth and the personal history of the cardinal: born Jewish, Aaron Lustiger was hidden by Catholic priests during World War II. The protection he received saved Lustiger, who converted to Catholicism at the age of sixteen; his mother perished at Auschwitz. He went on to become a favorite of Pope John Paul II, a member of the French Academy, and, interestingly, a leading Catholic prelate who also continued to regard himself as a Jew.

Saint Patrick's Cathedral in New York had its own flavor. It was packed with worshipers when Bishop Belo quietly visited there on a Catholic holiday in June 1995. Cardinal O'Connor was in Chicago at the time, so Belo only wanted to pray by himself in the crypt.

"Where are your papers?" demanded an attendant, as if the bishop might be a thief. Belo showed his passport, and was admitted to the inner sanctum with a profuse apology. It was just like New York—initially suspicious, then friendly, once one's bona fides were established, but for Belo it was a very strange world. Saint Patrick's had been the victim of a gunman weeks before who held up two priests and made off with the collections. In New York, one never knew who might be a thief or an assailant, and the staff was edgy. In East Timor, there was politically motivated violence, but a strong-arm robbery of a church was unthinkable. Belo could not understand it, and again, this state of affairs made him feel rich.

Belo's experience at Saint Patrick's was amusing to his host in Germany, Bishop Walter Kasper of Rottenberg. Kasper, a noted theologian and head of his church's overseas charity, Misereor, once taught at the Catholic University of America, knew his way around New York, and had an uproarious sense of humor similar to Belo's. He wanted to issue a statement supporting Bishop Belo almost immediately, but it might have been dangerous to do so while the bishop was abroad, especially in Germany, where recent statements by critics of Indonesia had resulted in their being charged with embarrassing the state. Kasper waited, issuing a strong declaration on August 17, Indonesian Independence Day, after Belo was safely back in Dili.

In Germany, Belo also went to meet Bishop Franz Kamphaus, in the storybook town of Limburg, its brightly colored, low-slung buildings as relaxing a contrast to the tensions of East Timor as one might find. Bishop

Kamphaus, who had first spoken out in support of Bishop Belo more than ten years before, was the head of his country's Catholic Justice and Peace Commission. He had a soothing, gentle manner.

It was in Germany, too, that Bishop Belo met the Dalai Lama, who had received the Nobel Peace Prize in 1989. The Dalai Lama and the bishop felt their countries had much in common: as in Tibet, invaded by the Chinese in 1950, the settlers in East Timor were overwhelming the East Timorese in their own country. Both Tibet and East Timor are threatened with cultural genocide.

"It was a great grace for me to meet the Dalai Lama," the bishop said. "I felt we had the same kinds of problems. The spirit of the Dalai Lama gave me a lot of courage and inspiration to continue to struggle for reconciliation and peace."

What may have been most striking, however, were their personal similarities. In fact, Pierre Pont, now a senior official for the International Committee of the Red Cross, who has met both spiritual leaders in the course of his work in Asia, said that "There is a similar quality of compassion" between the two. It was a comparison also made by U.S. Representative Tony Hall in his 1994 letter nominating Bishop Belo for the Nobel Peace Prize.

Bishop Belo soon met another Nobel Peace laureate, receiving a firsthand education on another terrible conflict—"the troubles" in Northern Ireland. Mairead Corrigan shared the prize in 1976, for efforts to organize a women's movement against violence. Over the years, working with her organization, the Community of the Peace People, based in Belfast, she had taken up the cause of human rights worldwide. In May 1994, she went to Manila for a conference on East Timor, but was prevented from entering the country. The Suharto regime had pressured the Philippine government to prevent the gathering from taking place. (Cardinal Jaime Sin of Manila sent a letter to Bishop Belo apologizing for the actions of his government.) In late 1994, Mairead Corrigan Maguire, as she had become known, also nominated Bishop Belo for the Nobel Peace Prize. "It defies imagination that so many people have perished in such a small place as East Timor," she lamented.

"I was very happy to meet her, a woman full of ideas who is also defending the principle of nonviolence," Bishop Belo remembered. "I was especially grateful to have had the opportunity to visit Belfast with her."

The bishop's visit, especially to the poorer, Catholic part of town, with its boarded-up windows and doors, made a strong impression on him. The conflict was vividly evident at the moment he came to Belfast. Dozens of vehicles had been burned the night before, in response to the early release of Lee Clegg, a British Army lieutenant who had killed an eighteen-year-old girl, Karen Reilly, a few years before—a youngster like Sebastião Gomes, whose death had set off the march to Santa Cruz.

Ireland might have seemed as distant from the repression in Timor as one could get, but Dublin was the one place in Europe where Bishop Belo was visibly followed by Indonesian agents, probably because of the large movement in Ireland on behalf of East Timor. Public concern had been sparked after Santa Cruz, perhaps because of the Irish historical experience of occupation by a powerful neighbor.

When Bishop Belo got off his Aer Lingus flight in Dublin, two men of Indonesian appearance waited in the front rows of the plane for him to pass. When the bishop went by, one of the men pointed his finger at him in a very obvious way, almost as a warning. Belo was completely unfazed. It was a warm, languid June evening, and the mood was relaxed. But the two men were clearly tailing Belo. His luggage hadn't arrived with his flight, and making arrangements for its delivery took about an hour. Still, the two men waited in the rear of the arrivals terminal.

The next morning, it became apparent why they had stayed in the airport, when Bishop Belo had his breakfast in the dining room of the Royal Marine Hotel, thirteen miles from the airport. Once again, the two men appeared. Belo noticed them as soon as they entered the room.

"Is this the only hotel in Dublin?" the bishop asked mordantly. But he shrugged it off; it was nothing, he said, nothing compared with life in East Timor. Nonetheless, one did not expect this kind of surveillance in Ireland, much less on a sparkling, sunny morning. It was spookier still, because there had been no public announcement of the bishop's schedule. At the buffet table, one of the men, feigning ignorance, asked the bishop's breakfast companion, "Is that man from Indonesia?"

Asked where he was from, the man, tall and well built, replied, "Jakarta," without hesitation. The man said he was in Dublin to sell insurance, but he had arrived on a Friday evening and this was a Saturday in summer: it seemed an unlikely story.

That wasn't the last of the two men. They appeared at the pro-cathedral in Dublin that night as Belo was about to concelebrate Mass with Archbishop Desmond Connell in a church with few empty seats: unlike in some other places, Irish churches remained well attended. Even with a million inhabitants, Dublin in some ways remained as tight-knit as in the early years of the century, and the prime minister and other notables would be among the worshipers on this sultry evening. The archbishop's security detail, elite anti-terrorist police, was notified by the organizers of Belo's visit, a Catholic aid agency called Trócaire ("Help" in the Gaelic language). The police were not amused that anyone, let alone a Catholic bishop nominated for a Nobel Peace Prize, was being followed by foreign agents on Irish soil.

At that point, police scanned the pro-cathedral even as the deacon made a strong statement about oppression in East Timor. But the men who had been following Bishop Belo were no longer around, and were not spotted again in Ireland. It was one thing to be visible in a public place like an airport or a hotel restaurant, quite another to be overly conspicuous in a church.

But it did not end there. A few days later a Dublin newspaper published a brief item about the Mass at the pro-cathedral, adding that Belo had also seen then President Mary Robinson, and Joan Burton, then minister of state for foreign affairs. They were supposed to be private meetings without press coverage, to avoid problems for the bishop, but news of them was published because of a misunderstanding. When Belo returned to Portugal a week later on his way back to East Timor, he received a phone call from someone known to be in contact with Indonesian intelligence, letting the bishop know in a pointed way that they were aware of what he had been doing in Ireland.

Belo's main fear had always been that he would not be allowed to return home. He had come back to East Timor after years abroad to render service, and wanted nothing to interfere with his mission. The Indonesians knew it, and also knew that, with death threats meaningless—how can you threaten someone who is so unafraid?—the only way to get to him was to put the fear of expulsion in his head. A game of psychological warfare had been played for years, in which Belo's trips abroad were accompanied by warnings, veiled or otherwise, that he might be denied reentry if he were too outspoken or engaged in certain kinds of actions. In the days before he was to return in July 1995, a rumor was spread that Belo might be barred from coming back: this was enough to cause anxiety on the trip home. The Indonesian regime knew precisely what Belo wanted most, and exploited this knowledge to the hilt. Of course, by 1995 there would have been a worldwide outcry if the Indonesian government had tried to stop Belo from returning. As with death threats, however, one could never be completely certain just what the outcome would be. That uncertainty had its own power.

The bishop's travels in Europe had been somewhat relaxed until Dublin, but after the news report appeared, he made sure that subsequent meetings remained private, and he avoided contacts that might have led to unwanted publicity: he did not want to give the Indonesian regime any pretext to deny him reentry. Thus in London, his last stop, in northern Europe, the bishop restricted his meetings largely to Church circles, notably with Cardinal Basil Hume, who had made a strong gesture by selling shares owned by the Archdiocese of Westminster in British Aerospace, manufacturer of Hawk attack aircraft sold to Indonesia. By the 1990s, Britain had replaced the U.S. as Indonesia's biggest arms supplier. On that subject, Bishop Belo told the Foreign Office in a private meeting that "If you want to help the people of East Timor, don't send arms, send potatoes."

While in London, the bishop met with an old friend of the late Archbishop Oscar Romero, Julian Filochowski, a close associate of Cardinal Hume and director of CAFOD, the Catholic aid agency which had come to play a leading role in support of the Church in East Timor in the 1990s. Belo also saw leaders of Christian Aid, an agency representing forty British and Irish denominations working in the areas of greatest need in more than sixty nations. In the minds of his friends, Bishop Belo's various international exchanges were aimed in some measure at ensuring that the Timorese prelate would never meet Archbishop Romero's fate.

Such grim matters were quite distant as the bishop walked along the banks of the Tagus River in Lisbon in the days before he headed back to East Timor in July 1995. His mood had vastly improved from when he was thinking of resignation the month before. As tiring as his travels had been, they were also exhilarating, and the bishop's face showed it. He sensed that he might be on the edge of momentous change.

Freed from his day-to-day duties, Bishop Belo even had a bit of time to reflect on his need for quieter moments, of his love for music, painting, and literature. He was wistful: "I very much like landscapes, especially the colors blue and green, very green landscapes; the mountains and valleys and blue sky give me a certain poetic inspiration. When I was young I wrote some poetry, but now life is so difficult that poetry sometimes disappears. But I should practice poetry, to turn real life into everyday poetry in order to be able to deal with the difficulties and problems."

That was his artistic, learned side, that was submerged. It was this aspect of his personality that brought him to listen quietly to big band jazz while watching the cockatoos play in the trees above his house. But some weeks later, back in Dili, Belo had no time for such luxuries.

Only a few days earlier, everything there had seemed quiet. Then, all of a sudden, trucks filled with heavily armed Mobile Brigade riot police—the Brimob—roared through Dili late at night, Plexiglas shields and batons visible by dim streetlamps. One truck after another headed for the Becora section of town, the same place where the uprising had begun during President Clinton's visit to Indonesia the previous year. As always, the area was a tinderbox, filled with unemployed youth resentful of their treatment by Indonesian authority, and, increasingly, not afraid to show it.

Seemingly out of nowhere, there had been a new set of religious disturbances. The spark was the so-called Maliana incident, in which, inexplicably, a prison warden in that small town insulted the Virgin Mary. There followed an outpouring of indignation among the local population and demonstrations in several towns. What was curious, however, is that reliable independent observers said it was the Indonesian authorities themselves who publicized this incident, guaranteeing further upheavals: it was the equivalent of yelling "Fire!" in a crowded theater.

It all had the air of being orchestrated: knowledgeable sources close to the Indonesian regime tied a string of religious incidents back to Prabowo Subianto, President Suharto's son-in-law, earlier one of the authors of the "ninja" phenomenon. Prabowo had continued his meteoric rise in the armed forces chain of command. His power in East Timor and elsewhere stemmed not only from his military rank and family connections, but also from intelligence operations under his personal control.

Sources close to the Indonesian government believe the bishop was one target of these operations. Belo became the object of a campaign of vilification in the Indonesian press, specifically in a newspaper owned by a crony of President Suharto's. By this time, Indonesian intelligence was said to be alarmed by reports that Bishop Belo might win the Nobel Peace Prize, according to a relative of a Timorese official in the Indonesian government. Clearly their task was to prevent this from happening. Belo was portrayed as a bigot, because of an interview in which the bishop said that East Timor should retain its historical Catholic character.

There was Muslim reaction against his statement, which the bishop insisted had been distorted. Conditions in East Timor were rarely mentioned and were in all probability unknown to most Muslim leaders. His statement was not meant to express religious prejudice, but to defend people being overrun in their own land, a very small territory, compared with Indonesia. It is extremely doubtful that any Muslim leader in Indonesia would have taken kindly toward similar encroachments in their own land. It was mentioned that "one hundred *Ulamas*"—Muslim religious leaders—had sought a meeting with the bishop to take him to task for his views: the statement seemed manufactured for the occasion.

Belo had traveled a tortuous road. First he was favorably regarded on Indonesian television when he was installed as bishop in 1988; now he was placed on the cover of a magazine next to the writer Salman Rushdie, with the heading, "Enemies of Islam." This, too, was almost surely propaganda orchestrated against his Nobel nomination. The underlying reasoning apparently was that the Norwegian Nobel Committee would recoil at the slightest suggestion of religious prejudice.

In those very same days, too, to add to the poisonous religious brew, a Protestant church was burned in the far-eastern part of the territory. It was unclear who was responsible, but again, the timing was suspicious. The church was one of many built since the 1975 invasion, with heavy support from the Indonesian Protestant churches. The indigenous Protestant community was tiny before the invasion, only slightly larger now, headed by an attractive young leader, the Reverend Arlindo Marçal, who was friendly to Belo. The bishop drove seven hours to reach the town of Uatolari to try to cool the situation.

Nothing was sacred: even as animosity was incited between Catholics and Muslims, and Catholics and Protestants, the Suharto regime was trumpeting its role in constructing the second-highest statue of Jesus Christ in the world, smaller only than the one in Rio de Janeiro. The statue was built together with Garuda, Indonesia's state airline, to be inaugurated in 1996, the twentieth anniversary of Indonesia's unilateral annexation of the territory. These gestures were intended to impress international public opinion by signaling support for Catholicism. In a bizarre twist, the construction of the statue coincided with renewed efforts to discredit Belo and have him removed. For the bishop's part, he said that rather than putting up statues, Indonesian authorities might behave decently toward the people.

There was little indication of decency by the authorities in September 1995. At a Mass one day that month at the home of Bishop Belo, there appeared a crippled boy, his face black and blue and caked with blood from a beating by security forces. Traumatized and barely willing to speak, he said he had been in a police station with thirty other young people who had been stripped naked and similarly assaulted.

On the morning of September 8, 1995, some of the most serious upheavals since the Santa Cruz massacre of November 1991 took place. Young student demonstrators in the Becora area of Dili confronted large numbers of Indonesian security personnel.

High tension was palpable, and the disparity between the two sides could not have been more clear. On one side were unarmed young people. On the other, heavily armed units of Indonesian Mobile Brigade riot police. There were countless trucks filled with machine gun–toting army troops, both uniformed and in plainclothes, some wearing ski masks in broad daylight in the oppressive tropical heat. Spies working for Indonesian forces were everywhere.

After hours of tense confrontation, the two sides were at an impasse, and the young people asked to speak with Bishop Belo.

With the smell of tear gas heavy in the streets, Belo arrived with his vicar general, Father José António da Costa. After the bishop spoke with both the young people and the military, the confrontation eased, for the rest of that day, at least.

That night, there was a special feast at the church of Balide in the outskirts of Dili, an area that had taken Indonesian forces three weeks to reach when they first invaded. Bishop Belo insisted the event go forward as planned. Before thousands, in very tough terms, he called on the youth to show restraint. The bishop criticized the Indonesian military and intelligence service as well. There were senior army officers there that night—the church lay across the road from one of the outposts of the regional military command. The officers glared at Belo: right to their faces, he had accused them of exploiting the unrest for their own ends. But this was no great secret. A senior Indonesian military official had recently told an independent witness, "We will use the East Timorese to destroy the East Timorese."

Now, however, the military were stepping up efforts to create divisions and otherwise exploit tensions. Intel seemed to have crafted a strategy of provoking "incidents" under the guise of religious confrontations, as a means of cracking down on the resistance, intimidating the local population, and justifying the continuing military presence. By now, the bishop had support for his tough stand against demonstrations: in September 1995, there was a strong consensus among the clergy that they must end, because escalating confrontations with the Indonesians would only lead to a bloodbath. By this time, it was not even clear just who the demonstrators were: some, desperate for money to help their families survive, may have been working for Suharto's son-in-law as provocateurs and spies.

Only a few hours after the Church festival ended, trouble started again, resulting from broken promises. As Bishop Belo put it in a later interview, "This was because the agreements we had reached were not kept. What we agreed was that the youth would all go home. They did as they were asked. But what happened then? The security forces went out that night and arrested these young people," some of whom were badly beaten. The market-place was burned, and smoke could be seen throughout Dili.

What helped illuminate my visit to Bishop Belo during this time was the perspective brought by my wife, Korinna, the first European who had lived for any length of time in East Timor before the Indonesian invasion to revisit the territory; possibly the only one. She insisted on walking the back streets during the disturbances to get a feeling for conditions. Occasionally it was frightening, as truckload after truckload of heavily armed Mobile Brigade police rumbled menacingly through the neighborhoods. But we saw how much the foreign visitor, without knowledge of local geography and languages, could miss in the normal course of a visit. No foreign journalists were on hand at the time. It was striking how third-hand articles in the international press that appeared on the disturbance while we were there seemed to capture only a small bit of the flavor and substance of what was going on.

During those same days, riding in the bishop's van, we saw a young man knocked off his motorcycle by a military truck while delivering cake to catechists at a rural church. The soldiers, dressed in jeans and batik shirts but armed with machine guns, wanted to take the young man, who lay crouched in pain, to the hospital. He resisted being taken by the military, and our presence allowed him to be taken to a small church clinic. Many East Timorese feared the Indonesian hospitals, seeing them as places of death rather than healing.

Such fear was not manifest under the Portuguese, whatever the many shortcomings of Portuguese rule. Korinna had lived in East Timor for nearly three years until the end of 1974, when she grew homesick for her family in Europe. There was a chance to visit them, which she gladly took. Had she stayed with her Timorese friends, in all probability she would have died.

As it turned out, that is what happened to most of those she had known. She learned this from an old acquaintance: most of the people they had known in common had died following the Indonesian invasion, while some of the surviving women had been widows for nearly 20 years. It was one thing to hear about death as an abstract statistic, quite another to learn of it in such a personal way.

Korinna had disliked the Portuguese colonial regime, which lent weight to her perceptions of Indonesian rule, and shed light on the upheavals we witnessed. For example, a market building of colonial architecture in the center of Dili was constructed by Portuguese authorities so local people could sell their wares out of the glare of the burning sun, or out of the pouring rain during the wet season. Under Indonesian rule, the Timorese had been evicted from the market building, consigned to a dusty strip of dirt road, much of it next to a police station known to be a detention and torture center. The inner market had been given to Indonesian traders who seemed to control the sale of manufactured goods. The Timorese sold only some tomatoes, garlic, and other vegetables, sometimes some fruit. In an ironic touch, among the books sold by the Indonesian traders inside was the orange-covered Tetum catechism, introduced by the late apostolic administrator, Martinho da Costa Lopes. "They're taking everything from us," said one man. "All that most Timorese have now is the skin on their bones."

In September 1995, Bishop Belo appealed again and again for calm, and for dialogue, but he also added an important point: "Reconciliation is a message from the Church which has a moral value. It is eternal. Reconciliation also contains the value of justice. If there is no justice there can be no reconciliation."

There were no portents of reconciliation in East Timor during those days of confrontations and burning. By the end of our visit in mid-September, the intense strain made Bishop Belo's face seem heavy, almost like a large mask. At breakfast on our last day, he seemed momentarily elderly, though the morning had scarcely begun. It contrasted startlingly with his appearance only a short time before in Portugal, where, for all the long days, his responsibilities were minimal compared with those at home. He soon left for a study course for bishops in Rome. There was a flurry of speculation that Belo would be the recipient of the Nobel Peace Prize as the day of the announcement of the winner drew near. Plans were made, not by the bishop, who remained skeptical about such prospects, but by others in Church circles. A special audience with Pope John Paul II was scheduled for the day after Belo's anticipated designation as laureate.

The day arrived, and so did Portuguese television journalists at the Salesian headquarters at Via della Pisana. They were seeking Bishop Belo's comment on the Nobel Committee's choice, Joseph Rotblat, a Polish-born British scientist who had resigned from the Manhattan Project once he realized that a nuclear bomb would not be needed to defeat Hitler. From then on, Rotblat, later with his Pugwash organization on science and world affairs, had pursued efforts to reduce the risk of nuclear conflict. The award had come on the fiftieth anniversary of the use of the first nuclear bombs on Hiroshima and Nagasaki. In his comments to the press, Bishop Belo noted the historical importance of this anniversary.

Within a few days of the 1995 result, a report surfaced that Indonesia's minister for religious affairs would visit Rome to demand Belo's ouster. "Do you think this will frighten me?" the bishop told me with rising anger at the thought that he could be intimidated.

The youth of East Timor were no less courageous. The action of the twenty-nine East Timorese at the U.S. embassy in Jakarta during the Clinton visit in late 1994 had drawn unprecedented international attention to East Timor, and this was a source of hope for the young people who scaled the embassy fence, giving them the aura of heroes. But afterwards the atmosphere within East Timor, and for Timorese students in Indonesia itself, was one of intense pressure from security forces and other agents of the regime. These circumstances were a big factor (the wish to keep international attention focused on East Timor was another) explaining why, from September 1995 on, dozens of young East Timorese entered embassies in Jakarta seeking asylum abroad.

Details of the lives of many of these young people told the recent history of East Timor: many had lost parents in the war, and nearly all had taken part in the demonstrations at Santa Cruz, at Taci-Tolu when the pope visited, or when U.S. ambassador John Monjo came to the Hotel Turismo. According to a number of testimonies, it was clear that they felt endangered. "We are not safe, we are persecuted and have no freedom," said one petition, which said they were taking this action "to save our lives and to escape the bleak future which threatens to overcome us and our people. . . . The situation has robbed us of our freedom to grow up as other young people in other parts of the world. We feel we have no future." Still, it pained Bishop Belo that these young people had to abandon their land.

Belo, however, could not leave; like his Makassae forebears, he was tied to the earth of East Timor. In early 1996, a TV interviewer asked Belo if he would leave East Timor. The bishop said: "Why should I leave? I'm from here."

The pugnacious ways of his paternal Makassae forebears often became evident. Told that he had been described as a remarkable person, the bishop responded: "I have no reaction to this; it is better to ask others and let them say if I am good or evil, a liar or lazy. It is better if others say it. I will not say anything about myself, only that I am a person who gets angry easily, who is dictatorial. In Dili I yell at people a lot, I lose patience, I'm nervous . . . I see myself as weak . . . I can be a dictator, I am proud and accept little of what others say. . . ."

But it was this very quality of pride, mixed with a fierce sense of identity as a member of one of the oldest ethnic groups in the territory, the

Makassae, and the vigorous self-confidence of the Waima'a, that together helped enabled him to be a leader in a place where so many had died. These qualities did not require a supportive audience.

Once, Carlos Filipe Ximenes Belo was stopped late at night at a military checkpoint not far from where his family had lived for centuries. The soldiers asked for his identification papers.

Belo exploded in fury: "I was born here. I grew up here. My parents were born here, my grandparents and many others before them. You came here. You never asked anyone if you could. Now you want my ID papers. I should be asking you for your ID papers. Now let me through," said the bishop, whom some people regarded as soft.

The soldiers were speechless. But they allowed him to pass.

The young East Timorese became increasingly audacious. On December 7, 1995, almost twenty years to the hour after Indonesian troops first attacked Dili, about one hundred East Timorese and Indonesian students acting in solidarity with them poured into the Dutch and Russian embassies in Jakarta. The purpose this time was not to win asylum abroad, but to heighten world recognition of the anniversary of the invasion. Although some were injured in the action, many were released unharmed, evidence of increasing international pressure on the Suharto regime coupled with the obvious presence of foreign journalists and other witnesses.

But the situation grew more dangerous still when in early 1996 a number of East Timorese trying to enter the German embassy were beaten by Indonesian security forces, who showed signs that they were prepared to open fire. In May 1996, while in Portugal, where most of the asylum-seekers had found refuge, Bishop Belo made a public appeal for an end to the embassy actions. The embassy actions soon decreased. Returning to East Timor from Europe in June 1996, the bishop rushed to his childhood home of Baucau to separate young demonstrators from security forces, who, like their colleagues in Jakarta, seemed all too ready to shoot.

Throughout many perilous moments from 1994 through 1996, Carlos Filipe Ximenes Belo gained increasing respect, though it was a rare moment when he was not the object of criticism by some who felt he was not supportive of their goals. Nonetheless, the bishop kept his equilibrium, at times under great strain, learning from past mistakes, and defending his people against attack at every possible juncture.

In February 1996, Bishop Belo was the subject of an admiring profile by journalist Paul Raffaele in *Reader's Digest*, which ultimately reached more than 100 million people throughout the world. Not surprisingly, the Asian edition, which carried the article, was banned by Indonesian authorities. The article, short but apt, ended with the bishop telling the journalist after a church service at his home in Dili, " 'We beg the outside world not to forget us,' " [the bishop] said softly. "If that happens, we are doomed.' "

As *Reader's Digest* put it in a coda the following year, "The world did not forget Belo and his people."

CHAPTER 9

NOBEL

❖ ❖ ❖ ❖

T HERE WAS SPIRITUAL RAPTURE of a kind rarely seen in this
primarily secular age. Thousands in East Timor, including many
working in the Indonesian administration, wept with joy at the
news that Bishop Carlos Filipe Ximenes Belo had won the Nobel Peace
Prize. The world at large finally knew of their tragedy. But peril was always
present as Indonesian military leaders absorbed the shock of the news
from Oslo. What international support would the East Timorese now receive, and what impact would the award ultimately have on Indonesia?

The news caught officials in Washington off guard. Only a few days before, a senior congressional aide visiting Jakarta had mentioned to U.S.
Ambassador Stapleton Roy the possibility that Bishop Belo might get the
award. The ambassador expressed surprise and countered that he thought
the Peace Prize would go to Richard Holbrooke, the Clinton administration's mediator of the Dayton accords on Bosnia. President Clinton also
had been nominated in connection with the Bosnia agreement.

The Nobel Peace Prize to Bishop Belo and the international spokesman
of the resistance, José Ramos-Horta, for "work toward a just and peaceful
solution to the conflict in East Timor" could not have arrived at a more
embarrassing moment for the Clinton administration. Campaign contributions with foreign links had become a visible issue in the final weeks of
his 1996 reelection drive. The Nobel Prize announcement came only four
days after an October 7 report in the *New York Times* alleging that Clinton's
policy on East Timor may have been influenced by various campaign con-
tributors and Arkansas friends with Indonesian connections.

Some accounts centered around an Indonesian banker named James
Riady, a one-time resident of Little Rock who had known Clinton there,

and the meetings—at least three by one count—that Riady had obtained in the Oval Office with the president himself. The issue of East Timor had been raised by Riady although details were never revealed. Then there was the question of sizeable payments the Riady family's Lippo financial group had made to former U.S. Associate Attorney General Webster Hubbell, a close friend of the president. The payments were made for unspecified services. Months later it became public that Hubbell had visited East Timor while employed by the Riadys in 1994.

Hubbell, a former law partner of Hillary Rodham Clinton's, was not the only Arkansan to have visited East Timor. There had been an earlier trip by a one-time presidential golfing partner, Mark Grobmayer, who went with James Riady in March 1993, the same month the United States supported a resolution on East Timor censuring Indonesia at the United Nations Human Rights Commission in Geneva. The purpose of the Grobmayer-Riady trip also remained unclear, but the Suharto regime had been concerned over the critical direction the Clinton administration had been taking on East Timor in its early days, and wanted to correct it. It appeared that the Riadys were anxious to curry favor with the Indonesian regime. Experts believe that trying to influence the Clinton administration on the East Timor issue, in part through arranging such visits, may have been one way for the Riadys to win points with Suharto. (Grobmayer had visited Indonesia with business cards introducing himself as "White House liaison.") It also became known that another former law partner of Hillary Rodham Clinton's, Joseph Giroir, who had long-standing business relationships in Indonesia, had drafted statutes that made Little Rock a "sister city" of Jakarta.

Had American policy been affected by such ties? Even if no wrong had been done, the maze of contributions and connections made it look as if it had. There was no question that the influence of U.S. commercial interests in Indonesia was pervasive enough to begin with, and that, combined with long-standing political interests, might have accounted for the basic thrust of American policy, which had not undergone any fundamental change in two decades. But the Arkansas connections and the campaign contributions combined to create at least the appearance of impropriety. One contribution, $425,000 from an Indonesian "landscape architect" in Los Angeles, had to be returned. No matter what could actually be demonstrated, the words and actions of the Clinton administration around the time of the announcement of the Nobel Peace Prize and through much of 1997 pointed to a weak American policy on East Timor. It left open the possibility that some degree of influence may have been exerted by Riady and his associates.

The issue of how Clinton had addressed or failed to address the plight of East Timor was made more complicated by the record of the president's most prominent critic, his Republican opponent, Bob Dole. "There are a whole lot of problems here that have been raised," Dole said. "Taking money from a foreign nation. They gave it back when somebody caught them, but why did they do it? Why did he [Clinton] meet with these people?" At a campaign rally he asked: "Did it have any impact on the policies in East Timor?"

But Bob Dole himself, as a United States senator, had done little on East Timor in the twenty-one years since the Indonesian invasion—far less, in fact, than had Clinton. He had not signed any of the more than two dozen letters of concern that had circulated in the Senate during those years. Worse, Dole worked actively to soften a Senate resolution critical of Indonesia soon after the Santa Cruz massacre, ignoring the pleas of a Republican colleague who tried to convince Dole to change his mind. But when news of campaign contributions and the Nobel Peace Prize raised the possibility of partisan political advantage, Dole suddenly became interested in the issue.

The shabby tone of the electoral arguments in the United States, characterized by self-serving one-upmanship on both sides, contrasted starkly with the language in the Nobel citation. The October 11 statement by the Norwegian Nobel Committee minced no words:

> In 1975, Indonesia took control of East Timor and began systematically oppressing the people. In the years that followed it has been estimated that one-third of the population of East Timor lost their lives due to starvation, epidemics, war and terror. Carlos Belo, bishop of East Timor, has been the foremost representative of the people of East Timor. At the risk of his own life, he has tried to protect his people from infringements by those in power. In his efforts to create a just settlement based on his people's right to self-determination, he has been a constant spokesman for non-violence and dialogue with the Indonesian authorities.
>
> In awarding this year's Nobel Peace Prize to Belo and Ramos-Horta, the Norwegian Nobel Committee wants to honor their sustained and self-sacrificing contributions for a small but oppressed people.

In East Timor itself, word of the Peace Prize was like a tonic. It arrived nearly seven years to the day that Pope John Paul II visited the territory, on October 12, 1989. The idea that the obscure young prelate embraced by John Paul in Dili would one day receive a Nobel Peace Prize would have seemed far-fetched at the time.

Yet, at the residence of the Canossian Sisters next door to the bishop's house, it was almost like a prophecy come true. When he first arrived at the bishop's residence in 1983, Mother Matilde and the other sisters had told the priests that they should have faith in Belo. Now, there was this wonderful international recognition.

For her part, Maria de Fatima, Belo's cook, wondered if life could be more than endless suffering. What would this prize really mean? What would really happen on a day-to-day level? Could people walk the streets the way they used to, without worry? Or would this only be excitement without results?

Bishop Belo had such thoughts as well. He had seen more than enough of people who allowed their feelings to get the better of reason. Since his early youth, Belo had seen the tragic results of actions driven more by passion than clear thinking. Keeping his distance from the emotions of the moment was his defense against disaster. For all of the complaints of his militant critics that he was too conservative or too willing to compromise, it was Belo's refusal to get swept up by the latest enthusiasm, even one based on himself, that made him an authentic leader, rather than merely a personification of the popular will.

It turned out to be a blessing that Belo had not won the year before: it would have been impossible for him to control the situation in East Timor from Rome. In 1996, he was home, but strangely enough, it seemed as though Indonesian intelligence operators hadn't the slightest inkling this time that Belo might win. For some reason, they were so fixated on the possibility of his receiving the Nobel Peace Prize in 1995 that they neglected to look ahead. Since the bishop had been nominated in each of the previous three years, the prospect was not a new one for him: Belo had sufficient time to ponder the consequences. He did not have to guess what they might be: after the street confrontations in 1995 and the press campaign waged against him, he could envision the territory, always on edge, might erupt altogether. The Indonesian authorities would surely be furious and might be looking for some pretext to take retribution.

As it happened, I had a premonition of victory the week before the announcement, and I informed the bishop of what had happened in Tibet in

1989 when the Dalai Lama received the award, as recounted by a researcher for Amnesty International. That year had seen a tough crackdown in Tibet, with checkpoints and riot police everywhere, making it impossible for Tibetans to stage anything like a large demonstration. Using traditional rites to celebrate, some people threw barley in the air, a practice later banned by Chinese authorities for a time when they realized how it was intended in this instance. But a handful of persons in the capital city of Lhasa were more vocal. Observers believe these people had said out loud, "Long live the Dalai Lama!", in the belief that the Nobel Peace Prize meant that the world finally understood their cause and would protect them from harm. It was a grave error, a misperception with severe long-term consequences: some of those detained in 1989 were still being held in Chinese prisons years later.

Belo's reaction to his selection illustrated how he had earned the award in the first place. Word arrived on a Friday at dusk. The bishop was presiding over a Thanksgiving Mass in the Comoro section of Dili to mark the fiftieth anniversary of the Salesian presence in East Timor, together with about twenty-five other priests. After his homily, he led the Prayer of the Faithful, when suddenly a priest came to his side and put a piece of paper on the altar telling him that he had received the Nobel Peace Prize together with Ramos-Horta. He immediately put the paper into his side pocket and continued with the Mass. Carlos Filipe Ximenes Belo was impassive: he did not even smile. "The responsibilities are all the heavier now," he said later, recalling his thoughts at the time, "to become more of a man of peace—in my actions, my thoughts, and my words, to be more patient, not to be angry, not to shout at others."

During Communion, the vicar general asked Belo if he wanted to have the message announced. The bishop declined. Some wanted an impromptu jamboree, others wanted to pay homage, but Belo simply wanted to be left alone, to avoid the slightest move that might create havoc. So he turned and quietly walked away, in the manner of one of his heroes, Mahatma Gandhi. Before long, so did everyone else. By dark, the streets in Dili are normally deserted, and Indonesian forces, always more insecure in the pitch black, become rougher the later it gets. But this time, there was a calm, happy silence in the town. Thousands had been at the Friday Mass but there was no disorder of any kind. Bishop Belo had instructed the clergy and, through them, contacts throughout Dili that there were to be no public celebrations, no crowds of people shouting "Viva" that might provoke Indonesian military retaliation. António spread the word among his network of young friends that this was the will of the bishop; he would not participate in any celebration. Belo let it be known that if anyone wanted to pay his or her respects or otherwise offer congratulations, he or she could simply attend Church services on the weekend. That is what many did.

So people went home and stayed there. They returned for an afternoon Mass the next day. The applause was thunderous, but the bishop soon asked for silence: he wanted sobriety above all. When it came time for refreshments, no one had champagne or even wine; even if any had been available, Belo would never have allowed such beverages to be served. (He normally restricts his own consumption to an occasional glass or two of wine on holidays and at special feasts.) Instead, there were tea and individual containers of iced mineral water—real luxuries in East Timor—together with butter cookies. In the end, there was no violence of any kind in the early days surrounding the announcement of the Nobel Peace Prize. Bishop Belo was jubilant about this.

If the streets of Dili were silent for the moment, the scene inside the bishop's house was one of near pandemonium. The phone rang continuously from six o'clock in the evening until two o'clock the following morning on that first day, with journalists and well-wishers calling from every corner of the globe. It started with CNN, which got the first call through after being alerted to the possibility of the award going to Belo, and continued nonstop, as António and his friends tried to keep track of the messages.

Dozens of congratulatory letters arrived on the bishop's old fax machine, which seemed as if it might short-circuit from excessive use. The phone grew warm from hours and hours of use. By the time the evening was over, Belo was hoarse, and there was a thick folder of tributes. Messages poured in over the following days, from Cardinal Roger Etchegeray, the pope's special envoy, several bishops conferences and church organizations, governments, parliamentarians, members of Congress and private groups, among many others. It contrasted greatly with the single letter of support Dom Martinho had received from a church organization in the eight years before Belo moved to the bishop's residence. All of this was amazing for a territory that not long before had been one of the most isolated in the world, a place dismissed by the great powers throughout its history.

Nonetheless, some things remained substantially unaltered. While statements of support had arrived from around the world, and public messages of congratulation were issued in many places, no letter of congratulations to Belo, not even a brief note, was forthcoming from the president of the United States. In striking contrast, Clinton had once sent a letter to James Riady in which (according to the *Washington Post*) he called the Indonesian banker "a treasured friend." Only when questioned by reporters did Michael McCurry, the White House press spokesman, acknowledge Bishop Belo. Ramos-Horta, however, went unmentioned by the press spokesman; only a State Department official, making it clear he was speaking for himself, offered congratulations to both. The protocol-conscious Indonesians, highly sensitive to questions of status, could not have missed the fact that no top-echelon American official had acknowledged Bishop Belo or his co-recipient. Some nations with heavy interests in Indonesia, such as Canada, had made straightforward congratulatory statements. Japan said nothing whatsoever, Australia very little. When pressed, the European Union declined to make a joint statement, though several countries (paradoxically, some of the same ones that vetoed a joint declaration) issued private congratulations.

But none of these nations had made such rhetorical flights as had Bill Clinton when he said during the 1992 campaign that East Timor had been ignored in an "unconscionable" manner. Bishop Belo received no direct communication from the United States for nearly a week, until a short, private note from the assistant to the president for national security affairs, Anthony Lake, finally arrived; while friendly in tone, his language was guarded: he offered his "personal congratulations" to Bishop Belo, making no mention of President Clinton or the administration as a whole.

A pattern became established during those days, in which the Clinton administration strongly defended its past record on East Timor, generally referring to actions taken years before, like the small arms ban, which was adopted only after Congress proposed stronger measures. At the same time, administration officials, including the president, seemed to take pains to avoid speaking about the current situation. This sent a more powerful message in late 1996 than Clinton's oft-repeated citation of his support for a United Nations Human Rights Commission resolution more than three years earlier, which had in fact never been implemented.

Still, armed with his new standing, the bishop acted on his own. On the following Monday, in his first interview after the award was announced, Belo made his most direct statement on the need for a fair solution in the territory since his 1989 letter to the United Nations secretary general. For those who harbored suspicions that he had changed his mind since drafting that letter, the bishop dispelled such notions.

Belo said he hoped the prize would increase international efforts to end the conflict once and for all and said a referendum was the best way to settle the issue. "Have you asked the people in villages what they really want?" he said, adding, "Don't think that all Timorese people have accepted the integration, and that everything is OK."

Responding to the Indonesian government's rejection of the idea of a referendum and its contention that the issue had been settled, Belo stated, "It has not been for the past twenty years, and may not be for the next twenty years. . . . Then what does it want?" he demanded, referring to the Indonesian government. "That the seven hundred thousand East Timorese people just bow their heads?"

The bishop's remarks were his bluntest on the subject of the territorial status of East Timor since he had replaced Dom Martinho thirteen years before. The importance of these comments, which he had wanted to say for so long, should not be underestimated: it would have been tremendously difficult for him to have said such things before winning the Peace Prize. It is here that some timely support from the Clinton administration on human rights and the need for a political solution might have helped. Instead, the United States remained silent.

One reason the Clinton administration might have waited almost a week before sending the Lake note to Belo was that President Suharto was making a visit to East Timor on October 15, a trip that had been arranged well before the Nobel news. The Indonesian leader had not been to East Timor since 1988. President Clinton had developed a personal relationship with his Indonesian counterpart over the years, or so a close aide to Clinton claimed, and for this reason the U.S. would not want to press Suharto on the question. The year before, when the Indonesian leader visited Washington after the September disturbances in Dili and other towns, a senior administration official told the *New York Times* that Suharto was "our kind of guy," even as Clinton "made the requisite complaints" about East Timor in response to a request from twenty-nine U.S. senators.

As things stood, even Indonesian journalists were grilled by military authorities before being allowed to board the press plane to Dili. Once in East Timor, Suharto attended a ceremony to dedicate the "Christ the King" monument, which Bishop Belo had agreed to attend despite his misgivings about the government's political use of the edifice. At the dedication Suharto appeared to avoid speaking with Belo, although they did talk during a helicopter ride around the monument. Suharto conspicuously declined to congratulate Belo on his receipt of the Nobel award. Curiously, other senior Indonesian officials, including armed forces chief General Feisal Tanjung, did make gestures. And, strangely enough, around this time the president's son-in-law, Major-General Prabowo Subianto, came to

Bishop Belo's residence to congratulate him on the award. The head of Suharto's state secretariat, Moerdiono, eagerly snapped photos of the bishop and arranged for pictures of the two of them to be taken together, although he had earlier criticized the award.

It was not only the Nobel award to Belo that bothered the Suharto regime. The naming of Ramos-Horta had made Jakarta positively wild. Some tried to ridicule the award, and a senior military spokesman went so far as to state that the Nobel Peace Prize "was like the Oscars," and as in Hollywood, "removed from reality." Despite such remarks, it symbolized a grand international rejection of their Timor policy, and this clearly stung. As for Ramos-Horta, he was extremely surprised at the news that he had received the Nobel Peace Prize. The award was "for all those who had fought against Indonesian oppression in East Timor," he told the news media. Reliable sources in Oslo indicated that because of the bishop's difficulty in making too many forthright public statements, and the need "to send a frankly political message," the Norwegian Nobel Committee decided to provide the award to Ramos-Horta as well. An exile and the special representative of the imprisoned resistance leader Xanana Gusmão, Ramos-Horta had established himself as East Timor's most effective overseas spokesman since the Portuguese dictatorship collapsed in 1974. He had been Jakarta's leading political nemesis with respect to East Timor throughout that period, refusing lucrative offers from the Indonesian regime to buy his silence. More to the point, Ramos-Horta could say whatever he wanted, whenever and wherever he chose—but not in East Timor itself, which he had left shortly before the 1975 invasion to plead the territory's case at the United Nations. He had not been able to return since.

The bishop operated in a totally different sphere, having day-to-day responsibility for the only sizeable independent institution in East Timor. He would speak out when he felt circumstances warranted it, but because of his position Bishop Belo was unable to act as a political leader or conduct international campaigns. As Bishop Belo noted in the days after they received the award, he had not had close contact with his fellow Nobel laureate. But in the very different world that he inhabited, seeds planted by Ramos-Horta in various places around the world had slowly created international awareness of the plight of his homeland. There is little doubt, for instance, that Ramos-Horta's efforts at the United Nations had kept the question of East Timor on the organization's agenda, without which the legal status of the territory would not have been the subject of ongoing international discussion. (It was the Dalai Lama who noted that "The Peace Prize is going to help the Timor struggle a lot, as it helped our own. From the legal standpoint, the Timorese have an advantage over us," he added. "The international community does not recognize Indonesia's occupation of East Timor, while it only refers to a single China, with Tibet inside it.")

Ramos-Horta had frustrated the full weight of Indonesian diplomacy, and for this reason alone, he was the object of the regime's enmity. In their fury, Indonesian spokesmen tried to link Ramos-Horta with violence committed by Fretilin during the 1975 civil war. But it was established that he had been abroad at the time and had no connection with any of these acts. Few of his critics were anxious to discuss the large number of friends and family Ramos-Horta had lost during the Indonesian assault, including a seventeen-year-old sister.

It was not as if the Indonesian regime had always treated Ramos-Horta as a pariah, no matter what their rhetoric after the Nobel Peace Prize. In the early weeks after the Portuguese revolution, twenty years earlier, Ramos-Horta had met with then Foreign Minister Adam Malik, who had assured him of Indonesia's peaceful intentions. Ramos-Horta than persuaded Malik to provide this in writing, which he did: "The independence of every country is the right of every nation, with no exception for the people of East Timor," the letter stated, and Ramos-Horta had distributed these words worldwide. To have elicited such a statement, made before the military overruled Malik, demonstrated Ramos-Horta's effectiveness. There was much more over the years, and now, to the regime's horror, Ramos-Horta had a "global soapbox," as one commentator put it.

If the Indonesian regime was relatively gentle in its public comments on Bishop Belo in the early days after the news of the Nobel, preferring to concentrate its anger on Ramos-Horta, this was soon to change. Clearly enraged over Bishop Belo's renewed call for a referendum, Foreign Minister Ali Alatas complained to Archbishop Jean-Louis Tauran, the Vatican's foreign minister, on October 18. Then the regime launched what had all the markings of a public campaign in response to an old interview with the bishop in the popular German weekly magazine *Der Spiegel*. Belo had made some acid comments on Indonesia's treatment of the East Timorese. He was quoted as saying that the Indonesians treated the East Timorese like "slaves" and "mangy dogs." Strangely, Indonesian officials did not react when the interview was published just after the Nobel news, in the October 14 issue. This may have been because German Chancellor Helmut Kohl was to visit Indonesia in late October, and an emphasis on the contents of the *Spiegel* piece before he arrived was hardly in Indonesia's interest. But once Kohl had gone home, weeks later, Indonesian authorities exploded, backed by the same sort of groups who had attacked the bishop in September 1995. This time the criticism went further, with suggestions in the highly controlled Indonesian media that Belo's Indonesian citizenship and passport might be lifted. No public incident during the Nobel period better illustrated the dilemma Bishop Belo faced throughout his years as head of the Diocese of Dili.

Eventually the bishop held a news conference in Dili to clarify what he had said in the interview, neither fully confirming nor denying it; it would have been difficult for him to do otherwise under the circumstances. Given the hostile mood of that moment, confrontation would have been senseless. In fact, the bishop once had said on camera that the Indonesians "treat us like dogs," without using the word "mangy." At the same news conference on November 8, Belo appealed to the Indonesian military for a better relationship in the future, but the military chose to ignore that part of the bishop's statement.

Of course, reconciliation was not on the Indonesian military agenda: intimidation and coercion prevailed. Far more was at stake than what Belo had actually stated in an old interview: the regime was most afraid of what the bishop might say in his Nobel lecture in Oslo, when the world would be paying especially close attention. Blunt language like that used in the *Der Spiegel* piece and the call for a referendum were things that they did not want to see repeated before the eyes of a global audience, yet by publicizing the interview well after it appeared, the Indonesian regime gave it a level of attention—indeed, worldwide notice—it could not possibly have received otherwise. But the Nobel ceremony, more than anything, explained the campaign Jakarta began about one month before the December 10 ceremony at Oslo City Hall.

Inside East Timor, the Indonesian regime seems to have conducted an elaborate game during this time. On the one hand, it was sensitive to international opinion, taking care to restrain the behavior of its forces where they might be seen in public. On the other hand, repression continued or even increased where it could not be seen.

Before the Nobel ceremony, Belo was to visit Jakarta. He was invited to the Indonesian Conference of Catholic Bishops, whose annual meetings he always attends as an observer. It was a strange combination of events. Some Indonesian Catholic bishops told Belo privately it was good that he received the Peace Prize, so that someone could speak out, because they themselves were not free to express themselves. On the other hand, the controversy over the interview in *Der Spiegel* showed how hard it could be for anyone who decided to be outspoken in Indonesia, even someone with world recognition. Belo had barely arrived in the Indonesian capital when he received rough treatment from demonstrators participating in a pro-government youth organization obviously acting under official influence. They shook his car and shouted epithets, in an ugly scene marked by banners saying such things as "Expel Belo!" The fifth anniversary of the Santa Cruz massacre had just occurred that November 12, and students in East Timor were ready to demonstrate in commemoration of their fallen compatriots. The insults to Bishop Belo could not have come at a more sensitive moment.

Yet in Dili the scene was apparently peaceful, at least during the day. More than a month after the initial news of the Peace Prize, despite a series of provocative actions from the Indonesian side, the crowds remained restrained. The faces of the East Timorese on five miles of roadway from the airport to Dili on November 16, 1996, when Belo returned from his visit to Jakarta, were joyous and free from fear. Nearly a third of East Timor's population filled almost every conceivable space for miles, waving fingers in "V for Victory" signs. Yet there had been no liberation, no end to the hated occupation of the *malae*, the foreigners. In fact, mistreatment of the East Timorese population continued during the period before the trip to Oslo and would intensify later. Arrests and beatings at night, when foreign witnesses were not present, particularly in the countryside, continued. A pattern had developed, especially pronounced since the worldwide embarrassment of Santa Cruz: the most severe kind of crackdown normally took place when it was most difficult for outside observers to witness it, though there were terrible exceptions.

Yet, the military did nothing of the kind on the day of Belo's return from Jakarta. The outpouring of affection that day, with a throng of as many as 200,000 people (twice as many as were able to greet the pope in 1989), coming from all thirteen districts of East Timor to salute Belo, was an answer to the harassment the bishop had faced in the Indonesian capital. But it was more than that: in its own way it was proof of the power of the Nobel Peace Prize to change official behavior, even if only for a short time. The year before, demonstrations of a few dozen people were all it took to bring down Indonesian military wrath. Small demonstrations had brought tear gas to the streets in 1995 as well as 1994, even in front of the cathedral: in both years there were savage beatings of East Timorese youths by security forces, despite the presence of foreign witnesses. On any previous occasion aside from the pope's visit, it would have been unimaginable that many tens of thousands of people, let alone hundreds of thousands, would have been able to gather in this manner.

In short, Indonesia was able to rein in its forces when it wanted to: the events in Dili in October and November 1996 showed that history could be determined by international factors with the power to put a brake on brute force, and also by the efforts of seemingly powerless individuals and movements. If something like this outpouring could happen in East Timor for those few hours, more could happen for longer than that. And if it could happen in East Timor, where for two decades people had been murdered, starved, and imprisoned with impunity, by concentrating attention on a particular place in the right way, the same could happen in other places, no matter how obscure they had been before.

Whatever the repressive capabilities of ABRI, on November 16, 1996, they were amazingly restrained, although clearly on full alert. While at Santa Cruz a small fraction of the number that appeared in Dili five years later were mercilessly attacked by the military (as, to a lesser extent, demonstrators and would-be demonstrators were set upon in 1993, 1994, 1995, and earlier in 1996), on November 16, 1996 there was no bloodshed whatsoever. On that day, it seemed there was only tolerance, however forced. Even though the peace of the early post-Nobel period did not last, it dramatically illustrated how violence in East Timor can be turned off or on at will, often depending on the inclination of the military powers that be.

After 21 years of atrocities, after the carnage of Santa Cruz, it was an uplifting time for the Timorese Church and people. The reception of Bishop Belo on November 16 could have been even larger—that is, even more than the one third of the population that did attend. A priest has said that Belo arrived in Dili a day earlier than expected to prevent even bigger crowds from assembling. Nonetheless, people had arrived early and had been waiting for many hours at the airport and beyond, lined up for miles on the road to Dili.

There, at the cathedral, Bishop Belo prayed the rosary with the people, then spoke for forty minutes. Referring to the actions of the mob in Jakarta, news of which had spread like wildfire in East Timor, he said, "I already have forgiven everything, because the Lord told us to forgive seventy times, that is, to forgive always. So if the shepherd acts this way, the sheep should do the same thing. . . . Remember, Jesus and the Holy Father have been more ill-treated than me. . . . It is the fate of a bishop to suffer," Belo emphasized, "otherwise he would not be a bishop."

Then Belo noted that a very important date was awaiting. "It will be the tenth of December 1996, when I will talk of the peace of Christ to the entire world for twenty-five minutes." He was, of course, speaking of the Nobel awards ceremony in Oslo.

Belo called for an end to the demonstration. He asked everyone to remain calm and prayerful and to go home in peace, "to give the bishop the opportunity to prepare for that great day."

They did so, which stupefied those watching. Within less than one hour, many tens of thousands of people had disappeared, returning to their homes and parishes. The peacefulness of the event offered great hope for the future. The Indonesian military, though on total alert, were not visible in public.

However exalted such developments may have been in absolute terms, Dona Ermelinda was not thrilled. Indeed, the bishop's mother could express only the same anxiety she had when her youngest son wanted to leave for studies in Portugal in 1968, after António's death: she feared the award meant she would never see Carlos again, that it would only bring trouble. While Julieta, the bishop's sister, did not believe that Carlos would disappear from their lives, she also thought that the Nobel Peace Prize would bring difficulties. Dona Ermelinda herself was too frail to make the trip halfway around the world to Norway for the award ceremony, so Julieta would represent the family. She would be joined by another family member, Sister Luisa Gusmão, their cousin. She was the daughter of Dona Ermelinda's brother, Lourenço, who had insisted more than seventy years before that Ermelinda be allowed to attend school over old Félix da Costa's objections.

After the resounding welcome he received on November 16, the bishop kept a low profile, gathering his list of people to be invited to the award ceremony in Oslo, concentrating mainly on a group of old friends, teachers, and benefactors, while showing indifference to celebrities, politicians, and millionaires. As it turned out, there would be little time to spend even with the ones he wanted most to see, the small circle of people who had assisted Belo with scholarships and otherwise guided the young Salesian in his studies from the time he was a teenager.

The trip to Oslo, unfortunately, was not simple. In exchange for allowing Bishop Belo to go there and return to East Timor, the Indonesian regime negotiated an agreement through the Vatican in which the bishop agreed to several conditions. He was forbidden to go to Portugal, where there would have been a resounding public reception in the immediate glow of the Nobel ceremony. In the end, Julieta was forced to visit their brother António's grave in Évora without Carlos: the bishop was unable to set foot on Portuguese soil at that time. Similarly, media interviews were to be severely limited if Belo did not want to jeopardize his return to East Timor.

These maneuvers were a reminder of the long history of dictatorial regimes that tried to blunt the impact of the Nobel Peace Prize. During Hitler's reign, for instance, the Norwegian Nobel Committee came under enormous pressure. In 1936, it selected a prisoner in a German concentration camp, Carl von Ossietzky.

The actions of the Nobel Committee could not save Ossietzky, who died two years later. But even so, only the prospect of the Peace Prize resulted in his release from the concentration camp to a hospital, demonstrating that even the Nazi regime could be moved. In Bishop Belo's case, it may well have kept the Timorese prelate in his office, the loss of which would have ended his unique ability to stave off violence, especially among East Timor's younger generation.

The story of the Nobel Peace Prize is the story of the past hundred years, of all this century's hope, tragedy and paradox. The paradox began with the man whose last will and testament created the award, the Swedish industrialist Alfred Nobel, inventor of dynamite and owner of a major munitions company. A man of extraordinary humanistic sensibilities and a talented writer, his interests were unusually broad, as evidenced by his endowment of the Nobel Prizes for literature, chemistry, physics, medicine and one for peace. Nobel lived abroad for much of his life—the French novelist, Victor Hugo, called him "Europe's richest vagabond"—and could speak, read and write five languages: thus Nobel was not tied to a narrow national outlook. He believed that as weapons were becoming all the more powerful, humanity would soon have the means to annihilate itself. Though he thought that possession of the most fearful weapons by contending sides might make use of them impossible, he saw an urgent need to work for peace in other ways.

Alfred Nobel was not simply a well meaning philanthropist, but a businessman and inventor rarely equalled in the 19th century; he who had made it possible for mining companies to go ever-deeper below the earth's crust would have needed few lessons in practicality from today's industrialists close to Indonesia's ruling circle. Yet Nobel was also disgusted by the senselessness of armed conflict, as typified by the Crimean War between Czarist Russia and Great Britain, Turkey, and France, from 1854 to 1855. Known to modern readers through the poem by Lord Alfred Tennyson, "The Charge of the Light Brigade," the Crimean conflict was emblematic of human heroism, folly, and sacrifice. Such conflicts compelled Nobel to explore ways of avoiding war. Perhaps because of his proximity to the political machinations of the corrupt Czarist regime, he developed a revulsion for war and an interest in international efforts to promote mediation and other peaceful means of averting or ending armed conflict. "War," he once wrote his close collaborator and friend, Bertha von Suttner, is "the horror of all horrors and the greatest of all crimes."

Nobel believed that his wealth could back peace initiatives by unusual individuals who otherwise might lack the financial resources to concentrate their attention on pursuits of this nature. Rather than taking a short-term view of personal gain, in which case his accomplishments would have been forgotten several decades ago, he would utilize his fortune from beyond the grave to address the ever more senseless conflagrations of the 20th century.

It has often been written that Nobel endowed the Peace Prize to ease his guilt over his invention of dynamite, then the most powerful weapon known to humankind. But the dynamite he had invented was of the industrial variety, used for underground blasting for the building of mines, bridges, and means of communication. Nobel asserted that if politicians or generals misused a product, that was not the fault of the inventor.

It was with the prodding of one of the most extraordinary women of that era, Bertha von Suttner, that Alfred Nobel made provisions to create an endowment for peace. Von Suttner, an Austrian noblewoman, was author of a best-selling anti-war book, *Lay Down Your Arms*: she was known as the "commander in chief" of international peace activism of her time, setting a standard for persistence. Nobel had first met von Suttner many years before when she worked as his assistant for a short time, and had fallen in love with her. But she was engaged to a young baron. Still, von Suttner and Nobel maintained contact, met occasionally, and kept up lively discussion and correspondence on issues of war and peace. Nobel, a skeptic by nature, doubted whether the peace movements and congresses favored by von Suttner would actually be effective: he wanted assurances before he would make a major commitment.

"Teach me, convince me—and then I will want to do something big for the movement," Nobel told von Suttner in a famous letter.

He kept his word. When Nobel died in 1896, his will stipulated that, in addition to the prizes for literature and science, one award be given annually "to the person who shall have done the most or the best work for fraternity between nations, for the abolition or reduction of standing armies and for the holding and promotion of peace congresses."

Unlike the other Nobel awards, which were to be awarded by Swedish committees, the Peace Prize would be decided by a committee of five persons to be elected by the Norwegian Storting, or Parliament. It is not known why Nobel made this choice, but historians have said that it may have been to encourage improved relations between the two nations: when the bequest was made, Norway was still ruled by Sweden. Others have argued one reason Nobel made his choice was that the Norwegian Parliament had shown an interest in the mediation of international disputes. In any event, well-placed observers in Oslo believe that Norway's long history as a foreign-ruled nation (by Denmark for hundreds of years before Sweden took over in 1814) gave it a special sensitivity to oppressed peoples.

The first Nobel Peace Prize, in 1901, was shared by Henry Dunant, the founder of the Geneva-based International Committee of the Red Cross, who had left the organization, ultimately becoming a leading advocate for peace in an increasingly militaristic atmosphere in Europe. Bertha von Suttner herself received the prize in 1905. But the award honored statesmen as well: President Theodore Roosevelt received it in 1906 for his mediation in the Russo-Japanese War: his maxim, "Speak softly and carry a big stick" was made popular. President Woodrow Wilson won in 1920 for his role in the establishment of the League of Nations, while General George C. Marshall received the award in 1953 for his work on the aid plan to Europe that bore his name.

Before and since, the laureates have been a mixture of activists, organizations, statesmen and religious leaders for a wide array of causes ranging from refugee work, Middle East peace, and the YMCA. Until 1960, when Chief Albert Lutuli of South Africa was honored, the Nobel Peace Prize had only been awarded in Europe and the Western Hemisphere. The Nobel Committee itself sees its omission of Mahatma Gandhi in the 1940s as its most notable mistake, based on an apparent unwillingness to offend Norway's traditional ally, Great Britain, the colonial ruler of India.

In historical terms, the award that is perhaps unparalleled in terms of sheer guts, and the one that put the Nobel Peace Prize on the world map as never before, was the prize to Carl von Ossietzky. A Catholic pacifist and journalist, Ossietzky courageously criticized the Nazis before Hitler took power in 1933. He remained in Germany when offered the chance to flee abroad; tortured in a concentration camp, he refused to recant his views. A free thinker, he criticized the excesses of both the right and the left. Ossietzky was previously unknown outside Germany when his friends abroad began a campaign to draw attention to his plight and win his release. They decided that a Nobel Peace Prize would be the best way to accomplish this.

The Nazi regime began to worry about the campaign for Ossietzky, coming as it did at the time of the 1936 Summer Olympics in Berlin. The

German ambassador in Oslo informed the Norwegian government that if Ossietzky won the Nobel Peace Prize, it would have "unfortunate consequences," writes Irwin Abrams, a leading historian on the Peace Prize. Coming at "a time when ruling circles in Europe were either denying that the Nazis were committing atrocities or looking the other way," giving the Peace Prize to Ossietzky took phenomenal courage, taking into account Norway's contacts with Germany and its vulnerability, as a nation of less than four million people as opposed to a German colossus more than fifteen times that size.

Though the Norwegian government argued that the Nobel Committee was entirely independent, the committee, in effect, took upon itself responsibility for any retaliation Hitler might have visited upon Norway. It is difficult to think of any prize that has been given at such potential risk to the awarding institution and its community. While the Peace Prizes awarded to Russian physicist Andrei Sakharov in 1975 and Lech Walesa, the leader of the Solidarity trade union in Poland, in 1983, surely antagonized the Soviet Union, with which Norway shares a border, the element of risk was hardly the same as that in 1936.

No award or awards committee can ever be perfect, and there has been criticism on occasion. The 1973 award to Henry Kissinger, then National Security Advisor to President Nixon, and North Vietnamese negotiator Le Duc Tho, drew fire from all sides, coming as it did after the United States had conducted one of the most massive bombing campaigns in modern history to force a peace settlement, which had collapsed. Norwegian peace groups were outraged, throwing snowballs on the day of the awards ceremony. For his part, Le Duc Tho declined to accept the award. (The bitterness remained nearly 25 years later: "What can you expect from people who would honor Le Duc Tho?" a former senior aide to Henry Kissinger complained when Ramos-Horta received the award.)

Lapses aside, the Nobel Committee's members, mainly former parliamentarians and other political or academic leaders, have acted as an entity with a worldwide constituency, taking a broad historical view. Indeed, the current chairman of the committee, Francis Sejersted, is a distinguished historian, as is the non-voting permanent secretary, Geir Lundestad. Another committee member, Gunnar Staalsett, the former general secretary of the Lutheran World Federation, which represents 57 million Lutherans, has a wide set of interests in international human rights, freedom of religion and the mediation of disputes. Consecrated Bishop of Oslo in 1998, he was honored himself late that year for his persistent and careful work on the peace process in Guatemala, where a long civil war had claimed many tens of thousands of lives. Staalsett received Guatemala's highest official decoration for his many years of personal involvement in the peace effort.

Through commitment of this kind, the Nobel award has helped facilitate social change in many places, and at strategic moments. The Rev. Dr. Martin Luther King Jr., the laureate in 1964, made it clear that the recognition provided by the Nobel Peace Prize had an energizing effect on himself as well as his movement. The timing could not have been better, a year after the 1963 march on Washington and only a few short months after three civil rights workers—James Chaney, Andrew Goodman, and Michael Schwerner—were killed while trying to register voters in Mississippi. King's receipt of the award sparked outrage in the segregationist South of those days and among the powerful, most notably F.B.I. director J. Edgar Hoover. Although the United States was an ally of Norway, the Nobel Committee did not hesitate to address America's most sensitive social issue.

Organizations have also benefitted, most notably, in recent decades, the 1977 winner, Amnesty International, the London-based human rights movement that has worked to free political detainees and end torture since it was founded in 1961. The Nobel award has helped give the organization worldwide credibility and visibility, and made it more effective. More recently, the International Campaign to Ban Landmines and its coordinator, Jody Williams, an American, were beneficiaries, addressing a crucial humanitarian issue. In another sphere, illustrating the diversity of recipients, the work of the Roman Catholic order, the Missionaries of Charity, received significant recognition when its founder, Mother Teresa, received the award in 1979. The Peace Prize was also of great importance to the cause of the 1984 laureate, Bishop Desmond Tutu of South Africa. It provided momentum for the anti-apartheid movement and protection for Tutu, who was later elevated to archbishop. And in 1986, the Nobel Committee commemorated the fiftieth anniversary of its award to Ossietzky by honoring Elie Wiesel, the writer, lecturer, and Holocaust survivor whose unflagging efforts have helped make it impossible for the world to forget the crimes committed by the Nazis against the Jews and other victimized groups: "a man who has climbed from utter humiliation to become one of our most important spiritual leaders and guides," in the words of the chairman of the Nobel Committee at that time. In 1987, the Committee honored President Oscar Arias of Costa Rica, whose newly developed peace plan ultimately helped lay the groundwork for a settlement in Central

America. In 1992, the Committee returned to the region, backing Mayan activist Rigoberta Menchu of Guatemala; this helped provide impetus for a peace agreement between the warring sides in that country which went into effect in late 1996. In 1994 the award was given to three recipients (the maximum possible in one year) for efforts toward peace in the Middle East: Yasser Arafat, Palestine Liberation Organization Chairman; Shimon Peres; and Yitzak Rabin, then Israeli Foreign Minister and Prime Minister, respectively. The fact that a Nobel Peace Prize is no guarantee of success has been amply illustrated in this troubled region, with Rabin assassinated in 1995 and future prospects uncertain. In 1998, the Nobel Committee returned to another of its longstanding areas of concern, Northern Ireland, honoring John Hume and David Trimble, prominent political figures who have taken great risks to help forge the peace effort. The decision drew criticism, with some saying that the Irish Republican Army leader, Gerry Adams, also should have been included, though others believed the choice of Adams would have infuriated many Northern Ireland Protestants and complicated peace efforts. It illustrated how very difficult it was for the Nobel Committee to please everyone.

Still, in Asia, the 1989 award to the Dalai Lama has given the Tibetan cause a worldwide platform and has helped make the Dalai Lama one of the world's best known people. The 1991 prize to Daw Aung San Suu Kyi, the leader of the National League for Democracy in Burma, has helped her become one of the world's most admired women. Despite continuing repression in Burma, the military regime that runs that country is more sensitive to international public opinion in the wake of the prize to Suu Kyi than it was beforehand; events such as the massacre of an estimated 3,000 people during the student demonstrations of 1988 have not been repeated on that scale, though the government remains harsh and brutal.

Even rumors that one might receive a Nobel Peace Prize have been known to have a beneficial impact. When longterm Chinese political prisoner and pro-democracy dissident Wei Jingsheng was released in 1997, it was said by one key expert to be in good measure because the government in Beijing had "a horror" that he might be more likely to receive the prize if he remained in jail. Throughout the world, speculation of this nature, however unfounded, has sometimes had a positive influence on events.

The trip to Oslo to receive the Nobel award was a short respite for Bishop Belo, though he was besieged by journalists, few of whom he was able to accommodate because of the conditions under which he was allowed to make the trip. Even at this historic moment, Oslo was swarming with Indonesian intelligence agents monitoring the bishop's every move. As is customary, Belo and Ramos-Horta stayed at the Grand Hotel, also the site of the Norwegian Nobel Committee's banquet honoring the laureates. It is a place of understated elegance, where the playwright Henrik Ibsen, the father of modern drama, whose works were marked by a vision of moral seriousness and responsibility to humanity, had once gathered with his friends every day in the cafe.

An ecumenical service the day before the Nobel ceremony set the tone for this extraordinary event, the granting of the world's most prestigious prize to two individuals from a place, as the chairman of the Nobel Committee put it, as far from Norway as anywhere on earth.

"The Church of Norway stands with the Church in East Timor," said the rector of Oslo Cathedral, illustrating the generosity of spirit that characterized the Nobel award. Here, in an overwhelmingly Lutheran nation, a Catholic bishop from a nation occupied by a regime with a vulnerable Protestant minority—indeed, a Lutheran minority as well—was being so recognized, without regard to religion. It was an eloquent message that the plight of East Timor was a world problem, not one of narrow parochial interests. (For its part, Norway has a community of only about 25,000 Catholics, but its aid agency, Caritas Norway, is in the forefront of international organizations working in East Timor.)

Alfred Nobel had died exactly one hundred years to the day before Bishop Belo and Ramos-Horta received the Peace Prize in Oslo's Town Hall on December 10, 1996. The bishop emphasized that

> . . . I believe that I have received this high tribute not because of who I am or what I have done. I firmly believe that I am here as the voice of the voiceless people of East Timor . . . And what the people want is peace, an end to violence and respect for their human rights.

But Belo's Nobel lecture, while making an urgent plea for the release of political prisoners in East Timor and measures that might support a just settlement of the conflict there, addressed a wide range of international human rights issues and struck a universal note:

> I stand humbled in the august presence of my predecessors in this place here in Oslo. I think of the Reverend Dr. Martin Luther King Jr., standing on the mountaintop, looking out at the promised land. These words remind me of the view of the majestic mountains in my beloved East Timor—Mount Matebian (the Mountain of the

Dead), near where I was born in the east; and Mount Ramelau in the west. As I look at these mountains in my frequent journeys throughout my native land, I feel ever more strongly that it is high time that the guns of war are silenced in East Timor, once and forever, it is high time that tranquillity is returned to the lives of the people of my homeland, it is high time that there be authentic dialogue . . .

And let us always think of many anonymous people throughout the world, struggling for the protection of human rights. Day by day, working to convince the international community of the justice of their cause; whether they be Moslems or Christians, Protestants or Catholics, Hindus or Buddhists, whether they be followers of age-old traditional beliefs, believers or non-believers, I say: press on, take courage, remain true to your ideals, you will not be forgotten . . .

Returning to the subject of the quest for peace and an end to suffering in East Timor, Belo said that

I speak of these things as one who has the responsibility to bear witness to what I have seen and heard, to react to what I know to be true, to keep the flame of hope alive, to do what is possible to warm the earth for another day. I speak as a spiritual leader, not as a politician, which in fact, I am not. In recent weeks, some articles have described me as "a former shepherd," not realizing that my vocation only evolved from a boyhood job of tending water buffaloes to the grave responsibility of trying to apply my fallible self to the difficult task of providing moral leadership in a situation where almost no one is ever completely happy with my actions.

Others have written that if there had not been a war in East Timor, I would be spending all my time tending to the needs of troubled youth . . . but this is only a matter of degree: even now, I spend an overwhelming amount of energy in listening to and counseling the youth of East Timor, who urgently need such help because of their history. This is my special obligation, and one which I welcome.

And the bishop, noting the way the United Nations helped bring independence to Indonesia in the 1940s, reminded the world of the role of UN efforts regarding East Timor, which have been of central importance in keeping the issue alive over many long years. . . . the United Nations have continued to persevere in the interest of generating dialogue that might one day create a lasting structure of peace in East Timor, and in many other places throughout the world.

The chairman of the Norwegian Nobel Committee, Francis Sejersted, gave a perspective in his own Nobel lecture that neatly summarized East Timor's struggle:

> The conflict in East Timor has been called 'the forgotten conflict.' It has not, however, been completely forgotten, having figured on the international agenda, with varying degrees of prominence, throughout those twenty years. But it has, so to speak, never caught on. There have been so many interests . . . to attend to, and East Timor is so small. Rarely has the cynicism of world politics been more clearly demonstrated . . .

After Oslo, Bishop Belo stopped in Norway's second largest city of Bergen for a torchlight parade, a meeting with schoolchildren and a ceremony at the town hall. Then he moved on to the traditional stop for Nobel Peace laureates in Stockholm. These were some of the darkest and coldest days of the year in frigid Sweden, but it was also a time when the festival of Santa Lucia was celebrated, marked by serenading and the lighting of candles. Bishop Belo was received by Sweden's royal family and other high government officials, just as he and his co-recipient had been in Norway. A memorable moment underscoring the universality of the occasion came in his homily at Stockholm's Catholic Cathedral, in which the bishop reflected on Santa Lucia—it was a miracle, he said, that an Italian saint, a Catholic, had become the centerpiece of Swedish Lutheran tradition.

From Sweden Bishop Belo traveled to Germany. In Bonn, Chancellor Helmut Kohl met with Belo for an hour and a half, considerably longer than Belo's later meeting with President Clinton. But Kohl, like Clinton, was not anxious to upset his relations with Indonesia.

Finally, it was on to Rome. In early 1996, all the talk had been not about whether Bishop Belo would receive the Nobel Peace Prize, but rather about whether he would actually remain as bishop of Dili much longer. Even Belo had his doubts about his fate when he met with a friend in Dili that February. His Indonesian antagonists were determined to be rid of this difficult character, once and for all. Without someone of Belo's visibility and moral stature in the territory, East Timor would have suffered a serious setback in the international arena. No matter how worthy any possible replacement, no matter how clever or reasonable or decent, a new bishop would be unknown internationally. The Suharto regime believed that removing Belo would remove a big international headache.

Bishop Belo had been aware of these maneuvers, as he walked through the grand corridors of the Apostolic Palace in the Vatican that May. But there were also friendly quarters in Rome. Earlier he had received a long-awaited visit in late February 1996 by Cardinal Roger Etchegeray, the French head of the Pontifical Council for Justice and Peace and one of the pope's leading diplomatic troubleshooters. The cardinal tackled some of the Vatican's most difficult problems, in China, Central America, Central Africa, and Cuba. Before leaving East Timor after a two-day visit, Cardinal Etchegeray called Belo "a brave bishop, close to his people." Upon returning to Rome, Etchegeray immediately met with the pope and informed him of his findings: essentially, that despite the criticism by his Indonesian opponents and some Vatican officials, Bishop Belo was probably all that stood between East Timor and a violent explosion. After Cardinal Etchegeray returned from Dili, the Vatican Secretary of State, Cardinal Angelo Sodano, said that "the Timorese must realize they are not alone, and Bishop Belo knows that." Thus, when Bishop Belo came to Rome for only three days in May 1996 he was quickly granted an audience with John Paul II. Soon after this meeting, Belo was more confident in his position than ever before.

Now, seven months later, on December 20, he was back at the Apostolic Palace with a Nobel Peace Prize in hand. Pope John Paul II was warm and gave words of encouragement about the bishop's receipt of the Nobel award: "I hope it will be a shield for you to work more for peace in East Timor . . . continue working for the people with the same enthusiasm, the same faith and the same loyalty." There seemed to be no doubt where the pope stood regarding the Peace Prize—hadn't Lech Walesa, the leader of Poland's Solidarity trade union, received it in 1983? Bishop Belo was buoyant after his meeting with John Paul, who had been represented at the Nobel ceremony in Oslo on December 10 by Cardinal Etchegeray. At the banquet honoring the recipients that evening, the cardinal nodded his head with vigor at the words of Francis Sejersted, who called for greater international attention for the East Timor problem. "I was proud to be standing next to you," he told Bishop Belo later.

But there were other, less hospitable quarters in the Apostolic Palace that the new Nobel laureate visited. He walked past intricate renditions of old maps of the world lining the walls in long marble corridors, packed with artifacts from all parts of the globe, a reminder of the historic progression of the Roman Catholic Church. In their own way, these maps symbolized the nature of Bishop Belo's problem, and the problem of East Timor in the international arena. The maps gave prominent notice to the East Indies for their abundant resources and immense political significance. However, one small part of the East Indies, the eastern half of Timor island, appears paltry compared with the Indonesian archipelago as a whole.

When Carlos Filipe Ximenes Belo reached the offices of the Secretariat of State, which deals with the international relations of the Vatican, a senior official was icy: "Now that you have won the Nobel Peace Prize, Monsignor, should I kneel before you?" he said to Bishop Belo, with the utmost sarcasm.

"Excellency, it is I that should kneel before you," replied Belo modestly.

"Because," another senior official added, "you may have the Nobel Peace Prize, but you still must win the pastoral prize," a reference to Belo's position as apostolic administrator, which is not a permanent bishop, only an acting bishop. But Bishop Belo and his supporters in Rome maintain that work in defense of the people *is* pastoral, not merely something incidental. Nonetheless, even after he received the Nobel award, one important Vatican official continued to press for Belo's removal, only to be told that this was now politically impossible. Despite the kind words of the pope and Cardinals Sodano and Etchegeray, Belo's problems with the Holy See—and East Timor's—were not over.

In the center of Saint Peter's Basilica in the Vatican, above the statue of Saint Peter himself, there is a statue of another saint. This one is of a hero of the modern Roman Catholic Church: Saint John Bosco, surrounded by young people in need of his protection. After his meetings in the Apostolic Palace, Carlos Filipe Ximenes Belo went to pray by the statue of Don Bosco, hoping this would give him strength in his difficulties.

The Indonesian military clearly wanted to send their own message after Bishop Belo left Rome and returned to Dili on Christmas Eve, and they lost little time in doing so. Only two hours after he landed, violence of a particularly insidious kind resumed like clockwork.

As Bishop Belo was saying Mass in Dili Cathedral, a struggle ensued outside, where a group beat to death a mentally disturbed Timorese soldier in the Indonesian Army who, it was claimed, planned to assassinate the bishop. There had, of course, been many rumored plots of this nature, including several after the Nobel announcement. Some knowledgeable sources insisted the mastermind was Major General Prabowo Subianto, the son-in-law of President Suharto. Well-placed sources in the diocese were convinced that the Indonesians themselves had provoked the murder of the alleged would-be assassin.

The bishop condemned the killing and went to visit the soldier's widow. "I don't agree with this radical action of killing that man," Belo said. He was deeply saddened by these violent actions and the way they desecrated the cathedral on Christmas Eve, ruining the holiday.

Representative Patrick J. Kennedy, Democrat of Rhode Island and the son of Senator Edward M. Kennedy, had arrived on the same flight with Bishop Belo, and felt he was in the midst of an historic event, joining a population that seemed awestruck until the murder took place. Afterward, Kennedy visited the bishop at his home, then returned for midnight Mass. Bishop Belo noted Kennedy's presence for those assembled, sending an unmistakable signal to the military that an important foreign witness was on the scene, which may have helped to avert further violence that night.

It was difficult to know if the murder at Dili Cathedral had been concocted by the Indonesian military to heighten the psychological strain on Belo and send tension in East Timor to fever pitch; it had long been a tactic of the Indonesian intelligence apparatus to create an atmosphere in which the situation seemed as hopeless as possible, the better to demoralize a long-suffering population. The bishop himself had questions about the authenticity of the plots, particularly the one on Christmas Eve, because its main aim seemed to be nothing more than destruction of the happy and festive mood.

In the months that followed, the Indonesian military used the murder of the soldier on Christmas Eve as a pretext to clamp down hard, as another important visitor, U.S. Representative Frank Wolf, a Virginia Republican, observed in mid-January 1997. Wolf, one of the first in Congress to nominate Bishop Belo for the Nobel Peace Prize, said that he had visited corners of the world where people live in fear: Sarajevo, before U.S. peacekeeping troops arrived in Bosnia; Chechnya, while its battle with Russia was raging; Sudan, in the midst of vicious conflict; and China. But the abject terror he found on his visit to East Timor was as bad as anything he had ever seen.

Photographs of Bishop Belo taken by Wolf during the visit showed years of hard toil etched on the Timorese prelate's face. His features were almost distorted, twisted in some excruciating kind of pain. A massive crackdown by Indonesian security forces had resulted in the beating and torture of hundreds of young people, many whose only "crime" was to wear a T-shirt with Belo's likeness on it. Around the same time, President Suharto, in what appeared to be another calculated snub to the Nobel Peace Prize, paid a visit to the military rulers of Burma, who continued to hold the country's main opposition leader, 1991 Peace laureate Daw Aung San Suu Kyi, under virtual house arrest.

Representative Wolf returned from East Timor outraged by what he had witnessed. Back at home, a powerful company in his Virginia district—Mobil Oil, with its sizeable stake in Indonesia—was not pleased with his interest in East Timor. The American Petroleum Institute, too, was unhappy with Wolf. During this time, BHP Petroleum and Phillips Petroleum announced a multibillion-dollar natural gas project centered in the Timor Gap region. Far from being warned off the issue, Representative Wolf became one of the most active members of Congress on the question.

Around the same time, a senior Clinton administration official stated bluntly in a private conversation that if Bishop Belo became too identified with the issue of self-determination for East Timor—that is, the goal of a free and fair election, which, among others things, might call into question Indonesian ownership of the Timor Gap—President Clinton and White House officials might refuse to see the bishop. In 1995, the World Court, which the United States has accepted as an authority in other disputes, had confirmed that the people of East Timor were indeed entitled to their internationally recognized right to self-determination. But the World Court's decision seemed to mean little to the Clinton administration in this case.

Meanwhile, in mid-March 1997, Pope John Paul II called for a "global solution" for East Timor, but this clearly was not an immediate prospect. Only days after the pope's statement, the special United Nations envoy, Jamsheed Marker of Pakistan, visited Dili with Fransesc Vendrell of Spain, the UN official who has played the most significant role on the East Timor issue since 1975 and a key player in bringing peace to Central America. East Timor seemed no less difficult. Indonesian authorities told Timorese students that Marker and Vendrell would meet them at the university, but when the UN officials failed to show up (in fact, the government had never informed the two diplomats about the meeting), a group of young people came to their hotel the next morning. It was another trick by the authorities, and a trap: police allowed the youngsters to enter the lobby of the Hotel Mahkota on Dili's waterfront, not far from the harbor where people had been shot when Indonesia first invaded. The military and police locked the glass doors and attacked the unarmed group with clubs. The students, some of whom tried to defend themselves and break through the glass doors to escape, came under ferocious assault. Dozens were arrested.

Bishop Belo rushed to visit them in jail. He was only allowed to see some of them. "But the faces of some that I did see were injured as if they had been beaten," he said. All told, the faces of at least thirty-six, including some young women, were black and blue—all for trying to meet with United Nations officials.

It was a sobering message. Belo went to Portugal in May to attend ceremonies at the Catholic shrine of Fatima marking the eightieth anniversary of the "apparition" of the Virgin Mary to three child shepherds. Immediately after he left East Timor, his mood was dominated by thoughts of the terrible crackdown that Indonesian forces had unleashed.

"The simple act of shouting 'Long Live the Nobel' or 'Long Live Ximenes Belo' set off arrests, questioning, and torture," Bishop Belo said soon after he arrived in Portugal. In fact, some in East Timor spread rumors blaming the bishop, saying that he had received a great award while the people paid the consequences. In reality, he had received little himself: the bishop's share of the prize money of about $1.2 million (equally divided with his co-recipient) was earmarked for a new major seminary to be built. But talk like this added to the disheartening atmosphere. The bishop needed relief.

He set out early one morning for southern Portugal with Father Mauricio de Bastos e Pinho, who had been part of the bishop's core of supporters during the darkest years of his ministry. He had spent a year with young Belo in Macau when the Indonesians first invaded East Timor. A key organizer of the Salesian mission in Portugal, Father Mauricio was strongly built with an affable manner: he sported a goatee and resembled the actor Fernando Rey. They set out across the Tagus River, stopping after a couple of hours for coffee and *bagaço*, a strong grape brandy. Surprisingly, the bishop downed his glass with gusto shortly after 10:00 A.M. Belo would never drink anything like that at such an hour at home—perhaps not at any hour—but this was Portugal, and the atmosphere was far lighter.

Around midday the bishop arrived in the coastal town of Albufeira in the Algarve region, once a center of the Moorish presence in Portugal centuries ago. It was a place of magnificent sunshine, fresh air, light, and relaxation, a universe away from the horrors in East Timor. Belo was toasted on all fronts and greeted like a hero, first by townspeople, then at school after school of applauding children who, in their own way, made it impossible for the Portuguese government to abandon the East Timor issue: leading politicians and diplomats made it clear that their own sons and daughters pressed them on the matter. The bishop warmed to his role. He was among friends in a country where he had spent many years as a student and, as an added relief, he was asked few political questions.

Sometimes it could be difficult for Belo in the Portugal of the 1990s, because there were many people who found it hard to grasp why he behaved as he did. Some did not see why Belo had to be careful in his public statements and actions—why, for instance, the bishop insisted that the time was not yet right to receive the Order of Liberty, an honorary award offered by the President of the Republic, Jorge Sampaio. Of course, acceptance of this award in 1997 from Portugal, Indonesia's diplomatic archenemy, or too many forthright declarations, might infuriate Indonesian forces marauding through East Timor. So the bishop chose to be circumspect.

It was easier when Bishop Belo crossed the Atlantic to receive an honorary doctorate at Yale University: no speech was required. Still, there was overwhelming applause from hundreds of students for Belo as he crossed the stage to receive his diploma on a sunny afternoon at the end of May. It was a measure of the widening public recognition of the East Timor cause since the Nobel Peace Prize.

But even as Bishop Belo was going to see the new United Nations secretary general, Kofi Annan, there came news of a series of military attacks carried out by Indonesian forces to coincide with elections being held throughout Indonesia. These elections, for a rubber stamp parliament largely controlled by Suharto, were not free, and in East Timor, where most were forced to cast a ballot and where people's nerves were already raw from the crackdown since Oslo, it rankled. Guerrilla commander David Alex and his men launched a series of attacks that had disastrous consequences for themselves and people living in their region, as military forces struck back harshly, with numerous arrests and terrible reprisals in these areas. Many were killed and others faced very long prison sentences.

If anything, the Nobel Peace Prize should have underscored the need to stop these kinds of offensive measures once and for all, Belo thought. He had long made it clear that such attacks and militant demonstrations should be abandoned. Soon Alex, a man with haunting, deep-set eyes who had an almost mystical reputation for his ability to hold out for so long, was himself killed. A senior international human rights expert said privately that such guerrilla attacks were "suicidal in terms of international public opinion and massive retaliation."

The situation at home preoccupied the bishop, but his meetings abroad were a vital counterweight. In the Netherlands, Belo was hosted by a fellow Salesian, Bishop Adrian van Luyn of Rotterdam. He also visited M.P.

Muskens, bishop of Breda and a distinguished historian of the Church in Indonesia. Muskens saluted Belo for his own spiritual strength and that of his people. The town was immortalized in the epic painting "The Surrender of Breda" by Diego Velázquez the seventeenth century, when the Low Countries were occupied by Spain. Except for the crucial fact that the Netherlands regained their independence, Breda might always have been a symbol of oppression. The parallels were not lost on Bishop Muskens's guest.

Neither were similar historical echoes in Ireland, where Bishop Belo headed next, surrounded by well-wishers in Dublin and County Waterford. It was at this time that a British TV documentary highlighted arms sales to Indonesia, specifically machine guns mounted on Land Rovers used by elite Red Beret troops in East Timor's countryside. Belo recognized them by sight, and was outraged. When he went on to Britain to deliver a lecture sponsored by CAFOD, the Catholic aid agency, he made a passionate appeal: "Please, I beg you, restrict still further the conditions under which this trade is permitted. Do not sustain any longer a conflict which, without these sales, could never have been pursued in the first place, nor for so long."

Arms sales were also a central issue when he went to Liverpool at the invitation of Archbishop Patrick Kelly, the chairman of CAFOD. In a 1996 trial in Liverpool, four women had been acquitted on charges of using hammers to inflict damage on Hawk fighter aircraft made by British Aerospace that were destined for Indonesia. The women, part of a group called "Seeds of Hope—Ploughshares," who had spent months in prison awaiting trial, made the argument that their actions were aimed at preventing crimes against humanity. Unexpectedly, their argument prevailed. Now, the Ploughshares women, as they were called, came to a religious service for Bishop Belo.

The bishop's brief visit to Liverpool, coupled with his next destination in the Italian city of Padua, provided an amazing illustration of the wide range of support that he, as a Nobel laureate and clergyman, was able to attract. Belo was invited to Padua by *The Messenger of St. Anthony,* an international Catholic magazine. The previous year a pilgrimage with relics of Saint Anthony had traveled throughout the world, including East Timor, where Anthony, originally from Portugal, was also the patron saint. Among them was Father Egidio Canil, a Franciscan priest who had spent time in East Timor and was the bishop's host in Italy.

The day of Saint Anthony was commemorated in Padua's cathedral. It was a warm evening, and afterward the Franciscan Friars, long associated with efforts for peace, took the bishop and local friends to have a refreshing *gelato*. Among them was an Italian brigadier general attached to NATO, upright in his blue uniform. Of course he was a supporter of Bishop Belo, the general stated robustly. From Liverpool to Padua, it was a broad coalition indeed.

There was something historically rich and symbolic about the meeting with the cardinal patriarch of Venice (from where five popes originated, including John XXIII and the short-lived John Paul I). Holding Bishop Belo's hand in Saint Mark's Cathedral, Cardinal Marco Cé told him that "East Timor was an unknown issue, but the Nobel Peace Prize elevated it to the top." Bishop Belo said that these words made his heart beat much faster. The bishop was also thrilled to be in a place where his hero, Saint Francis Xavier, had been ordained as a priest more than four hundred years before.

After Padua and Venice, Bishop Belo encountered an old Salesian friend, Don Giovanni Locatelli, whose nephew remained in East Timor running the Salesian school at Fatumaca after more than thirty years. Don Giovanni had tears in his eyes in the city of Ferrara as he described how he would invite Belo for holidays during his student days in Rome: he reminded the bishop of how far he had traveled since the time he would spend all day in Ferrara collecting scrap paper for recycling, to raise funds for Fatumaca.

The bishop's reception in Assisi was another milestone, in light of all the historical associations of the town where Saint Francis centered his efforts to assist the downtrodden. That East Timor was being linked with such a place was a testament to its newfound prominence on the world stage. At a dinner in the Franciscan refectory, the superior said he wished Bishop Belo was a member of their order.

Bishop Belo gave a homily on peace in the Basilica of Saint Francis, whose walls are adorned with the paintings of Giotto. At the end of the service, he seemed at ease as he walked through the church shaking hands with a warm, broad smile. He sang hymns at the tomb of Saint Francis. If he felt at home in Portugal, he felt only slightly less so in his other former place of study in Italy.

Just as he was preparing to return to the United States to address three hundred American Catholic bishops in Kansas City, Belo had news from Dili of arrests, torture with electric shocks, and attacks by the military throughout the territory. Bishop Belo wanted to return home immediately, but he did not. He needed the friendship of his American colleagues, and in Kansas City he received a standing ovation from the assembly of bishops, plus special support from the head of the U.S. Catholic Conference's international policy committee, Archbishop Theodore McCarrick of Newark, and powerful figures like Cardinal Bernard Law of Boston. Belo felt encouraged before his visit to Washington, where he thought President Clinton might be able to help.

Not long before Bishop Belo walked up the pathway to the White House, the *Washington Post* had revealed that Webster Hubbell, the disgraced former associate attorney general, had been taken to East Timor in 1994, at a time when he was still a close friend of the first family. During his visit to East Timor, Hubbell was on the payroll of the Lippo Group, an Indonesian conglomerate owned by the Riady banking family linked to the 1996 campaign finance scandal. An Indonesian official cited by the *Post* explained that the Riadys said "letting a friend of Clinton's see Timor might help change U.S. policy. So naturally we thought it was a good idea." Asked in April 1997 what influence the Riady connection may have had on American policy toward East Timor, a White House official replied, "I don't know and I don't want to know."

There was no hint of any of this in the meeting that finally took place, which the White House described as "very cordial." President Clinton, characteristically personable, was warm in his praise of Bishop Belo. The president asked the bishop why Indonesia wanted to hold on to East Timor. The bishop replied, "Perhaps because of the oil in the Timor Sea." Clinton then said, surprisingly, that a way should be found to share that money fairly—seeming to hold out the hope that the United States might ask Indonesia to do so. But the actual meaning of Clinton's words remained a mystery, because there was no indication of any subsequent action.

Soon after Bishop Belo returned to Dili following his meeting with Clinton, it was reported that he would be summoned to Jakarta to be questioned by government officials on his session with the American president. Washington was alerted to this turn of events, and it appears that a protest was delivered by the Clinton administration to the Indonesian government. "We do not take kindly to a Nobel Prize winner who met the president being interrogated about it," said a senior White House official privately. In the end, whatever their initial plans to query Belo, it appears that the Indonesian government quickly dropped the idea after signals from Washington of its displeasure.

Bishop Belo was surely grateful for this show of support, but he said that he had no real fear for himself. It was the young people who had none of the advantages available to him. What he wanted from the Clinton administration was action to create a better future.

The situation in East Timor remained difficult through the summer of 1997, but bad as it was, the Nobel Peace Prize still held out the promise of change. This was evident when Bishop Belo went to a conference sponsored by the president of the Czech Republic, Vaclav Havel, and Nobel Peace laureate Elie Wiesel in September in Prague. It was called "Forum 2000" and it involved discussions with scores of distinguished people from various fields.

In addition to his co-laureate Jose Ramos-Horta, a number of other Nobel Peace laureates participated in the gathering, and though they were not personally acquainted with the bishop, he had become a familiar face from newspaper photos alone. Several greeted him, including former President Oscar Arias of Costa Rica and former Israeli Foreign Minister Shimon Peres. Also in attendance was the Dalai Lama, with whom Belo had enjoyed a cordial exchange of ideas in 1995. And there was former South African President F. W. de Klerk, who shared the award in 1993 with his country's current president, Nelson Mandela. All of the Peace laureates present signed a letter to President Suharto asking him to reconsider Indonesia's policy on East Timor. (The former Australian Foreign Minister, Gareth Evans, who once said, dismissively, with reference to the illegality of the Indonesian presence in East Timor, that "the world is a pretty unfair place," also signed the letter, indicating a welcome change of heart.)

Though not at the Prague conference, President Mandela had become involved in East Timor diplomacy. On a visit to Indonesia in July 1997, he met with Xanana Gusmão, who was taken from prison to have dinner with the South African leader. Mandela then said that "We can never normalize the situation in East Timor until all political prisoners, including Mr. Gusmão, are freed."

President Mandela then met with José Ramos-Horta in South Africa, and invited Bishop Belo as well. But the bishop declined to go immediately, saying that Mandela "should talk to the Indonesian generals." It was characteristic Belo: he was concerned with substance rather than ceremony, believed there was little likelihood that the Indonesian regime would change its policy in the short term, and saw little point in raising unrealistic expectations in East Timor by immediately boarding a plane for South Africa.

The bishop finally was able to visit President Mandela several weeks later, and while there were no immediate results, there were, at least, possibilities that had not existed before: "I am very grateful," Bishop Belo said after they met.

A year after receiving the Nobel Peace Prize, there was, at the very least, a sense of being far less alone. The East Timorese people's crocodile-shaped island was illuminated in the world consciousness, and, despite all the difficulties, prospects for the future had been transformed. And the Nobel Peace Prize for East Timor was a signal to the world that every place, no matter how small, should know justice, and none should escape international scrutiny of abuses of human rights.

10

PERSEVERANCE

❖ ❖ ❖ ❖

THREE WEEKS AFTER returning from his visit to Nelson Mandela, Bishop Carlos Filipe Ximenes Belo began the day in his usual manner, praying the Psalms and the third part of the rosary in his little chapel, the sounds of the neighborhood rooster his only companion. Wherever he had been, whomever he had met there, the simplicity of Belo's life around his modest Iberian-style house was unchanged.

As he had done since childhood, he would awaken with the sunrise and devote himself to a day of prayer, hard work, and, sometimes, music, like a cassette tape of big band jazz or something classical. Despite all the horror that East Timor had endured and continued to experience, Belo believed that the beauty of life, like the starlit skies over the coast near Baucau, which his mother would point out to him when he would grow sad as a boy, transcended any hardship. One could see this attitude when the bishop watched with delight as the children sang in the church choir, played football across the road, or drank tea and ate cakes on festival days. It could also be seen in his delighted reaction when birds chased and teased each other in the trees above his house, even when he watched a small brown lizard on the ceiling. In a word, it was *alegria*, the Portuguese word for joy and happiness, especially in simple things, combined with a faith superior to human woes, that kept Carlos Filipe Ximenes Belo going.

It was nearly forty years since his boyhood apprenticeship as "bishop" on the coral hillsides of Baucau, a lifetime away from the bishop's hat that he made out of grapefruit peel, with a stick for a crozier. From those innocent early years, using whatever materials were at hand, the fatherless boy had learned to improvise. Without a sword or any kind of weapon, and though he was small in size, Belo had shown himself to be as sturdy in his own way as his grandfather, the warrior Félix da Costa Ximenes, had been in his. The bishop bristled at the comparison, disliking the notion that he was in any way like his violent forebear. To the grandson, what mattered far more than physical strength or fierceness was perseverance, and that, so far as he was concerned, was rooted in faith above all else. With this, the bishop felt, one could ultimately triumph over adversity.

With a mixture of goodwill, nonviolence, and the common sense of the gardener and buffalo herder that Belo once was, the people of East Timor might yet escape the darkness of the past twenty-two years. As he prayed alone in his little chapel shortly after dawn on this October morning, the bishop was confident of this: success could still be theirs.

The bishop's joy and faith were infectious: as he moved through the countryside, making one pastoral visit after another, the mood in the hamlets, villages, and towns was buoyant, despite the ugliness visited upon them and the attempts to destroy their euphoria. Bishop Belo had returned months before to Quelicai to say Mass, near the place of birth of his ancestors, within sight of Matebian. Spirits there were strong. There was always a renewal of the spirit that could never be extinguished. After the news of the Nobel Peace Prize, the Indonesian military went from hamlet to hamlet, warning the people that the award would not save them. But the people believed that this prize from a far-off place would eventually bring help. So after the merciless bombing of Matebian, the deportations to Ataúro, the "fence of legs," the disappearances at Quelicai, and the carnage at Santa Cruz, came a resurrection in the form of worldwide recognition that could not be erased the way whole villages had been obliterated by Indonesian forces.

So many had died in East Timor that the place had a spectral air. But the ghosts would not sleep quietly: they were heard eventually, the ghosts of the East Timorese and the small number of foreigners who had perished there. In the broad sweep of history, all the riches in Indonesia and all the influence that could be bought in the centers of power could not, in the end, buy silence.

"The dead are beginning to be noticed," Bishop Belo had said a few years before. And so they were, even if belatedly. It was not only in the Santa Cruz cemetery and sites like Mount Matebian. It was more than in the killing grounds at Taci-Tolu, made known during the pope's visit. From the seaside road leading to the bishop's house, for instance, one could see the beaches of Areia Branca, "white sands" in English, where bodies were thrown into the ocean after the Indonesian invasion. The beach huts at Areia Branca now were scrawled with graffiti saying, simply, in Portuguese, "East Timor suffers," over a map of the island drawn in crayon.

For all that had happened, the people of East Timor had retained and deepened their faith, and to Carlos Filipe Ximenes Belo, this mattered more than any worldly prize. It was a crucial factor that enabled them to survive the terrible onslaught since 1975. Strong expressions of this faith could be seen on any morning, but Sundays were special. On this Sunday, shortly after 5:00 A.M., as the sun began to rise over the mountains behind the city, the East Timorese population of Dili poured into the streets and, taking advantage of the coolness of the hour, walked briskly toward Bishop Belo's residence. Some came from miles away, setting out from all parts of town. In the back streets, and along the coastal roads, people marched alone or by twos and fours, amid the scattered chickens, wild pigs, and goats that belonged to the residents of nearby huts. Most walked with a quick step, thus bespeaking their mood. There was a palpable sense of hope in the early morning hours, as if the coming of a new day might somehow bring with it a change in the history of their beleaguered homeland. Whatever fear they may have felt the night before, the gentle morning breeze that drifted by the bishop's residence near the water brought with it a freshness of purpose.

The Sunday morning open-air Mass drew about three thousand worshipers. By 6:00 A.M. the people had quietly slipped in the gate. They entered the compound and took almost every available space in the garden area behind the residence, in all the pathways between the white statues of Christ and the Virgin Mary, in every corner in the rear under the large banyan tree. There were few chairs available, so most were obliged to stand.

Much care was taken in preparation for the event, from the sparkling neatness of the participants to the condition of the grounds. Every Saturday afternoon, dozens of youngsters swept the area clean of leaves and other debris that had sprung from the assorted oleander bushes, mango trees and coconut palms, and foliage that lined the garden. After working for hours, using palm leaves as whisk brooms, the youngsters left the area immaculate. Bishop Belo would watch the clean-up crew and smile.

For Belo, Sunday Mass was a major source of strength, as he looked out into the crowd, more than half of them young people and children, together with a large number of females. It was a gathering ranging from the tiniest of children to the very old. The crowd extended to the long fence beside the coastal road, with people's backs literally against the wall, to the perimeters of his residence and the small blue and white brick dwelling on the side of the garden where his staff lived and worked. Whatever else may have happened to East Timor, their church community had not only remained intact, but it was thriving.

There was a striking absence of men middle-aged and older—not for any lack of piety, but because most had perished in the war. This was seen most clearly at public gatherings. An old man, thin and wizened, clutched an old Portuguese prayerbook. Later, a woman who once taught Portuguese started to cry, telling a visitor, "We are longing for the olden days." She was bold; most East Timorese avoided speaking with foreigners. Even visitors to friends at parish churches were often urged not to remain long.

In the back of the garden, beneath large trees, there were two automobiles covered with plastic sheeting, presented to Bishop Belo and his colleague, the newly appointed bishop of Baucau, Basílio do Nascimento. They were gifts from Indonesia's national car project, developed by Hutomo Suharto, known as "Tommy," the youngest son of the president. The venture was favored with special tax advantages that had drawn much international criticism, as had the very name of the car: "the Timor." It was "infelicitously named," said an editorial in the *Financial Times* of London, which was surely at least part of the reason neither Bishop Belo nor his new colleague had ever driven them. Next to the unused "Timor" cars sat a scale model of the Christ the King monument built outside Dili by the government and the national airline—another unwanted gift.

The omnipresent spies from Intel were in the assembled throng, but they were unobtrusive on this special day of the week, even if most knew who they were. The discord and corruption they represented were what most had come to flee. What was most striking was the spiritual unity of the parishioners. At this hour in scores of Catholic churches throughout East Timor, Bishop Belo knew the same spirit was manifest.

Maria de Fatima was in the front row of the small group lucky enough to have seats. Next to her was Mother Matilde, who was wearing a crucifix made long ago by one of the island's traditional silver craftsmen. The two women were glad that the situation had been almost quiet in recent days, which seemed to be a happy, if temporary, result of a visit by four foreign bishops; when such dignitaries arrived, there was normally an atmosphere of surface calm.

Two of the visiting bishops were at the Sunday service. The senior figure, on his second visit to the territory since 1989, was the retired Episcopal bishop of New York, Paul Moore Jr., and his wife, Brenda Moore. My wife, Korinna and I were traveling with the Moores, who were joined by an old Anglican friend, Ian George, the archbishop of Adelaide, Australia, who had himself lived and trained in New York many years before. Just as Bishop Moore had ministered to some of America's most powerful figures in his years in New York and Washington, so Archbishop George had done in his own country. He, like Bishop Moore, had visited East Timor before, having been there the previous year. Two other bishops were traveling in the countryside: Bishop Kevin Manning of the Australian Catholic Social Justice Council and Bishop William Brennan, an old friend of Bishop Belo. The Indonesian military tried to be on their best behavior when people of this stature were present. But after what took place at Santa Cruz—or, for that matter, after Christmas Eve at the Cathedral, when Patrick Kennedy was there—one could not be absolutely certain.

António played the organ, even as he and the other young men who worked in the bishop's compound watched warily for any signs of trouble. The people sang hymns with intense devotion. A few minutes later Bishop Belo entered, taking his place at the wooden altar used on Sundays and holidays. He was quietly acknowledged by the thousands in attendance.

It was a special day for a homily. Today was October 5, 1997, the fifty-second anniversary of the founding of ABRI. Except in times of emergency, like after the death of Sebastião Gomes right before Santa Cruz, Bishop Belo has tended to avoid homilies of a direct nature, preferring the allegorical form. A military official had stated two years before that he would "use the Timorese to destroy the Timorese," and the past two years had seen signs of what he intended to do. Paramilitary groups of Timorese were created to fight their own countrymen, not simply in armed combat—there was far less of that now than in years gone by—but in supposedly civil settings. Fights were provoked at sporting matches and other public events, while groups of thugs would roam the neighborhoods at night launching attacks on suspected opponents of the regime. The subject of family and community togetherness had special meaning in such a setting, especially on Armed Forces Day.

Thus Bishop Belo chose to give his homily on family values, which he presented in a good-natured manner, making people laugh occasionally. It was not a speech devoted to clichés that might be heard in places at peace. With the crisis that Indonesia's occupation of East Timor had brought about, it was a fitting theme that the community should stay together no matter what the difficulties. With so many of their families separated or destroyed, the idea of family breakup was almost unthinkable to many Timorese. The stability of their fragile community depended on an extraordinary degree of togetherness.

Nearly everyone received Holy Communion, and after Mass hundreds came up to greet Belo. Many lingered in the garden afterward. As always, it was a refuge from the world outside the bishop's gate.

After that, Belo went inside, where Celestina was waiting with fresh papaya and coffee. She, like almost everyone else, was excited. The biggest religious event in East Timor in four years would begin the next day. It was a pilgrimage of a distinctive sort, and people had set out from all parts of East Timor days in advance. There had been a similar pilgrimage in 1993, at Mount Matebian, and there were good memories of it years later. This time, on October 6 and 7, tens of thousands of people would converge on Mount Ramelau, which was, like Matebian, a place where, in Timorese lore, the souls of the departed go to rest. At Ramelau, they planned to celebrate the mutual respect between the Catholic Church and the territory's ethnic traditions. The two-day gathering would harmonize the territory's traditional animism and its veneration of ancestors, the land as well as the sacred objects known as *lulik,* with the traditions of the Catholic faith. In light of the massive number of conversions that had taken place since the Indonesian invasion of the territory—Catholics had gone from barely 30 percent of the population to approximately 85 percent in a little more than two decades—the event had special weight. Many of those who had converted continued to venerate nature, the land, their ancestors and their *lulik* at the same time that they attended church services, which had themselves become a quiet statement of nationalist feeling.

A statue of the Virgin Mary would be carried to the summit of the mountain. It promised to be a unique occasion for East Timor's long-suffering people, and Carlos Filipe Ximenes Belo and his parishioners looked forward to it with great anticipation.

After breakfast, Belo went to have some rest and Sunday quiet. Most people had left the bishop's compound at Lecidere, and virtually the only company he had was the cockatoo and other birds in the trees above his house. It was as a Sunday should be, a chance to read, reflect, and write, something that was far more difficult to do over the past year. So he especially valued this occasion, and worked with great relish on his sermon for the Mass on Mount Ramelau. It would be the first public event of this magnitude since Bishop Belo had returned to Dili on Christmas Eve after receiving the Nobel Peace Prize in Norway. The joy on that occasion was blackened by the murder of the supposed would-be assassin outside the cathedral. What could interfere this time?

As Bishop Belo prepared himself for the historic trek the next day, the Indonesian Armed Forces were continuing their day-long celebration of the fifty-second anniversary of their founding. Festivities had started early that morning with a parade through Dili, and the streets were festooned with banners proclaiming ABRI's virtues. Bishop Belo had not been invited to the events, but he would have declined the invitation had he been asked to attend. This was for them, not for the people of East Timor. Often, as he ate his breakfast, Indonesian soldiers jogged by the bishop's window. The troops would sing merrily, oblivious to the effect it might have on anyone else.

In the center of Dili, perhaps a mile from the peaceful Mass that had just ended, Indonesian soldiers in jungle uniforms were going through their paces, first outdoors, then in an indoor sports arena. Most seemed easily twice the size of many of the Timorese at the church service. In the arena, few Timorese were present. It was, indeed, a ceremony for the conquerors.

Bishop Moore, Archbishop George, and Korinna and I approached an Indonesian officer outside the arena; we explained who we were, and asked if we might enter. A few minutes later, the officer returned with an affirmative reply. It was eerie, but we went in anyway.

In the cavernous arena, there was a world unto itself, and it had little to do with geographic location. Indonesian military leaders sat in the front row, together with a handful of members of the East Timorese elite working for the Indonesian administration. Most prominent among them was the governor, Abílio Osório Soares, who took over large coffee plantations from their previous owners and, not trusting his fellow Timorese, relied on employees from Java. In fact, Governor Soares had even made a "gift" of tens of thousands of acres of East Timor's most fertile soil to some of President Suharto's children, even as most East Timorese were undernourished and lacked access to good land. Soares smiled nervously as representatives of the branches of the armed forces marched.

The feared elite corps, the Red Berets, or Special Forces Command—"Kopassus" in Indonesian—were heavily represented. The Kopassus were then commanded by Major General Prabowo Subianto. The military commander in East Timor, Colonel Slamet Sidabutar, who addressed those gathered, was known as a protégé of Prabowo, as was the governor. With an air of satisfaction, the commander, a trim, well-built figure with straight black hair, announced the presence of Bishop Moore and Archbishop George, trumpeting the fact that they were from America and Australia. Both nations helped train the Kopassus, and the presence of the two bishops seemed to confirm the relationship in the mind of Prabowo Subianto's protégé. With hard gestures, he spoke of the success the military was having against the "security disturbers" in East Timor.

The stands were filled on all sides with Indonesian soldiers in their late teens and early twenties. After a progression of speeches, box lunches—a few pieces of fried chicken, sweet rice, and two small bananas—were served, and the soldiers devoured the contents. The commander then cut the ABRI birthday cake and handed out hundreds of slices to the troops. Afterward, many of the soldiers puffed away on *kretek,* the Indonesian-made cigarettes made from tobacco and cloves. Cloves, too, were one of the first family monopolies, this one also controlled by Tommy Suharto.

Then came entertainment, with a woman in a tan ABRI uniform simultaneously serving as singer and mistress of ceremonies. There was no band, and music blasted on a substandard stereo system. She began to sing, in English, the old Roberta Flack song, "Killing Me Softly." After that, the mistress of ceremonies broke into a rendition of the 1950s rock tune, "Be bop-a-loola, She's My Baby." Scores of soldiers came up to dance in a conga line. At that point, Korinna could take no more of the spectacle, and left to walk through Dili to pay homage to former friends and neighbors, now dead.

At the end of the ABRI show, a few local people in the rear of the arena extended their hands to wish the army well. One of them was a dwarf, from Bishop Belo's ancestral town of Quelicai. The dwarf from Quelicai, like many others, curried favor with the military for survival's sake.

But beyond the arena, people had scant time to dwell on the self-involved rituals of ABRI; they were nothing new. As ABRI strutted through Dili, it was the procession to Ramelau that was on people's minds. The ceremonies at Ramelau would unite the main voices of East Timor's religions and cultures. A holiday had been declared for three days. For a time, at least, the normal oppressiveness of life might be cast off, or so people hoped. Truckload after truckload of pilgrims made their way from every part of the territory. People put on special clothes for the occasion, from windbreakers with knitted messages to the traditional *tai* worn by thousands. Ramelau was a place where they felt they could be themselves.

As dusk began to set in, the streets of Dili near the central marketplace were teeming with many hundreds of people gathering provisions for the journey. Some stopped for a rest on the way to Ramelau. Among them, traveling in a jeep, was Bishop Belo's younger sister, Julieta. The climb at Ramelau was too difficult for Dona Ermelinda (or Mother Matilde), a trek of three hours or more over steep, rocky paths. Julieta was traveling with someone who had climbed the paths of Ramelau since he was a teenager: the bishop of Baucau, Basílio do Nascimento, named to the newly created second diocese in January 1997. Dom Basílio now lived a short distance from Bishop Belo's mother in Baucau. In an amusing touch, Bishop Nascimento, from the western part of the territory, now was the spiritual guide of the eastern flock where Bishop Belo had grown up, while Belo ministered to Nascimento's people in the west. Dom Basílio, stout and balding with a deep voice, an easy smile, and a friendly manner, would lighten the burden on Bishop Belo, who until 1997 had spent hundreds of hours a year traveling by road to all corners of his far-flung diocese.

The two were of like mind. For years there had been endless speculation about Belo's replacement, with mention given to Indonesian candidates or others from outside the region. Happily, the Vatican named Nascimento to the new position. Two years younger than Belo, he had been a classmate at the seminary in Dare, and they were old friends. After Dare, Basílio studied in Portugal, then worked abroad for more than twenty years, five of which he spent in France, before his return to East Timor in 1994. Now, the next morning, the two Timorese bishops would meet for breakfast at the home of Basílio's late father on the road to Ramelau.

Bishop Belo set out early. The journey would take several hours on narrow, winding roads. The pilgrims had prepared for this for many months. There were dozens of truckloads of people, with white banners on the side proudly announcing their parish, a dozen from the coastal town of Liquiça alone. There was a rare enthusiasm mixed with a quiet happiness and contentment, though they had to stand for many hours as the flatbed trucks slowly made their way through the hills, a bumpy ride with holes and curves above steep inclines. These were the roads that had been paved to transport the military in a big push to defeat Timorese resistance. Now, the military could be seen on denuded mountains as the motor caravan passed. The troops tried to be discreet, but they were barely hidden.

As Belo's motor caravan made its way through the interior the waving from people standing by the road became more intense, the jubilation more visible. "Hallelujah!" some cried out. Against the will of the bishop, there was a police escort, with a blaring siren. The escort seemed to have the purpose of calling attention to Indonesian control of the situation. (On the way back, the police car, a Volvo, nearly caused a bad accident; only the quick reaction of Belo's driver avoided it.)

Bishop Belo's driver seemed to know every hole and curve in the serpentine mountain roads. The passage to Ramelau was a mixture of festivity and iron oppression, with entire Indonesian military companies dotting the hills and police watching every move. In Dili, the military were holding exercises, spreading fear in the middle of all this joy. But the streets were lined with people, with an ocean of clapping hands wherever the bishop's jeep passed.

Bishop Belo stopped for breakfast in the town of Aileu, one of the centers of the Mambai people, East Timor's largest ethnic group. Freedom of choice was part of their tradition, as the Harvard-trained anthropologist Elizabeth Traube told Congress in 1977, based on her three years among the Mambai. They believed that "all things are part of an order": the Portuguese had been in East Timor for centuries, but by 1975 it was clear that the time had come for them to "surrender the flag" to new leaders, as the Mambai put it. How could this transition take place? The Mambai, Elizabeth Traube testified, "insisted that all the peoples of Timor must gather together to calmly and coolly discuss the situation. Independence, Indonesian rule, these were alternatives which Mambai had heard espoused, but they, themselves, wished for a time of peace and quiet in which all concerned might state their views, and so arrive at a consensual solution. As I understood them, and as I understood the legal principle, what the Mambai sought was their right to self-determination."

Traube, a native of the Upper West Side of New York's Manhattan, received a message from her Mambai friends shortly before the Indonesian invasion. "There are many words and our heads are aching," they told her. As she explained, "the Mambai expression for resolving conflicts means to cut words . . . that is, to separate the tangled strands of a dispute."

The Mambai were not given the slightest opportunity to do so, not in 1975 and not later. Aileu and other Mambai regions had been among the strongest areas of armed resistance to the Indonesian invasion; Fretilin forces had had their military headquarters in Aileu. When the Indonesians finally conquered the town, they chopped down many of the trees to deny the guerrillas cover. What was once lush and lovely now had a desiccated look. Bougainvillea, some that had taken many years to grow, were cut back, including an especially large one by the home of the military commander. It may have seemed like a small thing next to the terrible human toll, but it was one more symbol of the destruction of their land. Now, Bishop Nascimento said, Indonesian companies were systematically plundering the natural resources East Timor had to offer: oil, marble, manganese, and, quite possibly, gold.

Others had come to East Timor for more altruistic reasons. The town of Aileu, in fact, was also a small outpost of America: it was the home of a group of Maryknoll Sisters engaged in grassroots efforts to improve women's health and education. The Maryknoll women were in East Timor for several years, through some very difficult times, and Bishop Belo particularly appreciated their work. On his visit to the United States in May 1997, Belo went to the Maryknoll home base in Westchester, New York, overlooking the Hudson River, and it was evident from his relaxed demeanor that the bishop felt he was among close friends: their service in Aileu had left a strong impression.

After breakfast in Aileu, Bishop Belo's jeep proceeded through the mountains. Nearby was the village of Maubisse, not far from Hato Builico, the closest town to Mount Ramelau. Some of the strongest and richest-tasting coffee in East Timor comes from Maubisse, where the green hills that sustain the excellent crops have always provided a certain level of prosperity. Visitors are invariably given a taste of this local product, which graced the cafes of Lisbon and Oporto in the old days: coffee of this quality outshines most of that available in Rome, Venice, Paris, New York, or, for that matter, anywhere else in the world.

During Portuguese colonial times Maubisse had a *pousada,* or inn, that once provided panoramic scenery and bracing mountain air for its lucky visitors; it still stood, but was deserted. The temperature fell on some nights to forty degrees Fahrenheit in Maubisse, the town with the second highest elevation in East Timor (Hato Builico is the first). It was pointed out to Archbishop George, a former military chaplain, that Australian commandos had conducted their resistance in this region against the Japanese fifty-five years before. In fact, near the town of Ainaro, two Catholic priests had been executed by Japanese forces for allowing the Australian commandos to use their wireless radio transmitter.

It was not only the Australians and their Timorese allies who had fought here. Much more recently, the area was also the setting for the last stand of Nicolau Lobato, the leader of Fretilin for three years until his death on December 31, 1978. Carlos Filipe Ximenes Belo deeply admired Lobato: "He was a nationalist, a man of rectitude, just and humane," the bishop said simply but emphatically in 1997, in a tone of deep-felt respect.

During the 1975 civil war, UDT units executed some students aligned with Fretilin, including Nicolau's younger brother, sixteen-year-old Domingos Lobato. Nicolau knew who committed the crime, but refused to have him put to death. "Why did you do it?" was all he would say when he confronted the killer. Nicolau Lobato then lost his wife on the day of the Indonesian invasion, but he still refused to seek revenge against Indonesian prisoners or Timorese accused of working for Indonesia, the way some Fretilin commanders had done. Lobato maintained this stance even after nearly all of his family members were murdered over the next three years.

The people in Fretilin areas suffered unspeakable hardship in 1977 and 1978, and many tens of thousands of women, children, and the aged died from injuries or lack of food or medicine. That Lobato managed to maintain a reputation for decency that survived such horrors says something about his character. He was not a saint: it was said years later that there were killings of some Fretilin members who had tried to surrender, and that he might have stopped the killings from taking place but didn't. Nonetheless, even members of the clergy linked with the Indonesian military regarded him as a person of the highest moral integrity and mercy.

The end Nicolau Lobato met was not of the kind that befitted someone of his forgiving spirit. Indonesian intelligence agents learned of contact Lobato had with a family member in the mountains south of Dili—the very mountains through which Bishop Belo was passing on the way to Ramelau. Indonesian forces discovered that he was in the Maubisse region when they found a rolled-up field mattress and an abandoned machine gun—signs that someone of great importance in Fretilin was nearby. An operation of 2,500 troops in new helicopters swept from place to place over a three-week period, and finally came upon Nicolau on New Year's Eve, 1978. After three years of the fiercest combat East Timor had ever known, there was a shootout, and Nicolau Lobato, badly outgunned, was killed at the age of thirty-three. It was said that a Timorese sergeant had done the shooting, but this may have been highlighted for propaganda purposes, to buttress Indonesia's long claim that the East Timor conflict was a "civil war": in fact, the name given in the press report was not a Timorese name.

A little-known junior Indonesian officer came forward to take part of the credit for the killing of Nicolau Lobato. It was Prabowo Subianto, only a lieutenant at the time, who later became President Suharto's son-in-law. Prabowo's role in the death of Nicolau Lobato was given heavy publicity in the Indonesian media, and was seen as a big boost to Prabowo's military career. Suharto personally congratulated the troops that hunted Lobato down and announced that the Timorese fighter's weapon would be displayed in Jakarta's military museum. His body was, in fact, shown on national television. But while there was gloating in Indonesian military circles, in East Timor there was tremendous sadness: Nicolau Lobato had become a legendary symbol of resistance.

Now, almost twenty years later, Bishop Belo, Lobato's one-time fellow seminarian, was passing through the Maubisse region. A few hours earlier, as he passed the Dare seminary, the bishop had reminisced about his former colleagues, including Nicolau. "They were so pious," Belo said, "but then they became revolutionaries." In Lobato's case, he had remained a churchgoer, but the heavy irony would not have escaped him. His background had been similar to that of Carlos Filipe Ximenes Belo: both had fathers who were catechists, both grew up steeped in religion, both seemed destined for careers in the priesthood, but Nicolau Lobato had left the seminary for the civil service. He ultimately found himself as his nation's military and political leader in a brutal life-or-death struggle. And the Church, which some once considered a repressive tool of colonialism, had become a place where one might stay alive and work to defend the people, an institution that had vital links with the wider world.

Now it was up to the bishop to help lead his people into the next century, even as most of his contemporaries had perished in places like Maubisse, Matebian, and Ramelau. Going through the region where Nicolau Lobato and many others had made their last stand, Belo in his own way was a battle-scarred veteran. Many had scoffed at this young priest with a boyish appearance when he took over the diocese in 1983, after he had been away during the years of calamity that had claimed the lives of Nicolau Lobato and so many others. For all of that, Belo had prevailed.

Ramelau came into sight, a spectacular vista like an arrow aimed at the heavens. In fact, in the Mambai language of the region, *Ram Lau* means "arrow peaks" or "tip of the arrow"—it has had a military connotation, from the earliest times. Local Mambai people explain that, Ramelau is "a most sacred mountain"—simultaneously a place where the dead may rest in peace, the source of magic power, the source of life, the first witness of life on earth.

It was also a symbol of the East Timorese independence struggle, for which the national anthem written in 1974, "Foho Ramelau," was named. In the innocent days at Fatumaca in 1975, a lifetime ago, before the war broke out, Belo would sing "Foho Ramelau" with his students.

Finally, the bishop's jeep reached Hato Builico. Masses of people were there from all over East Timor. From the extreme east, or Ponta Leste, came the Fatalucos, craftsmen and builders of elegant gable houses on wooden pillars. Close kinsmen of the Fatalucos were the fearless Makassae, warriors haunted and driven by the ghosts of their sacred Matebian Mountains. "*Rau de nokorau?*", Bishop Belo said to them in their native tongue they shared with him. "Are you well or not?" They were well.

The smaller eastern tribes also sent their delegates. From the Tutuala district at the far eastern tip of the island came the Lovaia, descendants of immigrants from the South Moluccan islands. More numerous were the representatives of the four kindred tribes, the Naueti, Midiki, Kairui, and the Waima'a (the latter being Bishop Belo's maternal relations), all of whose curious, enterprising ancestors spearheaded the Austronesian invasion of Timor from Celebes a millennium ago.

From the environs of Laleia and Manatuto, hometown of Xanana Gusmão, came the Galolis, whose seafaring and fishing traditions were a response to the harsh realities of the most arid and inhospitable environment in East Timor. Represented, too, was Dili's small offshore dependency of Ataúro, called "the island of goats." The Ataurans were another fishing population linked for generations with the Galolis. Among the Ataurans were families from Biqueli, the only traditionally Protestant town in East Timor.

The language in which all the pilgrims shared their thoughts and feelings was, of course, the Tetum lingua franca, but prominent within the crowd were those who spoke it as a mother tongue. These included not only the cosmopolitan Dili folk, but indigenous Belunese from the northwestern district of Balibó (the place where the five Australian television journalists were murdered in 1975) near the old Portuguese-Indonesian border, and from the great, rainy southern plain, from Viqueque and Suai and the mountains of Samoro and Soibada.

The people of the governor's ethnic group, the Idaté of the central mountains, were there as well, as were the westerly Bunaks, whose Papuan speech, unintelligible to all other Timorese, makes them one of the oldest ethnic groups on the island. And pilgrims had traveled even from the distant Oecussi Ambeno enclave in West Timor, historic seat of the Topasses, or "Black Portuguese," and landing place of the first Catholic missionaries five centuries ago.

From the sharply eroded land sloping northwestward toward the sea from Ramelau came the Kemaks and the Tokodedes, quiet agriculturists whose languages point to an infusion of blood, somewhere in the past, from the easterly string of islands that link Timor with New Guinea. But no ethnic group was more strongly represented than the ancient inhabitants of the rugged ridges and hilltops fanning out in all four directions from the Ramelau peaks: the Mambai, whose religious attachment to their land has made them living symbols of all that is most deeply and intransigently East Timorese.

There was no sign of trouble, but the military and police were edgy. The police commander in the house where Bishop Belo took his afternoon rest in Hato Builico was friendly, but his hands were clammy and his face had a tense expression. Everything was peaceful now, but it could not be forgotten how difficult it had been to subdue the peoples of these mountain areas.

Ramelau and Matebian, the two sacred mountain ranges of East Timor, were also the areas of the toughest military resistance to the Indonesian takeover. All the East Timorese believed that the spirits of their ancestors dwell on the mountain peaks, so the higher the peak, the more sacred the site—and the greater the desecration when the Indonesian Army came to make their conquest.

There were improvised tent cities everywhere on the mountain around Hato Builico, along with makeshift straw huts, which seemed flimsy compared with the gigantic green ABRI bivouacs pitched in town, which looked like U.S. Army tents. Many traveled a long way to be at Ramelau, armed with blankets, food, water, and other provisions. There were few comforts of the kind that Westerners take for granted, but that seemed to be of little consequence. A number wore T-shirts with Bishop Belo's likeness, the same ones that had set off beatings by the military months before.

First, there was a welcoming ceremony by dancers wearing traditional Timorese clothes with headdresses made of cock feathers, and women with metal cymbals. The men wore big round traditional amulets on their chests with silver bracelets on their muscular upper arms, made from the Mexican coins that had found their way to the island many years before.

Both bishops were greeted by the highest priests of the various ethnic groups, but what was of much greater significance was the placement of the statue of Our Lady, in the sacred *lulik* house, on a stump of an ancient sacred tree trunk. It was a prelude to the great event the next day on the summit.

Bishop Belo was reminded of the offer he had rejected as a young man to become *liurai* of Quelicai. His lot was of the utmost difficulty, but there was no question of the wisdom of the decision. He noted that some of the *liurai* remained animists and waited to be baptized until they were old and sick. "They wait until the last minute," Belo said archly, with a hint of a smile.

Meanwhile, Bishop Nascimento told a visitor that the violence in East Timor was cyclical. Everything seemed normal for a while, then there were new provocations. One could never tell when. The Indonesian military and police were at the luncheon in plainclothes, watching everything.

In the late afternoon of October 6 there was a Mass in a Grand Canyon–like setting, entirely filled with tens of thousands of worshipers. A panoramic view of the mountain range loomed behind it, the different peaks that made up what was collectively known as Ramelau, through which missionaries had long ago passed. The sermon of this Mass, celebrated by Bishop Nascimento, contained strong references to Moses and the ancient Israelites, a theme often sounded by Belo himself.

Some of East Timor's peoples—the Bunak and the Kemak, for example—build their houses with the doors pointed toward the mountaintops to court the protection of ancestor spirits. Such beliefs have harmonized well with the Catholic traditions of apparitions of angels and the Blessed Virgin on mountains.

This Christian custom of worshipping on mountaintops in turn has deep Jewish roots, and links Ramelau with the Mount of Olives, Mount Tabor, Mount Carmel and, ultimately, with Mount Sinai itself. "I will lift up mine eyes unto the hills from whence cometh my help," sang the Old Testament psalmist. Hence the significance of erecting an image in a high place where modern Christian Timorese, like their animist forebears, looked for inspiration and help.

It became piercingly cold as dusk fell, yet the worshipers remained transfixed. The distribution of Holy Communion was an enormous logistical feat, with tens of thousands of people participating. Bishop Paul Moore was there, and said later he had rarely seen such a moving service in his life. "I have been to many Eucharists," he commented, "but this was one of the most memorable. The glory of the Eucharist and the beauty of that setting, together with the love of the bishops, seemed to give the young people hope that the Resurrection will come."

There was a brief supper in Hato Builico after the service ended. The atmosphere in the room seemed hospitable enough, but as always at public gatherings in East Timor, appearances were quite deceptive. Bishop Moore wanted to address the group, but Bishop Belo felt it was prudent to refrain from doing so. The room was filled with government agents, and any speech by an American was bound to be closely watched.

It was close to nine o'clock when the meal ended, but the night was only beginning; a march lay ahead, of nearly three hours in the darkness up the long, steep pathways of Mount Ramelau. Many thousands had carried walking sticks, some had tiny flashlights. It grew colder, but the vigor of the climb distracted the pilgrims' attention. The two Timorese bishops led the procession. Young people surrounded the bishops, in front and behind. They were accompanied by a group of elders outfitted with ancient symbols of Timorese religion. A group of young people carried the statue, dedicated to "Our Lady, Queen of East Timor," high over the crowd, with the yellow and white flag of the Vatican hoisted above. The statue was clad in a multicolored *tais*, imbued with nationalist feeling. It took an enormous effort to carry it because of the thinning air in the rising altitude. The culminating event was to be the placement of the statue the next morning at the top of the mountain, called Tata Mai Lau—"the peak of the ancient ancestors" in the Mambai language. It is akin to "the souls of the dead" of Mount Matebian. A funeral song, performed at the climax of the most dramatic play known to one of the local Mambai communities in Suru-Ainaro, refers to a spot leading to the peak of Mount Ramelau. The song, still performed by a traditional word-master, begins, "Where would you go and say your prayer?" and it seemed clear that the ceremony on October 7, 1997, at Tata Mai Lau was aimed at joining the Blessed Virgin to the ancestral pantheon of the island.

We made it to the plain below Tata Mai Lau around midnight. The excitement was palpable. Many thousands spent the night outdoors in biting cold in a clearing dotted by black eucalyptus trees at nearly ten thousand feet above sea level. It was very close to freezing, but people managed to bear it with equanimity, under the sparkling stars in the clear cold air. Almost no one had access to food or hot drinks. A lucky few with foresight wore ski hats more suited to Norway in the month of December.

A main source of warmth was the campfires lit throughout the gigantic natural amphitheater, where the Mass would be held in the morning. There was so much smoke that it stung the eyes and drew tears. Cold as it was on Ramelau, ill-clad as most of the pilgrims were, they were quite fortunate in comparison with those of the resistance who had struggled in these very hills twenty years before. After all, blankets were luxuries, and setting a simple fire, which might have attracted the attention of the Indonesian military, was impossible in those days. The main problem now was the presence of Indonesian spies around the campfires.

The buzz of conversation continued throughout the night, and music was heard through loud speakers, enough to make it difficult for anyone to sleep. Bishop Belo tried to doze without success on a simple mat in a traditional Timorese house built out of bamboo and decorated with Timorese fabrics for the occasion, transported stick by stick up the steep slopes.

The sun rose, providing a smidgen of warmth. *Tai* were omnipresent, in numerous designs. These fabrics may seem like a mere decoration in the heat of Dili or when they are presented as gifts to friends abroad, but on Ramelau there were thousands as they are traditionally used, as a means of warmth in the form of dresses, scarves, shawls, or kerchiefs. Here, too, the thousands of *tai* provided a kaleidoscope of color in the morning light.

Bishop Belo joked with a nun as he started the day with coffee. He needed it, for he had not been able to sleep. In the din of the crowd, Dom Carlos was preparing for Mass, quietly contemplating what he would tell the devoted ones who had come from all over the eastern half of the island and Oecussi Ambeno. Far from his little chapel, he was at peace in the midst of his people, who had gathered for a great Mass before the final climb.

Belo mounted the improvised staircase and the altar built with great care out of tree trunks, sticks, and stones. The lectern was made of wild cane. A choir of dozens of youngsters sang sweet hymns. Bishop Belo launched into a powerful oration, touching on the importance of joining East Timor's ethnic traditions with the Catholic faith. Then he devoted his homily to themes of peace, with allegorical references to the Virgin Mary, and citations of the Second Vatican Council and Pope John XXIII. Afterward, Bishop Belo seemed to be shaking everyone's hand.

The fact that so many people had gathered in a place as difficult to reach as Ramelau, bearing such good cheer and patience, had its own positive message. There was Holy Communion, amazingly disciplined with so many thousands receiving the sacrament. Once the Mass was over, there would be a short rest before the final leg to the top.

A man turned and said quietly to Korinna, in Portuguese, "We are under constant surveillance," adding, ominously, "All is not as calm as it appears to be." Spirits were high, however, as participants took refreshments before beginning the hour-long climb to the ultimate peak at Tata Mai Lau. All their provisions had been carried, pound by pound, up the long, steep paths of Ramelau, together with every piece of wood used to build the altar.

On the ground there was a wrapper from an ABRI ration bar, another reminder that the Timorese were not on Ramelau alone. Despite this, it was a wonderful day, the sky was brilliant, and there was every reason to celebrate. Some had already gone to the top to watch the sun rise, and many more were proceeding slowly up the mountain to precede the statue of Our Lady of East Timor.

The mood was festive, with people aware of the historic moment. But if it seemed too perfect for beleaguered East Timor, it was. So many people had made the long trek up the mountain, only to find the violence they had hoped to leave behind at home. After traveling in the back of trucks, some for days on end, in a remarkable outpouring of faith and hope, with many walking long distances to this singular event in East Timor's history, tragedy struck.

Only moments after Belo completed the Mass, the bombshell arrived; the priest who brought the news had an anguished look on his face, as if he himself had witnessed a murder. A man had tried to break through a cordon of Catholic Boy Scouts guarding the pathway to the top, where the statue was to be placed. (Later, there were reports from the Indonesian military that the assailant was a member of the Fretilin independence movement, but no evidence was ever produced to support this claim.) The intruder had been told to go back, whereupon he stabbed one of the scouts to death and wounded a girl; the assailant was in turn beaten to death by the crowd.

It was sacrilege of the worst order, a desecration of the site at a time when it should have been most holy. The statue of Our Lady of East Timor was to be placed at a spot where Mother Earth is united with Father Heaven, in the tradition of the religion of the Mambai, the guardians of Tata Mai Lau—it was almost too much to bear.

"Come down, come down, the pilgrimage is over," said a voice that all of those gathered had heard many times before. It was a voice of comfort and authority that came over the microphone. Sometimes it could be a tough voice, but this time it was mixed with a mellifluous quality. It was the kind of voice that a friend might hear at a weary moment.

"Come down, come down, the pilgrimage is over," Bishop Belo told the many thousands on Ramelau through the microphone on the makeshift altar made of tree trunks. Many had already reached the top of Tata Mai Lau, and there was a long procession winding its way up the hill to Tata Mai Lau, which could be seen amid the verdant hills.

"Come down, please, come down, the pilgrimage is over," Carlos Filipe Ximenes Belo repeated again and again, advising them with gentle but intensifying force. The bishop's plea came from simple loudspeakers. Thousands were still gathered around the makeshift altar with countenances of wounded shock. The people soon slowly turned around and did what Bishop Belo asked.

He repeated his message many times. Standing on the makeshift altar, without the benefit of sleep the night before, he continued his entreaty: "Come down, come down, the pilgrimage is over."

After Bishop Belo had said this many more times, he left the stage and began to lead his assembled parishioners, as many as thirty thousand strong, down the treacherous pathways that led back to Hato Builico. Bishop Basílio had spoken the afternoon before of Moses and the Israelites, and the scene this morning resembled a scene from the life of that Old Testament prophet. There were thousands above, and thousands below, but they moved in an orderly manner, obeying the voice of Bishop Belo.

The descent from the steep mountain was just the beginning of a long, arduous journey home for the many thousands who had gathered on Ramelau with great goodwill.

"They did it to us again," said a Timorese couple speaking to each other in Portuguese on the narrow precipice leading off the mountain, obviously wanting visitors to hear. "We should have expected this."

"The Indonesians staged this incident to prevent us from putting the statue of Our Lady up there," someone else said in Portuguese, not caring if spies heard him. "The Indonesians are behind it. They want to prevent us from showing our strength." Indonesian intelligence agents were indeed in the midst of the throng, watching everything.

Senior clergy had little doubt as to the source of the profanation of the event at Ramelau and the marring of the other celebrations. They attributed these incidents to crazed East Timorese, possibly badly tortured people turned into drug addicts by the Indonesian military. Some youngsters were paid by the army and taken in with promises of rescue. Later, some Church sources linked the stabbing to a military-inspired vigilante group called the Gardapaksi—said to be still another creation of Prabowo Subianto—which had been guilty of similar outrages in the past. Always, the Indonesians wanted to create the appearance of a struggle between Timorese. There was no absolute proof, but many knowledgeable people believed it.

There seemed to be no surprise in the expression of the crowd. In the eyes of a long-suffering people, there was a pattern. Something similar had happened only hours after Bishop Belo returned from Oslo on Christmas Eve 1996, after receiving the Nobel Peace Prize. The rock throwing by provocateurs at the cathedral when Cardinal Etchegeray visited East Timor in early 1996 was another blow. Many people, clergy and laity alike, complain bitterly that whenever there is an event that reflects the people's aspirations, the Indonesian military sets out to disrupt it.

Bishop Belo serenely led the thousands assembled at Ramelau down the steep inclines. The precipices dropped thousands of feet to the right of the narrow pathways, where rocks and stones could give way. At times the path seemed perilous, the mood extremely tense (if an individual could come out of nowhere to commit a stabbing, what else might follow?), but Belo reacted with aplomb, greeting friends and parishioners, even maintaining his teasing wit and easy humor. Inwardly, he was sad as well as furious over what he saw as a transparent attempt to denigrate the Church and dishearten the people, but he would not show it, as they looked to him for inspiration. The crowd, astonishingly, adopted his calm.

As well they might, for the East Timorese were a tough, stubborn people. If they had accepted Portuguese influence, illustrated most clearly in the mestizo roots of many of those at the Mass on Mount Ramelau, it was because they chose to do so, not the other way around. Similarly, many chose to become Catholic because it suited them, spiritually and otherwise. The interplay between the various ethnic groups on the island made the

East Timorese especially astute, good at weighing their options: one could only hope to convince them to accept something if they wanted to accept it for their own reasons.

Here in these mountains, the guerrillas had fought heavily armed Indonesian troops to a standstill for three years in the late 1970s, and in this region some guerrillas still remained. It was an area of unrest in other ways. The coffee-growing town of Ermera was as filled with discontented youth as any place in East Timor. It was the home of Tomás Ximenes, the mission teacher whom Bishop Belo had seen alive in the Santa Cruz cemetery on November 12, 1991, and who then disappeared, his wife and three small children left without support. Tomás Ximenes had come to Dili to commemorate the death of Sebastião Gomes; few had ever commemorated his own. Bishop Belo, though he might deny that he had such power, had greater ability than ever to deter actions that might lead to new sacrifices by the brethren of Tomás Ximenes.

Mayhem could have broken out at any time. If even the slightest physical struggle had taken place on the pathway, only a push or a shove—let alone a shot or a thrust of a knife as on Tata Mai Lau a few hours before—there could have been a human avalanche.

But Bishop Belo allowed nothing to disturb him, at least outwardly. He took careful steps in his white cassock with red trimming, only rarely allowing the Catholic Boy Scouts to support him. He made it very clear to them that he did not need their assistance, although on the one or two occasions when he slipped slightly on the rocky path, or stones rolled under his feet and he lost traction, the Boy Scouts moved swiftly to catch him. Mostly in their teens or early twenties, they eyed everyone with the determined air of those fully prepared to sacrifice their lives.

Greeting his parishioners heartily, he let none of his anguish about what had happened become apparent. "Hello, *katuas!*" he said cheerfully to one old man perched at the side of the cliff, wearing a traditional headdress and carrying a *katana* like that of Grandfather Félix da Costa Ximenes. He joked with friends. Making the best of a sad day, he tried to give what inspiration he could to those he passed.

In some sense he looked like Moses leading the Israelites out of bondage in Egypt, but Belo disclaimed any such pretension: "The people are not refraining from outbursts because of me," the bishop insisted. Yet it was evident that they were, in fact, following his lead. (Bishop Nascimento had remained in the back of the march, to provide supervision there.) Most people walking down had spent the night with little or no sleep and little or no food after days of exhausting travel. Yet however disgruntled, however discontent, however some may have wanted to vent their fury, they slowly made their way off East Timor's highest mountain in a spirit that was overwhelmingly tranquil. And the descent from the mountain was just the beginning of a long journey back. (Some would not make it: a flatbed truck crashed into a ravine later that day, costing nineteen lives.)

As the people slowly filed down the paths from Ramelau, ABRI units were dug in on the mountaintops above them. There was no real reason for them to be there. It was a religious procession and the crowd—except for the man who had committed the stabbing—was apparently unarmed. Still, the troops were present, guns in place, nearly twenty-two years after ABRI began its drive into the countryside. The day before, police and military units had stood nervously as the pilgrims gathered. Now they were seemingly ready to open fire if given the order to do so. The possibility may have been remote, but it existed. Who could guarantee that nothing would happen? Only a short time before, the sacred procession had been ruined. A further desecration of the event had a certain macabre logic to it, all the more so if anything happened to provoke it.

After the stabbing on Tata Mai Lau, there was heightened suspicion. Young men walked nimbly on other trails. Some were below where the bishop was walking, on steep, grassy terrain, while others were above. Some of the youngsters who were accustomed to climbing steep mountainsides took a shortcut. At one point near an especially narrow pathway where the bishop passed, a young man abruptly tried to enter. There was no sign that he meant any harm, but the bishop's Catholic Boy Scout guards and other friends were anxious not to allow a stranger to walk behind them: they stopped and waited for him to pass, taking care to allow the young man to get well in front of the bishop.

But if anything had happened to Belo on Ramelau, or any other place, for that matter, it would have been the subject of headlines worldwide. "Indonesia's relations with the rest of the world would not be repaired in our lifetime if any harm came to the bishop," someone had said months before, in a radio discussion with a State Department official, broadcast throughout the United States. For all the rumors and the scare tactics, this fact was as immutable as the stones on Mount Ramelau itself.

The bishop did not think of danger to himself. Instead, his thoughts turned to the Santa Cruz cemetery, where he had been unable to stop the killing, where he had wept in agony over his helplessness. Only a few months before there had been the scene at the Hotel Mahkota, where senseless beatings had taken place during the visit of United Nations officials. Following that there was the raid on Quelicai leading to the death of David Alex and others. Now, with the stabbing on Tata Mai Lau, disaster was again in the air.

Yet they were descending from Mount Ramelau, inching their way down, perhaps thirty thousand strong, in tranquillity. By now it was growing hot, after a two-hour march under the dark shadow of potential acts of violence. Belo pressed on, foot by foot. They were close to the road to Hato Builico. Looking out at this vast movement of his people, it was, he firmly believed, an omen for the future. Bishop Carlos Filipe Ximenes Belo and his people slowly descended, from the place of the dead, in a spirit of hope.

Epilogue

❖ ❖ ❖ ❖

T
HE SPIRIT OF hope among the people of East Timor managed to
outlast President Suharto's grip on office. In the months after the
pilgrimage to Mount Ramelau in October 1997, Indonesia's economy, hailed by its international backers earlier in the 1990s as a great success story, collapsed. By May 1998, when Suharto left office, the dollar value
of Indonesia's currency, the rupiah, had plunged 70 percent since July
1997, making it impossible for most Indonesian businesses to repay loans
from foreign banks or purchase necessary supplies from abroad. As a condition for a multibillion-dollar rescue operation by the International Monetary Fund, important governments that had long supported the
Indonesian strongman with few if any reservations—most notably the
United States—finally began to demand a dismantling of the system of
Suharto family monopolies that exercised heavy control of important sectors of the economy. Suharto balked, apparently hoping that the desire for
a stable ally by his longtime international partners would outweigh other
considerations.

But it was already too late to save his regime, as the ensuing economic
crisis threatened to cost many millions of jobs and place tens of millions of
people into abject poverty. The crisis triggered massive demonstrations by
students and others. Widespread rioting occurred, and hundreds of lives
were lost. Indonesia's most influential foreign friends evacuated their citizens, and there were days when it was uncertain if Jakarta's airport would
remain open. All of this was beamed to television viewers worldwide. It became clear that the large-scale financial help needed to restart the Indonesian economy would not be forthcoming as long as Suharto remained in
office. Suharto's support within the army eroded to the point where his position became untenable. His long reign as Indonesia's supreme leader had
finally ended.

It happened that Bishop Belo was in Lisbon, having received an honorary doctorate from the University of Évora, when Suharto resigned as president on May 21, 1998. As was the case when the old regime in Portugal fell in 1974, Belo remained wary over the changes in Jakarta in 1998. Better, he thought, to wait and see. The bishop and many other observers had long believed that a solution to the East Timor conflict required political changes far beyond ending Suharto's presidency, and there was little sign that the underlying system might be dismantled, since Suharto had been replaced by B. J. Habibie, who had been his vice president.

Nonetheless, the mood in East Timor could not but be different than before. There was sure to be turmoil ahead, and the bishop was worried. He was glad to be heading back to Dili.

A number of momentous events took place during this time, illustrating the fragility of the situation, both for the East Timorese and their military rulers. For instance, on the morning of June 4, scarcely two weeks after President Suharto left office, the Indonesian military commander of East Timor, Colonel Slamet Sidabutar—the same protégé of Major General Prabowo who had presided over Armed Forces Day in Dili the previous October—died in a helicopter crash in a mountainous area not far from Mount Matebian. His superior officer, Major General Yudomo, the newly-appointed head of the Udayana military command, which stretches from the island of Bali to Timor, was also a victim. Nine others perished with them. The official explanation was that the helicopter exploded into flames after hitting a mountain. An army spokesman blamed it on bad weather, and said it was not a result of a clash with Timorese guerrillas active in the area. Only a few days before he died, Colonel Sidabutar had insisted in a press interview that the Indonesian Armed Forces would never leave East Timor. The night of the helicopter crash, there was an eerie silence on the highway along the Dili shorefront.

The situation in East Timor seemed to ease for a few days. It may have been simply an odd coincidence, but what followed on June 6, 1998, would have been inconceivable at any time since the Indonesian invasion. A gathering organized by people who had been placed in local leadership positions by the Indonesian military took place in a hall behind the governor's palace in Dili. It was meant to be a meeting of six or seven people to discuss the future of the territory after the fall of President Suharto. From the government point of view, this handful of people was part of the sanctioned politics Indonesia had imposed from the time of the initial invasion.

However, this meeting turned into an outburst of voices that had long been muffled, in a stunning display of East Timor's long-suppressed nationalism. "This is the end and the beginning!" one man cried out. "Troops out!" said another. For most of the nearly twenty-three years since Indonesian troops had poured into the former Portuguese colony, people could do little in opposition unless they were willing to risk torture or death. Now, at least for this day, there was a rash of liberty.

"The intelligence officers are everywhere," said a young woman around that time. "They disguise themselves as meatball vendors and so on." But former Governor Mário Carrascalão, who chaired the event, told the audience not to worry about the omnipresent spies, because they had lost their power now that Suharto was gone.

In the hall, where the meeting took place, there was a sea of signs. "*Viva Independence!*" "We Want a Referendum!" and "Free Xanana Gusmão!" exclaimed banners unfurled for the occasion. Scarcely more than six years before, on the very same street lined with huge banyan trees, thousands of young marchers had passed by on the way to Santa Cruz cemetery, carrying similar signs. That time, inside the cemetery, they paid dearly for their defiance when Indonesian troops opened fire on the gathering. "I loathe the military," said a young woman shot at the Santa Cruz at the age of seventeen. "I just can't forget what has happened to me."

On June 6, 1998, such voices were heard worldwide, recorded by a TV crew from Britain's ITN network which was in the hall. Indeed, for the first time in twenty-three years, a meeting of this sort did not result in beatings, jailings, or deaths. The way the story goes in Dili, one of the six or seven leaders was asked to find a sampling of local people who might attend the session to present their views on the future of their homeland now that President Suharto had fallen. By the time everyone arrived at the forum building behind the governor's palace not far from the harbor, there were thousands—between three thousand and four thousand by one count. The group on June 6, 1998, wanted a real choice.

This is what Carlos Filipe Ximenes Belo had been pleading for over the past decade. He had made it clear beforehand that he would not attend the June 6 session, preferring to remain above the political fray, though he sent his vicar general, Father José António da Costa. Bishop Belo went instead to an engagement in the town of Ainaro, near Mount Ramelau. The bishop felt that his presence at the gathering in Dili was not really needed. He had already demanded a withdrawal of Indonesian troops, the freeing of all political prisoners, and the people's right to determine their own future through democratic means.

Belo had also publicly contradicted the new president's initial assertion that Indonesian government policy on East Timor should remain unchanged. Beyond that, the bishop advised East Timor's political leaders to act wisely and responsibly, and there was at least one hopeful sign: a committee was formed after the June 6 event to carry forward the political process in the period ahead.

At the same time, the bishop remained characteristically skeptical. After all, the armed forces had yielded to popular pressures in Jakarta, but there was no mandate for change in East Timor. Indeed, some in the military not only echoed the line of their dead commander, but they insisted that they had lost so many men in East Timor that they would fight to stay there. For Belo's part, he knew that despite the changes at the top, the structures that supported the Suharto system were still in place. For example, Suharto's son-in-law, Major General Prabowo Subianto, had been removed in May 1998 from his position as head of the strategic reserve command. (He had been promoted to that position from his former post as Kopassus, or Special Forces, commander during Suharto's last months in office.) His removal notwithstanding, Prabowo's ties with the feared Kopassus and with paramilitary youth organizations gave him the means to cause a good deal of trouble in Dili and elsewhere. The bishop was all too keenly aware of this. In addition, he knew that Timorese leaders needed the freedom to choose a different kind of future.

Therefore, Bishop Belo repeatedly called for the release of Xanana Gusmão as an indispensable step towards to resolving the situation. The United States, the European Union as well as South Africa and its president, Nelson Mandela, did the same: diplomats in Jakarta seem to view Xanana as a good negotiator whose freedom would help avert further violence and produce a settlement for East Timor. Xanana received visits in Jakarta's Cipinang prison from Stanley Roth, the U.S. Assistant Secretary of State for East Asian and Pacific Affairs, as well as parliamentarians and senior officials from several other nations. U.S. Representative Christopher Smith (Republican of New Jersey), chairman of the House subcommittee on human rights, seemed impressed by the Timorese leader's soft-spoken moderation. Some diplomats have predicted that Xanana and the other prisoners would be free within a year. In the early weeks after Suharto's fall, Xanana himself stated that "We are not in a hurry": he meant that from East Timor's perspective, it might take some time for the situation in Indonesia to move in a positive direction.

Despite this patience, the newfound freedom of expression took unanticipated turns, even though threats from the army were always there. A key student leader, Fernando de Araújo, demanded the release of Gusmão: "If Habibie won't release Xanana, we will continue to fight and die for the independence of our country." Araújo himself was only recently released from more than six difficult years in prison as punishment for providing information to the outside world about events at Santa Cruz, and organizing a demonstration in Jakarta after the 1991 massacre at the cemetery. Though he had been ill while in jail, now Araújo seemed remarkably hardy. And despite the severe punishment he had received for political protests in the past, he showed extraordinary courage, displaying no fear of the possible consequences of his current actions. Araújo was joined by other impressive young leaders, notably Antero Benedito da Silva, who was organizing gatherings in villages to counsel people on their rights.

Although people were taking great risks by doing so, there was one remarkable action after another. The next one occurred on June 10, when many hundreds of students staged a demonstration on the campus of the University of East Timor in Dili. At Belo's urging, however, they refrained from marching through the streets of the city, which could have provoked military retaliation. For the moment, things remained quiet, though banners minced few words: "Pull the armed forces out of Dili, end the bloodshed and free our leader Xanana Gusmão," said one.

Another challenge came in Jakarta on the morning of June 12. Word had spread days before that about 1,500 East Timorese studying in universities on the main Indonesian island of Java would converge on the capital to demand independence as well as freedom for prisoners. It was said that students sold all their belongings in order to board transportation and buy food for the journey to Jakarta. More than a thousand East Timorese entered the Indonesian foreign ministry, asking for a meeting with high-level officials to push their campaign for self-determination: "East Timor is not part of Indonesia," one banner proclaimed. They wore black headbands that bore the word "Referendum."

A petition handed to the authorities by the East Timor National Youth Front called on the government to revoke the 1976 law that made East Timor part of Indonesia, immediately withdraw its troops, and "open a serious dialogue on the political status of East Timor with Xanana Gusmão and other figures of the resistance movement."

The presence of the students at the foreign ministry was apparently too much for the military. General Wiranto, the commander of the armed forces and Suharto's former adjutant—and Prabowo's main rival in the armed forces—spoke the day before of "excessive demonstrations," warning that "We cannot allow these activities to continue indefinitely." Wiranto is actually seen by some Timorese leaders as being relatively enlightened, certainly in comparison with Prabowo. In the late 1970s, as deputy military commander in East Timor, Wiranto had a reputation as a man of his word: his promise to spare the lives of guerrillas who surrendered apparently was kept while he was there; resistance sources said it was only after Wiranto left that they were arrested and executed.

Whatever Wiranto's merits, they did not stop the Indonesian security forces who moved to end the protest by the East Timorese students at the foreign ministry. Troops and baton-wielding police charged into the students, whacking them with rattan sticks, fists, and boots, then forcing them into fourteen buses waiting nearby, which took them to be interrogated. Indonesian human rights sources said two persons were reported to have broken legs and one was stabbed with a bayonet. Two East Timorese women were knocked unconscious.

The next morning, Saturday, June 13, Bishop Belo openly worried about the possibility of new clashes, as another demonstration was about to take place in Dili. In fact, it happened without incident, but the situation remained dangerous, and in his Sunday sermon, Belo said that "In a critical situation like this, I ask all East Timorese to keep calm and restrained. Please don't create things which can disturb peace among people."

The bishop also said that Habibie's offer of a "special status" for East Timor could be a "transitional phase," though he said that the people must ultimately chose their own destiny. Regarding "special status," which despite rhetoric to the contrary, has never amounted to very much in other regions of Indonesia, Belo emphasized, "I'd like to see first. Not only promises."

In fact, "special status" and "autonomy," used interchangably by the Indonesian government, are not understood in East Timor the way they are defined elsewhere: many see these terms as only a fig leaf for continuation of Indonesian rule by another name.

Indeed, the idea of special status had been rejected as meaningless by the students and independence leaders, who were now demonstrating by the thousands. "We don't care about this special status thing," said one student. "We just want independence."

"East Timor should be free now," said a middle-aged woman, a vegetable trader in Dili. "So much blood has been shed . . . we are ready to have independence. I've witnessed the repression by Indonesia since the invasion. They have tortured and killed East Timorese. We don't want other people to rule our land anymore."

After talks with Bishop Belo on Monday, June 15, student leaders said they would suspend demonstrations. The demonstrators insisted on a referendum, which Habibie ruled out. The bishop feared that these differences could lead to confrontations with the military. "It is not only the students who are organizing, the other side is organizing, too," Belo told me, referring to provocateurs, linked to Major General Prabowo, who had engineered many violent incidents in the past.

Bishop Belo's fear of an outbreak of violence led him to adopt a cordial tone when he met President Habibie on June 23, 1998. Belo refrained from repeating his earlier calls for referendum, and in the immediate aftermath of this meeting in Jakarta, Bishop Belo praised the Indonesian president, some thought excessively. Reached shortly after his return to Dili, Bishop Belo told Oxford University Indonesia specialist Peter Carey that he felt quite positive about the encounter. Belo stressed that he and his fellow bishop, Basílio do Nascimento, had submitted a letter to Habibie containing about twenty-five requests, including withdrawal of Indonesian troops and the freeing of political prisoners. The two bishops were not taking a position on the status of the territory, Belo said, but leaving that to the United Nations, "the most competent forum" to reach a solution "that is fair, peaceful, and honorable as well as internationally acceptable."

Bishop Belo felt that the reception he received from Habibie was markedly different from his treatment in the past, under Suharto, but the crucial factor at work was the preoccupation of the two bishops, expressed by Belo on numerous occasions since the Santa Cruz massacre in 1991, that without demilitarization, there could be a renewal of large-scale violence. In Belo's view, any opportunity to make gains must be seized upon.

Nonetheless, many in East Timor, especially the youth, were perplexed and alarmed by the tone Bishop Belo had taken with Habibie, believing that he should have openly demanded a referendum. In terms that recalled the conflict between them during their confrontations in the early 1990s, the youth complained that Bishop Belo was too cautious, too conservative, that he did not represent their views. As one keen observer in Dili put it, some believed Bishop Belo should be using his standing to call for a referendum at every available opportunity. Others felt that in a tense and uncertain period, few, including the bishop, could afford to take too militant a position, or do anything that might foment further unrest.

At bottom, it was a question of what was really possible in the early days of the post-Suharto period. No one could claim to know.

Events the days after Bishop Belo returned to Dili from Jakarta in late June raised questions about Habibie's ability to deliver on promises of a more relaxed situation. Three Timorese were shot and killed by security forces in separate incidents around the time of the long-awaited visit of three European Union ambassadors, from Austria, Britain, and the Netherlands.

First, a twenty-one-year-old, Herman Soares, a nephew of Father Mariano Soares, the parish priest in the town of Manatuto, was shot by troops as he loaded firewood into his car: with no proper medical treatment available he bled to death on the way to Dili. Great fear seized Bishop Belo and other clergy that Soares's funeral could turn into another Santa Cruz. That did not happen, but neither did the violence end.

Indeed, once again in Manatuto, this time during the European ambassadors' visit, another man was shot to death. Many thousands of young demonstrators greeted the ambassadors, voicing their desire for independence. But small groups of demonstrators, said to be in the pay of the Indonesian military, tried to provoke violent incidents, apparently to "prove" to the European visitors that freedom would only bring more conflict.

The bishop was incensed over yet another incident, on June 29 in his hometown of Baucau. One person was killed and five wounded when Indonesian troops opened fire on a crowd of East Timorese who had come to greet the three European Union ambassadors, who were then meeting with Bishop Nascimento.

Bishop Belo said that eyewitness accounts affirmed that the shootings were carried out by special forces, still believed to be influenced by Prabowo just as the bishop had feared weeks before. The special forces also were set to open fire on people inside the Baucau church, Bishop Belo reported, but a priest managed to stop them.

"Now they are criminals," the bishop fumed. "Please tell the White House, and the foreign offices in Europe and everywhere."

Possibly because of pressure from such international sources, there were no further killings in the month that followed. Still, the next set of developments raised further questions about the government's intentions. Both East Timor's governor and military commander ordered the distribution of false documents which stated that the United Nations only envisioned autonomy for East Timor, not independence. But these were not official U.N. proposals, but rather only points that had been discussed in talks between the Indonesians and the Portuguese in their meetings under U.N. auspices. The United Nations denounced this misrepresentation of their position, and Bishop Belo criticized those in East Timor who had tried to mislead the public. Such misrepresentations did not cease. Indeed, there seemed to be a concerted effort by Indonesian authorities to push the East Timorese to accept a solution that would do little to address their basic concerns for freedom and self-rule.

Rumors surfaced that Prabowo might return to East Timor to lead a crackdown to end the growing pro-independence demonstrations that had become a feature of life since Suharto resigned. Other reports spoke of the distribution of weapons to pro-government groups. Accounts appeared in the Indonesian press of a mass exodus of Indonesian settlers that was taking place in East Timor, allegedly under pressure from pro-independence forces, but some Church sources saw such reports as exaggerated, designed to create an atmosphere of panic. Bishop Belo, in the spirit of reconciliation, called on the Indonesian immigrants to return.

Nonetheless, rumors circulated of an assassination attempt against Bishop Belo by Timorese vigilante squads created by Indonesian forces in a remote border village around July 12. Reached in Dili, Belo brushed aside the rumors, but the spreading of false reports like this was reminiscent of the situation in 1975 in the months leading up to the initial Indonesian invasion of East Timor: at that time, rumors presented a picture of chaos meant to justify military action by Indonesian forces.

The truth, Bishop Belo said, is that Dili is like it was in 1980, full of Indonesian soldiers who encircled the city. "Troops are entering houses at night," the bishop said, "and every day people are going to churches to take refuge."

In this atmosphere of high tension, Bishop Belo traveled again to the Indonesian capital in mid-July. Now, his approach was different. Belo seemed to operate according to a particular principle during this time, as he had on previous occasions: if it seemed that everyone was on the streets demanding action, he would speak softly, if at all. But once the demonstrators went home and things were quiet, the bishop would speak quite forcefully, sometimes surprisingly so.

His visit to Habibie had, after all, produced nothing tangible, and to Belo, the lack of concrete results was extremely disappointing, especially because he had bestowed praise on the new president in the hope of winning quick action to reduce the dangers in East Timor. Yet nothing positive had taken place, possibly because Habibie, unlike his predecessor, had little power over the military.

For its part, the army was not yet convinced that it should leave East

Timor, with some claiming to fear that doing so could lead to the breakup of the Indonesian republic. If East Timor won independence, so this reasoning went, other islands would demand the same, even though East Timor was different, in that Indonesia had no legal or historical right to the territory. Independent experts, noting the predominant role of ABRI in the vast archipelago, doubted that the independence of East Timor would lead to Indonesia's disintegration. Some believed the military was also worried about losing its central political role as well as its important economic interests in East Timor.

But other Indonesian political forces were becoming more open to the question of justice for East Timor. Indeed, the main purpose of Belo's visit in July 1998 was a meeting with two of Indonesia's foremost opposition figures, Megawati Sukarnoputri, a likely presidential candidate in elections slated for 1999, and daughter of the father of the nation, the late President Sukarno; and Abdurrahman Wahid, leader of the Nahdlatul Ulama, one of Indonesia's main Muslim organizations, with more than 30 million members. While Megawati was a new acquaintance of the bishop's, Wahid and Belo had met before. Wahid had given a positive interview about the bishop in a film produced for the Norwegian Nobel Institute after the 1996 Peace Prize, a courageous act at the time.

"Bishop Belo is the guiding star for the East Timorese people. We must of course follow the wishes of the East Timorese people. And I myself am quite convinced that Bishop Belo will do whatever is best for his people," said Megawati, in a pleasant surprise. She previously had taken the position that East Timor's status as part of Indonesia should not be changed. Another prominent opposition figure, Amien Rais, also shifted his stance, coming out in favor of an eventual referendum for East Timor.

In Jakarta, Bishop Belo was accorded the status of a statesman and given wide access to Indonesian television audiences. Dropping the softer approach he had taken after he saw Habibie, he was now outspoken, saying that the vast majority of East Timorese people want a referendum to determine East Timor's future. And if a referendum was held, he said, it should be supervised by an independent and authoritative body.

"As for me myself, I leave it to the people of East Timor to determine their own future," Belo emphasized, as he had at carefully chosen moments ever since he sent his letter to the United Nations in 1989. "Those in favor of integration are a small minority, while those wanting a referendum comprise the majority, whose numbers are growing all the time," he continued. "A referendum is the most democratic way to resolve the issue but this will have to depend on the talks between Indonesia, Portugal, and the U.N."

Bishop Belo also referred to the killing and rape of Chinese Indonesian women during riots in May 1998, crimes that have drawn worldwide attention. He added that such heinous acts happened regularly in East Timor, creating great trauma that few inside Indonesia had acknowledged.

Speaking of how East Timor had been regarded in Indonesia until then, Belo said, "It's a taboo subject, with the result that the general public in Indonesia does not know what is going on. And the situation today is the result of all this," he said.

While in Jakarta, Belo was allowed to meet with Xanana Gusmão for the first time since the resistance leader was imprisoned in 1992. The bishop asked for Xanana's agreement that large demonstrations should be avoided in East Timor to prevent violent clashes, and Xanana assented. "He was more cooperative than I was," Belo later joked. In contrast with their earlier encounters in 1986 and 1991, which were characterized by varying degrees of distance, Xanana in July 1998 was "closer, open, friendly," Belo said.

Despite sharp criticism Bishop Belo had received earlier from pro-independence advocates, and would receive again later, Xanana seemed to applaud the bishop's statements in Jakarta. This time, when Belo arrived back in Dili, Timorese close to the Indonesian government were furious. Those who had cast their lot with the Indonesians feared that they would have no place in an independent East Timor, and might be subject to persecution. It was Bishop Belo's unenviable task to mediate between the two sides and at the same time be true to the people's sentiments.

After what had taken place during the visit of the European Union ambassadors, Bishop Belo feared that a visit to East Timor by the United Nations special envoy, Jamsheed Marker, might spark demonstrations that could result in violence, and wanted to see the visit postponed. In the end, the bishop and Marker arranged for his visit to be switched from Dili to Baucau. Marker and Tamrat Samuel of Eritrea, a skilled diplomat in charge of day-to-day United Nations activity regarding East Timor, flew directly to Baucau on July 19. The U.N. officials spent several hours in numerous meetings with local leaders as well as the two bishops. There was talk of an interim agreement that would demilitarize the territory and provide for a United Nations presence, with a consultation of the population within five years. But the outcome remained unclear, with many expressing dissatisfaction with any plan that might fall short of independence.

On July 28, 1998, the Indonesian government, in a move obviously aimed at its aid donors, announced a withdrawal of some four hundred of its troops (out of about twelve thousand in 1998), bringing a hundred foreign journalists to East Timor for the occasion. Right from the start, there were questions as to whether or not the troops were actually being withdrawn.

Still, there seemed to be positive signs at the United Nations-brokered talks between Indonesia and Portugal in New York. An August 5 communiqué said that the two sides had agreed to consider the possibility of "wide-ranging autonomy" for East Timor, "without prejudice" to "basic positions of principle." This last part left open the possibility of an eventual referendum on independence. It was indeed encouraging that for the first time in the fifteen years of talks on East Timor under UN auspices, there was the possibility of substantial gains. But Foreign Minister Ali Alatas recognized that a show of flexibility wins praise from foreign governments whose goodwill is vital, in light of Indonesia's precarious economic situation. In fact, there are indications that Alatas has pushed the view that autonomy is a final status for East Timor, not an interim status.

Bishop Belo said on August 20, 1998 that the situation in East Timor remained substantially unchanged. Asked if he saw any concrete results after the UN talks, the bishop said firmly, "Not yet." Two weeks earlier, Belo stated, "There is still intimidation and terror."

A highly-qualified independent observer was also in East Timor on August 20. There was an appearance of openness in Dili, but reliable local people told this observer that such appearances are deceptive. And in East Timor's countryside, there was no change: "in the interior, no one has told the army about 'reformasi'," the source added.

There was another sign of hope in late August, however, when Major General Prabowo Subianto, already removed from his command position, was ousted from the army altogether. It seemed that the military career of Suharto's son-in-law was finished, but it was far from clear that Prabowo also would lose his power to influence political events. In addition, some army officers who had resented Prabowo's rapid rise through the ranks may have found it convenient to assign blame for atrocities largely to him, while absolving others no less culpable and the army as a whole.

Though no formal charges had been lodged against Prabowo, he stood accused by military investigators and the Indonesian public of engineering kidnappings of student leaders in Jakarta and killings in East Timor as well as in the predominantly Muslim province of Aceh on the island of Sumatra. Only a few days after Prabowo's ouster, Bishop Belo made an important ges-

ture of solidarity to Indonesia's Muslim community, when he issued a statement emphasizing that "I am horrified by the images of common graves . . .
of the brethren of Aceh . . . [and the] oppression and the suffering that the
Muslim brothers and sisters have had to endure over the past fifteen years."

This gesture towards Indonesian Muslims came at a time when the
bishop was preparing for a meeting on September 10 and 11 of dozens of
Timorese leaders at the site of the old seminary at Dare. The meeting was
aimed at averting violence and fostering reconciliation. A respected pro-
independence participant declared that Belo did an excellent job in facili-
tating dialogue among the different personalities and viewpoints. But the
atmosphere that the bishop tried to encourage at Dare was quickly undermined by Governor Abílio Osório Soares in early October. The governor
threatened to fire Timorese civil servants who failed to support the government's proposal of autonomy. Interestingly, in a September 16, 1998 interview based on answers he provided in Portuguese, Xanana Gusmão,
now president of the National Council of Timorese Resistance, took a similar position to that of Bishop Belo. Xanana said that "We accept autonomy
as a run-up to a referendum. A period of transition will create a climate of
political tolerance and wipe out the last vestiges of the legacy of vengeance
and hatred."

In contrast to Xanana's conciliatory statement, the governor's warnings
only inflamed an already tense atmosphere. Thousands demonstrated in
mid-October, demanding the governor's resignation. Bishop Belo called
on the demonstrators to keep their protests peaceful; over the next week,
he also told U.N. mediator Tamrat Samuel, "Here in the villages, people
don't talk of autonomy, only a referendum."

The bishop knew well from his extensive travels in the countryside in
September and October 1998 that people remained deeply frightened of
Indonesian troops, sometimes seeking refuge in churchyards until sunrise
at 5:00 AM, rather than spending the night in their own homes. The bishop
called on the government to make genuine troop withdrawals that could
be easily verified, but there was little response. This was the reality Belo and
his people experienced, even as the government announced that many, if
not most, of its combat troops had left East Timor.

On October 30, 1998 the *New York Times* and other papers cited leaked
Indonesian Defense Ministry documents showing that in August, immediately following the widely-publicized announcement of troop withdrawals, there were twice the number of troops that the government had
claimed. On October 31, a Western diplomat was quoted in the *Times* as
saying that "there was little doubt about the accuracy of the information in

the documents after comparing it with other information on military activity."

The discrepancy between Jakarta's public statements, and the official documents and reports from residents in East Timor, was a reminder of the Indonesian government's modus operandi in the period leading up to the tragic invasion of December 1975, when false announcements were issued by Jakarta as a matter of routine. The question in the late 1990s was what the rest of the world, which stood by silently during the worst of East Timor's catastrophe, would do this time.

In his 1998 New Year's address to the Vatican diplomatic corps, Pope John Paul II spoke of the "people of East Timor, and in particular the sons and daughters of the Church there, still awaiting more peaceful conditions in order to be able to look to the future with greater confidence."

But for this to happen, strong pressure on Jakarta is vital. A resolution adopted by the U.S. Senate in July 1998 called for an internationally supervised referendum in East Timor, at the same time that the European Union ambassadors issued a report saying that there would be no lasting solution "without a firm commitment to direct consultation" of the people of East Timor about their future. In September 1998, more than one hundred members of Congress wrote to Presidents Clinton and Habibie, giving strong verbal support to Bishop Belo's efforts, calling for a reduction in the Indonesian military presence, release of political prisoners and a democratic election on East Timor's future. The congressional letter to Clinton noted that "It is an unfortunate fact that the invasion was carried out with American weaponry and diplomatic support." While it was long overdue, in October 1998 Congress voted to ban the use of U.S.-supplied arms in East Timor.

Bishop Belo is painfully aware that such words and actions, as well as his own, have had limited impact. Some Vatican officials have long argued that although Pope John Paul II has spoken out on East Timor over the years, the nations with the greatest leverage (the U.S., Japan, Australia, Canada, Germany, Britain, France and other European countries) have placed their economic and political interests in Indonesia far above human considerations.

In fact, the historical record shows that in many instances, East Timor being only one of them, governments have chosen to ignore information from religious sources. In the case of East Timor, some Vatican officials have taken a coldly diplomatic view of the tragedy, but by mid-1998, some of those previously least supportive had become friendlier towards Bishop

Belo as his international standing as a Nobel laureate increased. Others, such as Archbishop Farano, the papal nuncio in Jakarta during the terrible years after 1975, Cardinal Etchegeray, the pope's special representative, and Archbishop Renato Martino, the papal ambassador at the United Nations, have been unquestionably humane. They, like their moral predecessor, the onetime papal nuncio in Istanbul, Angelo Roncalli, who rescued many endangered Jews during World War II, and later became Pope John XXIII, needed strong support from governments, which was not always forthcoming. The United Nations, for its part, has little power by itself to bring about change in East Timor and other places without the backing of powerful governments. And the permanent secretary of the Norwegian Nobel Committee, Geir Lundestad, states bluntly that the Peace Prize "is not a magic wand," stressing that the cooperation of others is vital if its promise is to be fulfilled.

While this remained true after the fall of Suharto, the situation had changed in at least one fundamental way. The difference is that now, and in the years to come, far more than when it invaded East Timor in 1975, Indonesia is desperate for international financial help. In 1998, Jakarta asked for twice the assistance it received in 1997 from members of the Consultative Group on Indonesia, the World Bank-sponsored aid consortium that meets in Paris every July (which includes the U.S., Japan, Australia, and European nations). During the very days of the 1998 Paris meeting, even as East Timor's capacity for independence was being questioned by some governments that supported Indonesia's invasion, the first oil to be produced in the Timor Gap had begun to flow.

People closest to the scene, both in the diplomatic arena and within East Timor itself, emphasize that the Indonesian government is unlikely to make major concessions unless pressed to do so: maximum world interest is needed if an end to East Timor's long nightmare is to be finally realized. For in the end, courageous individuals like Bishop Belo can only do so much without proper support. At a time when the Indonesian government needs tens of billions of dollars of assistance from publicly funded international financial institutions like the World Bank and the International Monetary Fund, not to mention direct aid from powerful governments, it is crucial that citizens demand that a commitment to a just solution to the tragedy in East Timor figure significantly on the world's agenda.

Carlos Filipe Ximenes Belo knows that the world has a responsibility to stand with East Timor, but is unsure if it will do so. "I'm not a prophet," the bishop told me in early November 1998. It certainly would have been impossible for Belo or anyone else to foresee the harsh future of East Timor in the days when Belo was a young, diligent student at the old seminary in Dare more than thirty years ago. Few outside of the region were even aware of the existence of East Timor during Portuguese colonial times. Without the invasion by Indonesia, it is likely that Belo would have spent his time educating and ministering to youth within sight of Mount Matebian.

The Indonesian military assault created conditions that imposed on him a unique role in the fate of his country. Two years after receiving a Nobel Peace Prize, he is in constant demand on the international stage. The bishop is grateful for the attention and support that this brings to his once-forgotten people, and he accepts invitations whenever possible. On December 10, 1998, for example, Belo joined other Nobel Peace Prize recipients in Paris at events organized by the government of France aimed at building international solidarity on the occasion of the fiftieth anniversary of the Universal Declaration of Human Rights.

With all of these honors, Bishop Belo's life remains difficult because the suffering and hardships of the East Timorese people have not ceased. And while the bishop worried about Indonesian troop movements and the terror that they create, he was also disturbed by several revenge killings and the intimidation of Timorese people who worked as spies for Intel or with government-backed paramilitary groups. Like Archbishop Desmond Tutu of South Africa, Bishop Belo condemns all atrocities, no matter what the source.

It is often lonely for Belo, and the stresses of his position can try his nerves and challenge his physical strength. Deeply tired at the end of October 1998, he felt compelled to escape the constant problems and ringing phone and take a week's respite near the eastern town of Lospalos to recuperate from a bout of malaria. This was the longest vacation he had had since he moved to Dili in 1983.

Bishop Belo turned down invitations he had received from many parts of the world where he might have taken a rest. Instead he stayed in East Timor. Speaking of his travels throughout his native land to be with the people, and of his visit to the region of his birth on "Matebian Day" on November 2, 1998, a festival commemorating the souls of the dead, Carlos Filipe Ximenes Belo said with great passion, "I don't want to be anywhere else. I want to be here. This is where I belong."

But no matter how pressed by the weight of his responsibilities, or the exhaustion he inevitably felt on occasion, Bishop Belo stated time and again, more strongly still, "The danger isn't for me, it's for the people." Indeed, the bishop showed flashes of irritation when people seemed overly concerned with his own state of being. After all, the average person was vulnerable in a way Belo was not.

This was demonstrated anew with attacks near the town of Alas in November 1998 and other places in 1999. In the Alas events, Indonesian troops killed a village chief and a young man, and perhaps others. The bishop said the military's actions were taken in revenge for resistance activity in the region, including the killing of six soldiers and a civilian working for the army, the capture of a cache of thirty-six weapons as hostage-taking. In response, Indonesian army battalions were "terrorizing the area," he affirmed. Church sources added that many young people had fled into the mountains. Thirty houses were burned, as the military cut water and electricity to many residents. Even kerosene lamps were banned. On November 19, 1998, at least 100 people were taking refuge in church buildings. Aid agencies were able to enter the area only after Bishop Belo spoke out, but local human rights organizations were denied access.

The army brought conscripts from throughout East Timor and conducted house-to-house searches, dragging people from their homes in the middle of the night and looking for those suspected of attacking their troops. The bishop begged for an end to this operation, which finally ceased after his entreaties.

Diplomatic sources said there was no doubt that the troubles were fomented in good measure by elements of the Indonesian military—first, through their obstruction of progress toward a settlement of the conflict and, second, through manipulation of groups they had armed. Such clashes gave the army an excuse to crack down on their opponents. In the case of Alas in November 1998, Indonesian troops launched brutal attacks on Timorese villagers, conducting retaliatory moves reminiscent of the "fence of legs" operation that was taking place when Belo returned to East Timor in 1981 as a young priest after completing his studies in Rome.

Outraged over the November 1998 military sweep, Bishop Belo spurned an invitation a few weeks later from President Habibie to meet in Jakarta. The bishop felt that nothing had come out of their previous meeting and believed another session would be a charade without concrete changes in the behavior of the Indonesian army. Pressed to the limit of his patience, Belo lashed out when word of Habibie's invitation arrived, saying it would be a waste of time to go to Jakarta. To the minds of some in East Timor, Belo had done exactly the right thing. After the earlier meeting with Habibie, Belo was heavily criticized by pro-independence groups, friends among them, for lavishing praise on Habibie. In fact, the bishop insisted that he had done so in the hope that President Suharto's successor would withdraw Indonesian troops and make other immediate moves to demilitarize East Timor. Belo had been more than willing to accept criticism, for he hoped that the "honey" (as the bishop himself termed it) he had bestowed on the new Indonesian president would be reciprocated with concrete deeds. When this produced no tangible results, the bishop adoped another approach.

Then, as if to stress that his tough standards applied to all, Bishop Belo in his Christmas Day homily chastised East Timorese on both sides, calling on them to stop taking vengeance against their brethren. New Year's Day was quiet, and for that day at least, Belo was delighted that the people appeared to be taking his words to heart. But the calm was short-lived. On January 3, 1999, in the town of Ainaro, near Mount Ramelau, an East Timorese group armed by Indonesian forces shot and killed two of their pro-independence countrymen who actually had come to talk about peace. A priest, who if anything had been inclined to cooperate with the Indonesian army when possible, described it best in a heart-wrenching report to Bishop Belo. He wrote that "[The military] do everything so that Timorese who are armed by them eliminate all those who are not on their side." Although those favoring continued Indonesian rule were vastly outnumbered by those favoring independence, with the backing of the military such groups clearly had the capacity to wreak havoc.

At the same time, tensions were fanned within Indonesia itself by elements of the military, part of the legacy of Suharto's rule. As before, ABRI would argue that its political role was indispensable to maintain order, when in reality some of their own forces were provoking confrontations. Much depended on the outcome in Jakarta, where on November 13, 1998, troops opened fire on student protesters, killing eight persons. The bishop condemned the violence by the military, the worst in Jakarta since Suharto's resignation in May 1998.

By early 1999, the Indonesian crisis had deepened: protests by students were taking place against the backdrop of a crippled economy with huge numbers of the country's 202 million people falling below the poverty line according to the government's own statistics, which put the figure at 130 million. It was becoming increasingly urgent for the world community to give generous backing to efforts by organizations like UNICEF to avert a catastrophe in nutrition, health and education. Doing so might help address the growing ethnic and religious tensions in Indonesia, which experts saw as largely economic and political under the surface. The future role of the military was unclear, but there were some worrisome signs, such as resumption of military operations and political killings in Aceh in late 1998 and early 1999. Bishop Belo had condemned such atrocities before: he was keenly aware that East Timor was not alone in suffering repression.

In the midst of this welter of problems, Carlos Filipe Ximenes Belo was angry and sad over the seemingly unending trials of his people, as well as the plight of ordinary Indonesians. He remained anxious about the future, but also determined to struggle on. For all the difficulties, there were reasons to be optimistic.

International interest in East Timor was a crucial factor. American diplomatic pressure was reportedly mounting, and in another sign of the changing times, the Australian government, one of the few nations that had recognized the legality of the Indonesian annexation, adopted a new policy accepting the principle that the people of East Timor must eventually have a choice of remaining a part of Indonesia or becoming independent. Bishop Belo asked Australia's Foreign Minister, Alexander Downer, to help East Timor through its crisis, and told Downer how his grandfather, António Filipe, had been tortured by the Japanese for providing assistance to Australians near Mount Matebian during World War Two.

Soon after Australia's statement, the Indonesian government stunned the world by mentioning the possibility of independence for East Timor for the first time since its 1975 invasion of the territory. Jakarta also announced that Xanana Gusmão would be moved from prison to house arrest. After refusing for so long to budge on the issue of independence, this was a tremendous breakthrough.

American diplomats said Indonesia's sudden turnabout was triggered when Bishop Belo refused to meet with President Habibie in January. Habibie was said to have felt hurt by the rebuff and became determined to rid Indonesia of the East Timor problem. In an interview, a top aide to Habibie, Dewi Fortuna Anwar, stated, in essence, that Indonesia had failed to win the hearts and minds of the East Timorese, drawing a comparison with the American experience in Viet Nam. Critics of the regime had long maintained this, but it was a surprising admission from a senior Indonesian official. At the same time, Muslims in Habibie's cabinet reportedly did not want to pour any more money into a Catholic province, especially not in a period of national economic crisis. When Indonesia's economy was booming, it could manage to afford a colonial-style occupation of East Timor. Now, however, such an adventure had become a big burden, costing at least $1 million per day. With deepening unrest in Indonesia stretching the army's capacity to meet its challenges, East Timor also was a drain on military resources. Nonetheless, Habibie's move obviously was aimed to a significant degree at gaining the good will of foreign donors; a statement on possible independence for East Timor by Indonesia's finance minister was regarded as important enough to be included as one of the pieces of good news to come out of the World Economic Forum meeting held in Davos, Switzerland, in February 1999.

Still, there was confusion about Jakarta's true intentions, and, indeed, questions about who exactly was in charge in Jakarta and East Timor itself, where there were brutal attacks against pro-independence groups. Thousands of villagers fled such violence, many of them taking refuge in churches. In this setting, top Indonesian officials stated that East Timor could either accept the government's autonomy plan or face an abrupt Indonesian departure.

A highly-informed diplomat stated privately that with military elements deliberately creating conflict by distributing arms and otherwise provoking confrontations, the idea of abrupt Indonesian withdrawal from East Timor had a sinister cast to it.

"The Indonesians have to leave East Timor properly. They have a responsibility to the East Timorese to do so after all the deaths that have resulted from their actions," this authoritative source stressed, saying that abandoning the territory as the Portuguese did in 1975 was not an acceptable solution: "Anything other than an orderly departure would be criminal."

Would the all-important military finally relent on its longtime insistence that East Timor must remain an integral part of the Indonesian Republic? Although some senior commanders seemed eager to be out of East Timor, the position of the army as a whole was unclear, and could pose the biggest obstacle to any just resolution of the conflict. A senior US official maintained that the Indonesian military had not been forewarned by Habibie of the change in policy. The army was "shocked" by the decision, this American official said and some sectors of the military could sabotage moves toward peace. One disturbing possibility was that army elements loyal to former President Suharto and his cashiered son-in-law, former Major General Prabowo Subianto were fomenting troubles throughout Indonesia as well as East Timor.

Alternatively, some experts believed that once the Indonesian government signaled its willingness to leave East Timor, the army's troops simply ceased its normal operations, ceding the initiative to its East Timorese collaborators, who were no longer under effective military control. But even if this was true, Indonesian forces formed and supported such groups in the first place, and had a grave responsibility to find ways of ensuring that they did not drive East Timor into a maelstrom of violence.

Thus, there was a chasm between hopeful reports emanating from Jakarta and the situation in East Timor itself. In Jakarta, Xanana Gusmão, released to house arrest, began to play a key negotiating role to reassure East Timorese working with the Indonesians that their rights would be respected after independence. In contrast, there was widespread fear in East Timor over the distribution of arms by the military to their local allies. Perhaps 20,000 modern weapons were distributed to these collaborators to confront the majority favoring independence, most of whom were unarmed.

Amidst this perilous situation, it seemed increasingly likely that East Timor might win its independence within the space of a year. President Habibie, anxious to shed a vexing diplomatic problem, said that he wanted to see East Timor become independent by January 1, 2000.

Many people in East Timor were in no mood to wait. Bishop Belo said that children from the age of three to elders of eighty years of age were jubilant, dancing and crying out that they would soon be independent under President Xanana Gusmão, who said he had no such ambitions. (A compromise candidate might be the able former governor, Mário Carrascalão.) The bishop also emphasized that those who backed the Indonesian government were downcast, even despondent.

All needed firm guarantees that their safety would be maintained. Fearing that they would face great dangers as well as lose their privileged positions, East Timorese on the Indonesian side, not surprisingly, were prepared to fight to protect their interests. It was vital to have peacemaking efforts among the East Timorese themselves, but this would be extremely hard if not impossible to accomplish if Indonesian forces continued to incite violence.

"It is time for a United Nations force to come here to prevent clashes and bloodshed," Bishop Belo pleaded. Although the efforts of the people of East Timor themselves would be the primary factor in determining their own future, it is indisputable that the actions of the rest of the world will play a critical role. International pressure might in the end prove decisive. US officials seem to have delivered the message to the Indonesian government that Jakarta will receive little credit for any policy changes on the East

Timor issue if the territory descends into bloody chaos. Other governments have apparently done the same. Thus, even if the military would like to hold onto East Timor or arm its local allies to enable them to win a struggle over pro-independence forces, the ultimate price for Indonesia may be too high. Indeed, the army high command must be prepared to take firm steps to prevent sabotage of a just settlement by elements close to leaders of the old Suharto regime.

The army must also offer complete cooperation to the United Nations, which helped Indonesia's own independence struggle half a century ago. The United Nations was trying to hammer out an interim agreement and, not surprisingly, a sticking point on the Indonesian side was who would retain control of East Timor's natural resources. On the other hand, there were encouraging signs, as Lisbon stated its willingness to fund an annual budget of more than US $100 million for East Timor. Still, it was vital that the United Nations oversee a transition to self-rule.

As for Bishop Belo, he remained wary, but that was his way: as always, he wanted to see what the concrete results for his people would be. He was worried about clashes between Timorese groups, while the Indonesian army, after having supplied its allies, looked the other way. "For me it is better to fight with diplomacy, with intelligence, with discussions, rather than with guns," Bishop Belo stressed, with passion.

In fact, the East Timorese leaders of two of the main pro-Indonesian paramilitary groups confessed to the bishop that they were provided weapons by the Indonesian army. These leaders were willing to disarm, and looked to Bishop Belo to mediate an agreement between them and the East Timorese resistance.

It will be vital to foster unity in a place where even the collaborators are loyal Catholics, and this is one reason why the bishop had adamantly refused to take sides in the conflict, other than to insist on the right of the people of his homeland to a democratic referendum. Bishop Belo called for the eventual formation of an independent truth and reconciliation commission of the kind led by Archbishop Desmond Tutu in South Africa as a means of building a firm foundation for East Timor's future.

So much of this would have been unutterable even only a short time before. In sum, prospects for the long-suffering people of East Timor had been turned upside down, and events were moving at a dizzying pace. The collapse of the Suharto regime had established a new international view of the situation. Coupled with the 1996 Nobel Peace Prize, the crisis in Indonesia made East Timor a global issue as never before, galvanizing public support in many countries, and offering many opportunities to further expand that support.

Bishop Belo was well aware of this, but he was not only thinking of the East Timorese. "Please remember East Timor, and other places, too" was his plea on a quiet Sunday morning in Dili in early 1999, a short time after Mass had ended and thousands of hopeful people had filed through the gates of his residence. "Work for reconciliation and peace and human rights in East Timor and around the world as we enter the new millennium, in places large and small" said Bishop Carlos Filipe Ximenes Belo. "Please try to be a force for good. Please help us and others in need, everywhere."

NOTES

■ ■ ■ ■

Page 3, "many others have died since": For background on the death toll, see "East Timor, Violation of Human Rights, Extrajudicial Executions, 'Disappearances,' Torture and Political Imprisonment," Amnesty International, London, 1985. For additional background see Peter Carey and G. Carter Bentley, eds., *East Timor at the Crossroads, The Forging of a Nation,* London: Cassell, 1995; James Dunn, *East Timor: A People Betrayed,* Jacaranda Press, Queensland, Australia, 1983; reprinted ABC Books (Australia), 1996; Jill Jolliffe, *East Timor: Nationalism and Colonialism,* University of Queensland Press, 1978; and John G. Taylor, *Indonesia's Forgotten War: The Hidden History of East Timor,* London: Zed Books, 1991.

Page 6, "David Alex": See "Urgent Action" from *Amnesty International* (London), UA 189/97, June 26, 1997.

Page 9, "The attribute of charisma had a special place in the intricate culture of Java . . .": See "The Idea of Power in Javanese Culture," in Benedict Anderson, *Language and Power: Exploring Political Cultures in Indonesia,* Cornell University Press, 1990.

Page 12, On the Ford-Kissinger visit to Indonesia and the diplomatic background leading up to the Indonesian invasion, see Hamish McDonald, *Suharto's Indonesia,* Victoria, Australia: Fontana Books, 1980, especially pages 207–8 and 211; Daniel Southerland, "U.S. Might Have Averted Tragic Timor Takeover," *Christian Science Monitor,* December 17, 1980; Arnold Kohen, "Invitation to a Massacre in East Timor," *The Nation,* (New York) February 7, 1981.

Page 12, "A key CIA official present in Indonesia at the time . . .": This was C. Philip Liechty, a former operations officer, interviewed in the 1994 Central Television (UK) film *Death of a Nation* by John Pilger. For a more extensive account of Liechty's recollections, see John Pilger, *Distant Voices,* Vintage (UK), 1994.

See also C. Philip Liechty, "How Indonesia Engulfed East Timor," *The Washington Post,* January 6, 1992.

Page 13, "his predecessor, Martinho da Costa Lopes, worked tirelessly . . .": See Michele Turner, *Telling East Timor, Personal Testimonies 1942–1992,* New South Wales University Press, Australia, 1992, pages 164–68. Also Amnesty International 1985 report, cited above.

Page 13, "A memorandum on a Washington meeting Kissinger held . . .": A transcript of this memorandum is published in Mark Hertsgaard, "The Secret Life of Henry Kissinger," *The Nation,* October 29, 1990. It is also cited by *New York Times* columnist Anthony Lewis on December 6, 1991, and May 25, 1998, and by Walter Isaacson, *Kissinger, A Biography,* Simon and Schuster, 1992. Isaacson states that Kissinger was "quietly content" that Indonesia launched its invasion of East Timor, page 680. See two articles by Anthony Lewis, "Realism and Evil," *New York Times,* December 6, 1991, and "Their Suharto and Ours," May 25, 1998.

Page 13, "roughly 90 percent": Testimony of George H. Aldrich, deputy legal adviser, Department of State, July 19, 1977, in "Human Rights in East Timor," Hearings before the Subcommittee on International Organizations of the Committee on International Relations, House of Representatives, 95th Congress, First Session," U.S. Government Printing Office, Washington, D.C., 1977.

Page 13, "there was no danger whatsoever of a takeover by communists": Also see interview with Bishop Belo in *Messenger of St. Anthony* (Padua, Italy), November 1996.

Page 14, "Photos of children . . .": For example, see *New York Times*, December 9, 1980, courtesy of *Sydney Morning Herald*.

Page 15, "two British journalists . . .": Photojournalist Steve Cox and filmmaker Max Stahl. For a collection of the photographs taken by Cox at Santa Cruz, see Steve Cox and Peter Carey, *Generations of Resistance*, London: Cassell (UK), 1995. Stahl's film footage of Santa Cruz is featured in *Cold Blood*, Yorkshire Television (UK), 1992, and *Death of a Nation*, cited above.

Page 16, "Bali . . . the scene of long-overlooked political violence": See Geoffrey Robinson, *The Dark Side of Paradise, Political Violence in Bali*, Cornell University Press, 1995.

Page 16, Prabowo Subianto: On Prabowo's eventual dismissal from the Indonesian Army, see "Suharto's Son-in-Law, a Much-Feared General, Is Ousted," *New York Times*, August 25, 1998.

Page 17, "The Catholic Church has quadrupled in size . . .": For a summary account of the role of the Church after the 1975 invasion, see Robert Archer's essay, "The Catholic Church in East Timor," in Carey and Bentley, *East Timor at the Crossroads*, cited above.

Page 17, "No less a personage": Tad Szulc, *Pope John Paul II, The Biography*, New York: Scribner, 1995, page 478.

Page 17, "The best opportunities," etc: See Mubyarto et al., Pat Walsh (ed.), *East Timor, The Impact of Integration, An Indonesian Socio-Anthropological Study*, Jogajakarta, Gadjah Mada University, Research Center for Village and Regional Development, published by Indonesian Resources and Information Program, Northcote, Australia, 1991. Also George J. Aditjondro, *In the Shadow of Mount Ramelau, The Impact of the Indonesian Occupation of East Timor*, Indonesian Documentation and Information Centre, the Netherlands, 1994.

Page 19, "neither the oil nor our freedom": Cited in Paulo Nogueira, *Publico* (Lisbon), March 23, 1995.

Page 19, For background on the dispute over Timor Gap oil, see Roger Clark's essay in *East Timor at the Crossroads*, cited above.

Page 19, "turned his back and walked away": See Paul Raffaele, "Champion of a Forgotten People," *Reader's Digest*, February 1997 (USA edition: the article appeared earlier in some other editions).

Page 19, "for their former Portuguese overlords": On visits to East Timor in 1995 and 1997 by the author there was evidence of nostalgia for the Portuguese in contacts with people from all walks of life throughout the territory.

Page 21, "British journalist": See Dom Rotheroe, "Maulindo's Feet," *Esquire* (UK), February 1997.

Page 22, "the first American president": For a summary account of Bishop Belo's meeting with Clinton and other events of 1997, see Arnold Kohen, "Shall I tell the President?", *Messenger of St. Anthony* (Padua, Italy: international edition), December 1997.

Page 24, "We will try to be more helpful": The author was present at Bishop Belo's meeting with President Clinton.

Page 24, "the White House press office repeatedly refused to release the photographs": The author learned of this from a White House official and through journalists who tried to obtain the photographs.

Page 24, "Suara Timor Timur": In fact, the photographs did not appear in this Dili newspaper. Associates of Bishop Belo considered it too provocative to military authorities for the paper to publish them at that tense time.

Page 25, "the people of East Timor played a valiant role . . .": See Dunn, 1996, cited above, pages 19–23, 110–114. For more on the Timorese role in World War II, see Turner, *Telling East Timor*, pages 6–51.

Page 25, "*Malae*": The author is indebted to Dr. Geoffrey Hull for his innumerable linguistic, ethnographic, and historical insights. Hull and his colleagues are struggling to conduct research on East Timor's threatened ethnic languages and cultures. Potential supporters of this work are urged to contact Dr. Geoffrey Hull, Faculty of Education and Languages, University of Western Sydney MacArthur, P.O. Box 555, Campbelltown NSW 2560 Australia.

Page 26, "able to endure untold suffering": See Taylor, cited above.

Page 27, "beautiful situations": William Bligh, *Bligh's Voyage in the Resource,* (Golden Cockerell Press, London, 1937), pages 243–44, in Jolliffe, cited above.

Page 28, "Whatever their differences": This is a central thesis in Taylor, cited above.

Page 29, "The religion of the Makassae": I am indebted to Shepard Forman and Leona Forman for the insights on the Makassae.

Page 30, *"nambu":* The definition of this word was provided by Bishop Belo.

Page 32, "can barely be noted": "Human Rights in East Timor," page 15.

Page 34, "value greatly": in Taylor, pages 1–2.

Page 39, "Estado Novo": Some of the insights on the Salazar period are taken from Antonio de Figueiredo, *Portugal: Fifty Years of Dictatorship,* Penguin, UK, 1975, and A. H. de Oliveira Marques, *History of Portugal,* Columbia University Press, second edition, 1976.

Page 40, "Finally": For more on the Japanese war years, see Dunn, cited above, and Jolliffe, pages 44–46.

Page 40, "Dom Jaime Goulart": See Louise Crowe, "The Impact of the Indonesian Annexation on the Role of the Catholic Church in East Timor, 1976–95, MA thesis, Northern Territory University (Australia), March 1996, pages 43–45.

Page 42, "few ever fully appreciated . . ." and "pleaded with us": Dunn, pages 20 and 21.

Page 43, "one former commando": Cliff Morris, *A Traveller's Dictionary in Tetum-English and English-Tetum from the Land of the Sleeping Crocodile, East Timor,* Photo Offset Productions, Australia, 1992, page 2.

Page 43, "From 1953 on . . .": Jolliffe, page 58.

Page 43, "Indonesia ultimately . . .": For background on the period leading to Indonesian independence, see George McT. Kahin, *Nationalism and Revolution in Indonesia,* Cornell University Press, 1952 (reprinted 1970), and Benedict Anderson, *Java in a Time of Revolution, Occupation and Resistance 1944–46,* Cornell University Press, 1972.

Page 44, "a thousand years . . .": Wm. Roger Louis, *Imperialism at Bay* (Oxford University Press, 1978), page 237, cited in Noam Chomsky, *Powers and Prospects,* Boston: South End Press, 1996, page 189.

Page 45, "As Bishop Belo stressed in an interview many years later . . ." Unpublished interview in 1994, courtesy of Pat Walsh, Australian Council for Overseas Aid Human Rights Office, 124 Napier Street, Fitzroy, Victoria, 3065, Australia.

Page 48, "If he was lucky . . .": Portions of the material from Belo's early years are taken from the magazines *Femina* (Jakarta), January 8, 1997, and *Maxima* (Lisbon), October 1995.

Page 49, "Makassae prayers?": From Forman's testimony in "Human Rights in East Timor," page 25.

Page 51, "in 1950 . . ." Statistics cited by Jolliffe, page 42.

Page 67, "1958": For background on the 1958 events, see Audrey R. Kahin and George McT. Kahin, *Subversion as Foreign Policy: The Secret Eisenhower and Dulles Debacle in Indonesia,* New York: The Free Press, 1995.

Page 68, "the 1965 coup": For a summary of these events, see Robinson, pages 280–86.

Page 69, "Seara": For an account of this period see Jolliffe, pages 55–56.

Page 74, "including that of the United States . . .": See Kahin and Kahin, page 230.

Page 79, "black propaganda campaign": See McDonald, pages 189–215, and Dunn (1996), especially pages 78–107.

Page 80, "This was very important": See Dunn (1996), XII.

Page 80, "a sacred cave": See McDonald, pages 1–2, 195.

Page 81, "Costa Gomes later claimed": See Anderson, 1995.

Page 81, "that governs ours": See the testimony of Shepard Forman, especially pages 13, 14, and 19.

Page 81, "the same day Jakarta launched": See Taylor, page 200.

Page 82, "it was only after returning": See McDonald, page 204.

Page 82, "ruled out independence for East Timor": See McDonald, page 204.

Page 84, "Ribeiro's march to the quay": See Dunn (1996), page 153.

Page 87, "Colby": From David Jenkins, Asia editor for the Sydney *Morning Herald*, writing for ABC ATVI News, September 17, 1993. It fits in with other disclosures on what the CIA knew of Indonesian actions in 1975. See Dale Van Atta and Brian Toohey, "The Timor Papers," *National Times* (Australia), May 30–June 5 and June 6–13, 1982.

Page 87, "effectively, quickly and not use our equipment": *Christian Science Monitor*, December 17, 1980, cited above. Full text published in George Munster and Richard Walsh, *Documents on Australian Defense and Foreign Policy, 1968–75,* Sydney, 1980, pages 192–93 and 199–200.

Page 87, "raged for months": See Daniel Southerland, "Indonesia's hidden hand in Timor," *Christian Science Monitor*, September 23, 1975.

Page 88, "American intelligence operatives . . ." See McDonald, page 211.

Page 88, "the Japanese rape of Nanking, China": See Iris Chang, *The Rape of Nanking,* Basic Books, 1997, page 4.

Page 89, "perhaps ten percent of the territory's population": *New York Times,* February 14, 1976.

Page 89, "As a disillusioned Indonesian soldier later put it": Transcript of interview with Radio Netherlands, May 1998, by journalist A. Santoso.

Page 89, "the social services building": Interview with a Catholic priest who had been near there that day.

Page 89, "a conscience-stricken ex-officer": See interviews in Pilger, cited above.

Page 89, "A crowd of onlookers . . .": See Amnesty International 1985 report, pages 24–29, for an account of the 1975 events.

Page 90, "Dom Martinho": See Turner, pages 164–68.

Page 91, "with no inconsiderable success": Quotation is from Daniel Patrick Moynihan, *A Dangerous Place,* Little Brown, 1978, pages 246–47.

Page 91, "one of the great horrors": Author's conversation with a Moynihan assistant, 1982.

Page 91, "the incursion into East Timor": *The Australian,* January 22, 1976. For a summary of what was known about the invasion by late 1977, see Arnold S. Kohen, "The Cruel Case of Indonesia," *The Nation,* November 26, 1977.

Page 92, "American nuclear submarines": See Michael Richardson, "Don't Anger Jakarta: U.S. Protecting Indon Channel for its N-Subs", *Melbourne Age,* August 3, 1976.

Page 92, "By the end of 1976": See Dunn, page 274.

Page 92, "In Dili Hospital": See Turner, pages 167–68.

Page 92, "Thousands in East Timor": See Richard Tanter, "The Military Situation in East Timor," *Pacific Research* (Palo Alto, California), Volume VIII, Number 2, December 1976, reprinted in *Dissent* (Melbourne, Australia), Winter 1977. Also see Daniel Southerland, "Indonesia faces guerrilla action in East Timor," *Christian Science Monitor,* December 8, 1975 and Anthony Goldstone, "No Glory in the Timor Secret War," *Guardian Weekly* (UK), April 22, 1976.

Page 93, "A retired Indonesian officer": Radio Netherlands interview, 1998, cited above.

Page 93, "A Catholic priest who lived in the mountains for three years": See Arnold S. Kohen and Roberta A. Quance, "The Politics of Starvation," *Inquiry,* San Francisco, The Cato Institute, February 18, 1980.

Page 94, "James Dunn": See "Human Rights in East Timor and the Question of the Use of U.S. Military Equipment by the Indonesian Armed Forces," Hearing before the Subcommittees on International Organizations and on Asian and Pacific Affairs of the Committee on International Relations, House of Representatives, 95th Congress, First Session, U.S. Government Printing Office, Washington, D.C., March 23, 1977.

Page 94, "A great wave of emotion . . .": This was from a letter brought to public attention by Australian Labor Parliamentarian Ken Fry, cited in the *Canberra Times*, February 14, 1978. Also see *Canberra Times*, March 25, 1978.

Page 95, "involved in the process": see Pilger, page 298.

Page 95, "Massive bombing campaigns . . .": see testimony of Father do Rego in Kohen and Quance, *Inquiry*, cited above. See also Amnesty International 1985 report, cited above.

Page 96, "the first international conference": The 1979 conference was held by CIDAC, Rua Pinheiro de Chajas 77, 1000 Lisbon, Portugal, from which the proceedings are available. Also see "Remember Us?" *The Economist*, London, May 26, 1979.

Page 96, "the only individual": Chomsky's address at the Lisbon conference, "East Timor and the Western Democracies," was published by Spokesman Books (Pamphlet No. 67), Nottingham (UK), 1979.

Page 96, "the news article that resulted was sketchy": "Timor Priest, Charging Genocide, Seeks U.S. Help," *New York Times*, December 14, 1979.

Page 96, "James M. Markham": see "Refugees from East Timor Report Famine Situation," *New York Times*, January 29, 1980, and "Refugees Say Rebels in East Timor Are Still Fighting the Indonesians," July 29, 1980.

Page 96, "sympathetic *Times* editorial comment": See the following *New York Times* editorials: "Tears for Timor," July 25, 1980; "The Shaming of Indonesia," December 8, 1980; "Christmas Beacons," December 25, 1981; "Forgotten Sorrows in Timor," October 9, 1982; "A Prison Called East Timor," July 11, 1984; "Honor Indonesia With Honesty," May 1, 1986; "East Timor: The Shame Endures," December 7, 1990, in addition to numerous editorials that have appeared since the November 1991 massacre at the Santa Cruz cemetery.

Page 97, "I felt like I was back in Saigon": Author's conversation with James Markham, January 1980.

Page 98, "David Jenkins": "Death of a Dream of Freedom," *Far Eastern Economic Review*, May 23, 1980.

Page 98, See "US Role in Plight of Timor: An Issue That Won't Go Away," *Christian Science Monitor*, March 6, 1980.

Page 99, "including the Thai-Cambodia border": Morton Kondracke, "Asia's Other Cambodia," *The New Republic*, November 3, 1979.

Page 99, "so have most of the casualties": *The New Republic*, November 3, 1979.

Page 99, "Edward Masters": His congressional testimony was published in "Famine Relief for East Timor," Hearing before the Subcommittee on Asian and Pacific Affairs of the Committee on Foreign Affairs, House of Representatives, 96th Congress, First Session, December 4, 1979: U.S. Government Printing Office, Washington, D.C., 1980, pages 20–22.

Page 99, "experienced journalist": Daniel Southerland, then chief diplomatic correspondent for the *Christian Science Monitor*, who had spent thirteen years in Asia and was acquainted with Ambassador Masters from previous assignments.

Page 99, *Christian Science Monitor*, March 6, 1980.

Page 100, "Makassae beliefs": The author is indebted to Shepard Forman for these insights. Also see *Human Rights in East Timor*, 1977, pages 11–39.

Page 102, "The people are now experiencing . . .": See "Reflection on the faith of the East Timorese people in the actual situation," July 31, 1981, presented to the Conference of Indonesian Major Religious Superiors. In Louise Crowe and Jack de Groot, *The Church and East Timor: A Collection of Documents by National and International Aid Agencies*, Catholic Commission for Justice, Development and Peace, Melbourne (Australia) Archdiocese, 1993.

Page 103, "white-robed Catholic priests": See Crowe's extensive account of the East Timor Church, 1996, cited above.

Page 104, "government officials spoke of 'improvements'": For an example of such talk by U.S. government officials, see "Recent Developments in East Timor," Hearing Before the Subcommittee on Asian and Pacific Affairs of the Committee on Foreign Affairs, House of Representatives, 97th Congress, Second Session, September 14, 1982, U.S. Government Printing Office, Washington: 1982. For articles and editorials illustrating the atmosphere of that time, see Arnold S. Kohen, "The Shattered World of East Timor," *Los Angeles Times,* January 7, 1982; "Timor Tragedy," *San Francisco Chronicle,* January 11, 1982; and "The Tragedy of East Timor," *San Jose Mercury News,* January 17, 1982.

Page 105, *"pemuda":* See Anderson, 1972.

Page 107, "CIA sources": Interview by the author with Senate staff, 1982.

Page 109, "Quelicai": See Amnesty International 1985 report, page 41 ("Quelicai" is spelled "Kelikai" in that document).

Page 110, "I decided there were no other means": See interview with Monsignor Lopes in East Timor Report, Australian Council for Overseas Aid, No. 5, November 1983. Also see "Justifiable concern," *The Tablet* (London), August 6, 1983.

Page 111, "The news from Timor is quite bad": The text of Monsignor Lopes's letter was inserted in the Congressional Record by Senator Paul Tsongas on December 16, 1981.

Page 111, "found their way to the international press": See, for instance, Daniel Southerland, "E. Timor may face food shortage," *Christian Science Monitor,* February 11, 1982.

Page 112, "Already resigned from office, Monsignor Lopes . . .": The account of the meeting with Cardinal Casaroli is based on the author's interview with Monsignor Lopes in 1984.

Page 112, "playing a leading role in the interreligious dialogue": See Desmond O'Grady, "Timor timebomb ticks on," *The Tablet* (London), June 1, 1996, for a discussion of the difficulties faced by Rome over the East Timor question.

Page 112, "Catholic leaders in Indonesia": See Pat Walsh, "The Pope rides the Indonesian rapid without rocking the boat," *National Outlook* (Australia), January 1990. For a discussion of the dilemmas facing the Indonesian Catholic Church, also see Pro Mundi Vita, East Timor, Dossier No. 4, Brussels, 1984.

Page 113, "Dom Martinho put it another way": Author's interview with Monsignor Lopes, 1985.

Page 114, "the Nazis had arrested the Salesians": See Carl Bernstein and Marco Politi, *His Holiness, John Paul II and the Hidden History of Our Time,* New York: Doubleday, 1996, page 59.

Page 115, "was likewise incredulous": Author's correspondence with Father José Luis Rodriguez, 1997.

Page 116, "die deserted": See "Reflection on the faith," Crowe and de Groot, cited above.

Page 116, For an example of how Belo was seen at the time in some international circles, see Carmel Budiardjo and Liem Soie Liong, *The War Against East Timor,* London: Zed Books, 1984.

Page 117, "There were many . . .": *Diario de Noticias,* (Lisbon) July 3, 1983.

Page 119, "Tetum language": See Anderson, 1993.

Page 120, "In a separate interview": See Budiardjo and Liem Soei Liong, 1984.

Page 122, "Belo's letter": See "Shultz Expresses Concern on Rights," *New York Times,* July 12, 1984, and "East Timor Prelate Reports Abuses," *Washington Post,* July 12, 1984, plus a *Times* editorial, "A Prison Called East Timor." Also see Martinho da Costa Lopes, "Shultz, Help East Timor," *New York Times,* July 8, 1984. For two analyses of events in that period by Daniel Southerland in the *Christian Science Monitor,* see "Congressional concern rises over E. Timor," December 21, 1983 and "Restrictions in East Timor spark US concern about human rights," October 24, 1984.

Page 122, "identity of the people": *New York Times,* "Pope Condemns South African Racial Policies," July 8, 1984.

Page 122, "Richardson": the interview with Belo in *The Age* was published on July 16, 1984 under the headline, "Fretilin hit hard by Jakarta: Churchman." For another brief account on Bishop Belo's comments at this time, see "Report on East Timor", *Washington Post,* July 27, 1984.

Page 123, The "confidential document of July 1984" from the Vatican is in the possession of the author. For related material, see "East Timor: Churchman, Pope Address Civil Strife," *National Catholic Reporter* (U.S.), July 20, 1984.

Page 123, "a critical document": the 1985 document was published in *Timor Link* (No. 2, June 1985), the newsletter of the Catholic Institute for International Relations, Unit 3, Canonbury Yard, 190A New North Road, London N1 UK. An account of the controversy over this document is given by Robert Archer, cited above.

Page 123, "on the eve of a visit,": See "Prelate in E. Timor Accuses Indonesia of Summary Killings," *Washington Post,* April 28, 1985.

Page 124, "'His Holiness said to me:": See *Público,* March 23, 1995.

Page 124, "don't forget to put it on": Interview with Timorese refugees in Lisbon, 1987.

Page 124, "ever let Dom Martinho leave": Monsignor Martinho da Costa Lopes made numerous statements that drew international notice, including testimony before the United Nations Special Committee on Decolonization in August 1986. In addition, he published several articles during this period, including "La Tragedia de Timor," *El País* (Spain), March 18, 1985; "Recalling Timor's Forgotten Voices," *Asian Wall Street Journal Weekly,* May 20, 1985; and "In East Timor, human rights are trampled upon . . .", *Boston Globe,* April 30, 1986. Also see various interviews, "The Timorese Will Fight to the End," *Newsweek* (international edition), September 3, 1984, and "Bishop Lopes Publicizes Plight of East Timor," *Maryknoll News* (US), July 1984.

Page 125, *"out of luck?":* The author was present at this 1986 meeting.

Page 125, "In a TV interview . . .": This was with Portuguese journalist Rui Araujo.

Page 126, "Sydney *Morning Herald*": The articles were by David Jenkins, April 10, 1986.

Page 126, "Barbara Crossette": See Arnold Kohen, "Indonesia's Press Needs Reagan's Help," *New York Times,* April 29, 1986.

Page 126, "Xanana Gusmão": A letter by Xanana Gusmão during this period, and material detailing the surveillance of Bishop Belo by Indonesian forces, was published in *Timor Link* (Number 9, March 1987). Also see Xanana Gusmão, *Timor Leste, Um Povo, Um Patria,* Edicões Colibri, Lisbon, 1994, pages 201–205.

Page 131, "letter of solidarity": See "Indonesian Church Hits East Timor 'Oppression,'" *National Catholic Reporter,* (U.S), February 24, 1984. The letter and other comments are included in Crowe and de Groot, cited above.

Page 133, "a delegation of West German Members of Parliament": See Hans-Ulrich Klose, "As If Everyone Were Under Arrest," *Der Spiegel,* April 29, 1985.

Page 133, "Ataúro": See "Filling the Void in Jakarta," *New York Times* (*The Week in Review*), October 17, 1982.

Page 134, *"Far Eastern Economic Review":* "Modesty Rewarded," October 22–28, 1982. Also see "Indonesia Accused of Abuses in Timor," *New York Times,* October 7, 1982.

Page 134, "congressional and press commentary": For such reports during this time, see Bernard Weinraub, "Indonesia Accused of Abuses in Timor," *New York Times,* October 7, 1982 and Anthony Lewis, "A Small, Far-Off Place," *New York Times,* October 11, 1982, in which Lewis spoke of how, on the eve of Suharto's visit to Washington, "an unusually broad group of Senators and Representatives expressed new concern about East Timor." Also see the editorial, "Forgotten Sorrows in Timor," *New York Times,* October 9, 1982 and a feature article in the same paper by Charlotte Curtis, "Dinner at the White House," October 19, 1982. In addition, see "What About East Timor?," *Washington Post* editorial, October 13, 1982; and Daniel Southerland, "Warm Welcome for Suharto—but Vexing Issues Lurk in the Background," *Christian Science Monitor,* October 12, 1982.

Page 136, "Jusuf Wanandi": See Martin Cohn, "Bitter Legacy of War Fading Slowly in East Timor," *Toronto Star,* February 5, 1989.

Page 136, "Suharto himself": Author's interview with Monsignor da Costa Lopes, 1984.

Page 137, "I am writing . . .": Bishop Belo's letter to Perez de Cuellar can be found in Crowe and de Groot, cited above. Also see in same publication the letter of support drafted by Bishop Aloisius Soma of Japan, cosigned by 5 cardinals, 32 archbishops, 77 bishops and other Church leaders of the Asia-Pacific region.

Page 137, "President Suharto himself": Dom Martinho confirmed this in a 1984 interview with the author.

Page 138, "the General Assembly": For a list of relevant United Nations resolutions, see *East Timor and the International Community, Basic Documents,* Cambridge University Press, 1997.

Page 141, "Gain the support of the Pope": For a retrospective view of these events, see Desmond O'Grady, *The Tablet,* cited above. For an account of how Belo was perceived by Rome at the time of the pope's 1989 visit to East Timor, the dilemmas facing Rome, as well as an interview with the bishop, see Desmond O'Grady, "Controversial East Timor bishop speaks out," *Our Sunday Visitor* (U.S.), October 15, 1989.

Page 141, "Carrascalão was "working very hard . . .": See Richardson article, cited on page 122.

Page 142, "The U.S. Bishops": for the text of the 1987 statement, see Crowe and de Groot, cited above.

Page 142, "The U.S. Bishops had made a statement:" For the full text, see "Bishops Join Hands in Condemning East Timor Tragedy," *Asian Wall Street Journal Weekly,* April 13, 1987 and *Congressional Record,* April 23, 1987. See Richard Halloran, "40 Senators Voice Concern for Timor Fighting," *New York Times,* August 9, 1987, which followed the U.S. Catholic Bishops' statement, and "U.S. is Nudging Indonesia On Rights in East Timor," *Washington Post,* November 3, 1988 (the latter article notes that "more than 200 U.S. senators and representatives" had urged the Reagan Administration to press the issue, also partly the result of interest by the Catholic bishops. In addition, see "Cardinal Voices Support for East Timor Catholics," Press Release from U.S. Catholic Conference, August 28, 1985.

Page 143, "without a voice to speak openly": See Lindsay Murdoch, "Bishop Calls for Poll in Timor," *Melbourne Age,* August 28, 1989.

Page 143, "are threatening me psychologically": Telephone interview with Bishop Belo, *Independente* (Lisbon), October 9, 1989, cited in Taylor, page 156.

Page 144, "emotional faith": Unpublished interview, 1994, courtesy of Pat Walsh, Australian Council for Overseas Aid Human Rights Office, cited above.

Page 145, "In his homily": The text of the pope's homily is in Crowe and de Groot, cited above.

Page 146, "For his part, John Paul II did not forget": See Desmond O'Grady, *The Tablet,* cited above.

Page 146, "This incident": *Ibid.*

Page 147, "resulted in the beating and torture": See Clyde Haberman, "Fear Expressed for 40 East Timor Protestors," *New York Times,* October 19, 1989.

Page 149, "The Ambassador's visit": see *Timor Link* (London) Number 20-21, January-February 1990 and "Violence in Timor protest," *Guardian* (London) January 19, 1990.

Page 153, "Oscar Romero": For a brief account of Romero's life and death, see Kenneth L. Woodward, *Making Saints: How the Catholic Church Determines Who Becomes a Saint, Who Doesn't, and Why,* New York: Touchstone, 1996, Pages 8, 36–49, 52, 153–54. For an account of Bishop Belo's comparison of the dangers he faced with the assassination of

Archbishop Romero, see "East Timor Bishop Writes of Torture," *New York Times*, February 11, 1990.

Page 154, "My position is very difficult,": Another protest demonstration during this time took place on September 4, 1990, at a Mass to celebrate the fiftieth anniversary of the Diocese of Dili, when the papal nuncio, Archbishop Canalini, came to East Timor for the occasion. About two hundred young people took part. For this and other details of the growing unrest during that period, see Steven Erlanger, "East Timor, Reopened by Indonesians, Remains a Sad and Terrifying Place," *New York Times*, October 21, 1990.

Page 156, "the actions of the young people": For a discussion of the youth movement in East Timor, see Benedict Anderson, "East Timor and the paradox of nationalism," *Arena* (Australia), No. 4, April–May 1993, and Steve Cox and Peter Carey, *Generations of Resistance*, cited above.

Page 156, See "East Timor: The Shame Endures," editorial, *New York Times*, December 7, 1990.

Page 156, "a campaign of terror": See *Publico*, October 17, 1991. Another important account that year, based on Belo's meeting with visiting parliamentarians, appeared in the *Catholic Leader* (Australia), April 21, 1991.

Page 157, "Clare Dixon": See her "Cry of a Forgotten Land," *Catholic Herald* (London), November 22, 1991.

Page 157, For an account of the world of double agents in East Timor at that time, see Constâncio Pinto and Matthew Jardine, *East Timor's Unfinished Struggle, Inside the Timorese Resistance*, South End Press, 1996.

Page 160, "Letter to the author": Excerpts of this letter and others were published in *Timor Link*, No. 27, October 1993, cited above.

Page 161, "General Murdani": See Adam Schwarz, *A Nation in Waiting, Indonesia in the 1990s*, Westview, 1994, page 345, note 56. Also see pages 194–229 for a summary of the Santa Cruz events and their aftermath. For eyewitness accounts, see Max Stahl, "Massacre among the graves," *The Independent on Sunday*, (London), November 17, 1991, and Allan Nairn, "I Witnessed and Survived the Massacre at the Santa Cruz Cemetery," testimony before the United States Senate Committee on Foreign Relations, "Crisis in East Timor and U.S. Policy Towards Indonesia," 102nd Congress, Second Session, U.S. Government Printing Office, Washington, D.C., February 27, 1992.

For a brief account of events during this period, see Arnold S. Kohen, "Making an Issue of East Timor," *The Nation*, February 10, 1992.

Page 163, "Hide us, or they will kill us!": Quotation from *Reader's Digest*, cited above.

Page 166, "Philip Shenon": "A Voice, Often Silenced, Speaks of East Timor's Fear," *New York Times*, April 24, 1993.

Page 166, "taken away and executed": See Lindsay Murdoch, "Dili deaths just the start," *Age* (Melbourne), November 18, 1998, in which former Governor Carrascalão reveals that dozens were taken away and executed in the weeks after the initial Santa Cruz massacre.

Page 167, "the *Wall Street Journal*": Helen Todd, "A Son's Death in East Timor," December 3, 1991. A longer version by the same author appeared under the title "Death in East Timor" in the *Asian Wall Street Journal*, November 25, 1991. Also see "West Cites New Excesses in East Timor," *International Herald Tribune*, November 20, 1991.

Page 168, "Priests suspected": Information here and on page 169 was provided to the author by clergy in East Timor. For an important account from the East Timor Church at that time, see Max Stahl, "A Church on Calvary," *The Tablet*, 25 January 1992. For an independent account by a visitor from the New York–based Human Rights Watch, see Joanna Weschler, "Another People Suffering Under 'Nation of Masters,'" *Los Angeles Times*, March 10, 1992.

Page 168, "Max Stahl wrote": See *Independent on Sunday*, cited above.

Page 170, "one prominent expert": The author is indebted to Benedict Anderson for his insights on military politics and many other matters. See "Indonesian Report on

Timor Shootings Draws Criticism," *Washington Post*, December 27, 1991 and "E. Timor Generals Fired," *Washington Post*, December 29, 1991.

Page 171, "described by Mário Carrascalão": Cited in Schwarz, page 194.

Page 172, "Fascell's reply": This account is based on the author's 1991 interview with Representative Hall.

Page 172, In Walter Isaacson's *Kissinger*, cited above, there are several references to Kissinger's work for Freeport.

Page 173, "told a Republican Congressman": Author's interview with Representative Frank Wolf.

Page 173, "oil companies signed new deals,": See, for example, "Canberra Braced for Protests over Timor Sea Oil Permits," *Financial Times* (London), December 6, 1991.

Page 175, "The Indonesians are saying one thing": Author's interviews with clergy, 1992.

Page 176, "It's just a fabrication": See *Público*, December 4, 1992.

Page 176, "I don't know what happened to make Xanana change so fast": See *Público*, December 4, 1992.

Page 176, "an editorial in the *Washington Post*": See "A Leading Asian Colonialist," December 5, 1992. Other *Post* editorials in the period after the Santa Cruz massacre were "Dead in East Timor", November 20, 1991; "Indonesia's Tiananmen", December 9, 1991; and "East Timor What?", February 29, 1992. *New York Times* editorials during this time were "Tears for East Timor," November 21, 1991 and "The Tiananmen in East Timor," January 25, 1992. Several also appeared in the *Boston Globe*, which has published numerous editorials on East Timor since 1980.

Page 177, "resolution on East Timor": See "U.N. Criticizes Indonesia About East Timor," *New York Times*, March 14, 1993.

Page 177, "Philip Shenon": April 24, 1993.

Page 180, "President Suharto was offended": See "Suharto Defends East Timor Takeover," *International Herald Tribune*, July 8, 1993 and "U.S. Criticizes Suharto on Rights," *Financial Times* (London), July 8, 1993.

Page 181, "On Sundays": For excerpts of Bishop Belo's letters during this period, see *Timor Link*, October 1993, cited above.

Page 183, "Feingold": The Senate action received editorial support from the *New York Times*: "A Different Message to Jakarta," November 1, 1993. While the Feingold amendment never became law, because it lacked the necessary votes, the measure became a symbol of what Congress might be prepared to do.

Page 184, "A Figure of Courage in the Midst of East Timor's Agony," *The Age*, November 17, 1993. Other quotations on this page are from that article.

Page 185, "It is great injustice and suffering": Representative Tony P. Hall inserted this letter from Bishop Belo in the *Congressional Record* on February 14, 1994.

Page 185, "East Timor is like hell": This quote is from *Reuters*, cited in William Branigan, "Christian-Muslim Clashes in East Timor Raise Tensions, U.S. Concerns," *Washington Post*, July 22, 1994.

Page 186, "Eat your God": see *Público*, March 23, 1995.

Page 186, "The young people . . .": Antonio Marujo, *Público* (Lisbon), June 1, 1994.

Page 186, "statements by Jewish and Protestant groups": For example, in the U.S., among Protestants, resolutions were adopted by the National Council of Churches and various denominations, including the United Methodist Church, Presbyterian Church and the United Church of Christ, as did the Lutheran World Federation (on the international level) and the Episcopal Church.

Among Jewish groups, the Central Conference of American Rabbis and the Commission on Social Action of Reform Judaism have passed measures.

Page 190, "*The Economist*": "Timor's Opportunity," November 19, 1994.

Page 190, "Editorials in the *New York Times* . . .": see "Indonesia's Embarrassment," November 15, 1994; "Indonesia's Opportunity Lost," *Washington Post*, November 22,

1994; "Rights and Wrongs in Indonesia," *Boston Globe,* November 25, 1994; "Grubby Little Secret," *USA Today,* November 15, 1994; "Eastern Fist," *Times of London,* November 17, 1994; "How to Move an Autocrat," *Globe and Mail* (Toronto), November 16, 1994.

Page 190, "The *Wall Street Journal*": "Indonesia's Pebble," November 17, 1994.

Page 191, "A United Nations specialist": See "Report by the Special Rapporteur, Mr. Bacre Waly Ndiaye, on His Mission to Indonesia and East Timor from 3 to 13 July 1994," *Economic and Social Council,* November 1994.

Page 194, "the standoff . . .": The author conducted an extensive interview with a European witness to that day's events.

Page 195, "*New York Times*": Andrew Pollack, "Roman Catholic Bishop Denounces Repression in East Timor," November 22, 1994.

Page 197, "Belo's ready answer": This was part of a long series of interviews by the author in 1995.

Page 198, "I accept their criticism": See *Público,* March 23, 1995.

Page 199, "change things": Paulo Nogueira, *Público,* March 23, 1995.

Page 200, "If I have to go to hell, then I'll go to hell": See *Público,* March 25, 1995.

Page 200, "*Público*": March 23, 1995.

Page 208, "Bishop Kamphaus": See introduction by Bishop Kamphaus in Klemens Ludwig and Korinna Horta, *Osttimor: Das vergessene Sterben: Indonesischer Völkermord unter Ausschluss der Weltöffentlichkeit, Gesellschaft für bedrohte Völker,* Göttingen, 1985.

Page 208, "Manila": For brief descriptions of these events, see two editorials in the *New York Times:* "Timorous on Timor," May 24, 1994, and "The Manila Folder," June 11, 1994.

Page 212, "trucks filled with": Much of the following account is based on the author's observations on his September 1995 visit to East Timor.

Page 213, "a crippled boy": For a first-hand summary of the atmosphere at that time, see Arnold S. Kohen, "Buried alive: East Timor's tragic oppression," *Boston Sunday Globe,* December 10, 1995.

Page 220, "Indonesian connections": See the October 7, 1996, *New York Times* column by William Safire titled "The Asian Connection." It notes the Grobmayer-Riady visit to East Timor and makes the allegation that Riady's actions may have caused the Clinton administration to "lose interest" in East Timor.

Also see Paul Moore Jr. and Arnold S. Kohen, "Clinton has solid cards to play on East Timor's behalf," *The Boston Globe,* November 16, 1996, and "For Sale: Foreign Policy," *Boston Globe* editorial, June 9, 1997.

Page 221, "while employed by the Riadys in 1994": See "Asian Donors Sought Prestige at Home," *Washington Post,* May 27, 1997. For more on the relationship of the Riadys and Clinton, see "Clinton's Asian Connection," *Newsweek,* October 28, 1996. Also see "By Courting Clinton, Lippo Gains Stature at Home in Indonesia;" also "Policy on Indonesian, East Timor Becomes U.S. Campaign Issue," *The Wall Street Journal,* October 16, 1996, and "Indonesian Magnate and Clinton Talked Policy, White House Says," the *New York Times,* November 5, 1996, which noted that while it was not known "precisely what policies Mr. Riady had pressed for" during his visits to the White House, "associates of the Riadys have said they were interested in American concerns about human rights in East Timor and worker rights more generally in Indonesia." For more on Hubbell, see the *New York Times,* March 20, 1997, "Asian Paid $100,000 to Hubbell Days After Visits to White House"; *Washington Post,* March 23, 1997, "Hubbell Meetings With Riady Draw Scrutiny"; *Washington Post,* March 25, 1997, "Crime Does Pay," (editorial); *Washington Post,* March 28, 1997, "What's His Secret?" (column by Richard Cohen).

Page 221, "sister city": See "Clinton's Early Link to Asia," *Washington Post,* March 7, 1997.

Page 223, "the week before the announcement": Coincidentally, the *National Catholic Reporter* published an editorial calling for Bishop Belo to be awarded the Peace Prize a week before he actually received it. See "A Courageous Voice Calling for Help in East Timor," October 11, 1996.

Page 223, "Tibet in 1989": I am indebted to Dan Southerland, now executive editor of the Washington-based Radio Free Asia, a Congressionally funded station, and Kate Saunders of the Tibet Information Network in London, for their assistance on matters pertaining to Tibet.

Page 224, "in the first place": see Arnold Kohen, "East Timor's peacemaker," *The Tablet* (London), October 19, 1996.

Page 226, "McCurry . . . State Department": Transcript of White House press briefing, October 11, 1996, and U.S. Department of State, daily press briefing, same date.

Page 226, "treasured friend": See "NSC Gave Warnings about Asian Donors," *Washington Post,* February 15, 1997.

Page 226, "Clinton's citation": See, for example, the *Washington Post,* November 9, 1996, "Clinton Denies DNC Funds Had Any Effect on Policy." Also see David Sanger, "Clinton Admits He And Indonesian Had Policy Talks," *New York Times,* November 16, 1996.

Page 227, "our kind of guy": See *The New York Times,* "Real Politics: Why Suharto Is In and Castro Is Out." October 31, 1995.

Page 228, "Ramos-Horta": For an autobiographical account of East Timor's diplomatic struggle, see Jose Ramos-Horta, *Funu, The Unfinished Saga of East Timor,* Red Sea Press, 1987 (reprinted 1997).

Page 228, "to send a frankly political message": See Irwin Abrams, "The Nobel Prize in Peace," *The Nobel Prize Annual for 1996,* New York: IMG Publishing, 1997, Page 57.

Page 228, "for all those who . . .": See Abrams, 1997, page 62: Here, Ramos-Horta also observes that he "suspected . . . that the Nobel Committee had decided to give [the award] to someone who had not been imprisoned and could keep speaking out about East Timor."

Page 233, "media interviews": The main interview Bishop Belo gave in Oslo to a Portuguese correspondent was to Adelino Gomes, then of RDP (Radio) News, who has followed the Timor case since 1975 more consistently than any other Portuguese journalist.

Page 234, "von Ossietzky": See Irwin Abrams, *The Nobel Peace Prize and the Laureates, An Illustrated Biographical History, 1901–1987,* G. K. Hall and Company, Boston, 1988, pages 125–29.

Page 234, "the man whose last will and testament created the award": See Kenne Fant, *Alfred Nobel, A Biography,* Arcade Publishing, 1993, Also see Abams, cited above.

Page 235, "one of the most extraordinary women of that era": See *Bertha von Suttner, A Life for Peace,* Brigitte Hamann, Syracuse University Press, 1996, and Abrams, and Fant, cited above.

The author is indebted to these three works for background information, especially that of Abrams, in addition to interviews at the Norwegian Nobel Institute, for information on Alfred Nobel, the Peace Prize and individual laureates.

Page 239, "The fact that a Nobel": See "The Nobel peace prize and the laureates: the meaning and acceptance of the Nobel peace prize in the prize winners' countries," Ed. Karl Holl and Anne Cecilie Kjelling, Frankfurt am Main: Peter Lang, 1994.

Page 240, "I stand humbled": The 1996 Nobel Peace Prize lectures are in *East Timor Nobel Peace Prize,* Edicões Colibri, Lisbon, 1997. Also see Carlos Ximenes Belo, "Time for Peace in East Timor," *New York Times,* December 10, 1996.

Page 243, ". . . Cardinal Sodano,": See Father Pat Smythe, "Bishop Belo, Advocate for Justice", in Torben Retboll, ed., *East Timor: Occupation and Resistance,* Document 89, IWGIA, International Working Group for Indigenous Affairs, Denmark, 1998, page 168.

Page 244, "Now that you have . . .": This is based on the author's interviews with two participants in the meetings in question.

Page 244, "only to be told this was now politically impossible": Well-informed diplomatic sources in Rome provided this account to the author.

Page 249, "Muskens, bishop of Breda": See M. P. Muskens, *Partner in Nation Building: The Catholic Church in Indonesia,* Aachen, Missio Aktuell Verlag, 1979.

Page 249, "four women had been acquitted": See "Protesters cleared over attack on jet," *Guardian* (London), July 31, 1996.

Page 250, "American colleagues,": For an interview with Bishop Belo during this time, see "Bishop Asks Help for East Timor Youth," *National Catholic Reporter,* June 20, 1997.

Page 252, "a letter to President Suharto,": See "Notables Seek Solution to East Timor Rebellion," *International Herald Tribune,* September 11, 1997.

Page 257, "*Financial Times*": "National Cars," June 13, 1996.

Page 263, "among the Mambai": See Traube's 1977 testimony in "Human Rights in East Timor," pages 21–36. Also see Elizabeth G. Traube, *Cosmology and Social Life, Ritual Exchange among the Mambai of East Timor,* University of Chicago Press, 1986.

Page 264, "The temperature fell": See Dunn, page 2.

Page 264, "two Catholic priests had been executed": See Turner, page 11.

Page 265, "Nicolau Lobato": For various accounts of the life and death of Nicolau Lobato, see Dunn, pages 280, 282; McDonald, page 214; Turner, pages 112, 155, 184.

Page 270, "The excitement was palpable": For a summary of these events, see Arnold Kohen, "Murder on the mountain," *The Tablet* (London), October 25, 1997.

Page 277, "President Suharto's grip on office": For analyses of this period and the months that followed, see the collection of essays in the journal, *Indonesia,* Number 66, February 1999, Cornell University Southeast Asia Program, 640 Stewart Avenue, Ithaca, New York 14850.

Page 278, "Outburst of muffled voices": For a summary of these events, see Arnold Kohen, "Muffled Voices," *Index on Censorship* (London), July–August 1998. For another account of events during this period, see Tony Jenkins, *Expresso* (Lisbon), June 6, 1998.

Page 279, "The intelligence officers are everywhere": Lewa Pardomuan, "Indonesia still enemy in East Timor 20 years on," *Reuters,* June 12, 1998.

Page 279, "I loathe the military": *Reuters,* June 12, 1998, same author as above.

Page 280, "We are not in a hurry," See article of that title by Tony Jenkins, *Expresso* (Lisbon), May 30, 1998.

Page 281, "East Timor is not part of Indonesia": See Andrew Marshall, "East Timorese raise voices against Indonesia," *Reuters,* June 12, 1998. Also see Kyodo News Service, same date.

Page 282, "I'd like to see first": See Geoff Spencer, "Indonesian leader predicts recovery," Associated Press, June 13, 1998.

Page 282, "We don't care about this special status thing": See Lewa Pardomuan, "East Timorese cool toward special status offer," *Reuters,* June 12, 1998.

Page 282, "East Timor should be free now": See Lewa Pardomuan, "Amid calls for freedom, some East Timorese wary," *Reuters,* June 15, 1998.

Page 284, "the bishop fumed": Author's interview with Belo.

Page 285, "immigrants": for Belo's remarks, see "Belo calls on U.N. envoy not to visit E. Timor", Kyodo News Service, July 15, 1998.

Page 285, "to take refuge": Author's interview with the bishop.

Page 286, "Bishop Belo is the guiding star": *Suara Pembaruan* (Jakarta), July 18, 1998.

Page 287, "It's a taboo subject": See *Detak* (Jakarta), July 16, 1998.

Page 287, "closer, open, friendly": Author's interview with the bishop.

Page 287, "Timorese close to the Indonesian government were furious": Author's interview with the bishop.

Page 287, "announced a withdrawal": See Sander Thoenes, "Indonesian troops start to withdraw from East Timor," *Financial Times,* July 29, 1998.

Page 289, "in a September 16, 1998 interview": The interview was with *Agence France Presse.*

Page 289, "leaked Indonesian Defense Ministry documents": See Barbara Crossette, "Indonesian Army Pullback in East Timor Disputed by Leaked Reports," *New York Times,* October 30, 1998.

Page 290, "the use of U.S.-supplied arms in East Timor": For a comprehensive study, see "U.S. Arms Transfers to Indonesia 1975–1997: Who's Influencing Whom?" by William

Hartung and Jennifer Washburn, Arms Trade Resource Center, World Policy Institute at the New School for Social Research, March 1997.

Page 290, "And some Vatican officials": See, for example, Thomas J. Reese, *Inside the Vatican,* Harvard University Press, 1996, page 265. The reference here is to "the world community," but privately some Vatican officials have implied that the most powerful nations in the world bear a special responsibility. See also Szulc, page 478.

Page 293, "Alas": There have been several conflicting reports on what took place in the Alas region, which was placed off-limits to a number of investigators. See "Indonesia Panel to Study Reports of Army Slayings in East Timor," *New York Times,* November 25, 1998. Also see "East Timor Massacre Reports Still Unconfirmed, Both Sides Must Respect Human Rights", Press Release by Human Rights Watch/Asia, November 23, 1998.

Page 294, "130 million": See Associated Press dispatch cited in "World Briefing," *New York Times,* January 16, 1999.

Page 295, "Aceh": See Geoffrey Robinson, "*Rawan* is as *Rawan* does: the origins of disorder in New Order Aceh," in *Indonesia,* Number 66, Cornell University Southeast Asia Program, cited above. *Rawan* is the Indonesian word for "trouble" or "tension."

SELECTED BIBLIOGRAPHY

◈ ◈ ◈ ◈

George J. Aditjondro, *In the Shadow of Mount Ramelau, The Impact of the Indonesian Occupation of East Timor*. Indonesian Documentation and Information Centre, The Netherlands, 1994.

Amnesty International, "East Timor, Violation of Human Rights, Extrajudicial Executions, 'Disappearances', Torture and Political Imprisonment." London, 1985.

Amnesty International, "Indonesia and East Timor, Power and Impunity, Human Rights Under the New Order." September 28, 1994.

Asia Watch, *The Limits of Openness, Human Rights in Indonesia and East Timor*. Human Rights Watch, New York, September 1994.

Benedict Anderson, *Java in a Time of Revolution, Occupation and Resistance 1944–46*. Cornell University Press, 1972.

Benedict Anderson, *Language and Power: Exploring Political Cultures in Indonesia*. Cornell University Press, 1990.

Benedict Anderson, *The Spectre of Comparisons: Nationalism, Southeast Asia and the World*. York: Verso, 1998.

Benedict Anderson, "East Timor and the paradox of nationalism." *Arena* (Australia), No. 4, April–May 1993.

Benedict Anderson, "Gravel in Jakarta's Shoes." *London Review of Books*, Nov. 2, 1995. Reprinted in Anderson, *The Spectre of Comparisons: Nationalism, Southeast Asia and the World. Verso*, 1998, pages 131–38.

"Breaking the Cycle of Human Rights Violations in East Timor": *Annual Report of Human Rights Violations in East Timor 1997*. Fitzroy, Australia: East Timor Human Rights Centre, February 1998.

Carmel Budiardjo and Liem Soei Liong, *The War Against East Timor*. Zed Books, London, 1984.

Peter Carey and G. Carter Bentley, eds., *East Timor at the Crossroads, The Forging of a Nation*. Cassell, 1995.

Peter Carey, "Surviving the Occupation: A Personal Journey Through East Timor," in Paul Hainsworth and Steve McCloskey (eds.), *The East Timor Crisis: The Struggle for Independence from Indonesia* (London: I. B. Tauris), 1999.

Noam Chomsky, *Power and Prospects: Reflections on Human Nature and the Social Order*. South End Press, 1996.

Noam Chomsky, *Towards a New Cold War, Essays on the Current Crisis and How We Got There*. Pantheon, 1982.

Noam Chomsky, "East Timor and the Western Democracies," was published by Spokesman Books (Pamphlet No. 67), Nottingham (UK), 1979.

Noam Chomsky and Edward S. Herman, *The Political Economy of Human Rights, Volume I.* South End Press, 1979.

Steve Cox and Peter Carey, *Generations of Resistance.* Cassell (UK), 1995.

"Crisis in East Timor and U.S. Policy Towards Indonesia." United States Senate Committee on Foreign Relations, 102nd Congress, Second Session, U.S. Government Printing Office, Washington, D.C., February 27, 1992.

Louise Crowe, "The Impact of the Indonesian Annexation on the Role of the Catholic Church in East Timor, 1976–95." MA thesis, Northern Territory University (Australia), March 1996.

Louise Crowe and Jack de Groot, eds., "The Church and East Timor: A Collection of Documents by National and International Aid Agencies." Catholic Commission for Justice, Development and Peace, Melbourne (Australia) Archdiocese, 1993.

Clare Dixon, "Cry of a Forgotten Land." *Catholic Herald* (London), November 22, 1991.

James Dunn, *East Timor: A People Betrayed.* Jacaranda Press, Queensland, Australia, 1983; second edition, ABC Books (Australia), 1996.

East Timor and the International Community, Basic Documents. Cambridge University Press, 1997.

East Timor Nobel Peace Prize. Edicões Colibri, Lisbon, 1997.

"East Timor: No Solution Without Respect for Human Rights": Bi-Annual Report for 1998, Fitzroy, Australia: East Timor Human Rights Centre, August 1998.

"Famine Relief for East Timor." Hearing before the Subcommittee on Asian and Pacific Affairs of the Committee on Foreign Affairs, House of Representatives, 96th Congress, First Session, Dec. 4, 1979: U.S. Government Printing Office, Washington, D.C., 1980, pages 20–22.

Herbert Feith, "The East Timor Issue Since the Capture of Xanana Gusmão." Fitzroy, Victoria, Australia, East Timor Talks Campaign, 1993.

Antonio de Figueiredo, *Portugal: Fifty Years of Dictatorship.* Penguin (UK), 1975.

Shepard Forman, "Descent, Alliance and Exchange: Ideology Among the Makassae of East Timor," in J. Fox (ed.), *The Flow of Life: Essays on Eastern Indonesia.* Harvard University Press, 1980.

Shepard Forman, "East Timor: Exchange and Political Hierarchy at the Time of the European Discoveries," in K. Hutterer (ed.), *Economic Exchange and Social Interaction in Southeast Asia.* Center for South and Southeast Asian Studies, University of Michigan, Ann Arbor, 1978.

Geoffrey C. Gunn, *East Timor and the United Nations, The Case for Intervention.* Red Sea Press, Lawrenceville, New Jersey, 1997.

Xanana Gusmão, *Timor Leste, Um Povo, Um Patria.* Edicões Colibri, Lisbon, 1994, pages 201–205.

Mark Hertsgaard, "The Secret Life of Henry Kissinger." *The Nation,* October 29, 1990.

David Hicks, "The Cairui and Uai Ma'a of Timor." *Anthropos,* 68 (1973).

Helen Hill, "Fretilin: The Origins, Ideologies and Strategies of a Nationalist Movement in East Timor." MA thesis, Monash University (Australia), 1978.

Geoffrey Hull, "East Timor: Just a Political Question?" North Sydney: Australia Catholic Social Justice Council, 1992.

Geoffrey Hull, "Mai Kolia Tetum, a Course in Tetum-Praca, the Lingua Franca of East Timor." Sydney: Australian Catholic Relief and Catholic Social Justice Council, 1993.

"Human Rights in East Timor." Hearings Before the Subcommittee on International Organizations of the Committee on International Relations, House of Representatives, 95th Congress, First Session, U.S. Government Printing Office, Washington, D.C., June 28, 1977 and July 19, 1977.

"Human Rights in East Timor and the Question of the Use of U.S. Military Equipment by the Indonesian Armed Forces." Hearing before the Subcommittees on International Organizations and on Asian and Pacific Affairs of the Committee on International Relations, House of Representatives, 95th Congress, First Session, U.S. Government Printing Office, Washington, D.C., March 23, 1977.

Indonesia: Arms Trade to a Military Regime. Amsterdam: European Network Against Arms Trade, 1997.

Jill Jolliffe, *East Timor: Nationalism and Colonialism.* University of Queensland Press, 1978.

George McTurnan Kahin, *Nationalism and Revolution in Indonesia.* Cornell University Press, 1952 (reprinted 1970).

Audrey R. Kahin and George McT. Kahin, *Subversion as Foreign Policy: The Secret Eisenhower and Dulles Debacle in Indonesia.* The Free Press, New York, 1995.

Arnold S. Kohen, "Buried alive: East Timor's tragic oppression," *Boston Sunday Globe,* December 10, 1995.

Arnold S. Kohen, "The Cruel Case of Indonesia." *The Nation,* Nov. 26, 1977.

Arnold Kohen, "Invitation to a Massacre in East Timor." *The Nation,* Feb. 7, 1981.

Arnold S. Kohen, "Making an Issue of East Timor." *The Nation,* Feb. 10, 1992.

Arnold Kohen, "East Timor's peacemaker." *The Tablet* (London), Oct. 19, 1996.

Arnold Kohen, "Murder on the Mountain." *The Tablet* (London), Oct. 25, 1997.

Arnold Kohen, "Shall I tell the President?" *Messenger of St. Anthony* (Padua, Italy), December 1997.

Arnold Kohen, "Muffled Voices." *Index on Censorship* (London), July–August, 1998.

Arnold S. Kohen, "The Shattered World of East Timor," *Los Angeles Times,* January 7, 1982.

Arnold S. Kohen and Roberta A. Quance, "The Politics of Starvation." *Inquiry,* The Cato Institute, San Francisco, Feb. 18, 1980.

Arnold Kohen and John Taylor, *An Act of Genocide: Indonesia's Invasion of East Timor.* Tapol (UK), 1979.

Morton M. Kondracke, "Asia's Other Cambodia." *The New Republic,* Nov. 3, 1979.

Pedro Pinto Leite (Ed.), *The East Timor Problem and the Role of Europe.* Lisbon: International Platform of Jurists for East Timor (IPJET), 1998.

Norman Lewis, *An Empire of the East, Travels in Indonesia.* Jonathan Cape, London, 1993.

Klemens Ludwig and Korinna Horta, *Osttimor: Das vergessene Sterben: Indonesischer Völkermord unter Ausschluss der Weltöffentlichkeit.* Gesellschaft fur bedrohte Völker.

Göttingen, 1985. ("East Timor, The Forgotten Dying: Indonesian Genocide Concealed from World Publicity." Society for Endangered Peoples).

Hamish McDonald, *Suharto's Indonesia.* Fontana Books, 1980.

A. Barbedo de Magalhaes, ed., *East Timor: Land of Hope.* Oporto University, Portugal.

Timothy Mo, *The Redundancy of Courage.* Chatto and Windus, London, 1991 (paperback by Vintage, 1992).

Cliff Morris, *Legends and Poems from the Land of the Sleeping Crocodile, East Timor.* Waverly Offset Publishing Group, Mulgrave, Victoria, Australia, 1984.

Mubyarto et. al., Pat Walsh (ed.), *East Timor, The Impact of Integration, An Indonesian Socio-Anthropological Study.* Jogajakarta, Gadjah Mada University, Research Center for Village and Regional Development, published by Indonesian Resources and Information Program, Northcote, Australia, 1991.

George Munster and Richard Walsh, *Documents on Australian Defense and Foreign Policy, 1968–75.* Sydney 1980. (Walsh and Munster, an imprint of Angus and Robertson)

Martinus P. Muskens, *Partner in Nation Building: The Catholic Church in Indonesia.* Aachen, Missio Aktuell Verlag, 1979.

Allan Nairn, "The Talk of the Town, Notes and Comments." *The New Yorker,* Dec. 9, 1991.

The Nobel Prize Annual for 1996, New York: IMG Publishing, 1997.

Desmond O'Grady, "Controversial East Timor bishop speaks out," *Our Sunday Visitor* (U.S.), Oct. 15, 1989.

Desmond O'Grady, "Timor timebomb ticks on," *The Tablet* (London), June 1, 1996.

A. H. de Oliveira Marques, *History of Portugal.* Columbia University Press, second edition, 1976.

Hugh O'Shaughnessy, *East Timor, Getting Away With Murder?* London: British Coalition for East Timor, 1994.

John Pilger, *Distant Voices.* Vintage (UK), 1994.

Constancio Pinto and Matthew Jardine, *East Timor's Unfinished Struggle, Inside the Timorese Resistance.* South End Press, [Boston,] 1996.

Pro Mundi Vita, East Timor, Dossier No. 4, Brussels, 1984.

Paul Raffaele, "Champion of a Forgotten People." *Reader's Digest,* February 1997 (USA Edition: the article appeared earlier in some other editions).

Jose Ramos-Horta, *Funu, The Unfinished Saga of East Timor.* Red Sea Press, 1986 (reprinted 1997).

"Recent Developments in East Timor," Hearing Before the Subcommittee on Asian and Pacific Affairs of the Committee on Foreign Affairs, House of Representatives, 97th Congress, Second Session, September 14, 1982, U.S. Government Printing Office, Washington, D.C.: 1982.

"Report by the Special Rapporteur, Mr. Bacre Waly Ndiaye, on his mission to Indonesia and East Timor from 3 to 13 July 1994," Economic and Social Council, November 1994.

Torben Retboll, ed., *East Timor: Occupation and Resistance.* Document 89, IWGIA, International Working Group for Indigenous Affairs, Denmark, 1998.

Geoffrey Robinson, *The Dark Side of Paradise, Political Violence in Bali.* Cornell University Press, 1995.

Timor's Anschluss, Indonesian and Australian Policy in East Timor, 1974–76. The Edwin Mellen Press, Lewiston, New York, 1992.

Sharon Scharfe, *Complicity: Human Rights and Canadian Foreign Policy: The Case of East Timor.* Black Rose Books, Montreal, 1996.

Abe Barreto Soares, *Come With Me, Singing in a Choir: Collected Poems.* Sydney, Australia: East Timor Relief Association, 1996.

João Mariano de Sousa Saldanha, *The Political Economy of East Timor Development.* Pustaka Sinar Harapan, 1994.

Adam Schwarz, *A Nation in Waiting, Indonesia in the 1990s.* Westview, 1994.

Kevin Sherlock, *A Bibliography of Timor.* Research School of Pacific Studies, Australian National University, Canberra, 1980.

Frans Sihol Siagan and Peter Tukan, *Voice of the Voiceless* (collection of interviews with Bishop Belo in Indonesian), Jakarta: Penerbit Obor, 1997.

Max Stahl, "A Church on Calvary." *The Tablet* (London), Jan. 25, 1992.

Keith Suter, *East Timor, West Papua/Irian Jaya and Indonesia.* Minority Rights Group, London, 1997.

Richard Tanter, "The Military Situation in East Timor," *Pacific Research* (Palo Alto, California), Volume VIII, Number 2.

John G. Taylor, *The Indonesian Occupation of East Timor 1974–89: A Chronology.* Catholic Institute for International Relations with the Refugee Studies Program, Oxford University, London, 1990.

John G. Taylor, *Indonesia's Forgotten War: The Hidden History of East Timor.* Zed Books, 1991.

Elizabeth G. Traube, *Cosmology and Social Life, Ritual Exchange among the Mambai of East Timor.* University of Chicago Press, 1986.

Peter Tukan and Domingos de Sousa (Eds.), *In the Cause of Justice and Peace,* Dom Carlos Filipe Ximenes Belo, SDB, Bishop of the Diocese of Dili, East Timor, 1997 (in Indonesian).

Michele Turner, *Telling East Timor, Personal Testimonies 1942–1992.* New South Wales University Press, 1992.

"U.S. Arms Transfers To Indonesia 1975–1997: Who's Influencing Whom?" by William Hartung and Jennifer Washburn, Arms Trade Resource Center, World Policy Institute at the New School for Social Research, March 1997.

Dale Van Atta and Brian Toohey, "The Timor Papers." *National Times* (Australia), May 30–June 5 and June 6–13, 1982.

Pat Walsh, "The Pope rides the Indonesian rapid without rocking the boat." *National Outlook* (Australia), January 1990.

Publications:

East Timor News Summary, National Council of Churches, 110 Maryland Avenue NE, Suite 108, Washington, D.C. 20002.

Timor Link, the newsletter of the Catholic Institute for International Relations, Unit 3, Canonbury Yard, 190A New North Road, London N1 UK.

INDEX

❖ ❖ ❖ ❖

About the Author

❖ ❖ ❖ ❖

A FORMER INVESTIGATIVE REPORTER at NBC News, Arnold Kohen has written articles for *The Nation*, the *Boston Globe*, the *Los Angeles Times*, the *New York Times*, *The Messenger of St. Anthony* (Padua, Italy), the London-based *Index on Censorship* and *The Tablet*, and other publications. He received a B.A. in English from the State University of New York at Stony Brook and an M.A. in journalism from the American University School of Communication. Kohen also has had a long association with specialists on Indonesia and East Timor at several universities. He has also lectured widely on these subjects as well as on other issues of international human rights and humanitarian interest. He lives near Washington, D.C.